SAILING DIRECTIONS

FOR THE

WEST COASTS OF FRANCE, SPAIN, AND PORTUGAL.

FROM USHANT TO GIBRALTAR STRAIT,

INCLUDING

THE AFRICAN COAST FROM CAPE SPARTEL TO MOGADOR.

FOURTH EDITION

(CONTAINING AN APPENDIX).

PUBLISHED BY ORDER OF THE LORDS COMMISSIONERS OF THE ADMIRALTY.

LONDON:

PRINTED FOR THE HYDROGRAPHIC OFFICE, ADMIRALTY,

AND SOLD BY

J. D. POTTER, AGENT FOR THE SALE OF ADMIRALTY CHARTS,

31 POULTRY, AND 11 KING STREET, TOWER HILL.

1885.

Price Four Shillings.

ADVERTISEMENT TO THE THIRD EDITION.

THE Sailing Directions for the West Coasts of France, Spain, and Portugal were originally compiled in 1867 by Staff Commander J. Penn. The coast of France being derived from the valuable surveys made by M. Beautemps Beaupré, between the years 1818–26, and the more recent charts published by order of the French Government. The Coast of Spain from the well known works of Tofiño, and the Derrotero de la Costa Septentriónal de España, 1860–61.

The general ·features of the Coast of Portugal were derived principally from the work of M. M. Franzini, as translated by Captain W. F. W. Owen, R.N., 1814 ; the directions for the Rivers Douro and Tagus being from the most recent surveys. The Strait of Gibraltar chiefly from the Manuel de la Navigation dans le Détroit de Gibraltar, 1857, and the Derrotero General del Mediterráneo, 1860.

A second edition, prepared by Lieutenant Dawson, R.N., and published in 1873, contained in addition a description of the coast of Africa, between cape Spartel and Mogador.

This edition has been revised to 1880, by Staff Commander Hitchfield, from various sources, including the most recent surveys undertaken by the respective Governments.

With a view to the general interests of Navigation, it is hoped that officers, both of the Royal Navy and Mercantile Marine, will transmit to the Hydrographer of the Admiralty notice of errors or omissions which may come under their observation, and also any fresh information they may obtain.

F. J. E.

Hydrograhic Office, Admiralty, London,
January 1881.

ADVERTISEMENT TO FOURTH EDITION.

In the fourth edition, an Appendix has been added, giving information that has been published in Hydrographic Notices, also other important information received since the publication of the third edition in the year 1881. The body of the work remains as in the third edition. Corrections are given for the alterations in lights since 1881, in a list at the end of the appendix.

W. J. L. W.

Hydrographic Office, Admiralty, London,
June 1885.

CONTENTS.

CHAPTER I.

USHANT TO ILE DE GROIX.

CHAPTER II.

ILE DE GROIX TO FUENTERRABIA.

CHAPTER III.

COAST OF SPAIN.—FUENTERRABIA TO CAPE PEÑAS.

CHAPTER IV.

COAST OF SPAIN.—CAPE PEÑAS TO THE RIVER MIÑO.

CHAPTER V.

COAST OF PORTUGAL.—RIVER MIÑO TO THE RIVER GUADIANA.

CHAPTER VI.

COAST OF SPAIN.—RIVER GUADIANA TO GIBRALTAR.
COAST OF AFRICA.—CEUTA BAY TO MOGADOR.

APPENDIX.

IN THIS WORK THE BEARINGS ARE ALL MAGNETIC,
EXCEPT WHERE MARKED AS TRUE.

THE DISTANCES ARE EXPRESSED IN SEA MILES OF
60 TO A DEGREE OF LATITUDE.

A CABLE'S LENGTH IS ASSUMED TO BE EQUAL TO
100 FATHOMS.

For later information respecting the lights which are described in this Work, seamen should consult the Admiralty Lists of Lights for north and west coasts of **France, Spain, Portugal, &c.** This List is published early in the current year, corrected to the preceding 31st December.

NOTE.—A list corrected to May 1885 of additions and alterations to lights, received subsequent to the publication of the Sailing Directions for the West Coast of France, Spain, and Portugal, 1881, will be found in the Appendix to this book.

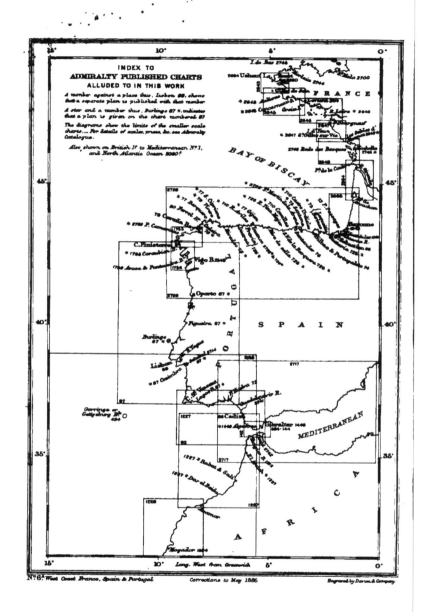

INDEX TO
ADMIRALTY PUBLISHED CHARTS
ALLUDED TO IN THIS WORK

A number against a place thus, Lisbon 98, shows
that a separate plan is published with that number

A star and a number thus, Burlings 87 *, indicates
that a plan is given on the chart numbered 87

The diagrams show the limits of the smaller scale
charts.— For details of scales, prices, &c. see Admiralty
Catalogue.

Also shown on British I? to Mediterranean N? 1,
and North Atlantic Ocean 2060?

N? 6? West Coast France, Spain & Portugal   Corrections to May 1886   Engraved by Davies & Company

SAILING DIRECTIONS

WEST COASTS OF FRANCE, SPAIN, AND PORTUGAL.

CHAPTER I.

INTRODUCTION.—The bay of Biscay, which takes its name from the province of that name on the north coast of Spain, extends from Ushant on the north-east to cape Ortegal (on the north-west coast of Spain) on the south-west, and is about 300 miles in breadth and 240 miles deep.*

The west coast of France between Ushant and the Gironde river varies in height, is broken, and skirted by numerous islands, rocks, and dangers; but southward of that river, as far as the Pyrenean chain of mountains dividing France from Spain, the land is lower and more uniform, with sandy downs, and the coast generally clear of dangers.

The north coast of Spain which forms the southern boundary of the bay, is bold and rocky, with lofty mountains and ranges, generally terminating in steep cliffs and inclines, which are the leading features of this iron-bound coast.

The coasts of the departments and provinces bordering on the bay of Biscay are, taken in order from north to south; in France,—Finistère, Morbihan, Vendée, Charente, Gironde, and Landes; in Spain from east to west, Guipúscoa, Vizcaya or Biscay, Santander, Asturias, and Galicia. The principal rivers which flow into the bay are the Loire and Gironde, in France; also among those of minor size and importance, the Vilaine and Adour in France, and Nervion in Spain.

The only islands of any magnitude are those situated on the north-west part of the French coast, the principal of which are Ushant, Belle Ile, Iles d'Yeu, de Ré, and d'Oleron.

SOUNDINGS.—The central part of the bay is very deep; the 100 fathoms line of soundings passes about 65 miles south-west of Ushant, and skirts the west coast of France at nearly the same distance, curving to within about 35 miles of the south-east angle of the bay. Beyond soundings of 100 fathoms the water deepens suddenly, and about midway between Ushant and cape Ortegal, attains a depth of 2,600 fathoms over a bottom of grey mud and shells. Along the coast of Spain, at 15 miles from the land, the depth is from 150 to 200 fathoms, rock and coral, but frequently

---

* *See* Admiralty chart :—British islands to Mediterranean sea, No. 1; scale, *m*= 0·02 inches.

i 17801.   Wt. 4225.   A

no bottom is to be found at that depth, even near the land, whilst at 40 miles off, no bottom is to be found with about 2,000 fathoms.

On the parallel of Ushant the whole extent of the edge of soundings may be traced in fine weather by the numerous ripplings in its vicinity, and in boisterous weather, the transition from deep water to comparatively shoal, is rendered apparent by the sudden alterations in the colour of the water, which changes from a dark indigo blue to various shades of green.   As Ushant is approached the depths slightly decrease, varying a few fathoms more or less; at the distance of 48 miles from, and on the parallel of the island, there are 72, 71, and 70 fathoms, with coarse pale yellow ground, resembling marl, with a mealy surface, interspersed with pieces of broken shells, and a substance like chaff.   At 27 miles from the island, the soundings are from 66 to 63 fathoms with the same bottom, and 61 fathoms will be found within 9 miles of the rocks.*

On the parallel of the Chaussée de Sein, commonly named the Saints, the transition from deep to comparatively shoal water is very sudden; in lat. 48° 2′ N. and long. 8° 4′ W. there are 326 fathoms water over dark bluish-gray mud, at only 10 miles westward of the 100-fathoms edge, and the whole of the south-western edge of the bank bordering the north-western coast of France appears to be equally steep.   In the parallel of Rochelle, a depth of 900 fathoms was obtained, 30 miles westward of the 100-fathom edge of the bank, and 2,275 fathoms at 60 miles.

Between the parallels of Penmarc'h point and Rochefort, or more precisely between the latitudes of 45° 50′ and 47° 53′, there is a remarkable bed of soft mud, limited to the south-east by the Plateau de Roche Bonne. It extends about 150 miles in a north-west and south-west direction, is 20 miles in breadth, and useful to verify a vessel's position.   The surface of this mud is very soft, especially on its edges, where it is mixed with a little very fine gray sand, and will scarcely adhere to the lead.   To the eastward the mud is more firm, and westward the bottom becomes more or less rocky. This difference between the qualities of the bottom leaves the bed of soft mud in a north-west and south-east direction.

Off the mouth of the Loire, between Belle Ile and Ile d'Yeu, the depths vary from 37 to 19 fathoms, and the difference between the two qualities of the bottom is less perceptible.   Between these isles the bottom is composed of sand and gravel, and of broken shells.   In the offing, westward of the

---

* Commander Methven, P. and O. Company's steamship *Kaisar-i-Hind*, 1880, when entering the English channel from the south-westward, in lat. 48° 4½′ N., long. 6° 19′ W. (54 miles W. ½ S. from Ushant), struck soundings in 60 fathoms, sand and shells.

Proceeding on a N.E. ¼ E. course, 2 and 5 miles respectively, depths of 63 and 69 fathoms were obtained; and, again, at a distance of 10½ miles on that course, 68 fathoms, sand and shells.

The attention of mariners is directed to the circumstance, that these depths lie some miles seaward of the 70-fathom line, as shown upon the charts to the south-westward of Ushant.

soft mud which has been described, the bottom is of sand, of a grayish colour, and frequently mixed with broken shells. This quality of the bottom continues westward to soundings of 180 fathoms, and extends in a north-west and south-east direction, between the parallels of about 45° 50′ and 47° 25′.

In concluding these remarks, the mariner is reminded that to judge correctly of a vessel's position, a continuous line of soundings should be taken over a considerable distance. Occasional casts are of comparatively little use.

WINDS AND WEATHER.*—The prevailing winds in the bay of Biscay throughout the year are those from N.W., West, and S.W. Severe gales are frequently experienced from the same quarters, often attended with violent squalls, rain, hail, and thick weather. These gales, blowing over the full extent of the North Atlantic, cause a mountainous sea in the bay, and at the mouth of the English channel.

A low barometer, heavy banks of clouds with lightning to the westward, threatening appearance of sunrise or sunset, and often an ominous westerly swell, are each and all indicative of the approach of one of these gales ; and as a rule, the longer these indications, the greater will be the force and duration of the coming storm. Commencing very often at South or S.W. with rain and thick weather, the wind gradually veers round to West and N.W. with clearer weather ; and perhaps after lasting from this quarter for a day or two, backs again to the old quarter ; a slight rise may then be perceptible in the barometer, indicating a greater force in the wind, which may continue for several days to blow in the same direction, shifting two or three points either way with occasional lulls, and finally with a decided rise in the barometer the gale blows itself out.

No fixed rule appears applicable to these gales ; they more frequently however commence in the south-west quarter, and blow themselves out in the north-west.

On the north and north-west coasts of Spain, as well as on the west coast of Portugal, the westerly gales are felt in full force. In these parts, if a calm with a westerly swell succeeds a south-west wind, it is considered a forerunner of one of these gales ; they become less frequent and violent as the latitude of Gibraltar is approached, and their influence may be said to cease about the latitude of the Canary islands (28° N.).

Easterly winds occur at intervals throughout the year, but are most common about the period of the equinoxes, when they often increase to gales of long continuance, generally attended with fine clear weather and high barometer. February and March are the months in which these winds may be said to be strongest and most frequent.

---

* *See* Admiralty Pilot charts for Atlantic ocean, 1875 ; and Wind and Current charts for Pacific, Atlantic, and Indian oceans, 1879.

· In the summer months, June, July, August, fine weather and light southerly and south-easterly winds are often to be met with in the bay of Biscay, and westerly gales are least frequent; but this time of the year is by no means exempt from the visitation of both easterly and westerly gales.

Fogs prevail in October and November, and on the coasts of the bay, as well as in the bay itself, are notably dense; they seldom last, however, for a longer period than 24 hours, before a change of wind causes them to disperse.

Rain is most common during the winter months, and at the season of the equinoxes.

For descriptions of the local winds and weather on the coasts of Spain, Portugal, and the straits of Gibraltar, the mariner is referred to the index of this book.

CURRENTS.—The easterly current from the North Atlantic ocean strikes the land near cape Ortegal, in Spain, and then appears to divide into two branches; the northern (Rennell current) flowing eastward along the coast of Spain, then north along the west coast of France, where it is felt at 30 or 40 miles off shore, and is 15 or 20 miles across; this current becomes wider as it proceeds northward, and is probably at times joined by the streams from the rivers of France. Near the parallel of 48° 20′ N. it is about 80 miles in breadth, and its direction nearly N.W., passing 15 or 20 miles westward of Ushant, it crosses the entrance of the English channel, and takes a westerly direction from the Scilly isles. At the entrance of the Irish sea it is divided into two branches, one of which is diverted into that sea, whilst the principal branch flows W.N.W. and West towards cape Clear. It has been found to run from half a mile to a mile an hour, and varies according to the strength and direction of the lately prevailing winds, those from the westward causing a heavy swell, and considerable augmentation in its force.

The southern branch turns gradually to the south-east and southward along the coast of Portugal until having passed cape St. Vincent, when it runs eastward towards the strait of Gibraltar. It must not, however, be presumed that the current along the west coast of Spain and Portugal always sets to the southward, for during westerly winds it sets strong towards the land, and immediately after the continuance of southerly gales or strong breezes the current will probably be found setting to the northward.

CAUTION.—The mariner will perceive that caution is necessary in crossing the bay, and that due allowance should be made both for the outset and indraft, but especially the latter, when standing to the southward during thick weather for a position westward of cape Finisterre.

PASSAGES.

ENGLAND to GIBRALTAR.—Steam Route.—Steam vessels proceeding from the English channel to Gibraltar should, if possible, sight and pass within 10 miles of Ushant; cape Finisterre should be passed about the same distance; Burling islands may be passed within 5 or 6 miles, and cape Rocca about the same distance, thence to cape St. Vincent, which may be rounded at a distance of 2 or 3 miles; care, however, is necessary when in the vicinity of this cape, as the currents generally set strong along shore, and have a tendency towards the cape. After passing cape St. Vincent, a direct course may be steered for the strait of Gibraltar. For the description, and directions for the strait of Gibraltar, *see* pages 309–326 and 338.

Sailing Route.—Sailing vessels bound to the southward from the English channel, and having a fair wind, should at once make westing, as the prevailing winds are from that quarter. It is usual, therefore, on leaving the Lizard, to shape a W.S.W. course, so as to be able the better to weather Ushant should the wind become adverse; but if it continue fair it is absolutely necessary to correct the dead reckoning as frequently as possible by astronomical observations, in order to reach the parallel of the north coast of Spain sufficiently to the westward for the safety of the ship.

Thus far the run across the bay of Biscay has been considered under circumstances of fair winds and fine weather, but if, on leaving England, an adverse wind and threatening appearance of weather, with low barometer, be encountered, the prudent mariner will do well to seek shelter in some safe anchorage, in order to save wear and tear, and be in an efficient state for prosecuting the voyage with the first favourable change. If, however, the vessel has advanced too far to sanction this retrograde movement, or it be determined to continue, the ship should be hauled to the wind on the tack which will best enable her to approach the proper course without drawing deep into the bay, which is especially to be avoided.

It would be better therefore to reach to the westward as far as 10° or 12° W. at some loss of ground, rather than risk being sent into the bay, as south-westerly gales frequently blow out by drawing round to the north-westward, which, if a tolerable board has been made in that direction, permits the ship to be tacked, and at once to proceed on her course a point or more free. It is during and after these gales that the indraft of the bay is most felt and to be guarded against, but with the above change of wind opportunities will most probably occur for taking observations, after which a safe course may be shaped.

Should the vessel have had to contend with southerly and south-easterly gales, she will have been driven to the westward, and in this case the aim should be to make the best progress to the southward possible under the circumstances. On the other hand, if westerly gales have prevailed, and the vessel has become embayed, it may be found difficult to weather cape Finisterre, or even cape Ortegal; under these trying circumstances refuge may be found in Ferrol, Coruña, Barquero, or Vivero, the two latter ports being about 10 and 15 miles respectively eastward of cape Ortegal. In extreme cases, with loss of masts and sails, the ports and roadsteads of France from the Gironde to Brest are under the lee, and the anchorage inside Belle-Ile and the Pertuis Breton, &c., are open and safe.

Proceeding to the southward from off cape Finisterre, a course should be shaped to clear the Farilhões and Burling island, the former of which lie about 205 miles to the southward of the cape, and 10 miles north-westward of the peninsula of Peniche, and should be avoided at night, or with south-westerly winds, which are frequently accompanied with thick weather, under which circumstances it is better to keep off the land, in order to escape the northerly current that sets along the coast with those winds, as well as to be in a position to profit by any change of wind to the west and north-west; in short, it is better to run to the southward at some distance from the coast of Portugal, as westerly winds make it a lee shore, and in winter these gales are frequent, blowing with great force, and continuing for several days together.

If the latter course be adopted it will be prudent to sight cape St. Vincent, and then steer for cape Spartel, which is safe to approach, being clear of danger, with 100 fathoms water, at the distance of 3 miles off shore. The land rises from the cape with a gradual slope to about 1,000 feet above the sea at a mile within, and consequently can be seen from a long distance. To the south of the cape the land falls, and has been mistaken at a distance for the mouth of the strait, which has led to the loss of several vessels; hence in dark unsettled weather, should the light not be in sight caution is necessary. After rounding cape St. Vincent, as the vessel proceeds to the south-eastward, the state of the wind and weather, and the indraft and current of the strait of Gibraltar, must be considered and allowed for.

CAUTION.—A vessel approaching cape Trafalgar in thick weather may assure her safety by the use of the lead and the chart, as the soundings extend some distance from the land; the shoals off the cape, and the Cabezos, westward of Tarifa, should be carefully avoided. With clear weather and common care no accident can occur, as none of these dangers extend more than 4 miles from the land; but with thick weather caution is necessary, the currents, tides, and eddies between cape St. Vincent and Tarifa being very variable.

The lighthouse on cape Trafalgar exhibits a *revolving* white light, whilst that on cape Spartel shows a *fixed* white light, and as they are 24 miles apart, N. ½ E. and S. ½ W., and either light in clear weather is seen at the distance of about 20 miles in all directions to seaward, the extreme range of these lights embraces more than 60 miles of latitude, and thus on approaching the strait, unless in very thick weather, the mariner should necessarily observe one or other of the lights.

GIBRALTAR to ENGLAND—Steam Route.—The homeward passage from Gibraltar for steam vessels is the reverse of the outward passage, but on entering the English channel much caution is requisite in rounding Ushant. That island is surrounded by dangers in all directions ; there are numerous rocks, the channels are intricate, the tides rapid, fogs and thick weather not uncommon, and, as might be expected, wrecks are frequent. No vessel should approach within 5 miles, or, if the weather be thick, come into less than 70 fathoms water until the parallel of the island be passed.

Tides.—Around Ushant the flood sets to the north-east, and the ebb to the south-west, and at springs the tides run at the rate of 3 or 4 miles an hour, the flood stream turning to the eastward as it slacks, and then setting more directly on the rocks. In the offing, the stream continues to run for 3 hours after the time of high water. Between Ushant and the Saints, the flood tide sets to the eastward, and ebb to the westward.

Sailing Route.—Sailing vessels bound from Gibraltar to England, after passing cape St. Vincent, with the prevailing northerly winds, generally endeavour to get an offing of 100 or 150 miles, to avoid the south and south-easterly currents near the coast of Portugal, mentioned in page 4 ; should, however, a southerly wind be experienced, it will not be necessary to keep so far from the land. For directions on approaching the English channel, *see* "Channel Pilot," Fifth Edition, Part I., pages 1-16.

Caution.—In approaching Ushant during thick weather it is absolutely necessary to keep the lead going.

USHANT TO ILE DE GROIX

VARIATION IN 1881.

Ushant   -   - 20° 30′ W. | Ile de Groix -   -   - 18° 00′ W.

USHANT, or ILE D'OUESSANT of the French, lies 10¼ miles westward of the north-west extreme of the coast of France. It is about 4¼ miles long, W. by N. and E. by S., about 2 miles broad, and its highest part, which is the north-east, 195 feet above the level of the sea. In fine weather the island is visible from a distance of 15 to 20 miles, the outline appearing rugged and uneven, being composed of high, craggy, and precipitous rocky cliffs of granite formation. There are two light-houses on the island; one on the north-east extreme, the other at the north-west.*

The inhabitants, about 2,500 in number, are chiefly employed in rearing cattle, and as fishermen, many of whom are well acquainted with and can act as pilots for the passages in the vicinity, rendered dangerous by the numerous hidden as well as apparent rocks and islets lying between the island and the main land. The people, generally, speak pure Breton.

The only village is named Lampaul or Portspaul, situated at the head of a bay on the south-west side, it is here that the pilots reside. In the other parts of the island the houses are scattered, forming only small hamlets. A post-boat sails twice a week for Conquet on the main land, at which place the produce of the island, consisting of soda, grain, sheep, and poultry is disposed of.

Supplies.—Wood is scarce, but water and other supplies can be obtained in moderate quantities; for fuel the natives find a substitute in dried seaweed.

LIGHTS. — North-east Light.—There are two lighthouses built on Ushant; one stands near its north-east extreme, from which, at an elevation of 272 feet above high water, is exhibited a *fixed* white light of the first order, visible in clear weather from a distance of 18 miles.

---

* *See* Admiralty charts :—France, west coast, channels between Ile d'Ouessant and mainland, No. 2,694; scale, m = 1·5 inches; France, north coast, sheet 8, No. 2,644; scale, m = 0·5 of an inch; Raz de Sein to Ile d'Ouessant, No. 2,643; scale, m = 0·5 of an inch; British islands to the Mediterranean, No. 1; and English channel, sheet 2, No. 2,675 b. Also Channel Pilot, Part I., fifth edition, p. 9; and Part II., third edition, p. 443.

North-west Light.—The other, at the north-west extremity of the island, is a circular tower, painted with black and white horizontal stripes, and, from an elevation of 223 feet above high water, is exhibited a *revolving* light, the eclipses of *twenty seconds* duration, being succeeded by *one red* and *two* white faces, each lasting *twenty seconds*, and visible in clear weather 22 miles.

Fog Trumpet.—A fog trumpet is sounded at the west point of the island, during foggy weather, at intervals of *ten seconds*, the duration of the blast being *two seconds*, the sound will generally be heard 3 miles in calm weather.

A Life Boat is stationed at Creac'h point.

Semaphores.—By using the Commercial code of Signals, passing vessels can communicate with either the semaphore on Creac'h point; or that on the N.E. point, and by this means telegraphic messages may be sent to all the countries of Europe.

Anchorages.—Notwithstanding the general dangerous character of the shores of Ushant, there are anchorages in which small vessels may find shelter from particular winds.

Baie de Lampaul, on the south-west side of the island, is the principal anchorage, and may be considered the port of Ushant. This bay is only used by small vessels, and affords good shelter from winds northward of West round to S.E., but it is exposed to the whole force of south-west gales. The water is deep, but shoals gradually towards the head of the bay, thus rendering the anchors less liable to drag with south-westerly winds.

The dangers to be avoided in entering this bay are the Jument rock and a ledge named the Basse Bridy, lying to the south-west of the southern point of entrance, and the Leurvas rock W.S.W. a long half mile from the northern point. The Jument lies S.W. ¾ W. 1¼ miles nearly from the southern point, and uncovers 19 feet at the lowest tides; the Basse Bridy lies 1¼ miles W. ½ S. from the same point. A rock near the Corce, the summit of which never covers, lies in the middle of the bay. The lighthouse on the north-east extreme of the island kept a little open north of this rock, leads between the Basse Bridy and the Leurvas. The best anchorage is on sandy bottom in 12 to 7 fathoms water, northward of the Corce, which may be rounded close to on all sides.*

Chaussée de Keller.—At 2 miles N.N.E. ¼ E. from the west extreme of Ushant, and 3 miles N.W. by W. ½ W. from the north-east lighthouse, lies a small patch of 11 fathoms (with 21 to 38 fathoms close around), named Basse Callet, at the west extreme of Chaussée de Keller,

---

* A beacon has been placed on Runiou point, the southernmost point of Ushant.

the name given to a chain or causeway of rocks extending N.W. by W. 1¼ miles from the western part of Keller islet. From the centre of Basse Callet, the north-east lighthouse is in line with Keller islet, bearing S.E. by E. ¼ E., and Bélanger mill (the westernmost mill of Ushant) is in line with the west end of Callet rock, S. by E. ¼ E.

The Baie de Béninou, between Keller islet and the north extreme of Ushant, affords good shelter in 7 to 12 fathoms water, sand and rocky bottom, during southerly winds, but the anchorage is quite exposed to the northward.

The Baie du Stiff, on the north-east side of Ushant, affords temporary anchorage for small vessels; but it is open to the eastward. The dangers to be avoided on entering are the Men-Corn rocks and Légounec bank lying off the southern point, and the Gorlè-bian rock in the middle of the bay; the former and latter uncover at half tide. The Men-Corn and Gorlè-bian rocks are both marked by stone beacons.

Pilots.—Should a vessel require a pilot, it is important that signals be made to attract attention, as many vessels pass near the island, both to the north and south, making it their point of departure when outward bound from British ports to the southward.

With south-west winds and flood tide, it is seldom possible for a pilot to come off.

Tides.—It is high water, full and change, around Ushant at 3h. 32m.; springs rise 12¼ feet, neaps 14 feet.

Haut Fond D'Ouessant.—At about 3¼ miles W.S.W. from the south-west point of Ushant is the northern end of a bank, about 1¾ miles long, north and south, and half a mile broad, on which are 25 to 32 fathoms water, over a bottom of broken shells. Around it on all sides are 50 to 60 fathoms, and between it and Ushant 50 to 26 fathoms.

Tidal Signals.—The following system of tidal signals was established in August 1855 by the French Minister of Commerce and Public Works, and as they are used at most of the French ports we need not repeat them for each place. The signals are made by flags and black balls hoisted on a mast, on which a yard is crossed.

A ball hoisted at the intersection of the mast and yard denotes a depth of 10 English feet in the channel between the jetties.

Each ball hoisted on the mast under the first denotes an additional depth of 3¼ feet.

Each ball hoisted above the first denotes an additional depth of 6½ feet.

Each ball hoisted at the right yard arm denotes an additional 20 inches.

A white flag with a black cross, also a black pendant, are used to indicate the state of the tide. These are hoisted at the masthead when there are 6¼ feet in the channel, and lowered when the water has receded to that depth. During the flood the pendant will be above the flag; at high water and during the top of the tide the pendant will be lowered; and during the ebb the pendant will be under the flag.

TABLE OF TIDAL SIGNALS.

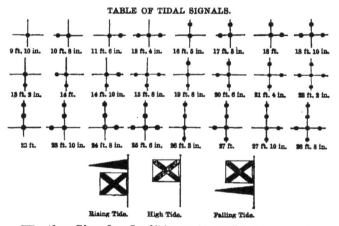

Rising Tide. High Tide. Falling Tide.

Weather Signals.—In addition to the established storm warnings, the following system of weather signals were adopted in 1870, for the principal ports, and shipping places on the coasts of France.

1. A flag of any colour indicates - Weather doubtful, barometer in-clined to fall.

2. A short pendant (cornet) - Appearance of bad weather, heavy sea, barometer falling.

3. A pendant - - - Appearance of better weather, baro-meter rising.

4. A ball above cornet - - The entrance of the port has become dangerous, be careful.

5. A ball before cornet - - The lifeboat is coming out.

Buoys and Beacons.—On the French coast, in entering a harbour, all buoys and beacons painted red must be left to starboard, and those painted black to port. The beacons below the level of high water and all warping buoys are painted white. The small rocky heads in the frequented channels are painted in the same manner as the beacons when they have a sufficiently conspicuous surface.

lights, ... or more ... upon it in full length or in abbreviation the name of the ... it marks and the number showing its numerical ... is the same channel. These numbers commence from seaward; the ... numbers ... the red ones, and the ... numbers on the black buoys. The letters and numbers are painted in white on the most prominent parts of the ..., and from 5 to 12 inches in length. The masts of the ... which in any present sufficient surface are surmounted for this purpose by a small board. All the jetty heads and turrets are coloured above the half-tide level, and on the former a scale of metres is marked commencing from the same level.[*]

The PASSAGE du PROMVEUR runs parallel with the south coast of ... among which are several rocks and rocky patches, but none extend more than half a mile from the shore. The principal danger lies in the southern side of the channel off the broken rocky isle of Loédoc, from which a rocky edge extends nearly half a mile in a W. by N. ¼ N. direction having at its extremity a detached rock, named the Men Tensel, which uncovers 12 feet at the lowest tides. Most of the rocks on this edge, however, are visible at half ebb, and there is generally broken water over them at some portion of the tide; but care must be taken to avoid a sunken rock with only two fathoms water over it, lying about 1½ cables north-west of the Men Tensel. Between this rock and the Darling ..., ... of ..., is the narrowest part of the channel, which is somewhat more than a mile across.

The streams run in the direction of the channel, about E. by N. and W. by S., and they are so rapid as to alarm any person unused to its navigation, particularly at the springs, when they run over 4 knots, and the ... surface of the water has the appearance of breakers.

When bound to ... the channel from the north-eastward—which in a ... ... should only be used in cases of necessity, and then only with the ... of ... east end of Ushant a berth of about three-quarters of a mile, and when the east end of the island is in line with the north-east lighthouse, bearing N.N.W. ¾ W., and the Loédoc islet just open of the west side of Ushant islet, about S.S.W., steer W. by S. ½ S. for 2½ miles, and until Ushant north-east lighthouse bears N.N.E. ½ E. and open westward of a mill on the north-eastern land of the island; when, if bound to ..., the lighthouse kept on the above bearing and S.S.W. ½ W. course under good for 2 miles, will lead westward of the Pierres Vertes. The north-west lighthouse seen just over the south-west point of the island bearing N. ¼ W. leads about three-quarters of a mile westward of the 4-fathom patch of the Pierres Vertes.

------

[*] The metre is equal to 3·2809, or nearly 3¼ English feet.

When Ar Men Guen Gondichoc is seen between the barracks and semaphore of Molène, steer S. by E. ½ E., which if made good will carry a vessel a mile westward of the outermost danger of the Chaussée des Pierres Noires, which should be rounded with discretion, and the tide considered.* The lighthouse on Petit Minou point, in line with the lighthouse on Portzic point, bearing East, leads towards the Goulet de Brest.

Pierres Vertes rises from a bank about 3¼ miles W. by N. of Molène island. The bank is more than three-quarters of a mile in length in an east and west direction, with several rocky patches on it. The Pierres Vertes in the centre of the bank uncovers 7 feet at low water, and at a third of a mile east of it the Gondichoc also uncovers 7 feet. From the west end of the bank, in 4½ fathoms water, the Men Du is in line with the Castel ar Mouliguet rock at the north end of Bannec, bearing N.E. ¼ E., and Ar Men Guen Gondichoc is seen between the barracks and semaphore on Molène island E. by S.

Béniguet is a low island, 1¼ miles in length, and about a quarter of a mile in breadth. It lies in an E.N.E. and W.S.W. direction, and its eastern end is about 2 miles from Kermorvan point. A large number of rocks and sunken ledges lie on its south-eastern side, most of which begin to uncover at one-third ebb, and show a great extent of surface at low water. A long ledge of rocks extends from its south-western point to a considerable distance, every part of which is visible at low springs; but as the sea breaks on them with the least swell, they may be easily avoided. At the extremity of the latter ledge are the Louedéguets, two small rocks a few feet above the surface at all tides.

There are also two small detached pieces of high rock, surrounded with low tide ledges on the northern and western side of the island, about a cable off; and a broken ledge of rocks extends from the north extreme, the whole of which are uncovered at low tide, and with the great Belveignou ledges form two small channels into the Four.

Almost the whole of this island is surrounded by a beach formed of small pebbles well calculated for ballast, and which may be obtained without risk and little trouble. Off the beach on the northern side there is anchoring ground for small vessels close to it.†

Le Cromic is a remarkable small rock, about 30 feet above high water, and at the distance of a few miles in hazy weather has much the appearance of a small vessel under sail. There are many-half tide and low water ledges extending from it to the southward; the outermost rock,

* *See* Views on Admiralty chart, No. 2,694.

† Capt. Hurd, R.N., 1806.

about half mile off, begins to uncover at about half tide. The marks for
the extreme point of this ledge are, the eastern Cheminées a little open of
the western side of Kérouroc, and Lochrist church spire a little within the
north point of Béniguet.

Morgol Isle has the appearance of a pebble beach, surrounded by
black ledges in all directions, and separated from Le Cromic and Lytiry
by small boat channels. · The ledges from its southern side extend to the
south-west and join the southern ledge from Le Cromic ; and from its
eastern side they extend off about a quarter of a mile, forming the western
boundary of the New channel into the Four, whilst the Belveignou ledges
form the eastern boundary.

Vieille Noire (Groac'h-du) is a rocky shoal about $1\frac{1}{2}$ cables in
extent, and uncovers 13 feet at low water springs. It lies with the town
of Conquet seen over the north end of Béniguet island bearing E.S.E.
nearly and the eastern Bossemen a little open of the ledge of rocks or
outermost breaker extending from that island S.E. $\frac{3}{4}$ S.

At 6 cables W. $\frac{3}{4}$ S. of the Vielle Noire is a small rock without a name
which uncovers 10 feet at low-water springs, with $3\frac{1}{4}$ and $3\frac{3}{4}$ fathoms
around it. The marks for it are, St. Mathieu lighthouse nearly in line
with the Louedéguet rocks at south-west end of Béniguet island bearing
S.E. by E. nearly, and Molène semaphore a little within the west end of
Triélen island North.

Cleu Basseven is a bank about half a mile in length east and west,
and a quarter of a mile in breadth. A small portion of the middle of the
bank uncovers 8 feet at low-water springs, but elsewhere there are from
one to $5\frac{3}{4}$ fathoms water. The eastern Serroux just open westward of the
west end of Triélen island leads eastward of the bank.

The Belveignou are a large group of black looking ledges, of considerable extent at low water, with two small spots only appearing above
the surface at high-water neaps; the remainder uncover gradually with the
ebb, and at low-water mark the eastern boundary of the new channel into
the Four. There are also two smaller channels on the southern and eastern
side of these ledges, between them and Béniguet island.

Lytiry is a small broken islet lying northward of Morgol and Le
Cromic, and only separated from them by a boat channel, through which
the tides run rapidly. It has two or three small beaches of fine sand, and
surrounded by ledges which show at half tide.

Quéménès, like Béniguet, is a low island lying in an E.S.E. and
W.N.W. direction, surrounded at low water with numerous ledges,
particularly to the northward, making it unapproachable but at high water,

except on its eastern side. The small islet Lédénès de Quéménès on the north joins it by a beach at half tides.

Triélen is another low island lying nearly east and west, but smaller than Béniguet or Quéménès. It has a salt water pond at its east end surrounded by a stone beach. Its southern side, like the other islands, is not approachable at low water within two or three cables, having rocky ledges at that distance extending from it. At a long half mile S.W. by S. of the west end of the island is a large bed of rocks called Les Serroux, visible at all times of tide, except very high springs, and of considerable extent at low water.

To the northward of the east end of Triélen at a distance of 2¼ cables, is a small beach-looking islet, with black ledges extending from it at low water in almost every direction.

CHAUSÉE des PIERRES NOIRES is a rocky bank extending E.S.E. and W.N.W. over a distance of about 6 miles, and terminating on the east at 1¼ miles from St. Mathieu lighthouse. Several of these rocks rise 15 or 20 feet above the level of high water, whilst others uncover at all times of tide, and show considerably at low-water springs. The soundings on the bank are very irregular, varying from less than one to 10 fathoms. There are passages between the rocks which with the aid of the chart may be taken if necessary. We shall begin the description of the rocks on this bank with the Basse Occidental des Pierres Noires, at the west end of the bank.

Basse Occidental des Pierres Noires, the most western shoal, has only 2 fathoms water on it, and lies with the eastern Serroux seen about a degree to the westward of the west end of Triélen island bearing N.E. by N. and Les Cheminées between the large group of the Pierres Noires or Black rocks and Le Diamant S.E. by E. easterly. To the westward of the bank the water deepens to 27 fathoms at the distance of a mile.

Les Pierres Noires or Black Rocks, are the western of the chain which uncover; they are about 15 feet above the level of high water, with a few ledges extending about a cable from them; on the largest of the rocks is a lighthouse. The south-western of this outer group is named Le Diamant, which is bold all round, with deep water between it and the other rocks; but at about a cable S.W. by W. of it is the Roux, a patch which uncover 2 feet at low-water springs.

Le Boufouloc, on which the *Magnificent* was lost in the year 1803, is a large uneven rocky bank, on which there are two small heads. The southern head lies N.W. ¼ N. distant 8¼ cables from Le Diamant, with St. Mathieu lighthouse in line with or a little open of the extreme north

end of Kérouroc islet bearing about E. by S. ½ S. The northern head lies
N.W. ¾ N. one mile from Le Diamant, with Lochrist church spire just
clear north of the Plaeen ar Béniguet. Between Le Boufouloc and the
Plaeen ar Béniguet, eastward of it, is a bank about half a mile in length
east and west, with 1¾ to 3½ fathoms on it at low water.

Plaeen ar Béniguet is a large ledge of rocks lying a long half
mile N.N.E. from Les Pierres Noires. These rocks uncover about 18 feet
at springs, and being at all times seen by the breakers are a good mark to
avoid other dangers.

Le Petit Taureau is a small rocky shoal which uncovers 9 feet at
low-water springs. It lies with Conquet church in line with the south-
east end of Béniguet island bearing E. ¼ S., and the Plaeen ar Béniguet
S.W. ¼ W. distant nearly three-quarters of a mile.

La Siège is a group of rocks, some of which are about 15 or 20 feet
above the level of high water, and surrounded by ledges that uncover at
low-water springs. These rocks on the west side, and the Pierre des
Poissons, Kérouroc, Les Cheminées, and Ranvel on the east, form a passage
for vessels having occasion to pass through the New Channel into the Four,
which is not, however, without sunken rocks, for the positions of which
the navigator is referred to the chart. There is also a channel north-west
of La Siège and Les Pierres Noires, or between these groups and the
Plaeen ar Béniguet, where also there are sunken rocks and shallow patches
to be avoided, and the chart must be the guide.

Kérouroc is a small islet, where a boat may find landing in almost
any weather. There are many half-tide rocks and shoals around it, and
about 1½ cables north of it the Pierre des Poissons rises 27 feet above low-
water springs.

Cheminées are three small rocks about 30 feet above high water;
the two easternmost being nearly joined together. There are a few half-
tide rocks, on which the sea breaks, on the eastern side; the western
Cheminée is bold, and lies on the south-east side of one of the passages to
the New Channel into the Four.

Le Ranvel is a ledge of rocks 5 or 6 feet above high-water springs.
To the westward and south-west are two patches which uncover 4 and
9 feet respectively at low water. These rocks are the outermost or most
southerly of this extensive chain, from the Pierres Noires to the eastern
Bossemen.

Western Bossemen is a circular rock about 20 feet above the
level of high water, having many detached ledges about it, which show at a
quarter and half tide in various directions to a distance of about 4 cables.

Eastern Bossemen is the easternmost of the Chaussée des Pierres Noires. It is small, circular, and about 15 feet above the level of high water. The Men Civien, a rock which uncovers 13 feet at low-water springs, is nearly 2 cables N.E. ¾ E. of it. The Basse des Bossemen is a small sunken rock with about 10 feet water on it, and lies with the Western Bossemen nearly in line with the south-east point of Béniguet island, bearing about N. by W. ¾ W., and the Eastern Bossemen W.S.W. distant about a third of a mile and open a little to the right of the town of Conquet.

Basse Large is a bank of about three-quarters of a mile in length N.E. and S.W., and half a mile in breadth. On its north part there are only 2 feet at low water, and on its south-east side one spot dries ; on other parts of the bank there are from 2 to 4 fathoms water. Vessels standing towards the bank should keep Le Diamant open southward of Le Ranvel. The south-east shoal spot lies with Le Diamant in line with Les Cheminées, and Lochrist church bearing E. by N. ¼ N., and well open of the Eastern Bossemen.

The Coast from Melgorne point, the north-west extreme of France, trends in a S.S.W. direction 11 miles to St. Mathieu point, at the entrance of the bay of Brest. It is moderately high, and the breaks and fissures in its granite formation, and the numerous and remarkably shaped rocks and islets near the land render its features easy of recognition. The shore generally is steep-to, but so bordered by the numerous dangers that it should not be approached by night, or in thick weather, within a depth of 45 fathoms, where the bottom will be generally of gray sand mixed with flints and other stones.

The whole space between the coast and Ushant is studded with islets, rocks, and shoals, and although pilots and persons well acquainted with the locality could conduct small vessels, and, more easily, steam vessels among them, yet for the general purposes of navigation, the passages of the Four and Fromveur are principally used.

At 2 miles southward of Corsen point, which is easily distinguished by its steep cliffs and semaphore, the shore curves round westward, forming Blancs Sablons bay, in which there is anchorage in 4 to 7½ fathoms water, sandy bottom, clear of dangers, but open to north and west winds. The head of this is separated from a small haven, named Le Conquet, by a narrow neck of land, the south-west extreme of which is Kermorvan point. Le Conquet dries at low water, and rocky ledges extend from both sides of entrance. On La Louve, north side of entrance to Le Conquet, there is a black beacon.

Kermorvan point is foul, and a short distance off it are two rocks, named Le Normand, and Petite Vinotière, which appear only at low water.

At half a mile S.S.W. of Kermorvan point is a shoal with 8 feet on it at low water, named the Renards, marked on its western side by a black buoy anchored in 19½ feet at low water; at a quarter of a mile east of this shoal stands a black beacon on Les Renards rocks. St. Mathieu point is distinguished by its lighthouse and the ruins of an old abbey, and by the rocks called the Vieux Moines lying half a mile south of the point, and which are about 4 feet above high-water ordinary springs. The point is bordered by rocky ledges, and about half a mile eastward of the lighthouse Les Rospects above water extend nearly half a mile from the shore. To the eastward of this ledge the shore is steep and may be coasted at the distance of half a mile.

LIGHTS.—On Le Four rock stands a lighthouse, 92 feet high, from which is exhibited a *fixed* and *flashing* light, showing a *fixed* white light during *thirty seconds*, and a *flashing* light of eight distinct flashes, followed by eclipses, during *thirty seconds*; thus the light will be alternately *fixed* and *flashing*; and should be visible in clear weather from a distance of 15 miles.

Fog Trumpet.—During thick and foggy weather a steam trumpet sounds a blast of *five seconds* duration, followed by an interval of silence of *twenty seconds*.

Corsen Point.—From a small structure attached to the south wall of the Semaphore building on Corsen point, is exhibited a *fixed* white light, visible through a sector of 8°, indicating the channel between Grande Vinotière to the westward, and Petite Vinotière and Basse des Renards to the eastward; it is elevated 105 feet above high water (5 feet above the ground), and should be seen in clear weather from a distance of 14 miles.

Note.—Mariners navigating the southern part of Chenal du Four should keep this light in sight, remembering that Basse du Chenal (page 20) is in the centre of the illuminated sector.

Kermorvan Point.—On Kermorvan point, at the north side of entrance to Le Conquet, is a square white tower, which exhibits at 72 feet above the level of high water a *fixed* white light, visible in clear weather at a distance of 11 miles.

St. Mathieu.—On St. Mathieu point is a round tower, exhibiting at 177 feet above high water a white light which *revolves* every *half minute*. The light is visible from a distance of 18 miles; the eclipses do not appear total within 8 miles.

Les Pierres Noires.—On the largest of Les Pierres Noires or Black rocks is a stone tower, which exhibits, at 90 feet above high water, a *red* flashing light showing a *flash* and an *eclipse* alternately, with an interval of *ten seconds* duration, visible in clear weather at a distance of 12 miles. The off-lying rocks extend three cables S.W. of the lighthouse.

Life Boat.—A life boat is stationed at Kermorvan point.

CHENAL du FOUR.—This channel is between the great cluster of islets and rocks southward and eastward of Ushant and the main. The dangers along the coast are two numerous for a detailed description, but the following are the principal in the neighbourhood of the channels, for the others the mariner is referred to the chart.

On approaching the coast from the northward the Four rock is a remarkable object; it is a large dark conical mass, broad at the top, and rises 17 feet above high-water mark, a long mile N.W. of Melgorne point, and E. $\frac{1}{2}$ S. 10$\frac{1}{4}$ miles from Ushant north-east lighthouse. It may be known by its vicinity to another large rock, named the Grand Château, lying between it and the Ile d'Iock.

On the eastern side of the channel, about one mile westward of the Four rock, is the Basse Boureau, a small patch with 5$\frac{1}{2}$ fathoms water on it. At 2 miles to the south-west of the Basse Boureau is the Basse Muer, a patch with two rocks having apparently less than 6 feet water upon them;* in shore of this is the Basse St. Jaques, with nearly 4 fathoms on it, and a number of dangerous reefs, some of which just dry at low water. At 2 miles S.W. $\frac{1}{4}$ W. from the Muer is the Basse St. Louis, with 2$\frac{1}{4}$ fathoms on it; and at 3$\frac{1}{4}$ miles S. $\frac{1}{4}$ W. from the Muer is the Valbelle, with only 11 feet water, of small size, and marked by a bell buoy; it lies with Plouarzel church, bearing S.E. by E. $\frac{1}{4}$ E. and seen between the Fourches islets. The channel between this latter shoal and the Platresses bank is only half a mile wide.

Les Platresses are a cluster of rocks three-quarters of a mile long, in a north and south direction, some of which uncover at half ebb. They lie about midway between the Plateau des Fourches and the Plateau de la Helle, the northern part of these rocks lies 1$\frac{1}{2}$ miles S. by E. $\frac{1}{4}$ E. from the Basse St. Louis. The north-east and south-east rocks are marked by buoys on their east sides.

The Tendoc Rock, with only 9 feet over it, marked on its western side by a black buoy, lies nearly a mile S.E. $\frac{3}{4}$ E. of the south-east rock of the Platresses, with the ruined mill of Trézien in line with the centre of a remarkable rock in shore, named Goaltock, bearing about E. by S. $\frac{3}{4}$ S.

The Basse St. Paul, with 2$\frac{1}{4}$ fathoms on it, lies one mile westward of Corsen point, which will be recognized by its steep cliffs and semaphore.

The Grand Vinotière lies three-quarters of a mile N.W. $\frac{1}{2}$ W. from Kermorvan point and in the middle of the Four channel; it dries 9 feet at the lowest tides, and is marked by a black and red turret beacon.

---

* The Pilote de la Manche, Cotes Nord de France, Vol. I., states : "The Basse Meur is a dangerous bank, having on it a depth of 8 metres (4$\frac{1}{4}$ fathoms)." The latest French chart (1873), No. 105, has the Basse Meur defined with two rocky heads, the depth upon which is not *exactly known*.

The Basse du Chenal, with 5 to 8 feet on it, having a red buoy on its eastern side, and steep close-to, is the south west danger of the Chenal du Four ; from it, St. Mathieu point bears E. ¼ N. 1½ miles, and Kermorvan point in line with Portzmoguer beach N.E. ¾ N.

Basse Royale, with 14 feet water and 10 to 16 fathoms close around, lies S.W. ¾ W. 1½ miles from Basse du Chenal. Basse Royale is marked by a red beacon.

Directions.—When bound through the Chenal du Four from the northward bring the lighthouse on Kermorvan point in line with that on St. Mathieu point, bearing South. By steering this course a wide berth will be given to the Boureau bank, and a vessel will pass to the westward of the Basse Muer, the Valbelle, and Tendoc, and to the eastward of the Basse St. Louis and the Platresses ; but on nearing the latter shoal, great attention must be paid to keep the mark on, as the channel between them and the Valbelle is but half a mile wide.

Continue to the southward with the above mark on until about three-quarters of a mile from Kermorvan point, when, by steering S.S.W., the vessel will pass westward of the Renards and Vieux Moines, and to the eastward of the Grand Vinotière and the Banc du Chenal, and may gradually steer in for the Goulet or entrance to Brest. A vessel of heavy draught should pass 2 cables westward of the Grand Vinotière, and steer about S.W. by S. for the eastern Bossemen until the town of Conquet bears East.

The least water in the channel is abreast Kermorvan point, where at low springs there are not more than 3¼ fathoms. A vessel in taking this or any of the other neighbouring channels should be well under command on account of the strong tide, which, at springs, runs 4½ knots ; the flood sets northward, and the ebb southward.

CHENAL de la HELLE is between the Platresses bank and the Plateau de la Helle, which latter is an extensive bank, 2¼ miles long, north and south, and dangerous throughout, as many of the rocky heads dry at low tide. A rock, named La Helle, lies on the north-western part of the bank, and is always uncovered. It has the appearance of a vessel under sail and bears S.E. ¼ S. 6½ miles from Ushant north-east lighthouse. The channel is 1½ miles wide, its direction is N.N.W. and S.S.E. nearly, and it unites with the Chenal du Four, about 3 miles northward of Kermorvan point.

The NEW CHANNEL into the CHENAL du FOUR, between the island of Béniguet on the east and those of Quéménès, Morgol, and Lytiry on the west, may be used by small vessels ; but as the tides in this passage run with great rapidity, every precaution must be taken to insure the vessel answering her helm quickly.*

To navigate this channel steer for the middle of Triélen island, on a N.N.E. ¼ E. bearing—keeping the eastern Serroux, which is always visible, well open to the left of the west point of Triélen, to clear the western 2-fathom patch of the Chaussée de Pierres Noires—and it will lead westward of the Boufouloc rock, on which there are only 2 feet water at low springs. When the lighthouse on St. Mathieu point is opened a little to the northward of the Placen ar Béniguet—which is always to be seen either as rocks or breakers—steer for Morgol isle until Lochrist church is just over the south end of Béniguet. Thence steer about East for the north-west end of Béniguet, taking care, on nearing the narrow part of the channel between the island and the ledge southward of Morgol isle, and that of Belveignou, not to shut in the two eastern Cheminées with Kérouroc isle, until the spire of Lochrist church is seen over the centre of Béniguet island.

From this point the channel becomes open to the N.E. by N., between Morgol isle and the Belveignou ledges, and may be steered for, carefully avoiding to open the inner or easternmost Louédéguet rock with the west end of Kérouroc isle, until Le Cromic appears over the centre of Morgol isle, when the west extremity of Belveignou ledge will have been passed, and the channel will begin to deepen and widen. Having passed the Belveignou, steer to the eastward, with Le Cromic open of the northern end of Morgol, which will lead into the Four channel, leaving the Petit Pourceau, as well as various ledges, rocks, and shoals, forming the Pourceaux bank on the port side; and the Petit Courleau, which dries 15 feet at low water, and other dangers, on the starboard side.

In cases of necessity and with the aid of the chart, the channel may be approached from the southward, between the rocks composing the Chaussée des Pierres Noires. The passages between Boufouloc and Pierres Noires, the Siége, and Kérouroc are apparent, and may be navigated by small steam vessels without danger.

The IROISE is the name given to the approach of Brest and Douarnenez bays; the depth of water over the outer part varies from 45

---

* In the French chart by M. Beautemps Beaupré, 1818, the soundings are sparsedly marked between Morgol isle and the Belveignou ledge, and at rather more than half a mile south-east of Morgol isle, as little as 6 feet water are shown on the chart. But in 1806, Capt. Hurd, R.N., says, "In every part of the channel to within half a mile of Béniguet island, there are from 10 to 6 fathoms water, and in the shoalest part, between Morgol isle and Belveignou, I have nowhere found less than 3½ fathoms at the lowest springs; and therefore on all neap tides you may fairly calculate on 4 fathoms at low water."

to 25 fathoms, but the inner part is encumbered with various shoals, the position of which, and the depth of water, will be best understood by referring to the chart. It is bounded on the north by the Chaussée des Pierres Noires, on the south by the Chaussée de Sein, commonly called the Saints, and on the east by an irregularly formed promontory which projects westward from the main land, separating and forming the above bays. Its northern projection is named the Presqu'île de Kélernn, and protects the bay of Brest.

The land of this promontory is high and steep, and many of its points projecting into the sea, are encumbered with rocks, and dangerous to approach. Toulinguet point, the western extreme of the promontory, is steep and cliffy, about 120 feet high, having on it a lighthouse. At 2 miles to the southward is a point off which lie 5 or six large rocks named the Tas du Pois, and between them and Dinant point to the south-east is the Anse de Dinant. Cap de la Chèvre, 4 miles to the south of Dinant point, is the southern point of the promontory and the northern headland of Douarnenez bay.*

Anchorages.—At about 1¼ miles eastward of Toulinguet point, is Grand Gouin, the western point of Anse de Camaret, in which there is good anchorage in 8 or 9 fathoms, muddy bottom, sheltered from all but north-westerly winds. Capucins point, the north-extreme of this bay, is the south point of entrance to Goulet de Brest.

On the north side of the Iroise, near the Pierres Noires, there is anchorage in fine weather and easterly winds; but the water is inconveniently deep.

There is good anchorage in 6 and 7 fathoms, sand, with the abbey on St. Mathieu point bearing S.E., and Kermorvan point N.E. by N.; but when working for this anchorage take care to avoid the Renard rocks and a small reef near the shore north of St. Mathieu point named Loquejou.

The Anse de Bertheaume between Créarc'hmeur point and Minou point, which latter is the north-western point of the Goulot, was formerly the outer anchorage of Brest; it affords shelter from all northerly winds, in 7 or 8 fathoms water. The shores of this bay and the adjacent coasts are studded with forts and batteries.

LIGHTS.—The lights seen from a vessel approaching the Iroise, in addition to those of Ushant, St. Mathieu, Kermorvan, and Pierres Noires already described in pages 8, 9, and 18, are the following:—

Minou Point.—On Minou point at the northern side of the entrance of the Goulet de Brest, a circular tower exhibits, at 105 feet above

---

* See Admiralty chart, Brest Roadstead, No. 2,690; scale, m = 1·5 inches.

high water, a *fixed* white light, visible in clear weather from a distance of 14 miles.

Portzic Point.—On Portzic point, the same side of the Goulet and 3¼ miles eastward of Minou point, is an octagonal tower, which exhibits, at an elevation of 184 feet, a *fixed* white light varied by a *flash* every *three minutes*, visible in clear weather 19 miles. The flashes are preceded and followed by short eclipses, which do not appear total within 8 miles.

Capucins Point.—On Capucins point, the north extreme of Anse de Camaret, is a square tower, which exhibits, at 207 feet above high water, a *fixed* white light, visible in clear weather from a distance of 13 miles, between the bearings of East northerly, and E. by S. (this bearing leads southward of Royale and Large shoals). To the northward a narrow ray of light is shown over the position of Les Fillettes rocks.

Toulinguet Point.—On Toulinguet point is a square tower, which shows, at 161 feet above high water, a *fixed red* light, visible 7 miles.

Tevennec Island.—On Tevennec island, north entrance of Raz de Sein, is exhibited a *flashing* light, showing a flash *every four seconds.* It will appear *white* between the bearings of N. ½ E. and N. by W., or between the rock of Cornoc Bras and La Vieille rocks; *red* from N. by W. to N.W. ⅔ W., and *white* from N.W. ⅔ W., through West and South, to E. by S. ¾ S., and from the last-named bearing to N. ¼ E. it will be obscured. It is elevated 92 feet above the level of high water, and in clear weather the white light should be seen from a distance of 13 miles.

Pointe Du Raz has a square tower standing on the highest part of the point which exhibits, at an elevation of 259 feet, a *fixed* white light visible 18 miles.

La Falaise.—From an iron tower on La Falaise, 220 yards from Pointe du Raz lighthouse, in the direction of La Plate rock, is exhibited a *fixed* white light having two sectors, one, visible between the bearings of East and S.E. ¼ E., covering La Vieille rocks; and the other between the bearings of S. by E. ¾ E. and S. by W., or between the Barillets and the dangers off Pointe du Van. It is elevated 207 feet above the level of high water, and in clear weather should be seen from a distance of 10 miles.

Ile de Sein has a round tower standing on the north point of the islet, which exhibits, at 148 feet above high water, a *fixed* white light, varied by a *flash* every *four minutes*, visible 18 miles. The short eclipses, which precede and follow each flash, do not appear total in ordinary weather within a distance of 12 miles. The upper portion of the tower is painted black.

Ar-Men Rock.—*Lighthouse building.*

Life Boats.—There is a life-boat station at Toulinguet point, Pointe du Raz, and at Ile de Sein.

DANGERS in the IROISE.—The approach to the Goulet de Brest is bounded on the north side by the Chaussée des Pierres Noires, Le Coq, and the Basse Beuzec. Le Coq rock, which is steep-to, dries 4½ feet at low water, and lies south-east 1¾ miles from St. Mathieu point, two-thirds of a mile off shore, with the chateau de Bertheaume in line with Créac'hmeur point E. by N. ¼ N., and a beacon on the shore between the Pignons de Kéravel N.N.W. ¼ W. Le Coq rock is marked by a black buoy. The Basse Beuzec is a patch with 5 feet over it. It lies E.S.E. 1¾ miles from Le Coq, with the Chateau de Bertheaume bearing N.N.E. ¼ E., distant rather more than a mile. Basse Beuzec is marked by a black and red buoy on its east side.

To the southward and eastward of the above, and on the south side of the approach to the Goulet de Brest, is an extensive group of dangers, having among them numerous passages, which should not be attempted by a stranger. The outermost of these is La Vandrée, a small patch with 6 feet water on it, and marked by an automatic whistle buoy (frequently adrift), from which the two peaks of the Siége group—Pierres Noires—are a little open eastward of the Cheminées, bearing N.N.W. ¼ W. A ridge of foul ground, having 10 to 19 fathoms water, and steep-to, extends from it one mile in a westerly direction. At half a mile E.S.E. from La Vandrée, is a small patch with 5 fathoms water on it named La Goémant; and at three-quarters of a mile N.E. by E. ¼ E. from La Vandrée, is another patch with 4½ fathoms on it named the Basse de l'Astrolabe.

Le Parquette is a rocky patch, marked by a beacon 23 feet high, lying S. ¼ W. 4 miles from St. Mathieu lighthouse, and nearly W. by N. 4½ miles from Toulinguet lighthouse. It is generally above water, and when covered the sea breaks, except in calm weather; another small head, that uncovers 6 feet at low water, lies E. by S. about 1¼ cables from it; and there is a patch having 7½ feet water in the same direction and half a mile from Le Parquette.

The passage between Le Parquette and the Basse de l'Astrolabe is 1½ miles wide, with 15 to 21 fathoms water, but the navigation between Le Parquette and Toulinguet point is dangerous from the many rocky heads which rise from the bank extending from Toulinguet point, several of which are seen at low water. The principal rocks are the Trépied, Louzaouennou, Corbeau, Corbin (the latter always above water), Pélen,

---

* The light will probably be exhibited in the autumn of 1881 or in the spring of 1882.

Mendufa-bian; and a small high rocky islet named Toulinguet, three-quarters of a mile W. by S. of Toulinguet point. The bank lies in an east and west direction, about 2¼ miles in length and 1¼ miles in breadth.

Le Trépied, which uncovers 9 feet at low water, lies with the south extreme of the Lignes de Kélernn just over Grand Gouin point bearing E. by S. southerly, and Lochrist church in line with fort St. Merzan N. by W. It is marked by a red buoy which is 2¼ miles S. by W. ½ W. of the buoy on Basse Beuzec, on the north side of the passage.

To the southward of these dangers are other shoal patches, the relative positions of which are best seen on the chart. The outer or south-western, with 4 fathoms water, named Basse de l'Iroise, lies S.S.W. ½ W. 2¼ miles from the shoal patch of La Vandrée, with Roscanvel mill in line with north rock off Toulinguet point, bearing nearly E. by N.

The Basse du Lis lies E. ½ S. 2½ miles nearly from the Basse de l'Iroise, with one to 3½ fathoms water, and is marked by a red buoy. It is about a quarter of a mile in extent, and from the shallowest part Lochrist church is in line with the western Pignon de Keravel bearing N. by E. ¼ E., and St. Sebastien mill in line with the summit of the Toulinguet rocks E. by N. ¾ N. The bank is steep-to with 18 and 20 fathoms around it.

The Passage du Toulinguet is formed between the Toulinguet rocks and La Louve with a beacon on it, at the extremity of the ledge extending from Toulinguet point the narrowest part of the passage is less than a quarter of a mile wide. Approaching it from the southward and westward, be careful to avoid the southern 2 feet patch of the Pélen, by not bringing Pen-hir point to bear southward of E. by S. ½ S. until at a distance of about three-quarters of a mile from the point; then skirt the shore and pass between the Toulinguet rocks and the point of the same name, but rather nearer the former.

The Passage du Petit Leach lies between the Pélen, Mendufas, and Toulinguet rocks on the one side, and Petit Leach and Le Corbin on the other. To run through this passage bring Roscanvel mill in line with the northern rock of Toulinguet point bearing E. by N., and steer for it until the west extreme of Cape de la Chèvre is seen midway between the two outer rocks of the Tas de Pois; then steer to the north-eastward. The summit of the road to Paris, behind the town of Brest, seen exactly in the middle of the Goulet, bearing E.N.E. nearly, leads also through in mid-channel clear of all danger.

The Passage du Corbeau, westward of the latter, is narrow but deep. It lies between the Corbeau, which uncovers 14 feet at low water, and the Pontchou bank, over which the depths are 6 to 13 feet.

These passages may be used by pilots and mariners with local knowledge.

Tides.—In the centre of the Iroise the tides have not much apparent strength, but their rapidity increases on approaching the openings of the Ushant channels and the Raz de Sein. The varying force of the tidal streams, in consequence of the influence of winds, renders the navigation of the Iroise difficult in thick weather, and under such circumstances it is recommended to anchor when practicable.

BREST is a strongly fortified town, and one of the chief naval arsenals of France. It is very advantageously situated near the west extreme of the department of Finistère, and on the north side of one of the finest ports in the world, nearly land-locked, accessible only through a narrow and well fortified passage, the Goulet, and extending far inland in two branches, one running up to Landernean, the other towards Châteaulin.

The Town stands on the summit and sides of a kind of projecting ridge, and some of its streets are too steep to be passable except on foot. It is situated on the left bank of the Penfeld river, which is a small stream flowing into the northern part of Brest road, and the communication is kept up with its suburb Recouvrance on the right bank by a bridge 65 feet above high water. The whole is encircled by ramparts, which, being planted with trees, form agreeable promenades, and afford a fine view of the port and shipping. The population exceeds 55,000, of whom about 13,000 consist of soldiers, sailors, convicts, &c.

Time Signal. *

Dockyard.—The mouth of the Penfeld is reserved exclusively as a port for vessels of the French navy, and although there are 30 feet in it at low water, it is narrow, and vessels lie in a single tier. The dockyard is on both sides of the river, and consists of graving docks, building slips, victualling department, and seamen's barracks. Above the dockyard is the naval hospital.

Commercial Port.—The commercial port, or port Napoleon, eastward of the mouth of the Penfeld, is an extensive artificial harbour, adapted for merchant vessels of large size, with two inner basins, containing respectively an area of about 11 and 8 acres. This is the established landing place for boats of foreign men-of-war.

Notwithstanding its great advantages, Brest has little trade, and no manufactures worth specifying. There are a few fishermen engaged in the cod, pilchard, and mackerel fishery.

LIGHTS.—A white iron turret on the western jetty, at the entrance

---

* At the Observatory of the Nautical schools, a flag is hoisted half mast at 5 minutes before signal, and hauled down at noon, Brest mean time.

to port Napoleon, exhibits at a height of 33 feet above high water a *fixed green* light.

A similar turret on the southern jetty, S.E. a little more than a cable from the former, shows a *fixed red* light at the same elevation. Both lights should be visible in clear weather at a distance of 7 miles.

At the southern, or last-mentioned turret, a fog bell is sounded in thick weather.

On the eastern pier head of the commercial port, a *fixed* white light is exhibited at an elevation of 21 feet above high water, and should be visible in clear weather from a distance of 7 miles.

The Goulet, or entrance to Brest roads, is a strait formed by the north shore of the Presqu'ile de Kélernn on the one side, and the coast between Minou and Portzic points on the other. It is nearly a mile to $1\frac{1}{4}$ miles wide; the shores on both sides are steep to, and may be coasted along at a distance of about 3 cables. The dangers to be avoided in sailing through are the Fillettes, Goudron, and the Mengam, all of which lie in mid-channel.

The Fillettes rocks lie at the west end of a shallow bank, uncover 5 feet at low water, and its north side is marked by a buoy striped red and black. The Mengam lies a mile farther eastward and does not cover except at very high springs; it has a beacon on it 26 feet high. Directly in a line between these dangers is the Goudron, a rocky bank on the extremes of which there are not more than 2 and 3 feet water. The passage between these rocks should not be attempted, there being several others under water. The approaches to Brest are marked according to the French system:— black buoys to the left or the port hand in entering the road, and red on the starboard. Buoys coloured black and red mark the central shoals.

Tides.—The tides run strongly in and out through the Goulet, and springs at about 3 miles an hour.

RADE de BREST.—This extensive roadstead or harbour contains an area of about 15 square miles, but its breadth varies considerably from the irregularity of its shores, and in some places it is more than 3 miles across. There are numerous streams running into it, one of which, the river Chateaulin, is navigable for steamers. In taking up a berth, if the vessel is of large draught, avoid the Banc de St. Pierre, the edges of which are buoyed; on one part of it there are only $4\frac{1}{2}$ fathoms of water. If anchoring in the southern part of the harbour, care must also be taken to avoid a small patch with 9 feet water on it, called the Basse du Renard, marked by a red and black buoy ; it has 9 fathoms close to and lies $1\frac{3}{4}$ miles southward of the Banc de St. Pierre, in a direct line between the Cormorandière rock and Ile Ronde, distant from the latter about three-quarters of a mile.

Storm and Weather Signals, the latter, as described in page 11, are shown from the entrance of the Man-of-war harbour, and at St. Mathieu point.

Tides.—It is high water, full and change, at Brest, at 3h. 47m. ; springs rise 19 feet, and neaps 13¾ feet.

Directions.—Vessels bound to Brest, and being in the fairway, should bring Minou and Portzic lighthouses in line bearing East, which leads southward of all dangers of the Chaussée des Pierres Noires, Le Coq, and Basse Beuzec; and northward of La Vandrée, Le Parquette, Le Trépied, &c., to the entrance of the Goulet. Then run along the north shore at a distance of about a third of a mile between it and the shoals in mid-channel. When the town of Brest is seen open of Portzic point haul up, and anchor off it in 8 or 9 fathoms water, muddy bottom ; or to the southward of the the Banc de St. Pierre in 10 to 15 fathoms.

The Coq will be avoided by keeping the north end of Beniguet isle open of St. Mathieu point, until the Pignons de Kéraval is seen open to the eastward of the beacon on the shore.

The Bouzec may be passed on either side, and if convenient a vessel may run to the northward of it, and cross the entrance of Bertheaume bay. In the Goulet, the Filletes, Goudron, and Mengam banks may also be passed on either side. In entering the Rade de Brest, give Espagnols point a wide berth, so as to avoid La Cormorandière rock, which is always uncovered.

At Night.—The *fixed* white light on Capucins point is only seen between the bearings of E. by S., and E. ¼ N., and when kept in sight clears all dangers. The lights on Minou and Portzic points in one bearing East, is the leading mark towards the Goulet; when on this line and within a mile of the former light, a vessel should steer a little to the southward, so as to give the point a berth of about a third of a mile, and then steer on for the Portzic light.

ANSE de CAMARET is formed between Capucins, the south point of entrance of the Goulet and Grand Gouin point, at 2 miles S.E. of it. The bay is about a mile deep, with 5 to 6 fathoms water, over sand and mud, and free from danger. The town and small port of Camaret is in the south-west corner of the bay, but as the latter dries 4 or 5 feet at low water, it is only adapted for small vessels, which lie sheltered from all winds. The port is protected by a peninsula several yards above high water, and near its extremity is the chapel of Nôtre Dame de Roch Madou, a small fort with moats and a drawbridge. Vessels of 150 to 200 tons, drawing less than 12 feet, can enter the port, but cannot at times approach the quays. The bay affords shelter from all winds except the north. The prevailing winds in the fine season are N.W., N.E., and S.E., but towards the equinoxes and during winter severe northerly gales are common, when the bay should be avoided. There are numerous batteries along the shore. A chain mooring, marked by three buoys, lies across the entrance to Anse de Camaret.

Coast.—Toulinguet point, at 1¼ miles westward of Grant Gouin point, is bordered by a ledge of sunken rocks extending about a cable from the point ; the narrow passage between this ledge and the Toulinguet rock has from 6 to 4½ fathoms water in it. In the bay, between Toulinguet and Pen-hir points, there is anchorage off the sandy beach in 5 to 7 fathoms water, sand, with the extremity of Toulinguet point bearing about North, distant half a mile.

Pen-hir Point, at 1½ miles southward of Toulinguet point, is steep and rocky, and off its south extreme are five or six large rocks named Les Tas de Pois. They extend nearly two-thirds of a mile in a south-west direction from the point, are always above water, and steep-to on all sides ; but there is a patch (Basse de Dinant), with 8 feet water on it, at half a mile S.E. ¾ E., from the outermost rock. From these rocks the shore bends round to the E.S.E., forming the two small sandy bays of Pen-hir and Dinant.

From Dinant Point, the south extreme of Dinant bay, the coast trends in a southerly direction 4 miles to cape de la Chèvre which has some small rocks scattered about it, also a sandy spit with 2¼ to 6 fathoms water on it, extending about a mile in a W. by S. direction. Between these points there are several dangerous rocks lying about one to 4 miles from the shore.

Basse Ménéhom, which is 1¾ miles eastward of the Basse du Lis (page 25), consists of three rocks, extending about three-quarters of a mile in an E.N.E. direction. The S.W. rock, with 13 feet water on it, lies with Lochrist church bearing North a little westerly, St. Mathieu lighthouse N. ¼ W., and Toulinguet lighthouse N.E. by E. ¼ E. The N.E. rock, with 3½ fathoms on it, lies with St. Mathieu lighthouse bearing N. by W. ¼ W., and Toulinguet lighthouse N.E. by E. easterly. The third rock, having 3¾ fathoms on it, is nearly midway between them.

La Chèvre, Le Chevreau, and Le Bouc, are three rocks rising respectively about 3, one, and 4 feet above the surface at high-water springs, with deep water around them. The first of these rocks lies W. ¾ N. a long mile from the southern extremity of Dinant point ; and the second W. ¼ S., 6 cables beyond it ; the third bears N.W. ¾ N., rather more than 2¼ miles from the western extreme of cape de la Chèvre.

Ile de Guénéron which is small lies near the shore, but there is no passage between it and the main land except for boats.

The **Basse Vieille** uncovers about 5 feet at low water, and is steep-to, having 12 and 17 fathoms close around.   It lies with Kidizient mill in line with a small rock, named Men Cos, lying off the south-east extreme of cape de la Chèvre, bearing E. by N. ½ N., and the western Tas de Pois in line with the Toulinguet rock, N. ¾ E.   It is marked by a black buoy.

The **Basse Laye**, a rock having on it less than 6 feet of water, lies S.S.E. ½ E. 9 cables from cape de la Chèvre, and S.W. two thirds of a mile, from the Men Cos rock.

BAIE de DOUARNENEZ.—This bay is 10 miles deep and about 7 miles wide.   The soundings decrease from 18 to 8 fathoms, sand, shells, and mud, and the entrance is so wide that no leading mark is required to enter, provided a berth is given to the Basse Vieille, and the foul ground off cape de la Chèvre on the north.

In the northern part of the bay there are several rocks, some of which are uncovered, whilst others appear only at low water.   The outermost of these is La Pierre Profonde, which is always above water; a little to the northward of it are Le Taureau, which uncovers 5 feet, and the Basse Rip, a knoll with 5 fathoms water.   At about half a mile eastward of the Taureau are Les Verrès, north of which, and near Laber isle, is the Laber rock, always showing above water.   Elsewhere the bay is clear of dangers, except near the shore.

The village of Douarnenez stands on the southern shore of the bay. Here is a little harbour, at which about 500 small vessels are annually fitted out for the sardine fishery.   The church of Plouaré, on a high hill to the south-east of Douarnenez, is a fine specimen of architecture.   Tristan island lies off the village, and at about three-quarters of a mile northward of it is the outermost of two small sand patches, named the Basse Muer and the Basse Neuve, the former with 17 and the latter with 8 feet water over it, these shoals lie with the centre of Tristan island in line with Plouaré church.

From Douarnenez the southern shore of the bay trends in a westerly direction for nearly 16 miles to Pointe du Van, the coast being high and steep, with several projecting points, some of which are encumbered with rocks and dangerous to approach.   At one mile N.E. of Pointe du Van is the Basse Jaune, a rock which uncovers 2 feet at low water, with 7½ to 10 fathoms around it, and in line with Le Chlec rock—just off Pointe du Van—and the extremity of Pointe du Raz.   There is a deep channel between it and the point, but it will be prudent for a stranger to pass to the northward of the rock.   A buoy, painted with black and red bands, is moored about one-third of a mile West from Basse Jaune.

Anchorage.—For vessels of heavy draught there is fair anchorage off the village of Douarnenez in 5 fathoms; Tristan island lighthouse bearing W. ¼ N. and Plouaré church S.W. by S., but a vessel should be prepared to proceed to sea at the first appearance of bad weather, as with northerly and westerly winds a mountainous sea rises immediately. There is good shelter inside the mole for vessels, with good holding ground in 12 feet at low spring tides.

LIGHTS.—On the summit of Tristan island is a round tower 32 feet high, which exhibits, at 114 feet above high water, a *fixed* white light, visible in clear weather at a distance of 10 miles.

An iron pillar on the extremity of Rosmeur mole, Douarnenez bay, exhibits, at an elevation of 23 feet above high water, a *fixed red* light, visible in clear weather at a distance of 5 miles.

Point Millier.—*Light proposed.*

A Life Boat is stationed at Tristan island.

Directions.—The best landing mark into Douarnenez bay is the high mount of Locrenan (to the south-east), just shut in to the southward of Léidé point, which is about 1¾ miles westward of the village of Douarnenez. This will lead to the southward of the Basse Vieille, the marks for which should be kept open. The town of Crozon, on the north shore of the bay, is distinguished by a high black tower, and the village of Beuzec on the south shore by a church with a high Gothic spire. If making for the anchorage off Douaranenez in hazy weather, the Plouaré church steeple forms a conspicuous mark, and is very often distinguishable before Tristan island. On advancing into the bay, mount Locrenan will appear well cultivated; the village on its side is large and surrounded by trees.

POINTE du RAZ—Bec du Raz.—From Pointe du Van, the south-west extreme of Douarnenez bay, the shore trends nearly south and then west for about 2½ miles to Pointe du Ras, forming the sandy bay of Trépassés. Pointe du Van is surrounded by rocks, and the outer one, named Cornoc an Tréas, at three-quarters of a mile from the shore, uncovers at low water. A chain of rocks, some of which are above water, extend W.N.W. from Pointe du Raz; the largest is named La Vieille or Old Woman, and a cable from it and three-quarters of a mile from the shore is La Plate, which is the outer danger, and uncovers 11 feet at low water. All these rocks are steep-to. The lighthouse, 259 feet above high water, stands on the highest part of Pointe du Raz, for which see page 23.

The CHAUSSÉE de SEIN, commonly called the Saints, is an extensive cluster of islands, rocks, and shoals, occupying a space of 11 or

12 miles in length, in a N.W. by W. and S.E. by E. direction, and of an average breadth of 1¼ miles. Ile de Sein, the largest island near the eastern end of the Chausée, is low, flat, and inhabited by few fishermen. On its north extreme is the lighthouse (page 23), and at its north-eastern part is a small harbour, with gravel and mud bottom, which dries at low tide. It is frequented by coasters, but the many rocky ledges render its approach dangerous to strangers.

The eastern dangers on the Chausée are named Pont des Chats, (Catsbridge), and from Le Chat, a rock about 4 feet above high water, and S.E. ½ S. 2¼ miles nearly of Ile de Sein lighthouse, the Ponte du Raz lighthouse bears E. ¼ S. 8¼ miles. The extremity of the reef is about half a mile eastward of Le Chat. For a distance of about 4½ miles westward of Ile de Sein the Chassée is studded with rocks more or less above water, and which is named Pont de Sein or Saints Bridge. The western part of the Chaussée is named Basse Froide, having several rocks, which uncover at low water. From the outer or most western 3½-fathom patch, Ushant north-west lighthouse or *revolving* light bears N. by E. ¼ E., distant 24 miles, and Ile de Sein lighthouse or *flashing* light S.E. by E. ¼ E. 8¼ miles, and a little open southward of Pointe du Raz lighthouse or *fixed* light.

The Chaussée de Sein should not be approached too near, as little or no warning is given by the lead, there being from about 30 to 40 fathoms rock and broken shells, within a mile of the bank, and as the tides are strong and uncertain in its vicinity, and probably all the dangers not yet known, the mariner will do well to give it a wide berth. At about 3¼ miles S. by W. from the western danger is a patch with 18 fathoms water over it, named Haut Fond Fouquet, on which it is said the sea occasionally breaks. It is of small extent, and has 30 to 33 fathoms close-to.

Tides.—It is high water, full and change, at Ile de Sein, at 3h. 22m; springs rise 17½ feet, and neaps 12 feet. In the Raz de Sein the flood runs nearly due north. To the north and north-west of the western extremity of the Chaussée the flood runs to the N.E. 1¼ miles an hour, and the ebb S.W. about one mile an hour, the flood commencing 5h. 50m. after high water at Ushant.

The RAZ de SEIN, between the eastern extreme of the Chaussée de Sein and the chain of rocks extending three-quarters of a mile from Pointe de Raz, is about 1¼ miles wide, with 11 to 20 fathoms water, but as there are many dangers to be avoided, it should not be entered by a stranger without a pilot.

The northern part of the passage is divided into two channels by a bank, in the middle of which is a large conspicuous rock, named the

Tevennec, from which the lighthouse on the Ile de Sein bears about W. ¼ S. 3¼ miles, and that on Pointe du Raz S.S.E. ½ E. nearly the same distance. The Tevennec is surrounded by rocky heads, principally covered, which are the more dangerous in consequence of the tides setting strongly over them.

In the southern part of the passage are two patches, three-quarters of a mile apart, named Cornoc Bras and Masclougréiz, the former with 10 feet over it at low water, and the latter with 27 feet. The Cornoc Bras lies with Ile de Sein lighthouse just over the north-east part of that island, bearing N.W. 3¾ miles nearly, and Le Chlec the outer and westernmost rock off Pointe du Van, in line with the rock next east of La Vieille, E.N.E. Le Chlec open or shut in with the extremity of Pointe du Raz clears the Masclougréiz.

Directions.—The Ile de Sein and Pointe du Raz lights in line, bearing S.E. by E. ¾ E., mark the general trend of the Chaussée de Sein. In approaching these rocks from the westward at night, the first light seen will be the *flashing* light on Ile de Sein, and a single bearing of it will indicate if the vessel is to the northward or southward of the line of direction of the lights. In clear weather Pointe du Raz light will not be seen until the vessel is within 4 or 5 miles of the western extreme of the Chaussée. To pass southward of these rocks keep the light on Pointe du Raz well open southward of that on Ile de Sein; but if intending to pass northward or to enter the Iroise, no time should be lost in opening the Pointe du Raz light to the northward of Ile de Sein light.

In proceeding through the Raz du Sein from the southward, the Tevennec bank may be passed on either side; but the eastern channel is considered the best, although the other, with a scant wind, may give a vessel the advantage of laying through without tacking, and the stream within it is weaker. The Vieille rock in line with a small detached rock off a point southward of Pointe du Raz, bearing S.E. nearly, is a good leading mark through this passage, borrowing on the Tevennec with the ebb, and on the Saints with the flood.

At night, vessels passing through the Raz de Sein from the southward, should get within the white sector of Tevennec light (page 23), and keep in it until the Falaise and Pointe du Raz lights (page 23) are in line; an E.N.E. course will then lead into the red light of Tevennec, and out of the western sector of Falaise light; and on Falaise light being again seen in the northern sector, a North course, or keeping the light in sight, will lead clear of all dangers.

From the northward, having Falaise light bearing South, keep it so until the red light of Tevennec is seen, when the course should be altered to

W.S.W. until the white light of Tevennec opens out, then proceed south in the sector of white light.

Attention must be paid to the currents prevalent in the Raz de Sein, and the channel should not be attempted in bad weather at spring tides when the winds are against the current.

The flashing light on Ile de Sein presents the same appearance as Penfret light—on the island of that name of the Glenan group—but this resemblance cannot be mistaken, as Penfret light is within the horizon of Penmarc'h point light, the flashes of which are at *half minute* intervals.

The Coast from Pointe du Raz trends to the south east and southward for about 24 miles to Penmarc'h point, forming the extensive bay of Audierne, in which the soundings are from 30 to 6 fathoms. In the northern part of the bay, and 1½ miles from the shore, is a cluster of shallow patches having from 2 to 5 fathoms water over them, with 8 and 9 fathoms between them and the shore, and 13 and 14 fathoms close-to outside. From the 3½ fathoms patch of Les Ninkinou, Plougof church bears N.E., and Pointe du Raz lighthouse N.N.W. distant 2¾ miles.*

At about 6 miles from Pointe du Raz is Cabestan bay, with a sandy beach, which is occasionally visited by small vessels, but it affords no shelter except with off shore winds. The extreme points of this bay are foul, and the rocks dry at low water; a detached rock named the Guilcher lies near the north entrance point.

At 1½ miles south-eastward of Cabestan bay is the entrance to port d'Audierne; thence the land is high until within a few miles of Penmarc'h point, where there is a valley, in which are a village and several churches. To the northward of Penmarc'h point is the small bay of La Torche, in the southern part of which, at Portz-carn, small vessels can take the ground without risk when embayed or unable to double the Penmarc'h rocks. At about 14 miles south-east of Penmarc'h point are the Iles de Glenan, and 18 miles farther eastward the Ile de Groix, which fronts the entrance of Port Louis. From La Torche bay, round eastward as far as Ile de Groix, the whole coast is studded more or less with dangers, lying nearly 3 miles from the coast and surrounding the Isles de Glenan, for the position of which the mariner is referred to the chart.

PORT AUDIERNE can only be entered at high water, but it shelters vessels that can take the ground from all winds. The town of Audierne stands on the west bank of the river, about three-quarters of a mile from the entrance. To the south of the town is the garden and old

---

* *See* Admiralty chart :—Ile de Groix to Raz de Sein, No. 2,645; scale, *m* = 0·5 of an inch.

convent of the Capuchins. On Raoulic point, at the west side of entrance, is a battery and a jetty constructed on its projecting rock. The bar dries 4 feet at low water.

Fronting the port about a mile from the entrance is a rocky bank, named La Gamelle, which dries 5 feet at low water ; a red buoy marks its western, and a black buoy its eastern edge, the position of these buoys cannot always be depended upon ; vessels entering the harbour may pass on either side of this bank, but between it and the shore there are several patches of sunken rocks. Basse Fornic, with 9 feet water, is the most easterly of the shoals at the entrance to port Audierne, and is separated from La Gamelle by a narrow channel.

LIGHTS.—A *fixed red* light, elevated 36 feet above high water, and visible 7 miles, is exhibited from a tower on the extremity of the jetty on Raoulic point ; and N.E. ¼ N., about sixth-tenths of a mile from this light, near the garden of the Capuchin convent, is another tower which shows, at an elevation of 69 feet, a *fixed* white light visible 12 miles. The two lights in line, bearing N.E. ¼ N., lead through the channel westward of La Gamelle bank, in 2½ fathoms water, and up to the entrance of the port. There are two white beacons west of Raoulic point, which when in line lead through the Grand channel in 4 fathoms water.*

A Life Boat is stationed at port Audierne.

Tides.—It is high water, full and change, at port Audierne, at 3h. 15m.; springs rise 13 feet, and neaps 6½ feet.

The PENMARC'H ROCKS are a group of dangers that surround Penmarc'h point and extend several miles along the coast to the eastward. These rocks, many of which are above water, lie 1¼ to 2½ miles from the shore, having between them passages for small vessels, but they are dangerous, and cannot be used by a stranger. There are depths of 20 to 30 fathoms sand, gravel, and shells close to the outer edge of Penmarc'h rocks.

Port Guilfinec, situated about 4 miles E.S.E. of Penmarc'h point, dries at low water, but is available for vessels of 8 feet draught ; its approach is difficult, and should not be attempted without local knowledge or the assistance of a pilot ; it is principally a resort for fishing and small coasting vessels.

LIGHTS.—Near the church of St. Pierre, on Penmarc'h point, is a circular tower which exhibits, at an elevation of 135 feet above high water, a white light *revolving* every *half minute*. The light is visible in clear

---

* *See* Admiralty plan :—Port D'Audierne, on chart, No. 2,645.

weather from a distance of 22 miles; the eclipses will not appear total within the distance of 12 miles.

On the eastern point of the entrance of port Guilfinec, two *fixed red* lights are shown W. by S. ½ S. and E. by N. ½ N. of each other, and 620 yards apart. The upper or easternmost light is elevated 50 feet above high water, and in clear weather visible through an arc of 10 degrees on each side of the centre of the channel, and, if the observer be in the centre of the channel, should be seen from a distance of 9 miles, decreasing to 6 miles to 10 degrees on either side.

The lower or westernmost light is elevated 19 feet above high water, and should be seen 6 miles in clear weather.

The GLENAN ISLANDS are an extensive group of islands and rocks within which there is no anchorage nor passage, unless for vessels of light draught, which must pass within range of a fort, said to be bomb-proof, which stands on Cygogne islet, near the centre of the cluster. The security of this defence lies in its being surrounded with water, which is, in places, so shallow that a man may cross to the rocks and islands next to the north-west.

The largest and principal islands of the group are Penfret, St. Nicholas, Loc'h, Drenec, and Castel-bras. Penfret, the most easterly and largest, is nearly a mile long, low in the middle, but rises at each end, so as to form two hills. A lighthouse 79 feet high stands on its northern end, and a semaphore on the southern. On the rising ground of the island are several large gardens, near which are three wells of excellent water, whence from 30 to 40 tons have been obtained daily. There are sandy bays on both sides of the island, and boats may always land to leeward. The islands are destitute of wood.

La Jument, the southernmost of the dangers of this group, is a reef half a mile in extent, the eastern part of which is the shoalest, one part being awash at the lowest tides; the depth increases quickly to the southward, but between the reef and the islands there are various sunken rocks. From the shoalest part, St. Philibert church is in line with the low south point of Penfret island, bearing N.E. by E. ¼ E., and the flagstaff on fort Cygogne seen nearly over the middle of Loc'h, a low flat island, N.E. ¼ N.

The Basse an Ero is a small reef awash at low water, lying 9¾ miles eastward of the Jument, with the highest of the rocks south-east of Penfret, about 3° open of the north-east part of that island, N. ¼ E.; and the upper part of a remarkable peaked rock, which is seen just over the south point of Loc'h island, N.W. ¼ N. At about 1¼ miles southward of this reef are some patches with 5 to 8 fathoms water, named the Laouenou, having 10 and 15 fathoms close to, and 30 fathoms at the distance of about half a mile to the east and south of them.

Basse Pérenés, with 11 feet water, is the westernmost danger of this group, and lies 3¼ miles N.W. ¼ N. from La Jument.

At about 3 miles S.E. by E. from Penfret are several shallow rocky patches, at the east end of an extensive bank named the Basse Jaune, one of which uncovers a foot at the lowest tides. From this rocky head the flagstaff on fort Cygogne is a little open to the south of Castel Raet, a rock in the sandy bay on east side of Penfret N.W. by W. ¾ W.; the western part of the summit of Locrenan mountain on with eastern slope of Beg-meil high land, N. ¾ W.; and St. Philibert church, N.N.E. easterly, open eastward of the Men-Disu rock, which dries 15 feet at low water. On other parts of the bank there are from 5¼ to 16 fathoms water, rocky bottom.

Within, and to the northward of the Glenan islands, is the Pourceaux bank, with many rocks appearing above the surface, and others which uncover at low water. To the northward of this bank is Ile aux Moutons and bank; and within these are numerous other rocky patches and shallows too complicated for descrpition.

LIGHTS.—On the north end of Penfret island is a square tower, which exhibits, at an elevation of 118 feet above high water, a *fixed* white light, varied every *four minutes* by a *flash*, visible in clear weather at a distance of 14 miles. The faint light which is perceptible during the intervals is preceded and followed by short eclipses, but these are not total within the distance of 6 miles.

There is but little apparent difference between this light and that on Pilier islet (page 65), but there is no danger of mistaking the one for the other, as it is not possible for any vessel from seaward to arrive in sight of the Penfret light without having previously seen either the *revolving* light on Belle-ile or that on Penmarc'h point; and when approaching the Chaussée de Sein, there are visible at the same time the *flashing* light on the Ile de Sein, and the *fixed* light on Pointe du Raz.

Isle aux Moutons.—On isle aux Moutons stands a lighthouse 49 feet high, from which, at an elevation of 59 feet above high water, is exhibited a *fixed* light:—showing *red* through an arc of 60°, between the bearings S. 19½° E. and S. 79½° E. (over the dangers included between les Polains and Karekgrèis); *green* through an arc of 31°, between S. 79½° E. and N. 69½° E. (indicating the position of Basse Rouge shoal); *white* over the fairway of the channel, through an arc of 22° between N. 69½° E. and N. 47½° E.; *red* through an arc of 96°, between N. 47½° E. and N. 48½° W (covering the dangers between Bluiniers and Basse Jaune shoals); and *white*, between N. 48½° W. and S. 19½° E.

The white light should be visible in clear weather from a distance of 12 miles; the red, 8 miles; and the green, 7 miles.

Anchorage.—At one to 2½ miles distance east and north-east of Penfret, on which side the island is steep-to and free from danger, there is good anchorage in 15 to 18 fathoms water, muddy bottom. Here vessels will lie well sheltered with winds from S.W. round westerly to N.E., being exposed only to those between East and South, and in that direction the Basse Jaune reduces the force of the sea.

In the winter the safest anchorage is well to the northward, in 15 fathoms, 2 miles nearly from the north end of Penfret, with the flagstaff of fort Cygogne bearing about W.S.W., and the Ile aux Moutons N.W. For watering or other reasons, in order to be nearer Penfret, the flag-staff of fort Cygogne may be brought in line with the north end of Penfret about W. ¾ N., and Ile aux Moutons N.W. by N.; this position will be about a mile from Penfret in 15 fathoms, muddy bottom, but more exposed to southerly winds.

Tides.—It is high water, full and change, at the Glenan islands at 3h. 12m.; springs rise 13 feet, neaps 10 feet. The eastern or flood stream usually runs an hour longer when it is uninterrupted. The rate of both streams is from half a mile to 2 miles an hour.

Directions.—When bound for the above anchorages from the southward, bring Ile aux Moutons to bear N.N.W. ½ W. and open a little northward of the north point of Penfret, which will lead between the Glenan islands and the Basse Jaune, in from 25 to 15 fathoms water.

There are passages between the Glenan islands and the Ponceaux bank, and between Ile aux Moutons and the main; but the dangers in them are so numerous that they should not be attempted by strangers unless in cases of necessity, and then the chart and the eye should be the guide.

PONT-L'ABBÉ RIVER.—Anse de Benodet, at about 10 miles eastward of Penmarc'h point, is so studded with dangers, that to a stranger the services of a pilot are indispensable. On the west side of the bay is the entrance to the little river Pont-l'Abbé, which is almost barred by banks, and accessible only at high water, through a small navigable channel. When within the entrance the water deepens, and small vessels may anchor near Tudy isle, abreast of Loctudy.

LIGHT.—On the south side of entrance to Pont-l'Abbé river is a circular tower, showing a *fixed* white light, at an elevation of 36 feet above high water, and seen in clear weather from a distance of 10 miles.

ODET or **QUIMPER RIVER.**—At the head of Benedot bay and 2¾ miles eastward of Pont-l'Abbé river, is the mouth of the Odet or

Quimper river, which is nearly half a mile wide at the entrance, but the navigable channel, with 3½ to 4½ fathoms water, is narrowed considerably by ledges running off on either side, by two rocky banks, named Les Verres and Le Four, each marked by a red beacon, lying in mid-channel, and by another, La Rousse, near the western point, and marked by a black beacon : these latter dangers uncover respectively 11, 6, and 8 feet at low water. There is a battery on the western point, and one on Pointe de Coq, on the east side within the entrance.

At a mile within the entrance, on the east bank, is the village of Benodet, and at 10 miles, following the windings of the river, is the town of Quimper, the capital of the department of Finistère, which possesses a cathedral, contains about 12,000 inhabitants, and bears the stamp of antiquity as much as any town in Brittany. The manufactures consist of earthenware, leather, and beer. The trade is important. There are also building yards. Imports consist chiefly of coal, timber, wine, and resin. Exports are grain and wine barrels, of which latter there is a large manufacture.—Vessels of 9 feet draught can ascend the river as far as Quimper at low water, and steam vessels of heavy draught can remain off Benodet, or in the cove of Kerandren ; it is requisite, however, to moor head and stern.

LIGHTS.—On the east side of entrance to the Odet there are two lighthouses ; one on Coq point, at half a mile within the entrance, which shows a *fixed red* light, at 33 feet above high water, visible 7 miles ; and the other at 284 yards, N. ¾ E. from it, exhibits a *fixed* white light, at 56 feet above high water, visible 9 miles. The *red* or southernmost light, is visible through an arc of 15 degrees on each side of the centre of the channel. The two lights in line are the leading mark for the channel into the river.

Directions.—The best anchorage in Benodet bay, off the entrance of the Odet, is in 5 or 6 fathoms water, with the east side of Pen-an-Guern rock (at the north-east side of Ile aux Moutons), in line with the lighthouse on Penfret, bearing S. by E. ¾ E. In steering from this anchorage towards the river, take care to avoid Le Taro, Les Mats, and other dangers about 1¼ miles off the eastern shore of bay. Le Taro, the western of these dangers, uncovers 7 feet at low water ; it is marked by a red and white beacon, and lies with Tregunc church in line with Mousterlin point bearing E. by S. ¼ S., and Bonodet church on with fort Coq. This latter mark leads westward of the reefs, which extend 2 miles southward of Mousterlin point.

The two lighthouses in line bearing N. ¾ E., lead in to the river in mid channel between the Verres and Four Rocks on the east, and

La Rousse on the west, the least depth will be about 20 feet. A black buoy lies on the east side of La Rousse. Continue with this mark on until well up to Coq point, when keep in mid-channel, and anchor abreast the village of Benodet in 5 to 7 fathoms water, sand and mud. Strangers are recommended to take a pilot in the bay, before entering the river.

BAIE de la FOREST.—At about 6 miles eastward of the entrance the Odet is the Baie de la Forest, the coast between being bordered with rocks and shoals, many of which appear at low tide. The entrance, $2\frac{1}{4}$ miles wide, is between Beg Meil point on the west and Cabellou on the east, and on each point there is a fort. A rocky ledge extends nearly a mile from Beg Meil, and there are dangerous ledges off Cabellou point. The bay is also studded with dangers, but with local knowledge, anchorage may be obtained in 5 to 6 fathoms, mud bottom.

Concarneau.—On the eastern side of Forest bay is the little harbour of Concarneau, which has good anchorage, and will receive vessels of 500 tons burden, but its entrance is obstructed by rocks, and should not be attempted without a pilot. The town, which stands on a small island in the middle of the harbour, is surrounded by thick stone walls, with a projecting parapet, and towers at regular distances. The suburbs are more extensive than the town, and are better built. The island is 400 yards long, and 120 broad. About 300 boats belonging to the place are engaged in the pilchard fishery. Besides pilchards and other fish the exports are cider, wood, and grain ; the imports, salt, wine, spirits, and Norway deals. Population, about 3,000.

Most of the dangers at the entrance of Concarneau dry from one to 16 feet at low water, but there are others with only 2 to 5 feet over them at that time of tide; some of these are buoyed. The Men Cren is a rock, with a beacon on it, lying on the west side of the channel into the harbour ; it never covers, and eastward of it is an outer anchorage in 5 to $6\frac{1}{4}$ fathoms, sand, mud, and shells. From this to the town, the depths are 20 to 11 feet at low water.

LIGHTS.—There are three lights at Concarneau—two as a leading mark for the entrance channel, and one to guide to the anchorage. The first is a *fixed* white light exhibited from a circular turret in the Croix fort, on west side of entrance ; it is elevated 46 feet above high water, and visible 9 miles.

At about a mile N.E. $\frac{1}{4}$ E., from the above, is another turret, which also shows a *fixed* white light, elevated 148 feet, and visible 12 miles. These lights in line lead in through the channel between the Men Cren, and Men Fall shoal, which is marked by a buoy.

The other is a *fixed red* light shown from a house at Lanriec, on the eastern shore; it is elevated 43 feet above high water, visible 9 miles, and is intended to guide vessels to the anchorage after passing the Men Fall shoal. It only lights an area of 19° free from danger, and the southern limit of the light passes about 90 yards northward of the Men Fall; it will also be lost sight of before the vessel reaches the shore where it is shown.

Medée Rock.—*Lighthouse building.*

Tides.—It is high water, full and change, at Concarneau at 3h. 12m.; springs rise 13 feet, neaps 9½ feet.

Directions.—When bound to Concarneau harbour from the southward, after passing on either side of the Basse Jaune, keep the lead going and preserve the depth of 15 to 16 fathoms to avoid the dangers off Trévignon point, for they are steep-to and most of them covered, except at low water, when the Flaharn and others show. Some of the Soldats are uncovered. The general nature of the bottom will be green mud and clay, and the soundings will decrease to 12 and 11 fathoms, as the leading mark for the entrance is approached.

Beuzec church in line with Concarneau church leads in the deepest water through the channel between the Lué-vras rocks, and Men Cren on the west side, and the Men Fall, Barzic, and Cochon rocks on the east. When close up to the Men Cren, steer for the windmill on the eastern shore, passing at least 1½ cables southwards of the west point of entrance of the harbour to avoid the shallow ground around it, and steer in along by the eastern shore.

At night keep the two *white* lights in line bearing N.E. ¼ E. until the Men Fall is passed, when steer towards the *red* light, and anchor in the outer road.

The Coast from Cabellou point trends in a S. by E. direction, 5 miles to Trévignon point, on which is a fort and signal house with a semaphore. At 1½ miles from the former point is Jument point, with rocky ledges extending from it, and from half to about 1¼ miles off the point is an extensive flat, having shoal patches with 2 to 18 feet on them at low water; the outermost, named Le Corven, has 16 feet on it. Hence to Trévignon point the coast is bordered with rocky patches, the outermost of which, with only 7 feet on it, and named Le Corven de Trévignon, lies nearly 1½ miles from the point, with St. Philibert church bearing E. ¾ N. At 6 cables N.E. by N. of this patch is the Flaharn, which dries 5 feet, and to the northward, 3½ cables from the Flaharn, are Les Soldats, of which some are uncovered.

From Trévignon point the coast trends easterly for 5 miles to the entrance of the little rivers Aven and Bélon, both of which are shallow and have bars that dry one foot at the lowest tides; the former has a lighthouse

on the western point of its entrance. At about midway and a mile off
shore, is a small islet, named Ile Verte or Green isle, and within this is
Raguénèes islet.   There are several shoal patches outside Verte isle, the
Men an Tréas, at a mile west of it, uncovers 4 feet at low springs, a near
approach to the shore is therefore dangerous.   Before the entrances to the
rivers are Le Cochon and Les Verrés ledges, which dry 2 to 8 feet, the
latter is marked by a beacon, and Le Trépied bank with 3¼ fathoms on it
at low water; these must be left to the eastward when steering for the
entrances, off which the depths are from 2 to 3 fathoms.

At 2¼ miles S.E. by S. from the entrances of Aven and Bélon rivers is
Beg-Morg point, close to which are Les Cochons rocks awash at low tide.
Immediately eastward of this point is a small inlet, named port de Brigneau,
with rocks at either side of its entrance ; and at three-quarters of a mile
farther is port de Méryen, the entrance to which is also rocky. On the
shore, a mile eastward of Méryen, is a signal house, and half a mile farther
is port de Douélan creek.

LIGHTS.—On Bec-ar-Vechen point, at the western side of the
entrance of the river Aven, is a stone turret which exhibits a *fixed* light,
showing *white* between the bearings of E. by N. ¾ N. around north to
N. by W. ¼ W.; *red* between N. by W. ¼ W. and N.N.W. ¼ W.; *white*
between N.N.W. ¼ W. and N.W. by N.; and *green* from N.W. by N. to
the land. The light is elevated 125 feet above high water level, and visible
in clear weather at a distance of 8 miles.

Port de Douélan.—A *fixed* white light is exhibited from a round
turret on either side of the entrance to port de Douélan 356 yards apart,
bearing N. ¾ E. and S. ¾ W. of each other, and both visible at a distance
of 8 miles.*

The two lights in line lead into port.

QUIMPERLÉ RIVER.—The entrance to this river, 3 miles
eastward of port de Douélan, is narrow and barred, but vessels of 150 tons
burthen ascend to the town of Quimperlé (about 6¼ miles from the entrance), which has 6,000 inhabitants and a considerable trade.   Close off
the entrance of the Quimperlé are some rocks which dry 4 feet at low
water marked by beacons.

The Coast from Quimperlé river trends to the southward for 2 miles
to fort Kergan standing on a rock close to the shore, forming Pouldu bay,
in which the soundings decrease gradually to the shore.   Thence the coast
for 8¼ miles, to Talut point, is bordered by rocky patches, many of which
are dry at low water, extending at least 1¼ miles from the shore. From

* The upper part of the lighthouse on le Four, port Douélan, has been carried away
by the sea, and is not much above high-water mark ; it is said this lighthouse will be
repaired in the course of the year 1881. *Annonce Hydrographique*, No. 150 of 1880.

Talut point the shore trends round to the eastward for 3 miles to the entrance of port Louis, and is skirted all the way by rocks.

L'ILE de GROIX lies 18 miles S.E. by E. of the Glenan islands, and between it and the main land, from which it is distant 3 miles, is a good channel with 14 to 19 fathoms water in it, leading to port Louis and L'Orient. The island, which may be distinguished by a lighthouse at each end, is 4¼ miles long N.W. ¼ W. and S.E. ¼ E., and 1½ miles broad. The population is mostly seafaring, and their chief occupation is fishing.

The coasts of this island are free from danger, excepting near the north-east and south-east sides, particularly the latter, off which dangers extend nearly 1¾ miles. At three-quarters of a mile north-west from the light-house on the eastern part of the island, and about a third of a mile from the shore, are rocks and shallow patches named Basses Milit, which are steep-to, and therefore dangerous to approach. From Pointe des Chats, the south-east extreme of the island, a reef extends three-quarters of a mile to the southward, terminating in the rocks named Les Chats, which are occasionally uncovered. At nearly 1¾ miles S. by E. from this point is the Basses des Chats, over which there are only 13 feet water. The marks for it are, Enfer and St. Nicolas points on the south side of Ile de Groix in line bearing N.W. ¼ N. nearly, and the tower of port L'Orient in line with the citadel of port Louis, N.E. by N. There is also a small patch, with 4 fathoms water on it, to the north-west of this shoal, but between it and the Chats rocks there is deep water.

This island is bordered on the north side by the Basse des Bretons, with depths of 6 to 15 fathoms, sand, mud, and gravel, which extends nearly half way over from the island towards the main.

LIGHTS.—There are two lighthouses on Ile de Groix; one standing S. by E. ¾ E., at about a quarter of a mile within Pen-Men point, the north-west extreme of the island, the other in fort de la Croix, at the eastern extreme.

Pen-Men Point.--The lighthouse of Pen-Men point has a square tower which exhibits, at 194 feet above high water, a *fixed* white light, visible in clear weather at a distance of 18 miles.

Fort de la Croix.—The lighthouse in fort de la Croix exhibits a *fixed* white light, varied every *three minutes* by a *red flash*. The light is elevated 171 feet, and visible 10 miles, except towards the Glenan islands, in which direction it is masked by the heights of the western part of Groix.

It should be remarked that, except in foggy weather, vessels coming from the southward will perceive the light on Belle-Ile, which *revolves* every minute, before the light on Pen-Men point can be seen; and that in approaching Ile de Groix, the *flashing* light on its eastern point will be

seen shortly after the light on Pen-Men point. In like manner, vessels
coming from the westward will not be exposed to the risk of mistaking the
lights; for, before the light on Pen-Men point will be visible they will
almost always have seen Penmarc'h point light, which *revolves* every half
minute, and also Penfret island *fixed* and *flashing* light, both of which have
been described in pages 35 and 37.

Life Boat.—A life boat is stationed at L'Ile de Groix.

CHAPTER II.

ILE DE GROIX TO FUENTERRABIA.

VARIATION in 1881.

Ile de Groix	- - 18° 00′ W.	Ile d'Oleron -	- - 18° 30′ W.
Gironde river, entrance	17° 30′ W.	Adour river, entrance	- 17° 30′ W.

PORTS LOUIS and L'ORIENT.—At 4 miles N.E. by E. easterly from the lighthouse on the eastern end of Ile de Groix, is Pointe de Gavre, the south extreme of a peninsula on the east side of entrance to the harbours of ports Louis and L'Orient. On the eastern shore, at about 1¼ miles within Pointe de Gavre, is the strongly fortified town of port Louis, and at about 2 miles northward of the latter is the town of L'Orient, on the right bank of the river Pont-Scorf, a small stream which unites at half a mile below the town with the river Blavet, from the eastward, and they both fall into the northern part of the harbour of port Louis.*

L'Orient is strongly fortified, and is one of the five naval ports of France. The naval arsenal is large and commodious, and has accommodation on the buildings slips for the simultaneous construction of several vessels of war. There are also factories for steel ship building; and two dry docks. A school of gunnery is established on Pointe de Gavre, where experiments are constantly carried on.

There is an extensive trade in sardines, marine stores, iron, wax, and honey.

The entrance to the harbours is bounded on the east by the rocks lying off the peninsula of Le Gavre, on the south by the Bastresses, Errants, and Truies rocks, and on the west by the ledges extending from that shore. The channel gradually narrows, and between the Jument rock and the citadel of port Louis it is not more than 150 yards wide at low water, immediately within which is the harbour of port Louis, occupying a space of nearly 2 miles in length in a north-east and south-west direction, and an average breadth of half a mile; but the depths are irregular, and the anchorage much contracted by banks and shoal patches. In the centre of the harbour is Ile St. Michel, which is covered with the yellow buildings of the Lazaret. A vessel may pass on either side of this islet in proceeding towards L'Orient, but the western channel is the deeper, and if it be necessary to wait for the tide there is anchorage in 6 or 7 fathoms water, in the southern part of the harbour.

---

* See Admiralty chart:—France, west coast, sheet 5, Bourgneuf to Ile de Groix, with views, No. 2,646; scale, m = 0·5 an inch.

The port of L'Orient is abreast the town of the same name, and is occupied only by vessels of war. It is about three-quarters of a mile in extent, north and south, but not more than a cable wide at low water, at which period the average depth is about 25 feet. At half a mile above the port is a suspension bridge, near which are more establishments belonging to the arsenal. On the south side of the town is a narrow creek, dry at low water, leading to the commercial port, which is 760 yards long, and communicates with a basin 430 yards long.

Time Ball.*

LIGHTS.—On the hill of La Peyrière, at the north-west side of port Louis and about a third of a mile north of Ile St. Michel, is a square tower, which shows, at 75 feet above high water, a *fixed* white light, visible in clear weather 12 miles. At the distance of nearly a mile N.N.E. ¾ E. from the above light-tower, another *fixed* white light is exhibited from L'Orient church tower, at 148 feet above high water, visible 12 miles. These lights in line lead through the eastern channel or Passe de Gavre.

On the end of the Breakwater, a fixed *red* light is exhibited, visible 5 miles.

On the south bastion of the fortifications of port Louis, a *fixed* white light is shown at 20 feet above high water, visible at the distance of 6 miles. At E. ¾ N., distant nearly a mile from this light, is a circular turret, which exhibits another *fixed* white light at 62 feet above high water, and visible 12 miles. These two latter lights in line lead in through the Great channel.

At Keroman Creek two leading lights are exhibited.

The high light is a fixed *red* light, shown from the keeper's dwelling, elevated 44 feet above high water, and should be visible in clear weather from a distance of 9 miles.

The low light is a fixed *green* light, shown from a hut constructed of sheet iron, situated S. 12° W., 372 yards from the high light ; it is elevated 10 feet above high water, and should be visible in clear weather from a distance of 8 miles.

These lights lead between Turc bank and the shoal ground extending from the western shore.

In Kernevel Bay two leading lights are exhibited.

The high light is a fixed *red* light, shown from the keeper's dwelling, elevated 30 feet above high water, and should be visible in clear weather from a distance of 9 miles.

The low light is a fixed *green* light, shown from a hut constructed of

---

* At the mast of the Harbour tower, a black ball is hoisted close up at 5 minutes before signal, and dropped at noon L'Orient mean time.

sheet iron, situated N. 54° E., 328 yards from the high light; it is elevated 5 feet above high water, and should be visible in clear weather from a distance of 8 miles.

The Kernevel lights in line indicate the channel from their intersection with the line of Keroman leading lights, to the anchorage of Penmane.

These leading lights are visible only through an arc of about 16° on each side of the mid-channel courses, and will diminish in brilliancy as those lines are receded from.

Tides.—It is high water, full and change, at port Louis at 3h. 11m.; ordinary springs rise 13 feet, neaps 9½ feet.

Directions.—The great or western channel into port Louis is between Les Truies bank and rocks on the east, and Basse de la Paille and Basse du Chenal on the west; the Paille has 4 feet least water on it, the Chenal 11 feet, and the Truies bank 10 feet; one of the Truies rocks is always above water, and has a beacon on it, the others uncover 2 to 12 feet at low water. The eastern channel is between Les Bastresses on the east and Les Errants rocks on the west; the former is a bank with numerous shallow heads on it, one of which, Le Baril Rond, is awash at low water; Les Errants are never completely covered, and a beacon marks the eastern rock. The least depth in either channel with the leading marks on is 16 feet at low water; but the eastern channel is narrow, and should not be attempted without a pilot.

Approaching by the western channel, steer mid-way between Ile de Groix and the coast, until the lighthouse at Kerbel is in line with the one in the south bastion of the fortifications of port Louis, bearing E. ¼ N.— or at night the two lights in line,—which leads between the dangers on either side. Continue with these marks on until L'Orient church is in line with the lighthouse at La Peyrière. Then steer N.N.E. ¾ E.—or at night the lights in line—and with this mark kept exactly on a vessel will pass westward of La Paix bank and Potée de Beurre rocks on which there is a beacon, and mid-channel between the Jument rock also marked with a beacon, and the foot of the citadel of port Louis. Having passed the citadel, if the vessel is of large draught and bound to L'Orient, anchor in 6 or 7 fathoms, and wait for high water.

The leading mark through the eastern channel between the Errants and Bastresses, is L'Orient church tower in line with the lighthouse at La Peyrière bearing N.N.E. ¾ E.—or at night the lights in line—but this mark must be kept exactly on, as it leads close to some of the dangers which are buoyed. There is also a narrow channel used by coasters between Pointe de Gavre and Les Bastresses.

Vessels entering port L'Orient at night, and proceeding to the inner harbour, should keep the fixed white lights of L'Orient church tower and

La Peyrière in line until Keroman leading lights come in line, when those lights should be steered for until Kernevel lights appear in line astern for leading to the anchorage of Penmane. The fixed white light of the landing place at L'Orient is also a guide to the anchorage at Penmane.

The COAST from Pointe de Gavre trends to the southward for about 14 miles to Beg en Aud, the north extreme of the Presqu'ile de Quiberon. The land between is generally low, with downs, and the shore—which forms a bend to the north-east—a sandy beach, and as in places several dangers lie a considerable distance off, it should be approached with discretion.

The first danger south-eastward of Pointe de Gavre, is a shallow patch having $2\frac{1}{2}$ fathoms on it at low water, with a reef of rocks northward of it; and three-quarters of a mile southward of the point lies a rocky patch with 16 feet on it, and steep-to, named Basse de Gavre.

At about 4 miles south-eastward of Pointe de Gavre, and a long half mile from the shore, are the Magoëro rocks, which uncover 18 feet at low water. On the land abreast this ledge is a semaphore.

At 2 miles south-east of the Mogoëro rocks is the Rivière d'Etel, a small stream, the entrance to which is obstructed by a bar with only 2 feet over it, but the water deepens to 20 and 25 feet within. At about $1\frac{1}{4}$ miles W. by N. $\frac{1}{4}$ N. of the entrance are the two Roheu rocks, which uncover 17 and 19 feet at low water. Pointe d'Ardevenne, at $1\frac{1}{4}$ miles south-east of the entrance, is bordered by a rocky ledge, and southward of it are several rocks, the principal of which, the Rohellan, is always uncovered.

At about 2 miles S.W. of Ardevenne point, is the centre of a rocky bank, which is a mile in length east and west, with general depths of 4 to 6 fathoms on it, but there are several patches with 10 to 16 feet water, and on its western part are some heads which uncover 10 feet. From these latter, which are named Les Pierres Noires or Chiviguete rocks, the church of Ardevenne is in line with the Rohellan rock, bearing N.E. by E. $\frac{1}{4}$ E., and the Men-Toul rock is in line with the south part of Penthièvre fort, S.S.E. $\frac{1}{4}$ E. nearly. The soundings around the bank are 8 to 10 fathoms, gray sand, and rocky bottom.

The shore from Ardevenne point continues low until near the north end of the peninsula of Quiberon, when it rises a little and becomes bolder. On the narrow neck of the isthmus connecting the peninsula with the main land, is fort Penthièvre, abreast of which is Ile Teviec, surrounded by numerous rocks which extend fully 3 miles northward of Beg en Aud, and 2 miles from the shore, so that a vessel should not approach this part of the coast too near.

The peninsula of Quiberon, 5 miles long north and south, and about 1¼ miles wide, is high, and the western shore is bold and cliffy, but off it. southern end are numerous rocks, many of which are covered at low water. The principal of these rocks, named La Teignouse, is 1¼ miles S.E. ½ S from the south-east extreme of the peninsula; it is large, high, round, and distinguished by a lighthouse. Within the lighthouse there is no passage, being all foul ground, but south of the Basse du Chenal and the lighthouse, between them and the Chaussée du Beniguet, is the Passage de la Teignouse, which is frequently used. The Basse Cariou and Basse du Chenal, the southernment of the dangers extending from the peninsula, are marked by black buoys.

LIGHTS.—The river Etel is pointed out at night by a *red* light, which is exhibited from a tower at the north point of entrance, at an elevation of 40 feet above high water, and visible in clear weather 7 miles.

A life boat is stationed at Etel river.

Teignouse Rock.—The lighthouse on the Teignouse rock shows, at an elevation of 59 feet above high water, a *white* light varied by a *flash* every *three minutes*, visible 11 miles.

PLATEAU des BIRVIDEAUX.—This rocky bank, at about 5¼ miles westward of Beg en Aud, is a mile long east and west, and with general depths on it of 4 to 7 fathoms; but near the centre of the bank are shoal patches with 8 to 21 feet water on them. From the 8 feet patch, Portivi windmill is in line with Portz-Guen point bearing E. ¼ N. and Borderun semaphore, on Belle-Ile, in one with the guard-house of the battery on Vieux Chateau point, S. ¾ W. nearly.

BELLE-ILE, 9¼ miles long N.W. by N. and S.E. by S., and 5 miles wide at its broadest part, affords shelter during west and south-west winds. Its shores are generally high and steep, and its natural strength is much augmented by fortifications on its accessible parts. Near the middle of its north-east side is Le Palais, the chief town, defended by a citadel, the walls of which bound the northern side of a small artificial harbour with only 5 feet in at high water.

On the north side of the island, 3 miles north-west of Le Palais, is port Sauzon, which is said to be capable of receiving vessels of 50 tons, but they lie aground at low water. This harbour is easy of access, and considered preferable to that of Le Palais, although the latter is the more frequented. The island is well cultivated, and produces excellent wheat; fresh water is abundant; population about 6,000.

Several rocks and shallow heads lie along the shore of Belle-Ile, but none of them are farther off than three-quarters of a mile. Vessels, however, bound round the north-west point of the island must give it a berth of at least 1½ miles to avoid Les Poulains reef, which extends nearly that distance in a N.W. by W. direction from the point. Some of the rocks on this reef uncover at low water, whilst others have only 6 to 8 feet on them at that time of tide.

The general soundings in the channel on the north-east side of the island are from 8 to 15 fathoms, excepting on the Bancs de Taillefer, which are three distinct ridges lying parallel to each other in mid-channel. They have from 6 to 8 fathoms water on them, but on the centre ridge is a shoal spot with only 21 feet on it, from which the citadel of Le Palais bears S.W. ½ W., distant nearly 2¾ miles. Other shoal patches lie to the southward of these ridges, but none have less than 10 fathoms on them, except a rocky patch of 4½ fathoms, named Basse du Palais, lying E.S.E. 1½ miles from the citadel.

Semaphores.—There are four semaphores on Belle-Ile, and communication with the main land by electric telegraph. Vessels by using the commercial code of signals can transmit messages to any of the provincial towns in Europe.

LIGHTS.—There are five lighthouses on Belle-Ile; one on the table land above port Goulfar, near the middle of the south-west side of the island; another on Ile aux Poulains, near Pointe de Poulains (the north point of the island); a third on the mole head on the west side of entrance to port Sauzon; the fourth on the mole head on south side of entrance to port Le Palais; and the fifth near Kerdonis point, the east extreme of Belle-Ile.

Port Goulfar light-tower exhibits, at 276 feet above high water, a white light, which *revolves every minute*, and is visible in clear weather at a distance of 27 miles. The eclipses do not appear total within 10 miles.

Ile aux Poulains.—The light-tower on Ile aux Poulains, at the north extreme of the island, exhibits a *flashing* white light which eclipses for *five seconds* at intervals of *five seconds*, elevated 112 feet above high water, and visible in clear weather at a distance of 14 miles. This light when in line with port Goulfar *revolving* light, leads about three-quarters of a mile to the eastward of the Plateau des Bervideaux.

Le Palais and Sauzon.—The tower at Le Palais shows, at an elevation of 30 feet above high water, a *fixed* white light, visible 9 miles. That at Sauzon shows at the same elevation a *fixed red* light, visible 7 miles.

Kerdonis Point light exhibits alternately a *fixed white* light of *twenty-five seconds* duration, and *five red flashes* during the following *twenty-five seconds;* it is elevated 116 feet above high water, and should be visible in clear weather from a distance of 12 miles.

CAUTION.—When approaching from the southward or westward, that the revolving light on the south-west side of Belle-Ile may not be mistaken for the revolving light on the Plateau du Four, at about 25 miles eastward, it must be remembered,—that the Belle-Ile light is much more brilliant than the Four light, that it revolves only *once* in a minute, that it is 197 feet higher than the Four light, and that on approaching the former the high land of the island can generally be distinguished at night.

Tides.—It is high water, full and change, at Le Palais at 3h. 18m.; springs rise 14¼ feet, neaps 10¼ feet.

Anchorage.—There are several anchorages along the shores of Belle-Ile, but those principally used by small vessels in south-west and westerly winds, are on the north-eastern shore, under the citadel of La Palais, and about 3 miles eastward of the citadel; during north-west winds they find shelter on the eastern side of the island, under Kerdonis point. Large vessels will be well sheltered from south-west winds by anchoring in from 8 to 15 fathoms, sand, mud, and shells, on the north-east side of the island, anywhere between Kerdonis point and Sauzon. The only precaution to be taken is to keep about a mile off shore and to avoid the Basse du Palais.

QUIBERON BAY is about 9 miles wide at the entrance between Les Grands Cardinaux and Point de St. Jacques, and affords capacious anchorage in 6 to 10 fathoms, mud, sand, and shells.* It is protected on the west by the Quiberon peninsula, and on the south-west and south by groups of islands and rocks named Beniguet, Houat, and Haedik, which extend in a S.S.E. ¼ E. direction for 14 miles from the south-east extreme of the peninsula, terminating in high rocks named Les Grands Cardinaux.

The northern shore of the bay is indented by numerous small inlets, some of which dry at low tide, and is fronted by banks and rocks. In the north-east part of the bay is the entrance of the Morbihan, which is so called from two Celtic words, meaning inland sea. Its shores on all sides have a most broken and jagged outline, and it is for the most part occupied by numerous islands and shoals, between which are narrow channels leading up to Vannes and Auray, but local pilots are necessary for their navigation.

Water.—Excellent water can be obtained from Haedik, the south-west island of the bay.

---

* Several sunken dangers have been found in Quiberon bay, for the position of which the mariner is referred to the chart; caution should be used in navigating this bay, as it is probable that others may exist.

The town of Vannes (signifying handsome) stands at the head of an inlet in the northern part of the Morbihan. It has two suburbs, Manche and St. Paterne, each larger in extent than the town. The harbour is small, and bordered with quays capable of admitting vessels of small tonnage. The trade is chiefly in corn, salt, hemp, butter, wax, honey, iron, cider, brandy, and wines; and the industrial products are coarse woollen cloth, linen, calico, lace, ironmongery, leather, beer, and salt. Population about 14,000.

The River Auray flows into the western part of the Morbihan near its entrance. Small vessels can ascend it at high water as far as the town of Auray, which stands about 7 miles from the entrance, and contains nearly 4,000 inhabitants employed in the coasting trade and fisheries.

Passage de la Teignouse, formed between the rocks off the south extreme of Quiberon peninsula, the southernmost of which are marked by black buoys, and the Chaussée du Beniguet, is nearly $1\frac{1}{4}$ miles wide; but nearly in the middle of the western entrance is the Goué-Vas, a shoal about half a mile in extent, upon which there are patches of only 4 to 9 feet water; it is marked by a red buoy on its northern and a black buoy on its southern edge. The Vieille, Fourchec, and Sœur rocks in line, S.E. $\frac{1}{4}$ E. easterly, is the cross mark for the 4 feet; and from a patch of 17 feet on the south-east extreme of the shoal, Le Petit Mont in the north-east part of Quiberon bay is open a quarter of a point south-east of La Teignouse lighthouse, E. by N. $\frac{3}{4}$ N.

The soundings around the Goué-Vas are 6 to 11 fathoms, but to the southward between it and the Beniguet are patches of $4\frac{1}{2}$ fathoms, named the Basse du Milieu, which narrows the deep water channel south of it to about half a mile. The channel north of Goué-Vas is about one-third of a mile wide, and has a depth of 6 fathoms; being buoyed it will be found preferable. To the eastward of the before-mentioned banks the soundings deepen to 14 and 18 fathoms, the passage widens to a mile, and is clear of danger, excepting a small patch with 6 feet water on it, named Basse Nouvelle, which lies a third of a mile from La Teignouse lighthouse, and in line with Loc Maria church, bearing N.W. $\frac{1}{4}$ N.

Tides.—The tides set E.N.E. and W.S.W. through the passage, and at springs the rate is 2 to $2\frac{1}{2}$ miles an hour.

Chaussée du Beniguet is a cluster of islets, rocks, and shallow heads, on a bank of about $2\frac{1}{4}$ miles in extent S.S.E. and N.N.W., and a mile wide. Near the north end of the bank are Les Esclassiers rocks, from which the Vieille, Fourchec, and Sœurs rocks are in line, S.E. $\frac{1}{4}$ E. easterly, and fort Penthièvre is a quarter of a point open eastward of fort Riberen, on Quiberon peninsula, about N. $\frac{1}{2}$ W. The Esclassiers dry from

5 to 15 feet at low water, and near them are patches with 1½ to 3 fathoms on them.

Houat Island, separated from the latter group by the Passage du Beniguet, is 2¼ miles long, of an irregular shape, and surrounded by rocks and shallow heads, particularly off its southern end, where, lying parallel with the island, is an extensive rocky flat, named Chaussée de Chevaux, on which is a small islet. Many of the rocks on this flat uncover, and others have but little water on them at low tide. From a patch of 2¼ fathoms, named Basse Occidentale, at the north-west extreme of the flat, the north point of Chevaux isle is in line with the south point of Haedik island, bearing about S.E. ; and the Rouleau rock, off the west end of Houat, is just open westward of the Men er Broc rock, N.E. ¼ E.   The Banc de Houat, with 2 to 4 fathoms water on it, extends 2½ miles in an E.S.E. direction from the east end of Houat, and bounds the northern side of Haedik road. On Er Spernec bihan, south side of Banc de Houat, stands a beacon tower, painted black.

Passage du Beniguet is not more than 2 cables wide, with 10 and 12 fathoms water in mid-channel, and 7 fathoms near the rocks, which bound the passage on either side, but in the north-east entrance is a small patch of 3¼ fathoms, with 8 and 9 fathoms close to. The tide sets directly through, about E. by N. and W. by S., with greater strength than it does in the Teignouse passage.   In December 1795 H.M.S. *Orion* led more than 150 sail of transports and store ships through this passage.

HAEDIK ISLAND, lying 3 miles south-east of Houat, is about 1¼ miles in extent, and here excellent water, shingle ballast, and fine sand in abundance may be obtained.   The Passage des Sœurs, between the shoals on its north-west side and those southward of Houat, has from 3¼ to 7 fathoms water, but is narrow and intricate, and no stranger should attempt its navigation, as the tides run through and over the ledges with great velocity.

This island is surrounded by a rocky bank, many of the rocks on which are always uncovered, and others only show at low water. At 1¼ miles from the south-east point are Les Grands Cardinaux, some of which are always above water, but they have foul ground extending some distance from their south-east side, and therefore should be given a good berth in passing. One mile to the S.S.W. of these rocks is a small patch of 3 fathoms, called Basse de Cardinaux, with deep water close to.

LIGHT.—On Grongue-Gues rock stands a lighthouse 80 feet high, from which is exhibited, at an elevation of 89 feet above high water, a *fixed* white light, visible in clear weather from a distance of 12 miles.

PLATEAU de la RECHERCHE, lying in an east and west

direction, parallel to the northern shore at the entrance of Quiberon bay, is nearly 5 miles in length, and its average breadth is about half a mile. The general soundings on it are 5 and 6 fathoms, but there are several shallow patches of one to 4 fathoms. Around the bank there are 7 and 8 fathoms water, mud, and clay, and from its west end, in 4 fathoms, Lomariaker church is open a quarter of a point westward of Pointe de Port Navallo, bearing about N. ¾ W.

From Basse Lomariaker, a rocky patch with only 6 feet on it at low water, marked by a black buoy, near the middle of the Recherche bank, and 2 miles from its west end, Lomariaker church is in line with Pointe de Port Navallo, bearing N. by W. ¼ W., and the north point of Dumet islet on with the south summit of Beaulieu wood, S.E. by E. ¼ E. The Sarzeau, another rocky patch with 6 feet on it, lies 1¼ miles eastward of the Lomariaker, with Pointe du Petit Mont just seen open westward of Pointe du Grand Mont, about N.N.W., and the north point of Dumet island S.E. ¾ E. easterly 6 miles.

The COAST.—To the northward of the Recherche bank, the eastern shore of the bay Pointe de St. Jacques to the entrance of the Morbihan, is bordered by flats, on which are several shallow rocky patches. The Basse de Thumiac, the outer of these patches, at nearly 2¾ miles from the shore, lies with Badene church, in line with Navallo point, bearing N.N.E., and St. Gildas monastery in line with Trest windmills, E. ¾ S. Nearly midway between the Thumiac and the bar of Morbihan lies Basse du Morbihan, with 12 feet water, and Basse di Ker Granno with 18 feet water; between Thumiac and Pointe du Grand Mont lies Basse de St. Gildas, with 2 feet water, from which the monastery bears E. by S. ¾ S., distant 1¼ miles. The bank near the outer extremity of this shoal is marked by a buoy, striped black and white. There is also another rock named the Basse du Grand Mont, awash at low water; it lies nearly a mile S.S.W. of Pointe du Grand Mont, with Lomariaker church in line with Navallo point N. by W. ½ W., this rock is marked by a buoy chequered black and red.

For the contour of the coast bank, and the detail of the many other dangers in Quiberon bay, the mariner is referred to the chart.

LIGHTS.—On the north jetty at Portaliguen, on the eastern side of Quiberon peninsula, a circular tower exhibits a *fixed* white light at an elevation of 39 feet above high water, and visible 10 miles in clear weather.

River Crac'h.—The river Crac'h empties itself into the northern part of Quiberon bay, and two lights are shown from the left bank at the entrance; the southern one is a *fixed red* light, elevated 30 feet above high water, and visible at a distance of 9 miles; the northern is a *fixed* white light, elevated 69 feet, and visible 10 miles. They are 574 yards apart, and when in line bearing N. by E., lead into the river.

Pointe de Port Navalo.—On Pointe de port Navalo, at the east side of entrance to the Morbihan, is a circular tower, which exhibits, at an elevation of 72 feet, a *fixed* white light, visible 10 miles.

Tides.—It is high water, full and change, at port Navalo, at the entrance of the Morbihan, in the north-east part of Quiberon bay, at 3h. 42m.; springs rise 13 and neaps 9¾ feet. The tides are weak in the bay, but they run strong in the western passage leading to it, and at the entrance of the Morbihan.

Directions.—Entering Quiberon bay from the westward through the Teignouse passage, give the north extreme of Belle-Ile a berth of more than 1½ miles in passing, to avoid Les Poulains, and then steer about E. by S. ¼ S. until La Teignouse lighthouse bears N.E. by E. ¼ E. The lighthouse kept on this bearing will lead between the Goué Vas and Milieu patches, until fort Penthièvre—at the north end of the peninsula—opens a quarter of a point eastward of fort Riberen, N. ¼ W., when steer E. ¾ S. into the bay. A vessel may clear the buoy on the Basse du Chenal, and pass through the channel northward of the Goué Vas, by keeping the lighthouse E. ¾ N. until fort Ponthièvre opens out, when steer about E. by S. This channel is narrower than the former, but being buoyed on either side will be found preferable.

Proceeding through the Teignouse from the south end of Belle-Ile steer northward until the lighthouse bears N.E. by E. ¼ E., when proceed as before.

‾- The western entrance of the Beniguet passage bears E. by S. ⅛ S. from the lighthouse on the north extreme of Belle-Ile, and N.E. ¼ N. from the south-east extreme. Approaching from the southward, a berth should be given to the dangers on the Chaussée de Chevaux, and the Basse Occidentale will be avoided by keeping the west end of Haedik island open west of Chevaux islet until the Men er Broc rock at the south side of *east* entrance of passage is well open northward of Le Rouleau rock at the south side of *west* entrance. Le Rouleau, Ile Guric, and the Men er Broc bound the south-east side of the passage, and Le Grand Coin rock, and the 3½-fathoms patch east of it, the north-west side; all these rocks have beacons on them, and should be given a fair berth in passing.

To sail through from Quiberon bay keep St. Gildas monastery on an E. by N. ¼ N. bearing until abreast the Men er Broc, then steer West or W. by S. In a vessel of heavy draught, when about 1½ or 2 miles off Le

Grand Coin it should be brought to bear about East, so as to pass between the two Houat banks.

Entering Quiberon bay from the south-westward, steer northward for Haedik lighthouse until the Plateau du Four lighthouse bears E.S.E., then steer for the latter, passing Haedik lighthouse at the distance of 2½ or 3 miles, and when it bears N.N.W. steer N.E. into the bay; this latter course should lead about a mile eastward of the Cardinaux and all dangers near them, and the vessel should haul to the northward round the shoals of Haedix island with discretion, for the intended anchorage.

If bound into the Morbihan, from a mile eastward of the Cardinaux about a North course will lead up to the bar, which has 18 feet on it at low water, passing westward of the Plateau de la Recherche, the Basse du Grand Mont, and Basse de St. Gildas; and eastward of Basse de Thumiac, the 2 and 3 fathoms patches northward of it, and the bank on which is Méaban isle and several rocks. Within the bar the water will deep to 11 and 15 fathoms, but a stranger should not attempt to enter without a pilot, for the channel is narrow and the tides strong.

Anchorage.—There is good anchorage in Haedik road in 9 fathoms, clay and mud, with the Cardinaux bearing from South to S.S.W.; by anchoring between these bearings a vessel will avoid the rocky ground on the Plateau de l'Artimon. There is also good anchorage northward of Houat island, between it and the north-east shore of the bay; also in the north part of the bay, north-east of the Quiberon banks, in 6 to 10 fathoms, with Teignouse from W. by S. to S.W. by S.

The COAST from St. Jacques point trends E. by S. for 10 miles to Kervoyal point, at the north side of entrance to the river Vilaine. It is of moderate height, indented by little bays and inlets, and bordered in places by flats and shallow patches, which lie 1½ miles off shore. Nearly midway is Penvins point, on which is a battery, and immediately eastward of the point is a little inlet, named port Penerf, and has 3 fathoms water over the bar, and 5½ fathoms within it. The village of Penerf stands on the east bank, about 2 miles within the entrance.

Between Penvins point and Kervoyal point is an extensive rocky flat named Plateau des Mats, which extends in some parts 1½ miles from the shore. Many rocks on it uncover at low tide, and southward of it is a patch of 6 feet named Basse de Mats. There is a red beacon with a white band on Le Borénis rock, near the south-west edge of Plateau des Mats.

From the entrance of the Vilaine the coast trends abruptly to the southward, and has several inflections, but its general trend is S.S.W. ¼ W. to Croisic point, which is distant 12 miles. The shore is generally low, and at a short distance eastward from Croisic will be seen the spire of

Bâts church, 200 feet high, standing on the shore 3 miles south-east of Croisic point, and the spire of Croisic church, 180 feet high, will materially assist to identify the coast.

Dumet islet, lying N.N.W. ½ W. 3¼ miles from Castèlli point, is of an irregular shape, not more than half a mile in extent, and surrounded by a flat, on which are several shoals of 3 to 9 feet; a rock which only appears at low water lies half a mile from its east end. The passage inside this island should not be attempted by vessels of large draught, for the deep water channel is narrow between it and the Plateau de Piriac, which extends nearly 2 miles from Castelli point, and has shoal patches with 5 to 15 feet water on them.

Le Croisic.—Between Castelli and Croisic points is the haven of Le Croisic, which is difficult of access, the entrance being encumbered with rocks, of which a patch called Basse Hergo dries 3 feet and is marked with a red buoy. Croisic roadstead, outside the harbour, has good anchorage in 6 and 7 fathoms water, sand and shells. The town, having a population of about 3,000, has become a favourite watering place, and a road leads from Guérande. In 1865, 1,340 tons of salt were exported to Nantes from this place, and about 80 boats are employed in the sardine fishery.

A jetty extends from the town nearly 9 cables to what was formerly the Trehic rock; inside of this the haven dries at low water; the tides in and out are very strong.

PLATEAU du FOUR.—This dangerous rocky bank, lying from 3½ to 5½ miles westward of Croisic point, is about 3 miles long and from one to 2 miles broad. There are numerous shallow patches with 4 to 12 feet water on them, and a ledge on its northern part which dries to a considerable extent at low water; the northern part of this ledge is marked by a round stone light-tower, 92 feet high. From a patch with 5 feet on it, named Goué Vas, at the south extreme of the bank, the semaphore of Romaine is just seen south of the steeple of Guérande church, bearing E. ½ N. northerly. Northward of this patch, between it and the ledge, is a small rock that dries 3¼ feet, and another near the east edge of the bank awash, at low water.

There is a passage with 8 and 9 fathoms water between the Plateau and Croisic point; but the Basse Hikeric, a patch of 2¼ fathoms, lies in mid-channel, and another, the Inconnu, of 3¼ fathoms, between it and the light-house. Croisic point is rocky for some distance off in a northerly direction, and at nearly a mile are shallow heads with 2 feet on them, named Basse Castouillet.

To the southward of the Plateau du Four is the Banc de Guérande, with 5½ to 8 fathoms water over it, rocky bottom, 6 miles in length, north and south, and one to 2 miles wide. On its northern end is a rocky patch of 3½ fathoms, named Basse Capella, from which Du Four lighthouse bears E. by N. ¾ N. 3⅜ miles, this patch should be avoided by vessels of heavy draught.

RIVER VILAINE rises near Vitré in the department of Mayenne, and its course is about west to Rennes. From thence it takes a south-westerly direction to the ocean, passing by Redon and Roche Bernard. Its entire length is 135 miles, of which 90 miles are navigable. Vessels of 250 tons burthen can ascend as far as Redon.

Rennes has a population of 40,000, and a trade of considerable extent. It stands on the acclivity and at the foot of a hill on the canal of Ille and Rance, at the confluence of the Ille and Vilaine. It is traversed from east to west by the Vilaine, which divides it into the high and the low town, and is crossed by three bridges. There is water communication from it by canal with St. Malo, Nantes, and Brest.

Redon, at 39 miles S.S.W. of Rennes, is built at the foot of a hill on the Vilaine, and contains about 4,000 inhabitants. It has a good harbour, in which the tide rises 9 to 12 feet, and there is a considerable foreign and coasting trade. There are also building yards, in which vessels of 400 tons have been constructed, and extensive slate quarries.

La Roche Bernard is 9 miles from the sea on the left bank of the Vilaine, which is here crossed by a fine suspension bridge of iron wire, supported on 2 piers of granite. The opening between the two points of suspension is 626 feet wide, and the elevation of the roadway above high water is 108 feet.

LIGHTS.—Four lights are exhibited on the part of the coast just described,—one on Penlan point, at the north side of entrance to the river Vilaine; one from the tower on the ledge of the Plateau du Four; and two harbour lights at Le Croisic.

Penlan point.—The round tower on Penlan point exhibits, at an elevation of 52 feet above high water, a *fixed* white light, visible in clear weather at a distance of 10 miles.

Plateau du Four.—The round tower on the Plateau du Four shows a white light which *revolves* every *half minute*. The light is elevated 79 feet above high water, and visible 18 miles; the eclipses do not appear total within 8 miles.

Tréhic.—On the outer extremity of the jetty of Tréhic, at the entrance of Port Croisic, stands a lighthouse 33 feet high, from which at an elevation of 39 feet above high water is exhibited a *fixed* light, showing white between the bearings of S.S.E. (easterly) and E.S.E. On either side of these bearings the light will show *red* until obscured by the land.

In clear weather the white light should be seen from a distance of 10 miles.

Le Croisic.—The two *fixed* white harbour lights at Le Croisic are 50 yards apart, and when in one, bearing South, show the direction of the channel into the harbour, but lead close to two rocks lying S. ½ E. half a mile from the outer extremity of the jetty. The northern light, elevated 13 feet, bears N. ¼ W. 492 yards from the church, visible 12 miles ; the southern light is 33 feet high, and visible at 6 miles.

Pilots for the Vilaine and for the Morbihan cruize off Les Cardinaux, and their services are indispensable to strangers.

Directions.—The best passage for a vessel from the westward bound to the river Vilaine is between Les Cardinaux and the Plateau de Four, and north of Dumet isle. Steer so as to bring the Plateau du Four lighthouse to bear E. by S. ½ S., and Haedik lighthouse N.N.W. ; then steer N.E. ¼ E. until Dumet isle bears S.E. The Penlan lighthouse at the entrance will then bear about E. by N. ¼ N., distant 8 or 9 miles, and to clear the Plateau des Mats, keep the wall beacon N.E. by E. of Kervoyal point, open east of the point. The soundings on these courses will shoal gradually from 18 fathoms abreast Les Cardinaux, to 8 fathoms off Dumet isle, and to only 10 to 4 feet at low water at the entrance of the river. In entering keep in mid-channel to avoid the rocks extending half a mile from the southern shore. A stranger should have the services of a pilot, as the river navigation is intricate.

Tides.—It is high water, full and change, at the entrance to the river Vilaine at about 3h. 40m. ; springs rise 13 feet, neaps 6 feet.

CHENAL du NORD or North channel to the river Loire, is bounded on the north by the ledges off the shore between Croisic point and the entrance of the river, and on the south by La Banche and La Lombarde banks. From Croisic point the coast trends S.E. 6 miles to Pain Chateau point, and is nearly clear of dangers, excepting those lying close in, and the Basse Lovre, a rocky bank with 3 feet water on it, lying three-quarters of a mile off shore abreast of the Tour des Bâts. The southern edge of Basse Lovre is marked by a buoy.

To the south-east of Pain Chateau point the shore forms an extensive shallow bay, at the back of which are some sand-hills and the church and mill of Escoublac. In the north-west angle of this bay is the little port Le Pouliguen, where there is a harbour light, but the narrow channel leading to it dries 4 to 6 feet at low tide.

Fronting this bay and extending in a S.E. by S. direction from Pain Chateau point are a chain of rocks and shoals, some of which are always above water. The shoal nearest the point, named Leven, is covered at about half tide, and marked by a pole; near it are several other ledges which cover at high water, and are separated from the point by a narrow channel. The Troves, a mile to the south-east, are ridges which dry 6 feet at low water.   The Pierre Percée, a mile further south-east, is a small islet about 15 feet above high water, with a beacon upon it ; about half a mile northward of it is the Baguenaud rock, which covers at about half tide, and is marked with a pole.   To the eastward of these, but close in shore, are the Vieille rocks, which dry 9 feet, and the Fromantières, which dry 2 feet, at low water.

South-east of the Pierre Percée, about half a mile, is Longue Folle reef, upon which the depth is only 5 feet.   To the eastward of this reef is the Banc des Charpentiers, which lies on the northern part of the bar at the entrance of the Loire, and has not more than 7 feet on its outer edge ; the bank is of sand, and on its western part are two rocks, Le Petit and Le Grand Charpentier, both of which uncover about 14 feet at low water springs, and each is marked by a small black tower.   To the eastward and inshore of this bank are several other shoal patches, all of which are more or less dangerous.

La Banche and La Lombarde banks, on the south side of the Chenal du Nord, are extremely dangerous.   La Banche, lying from 5 to 7 miles from the coast, is nearly 4 miles long, N.N.W. and S.S.E., and 1½ miles at its broadest part.   From the rock of 8 feet least water on the north-west extreme of the bank, Escoublac church is just seen inside and over Pain Chateau point bearing E. by N. ¾ N. northerly ; and from the rock with 7 feet on it at the south-east extreme, Poulhaut windmill is in line with Pierre Percée rock, E. by N. ¼ N.   At a mile within the south-east extreme of the bank is Le Turc ledge, which uncovers 9 feet at low water, and has a light-tower on it 87 feet high ; and at about a mile to 1¾ miles north-west of the tower are other ledges called Les Trois Pierres, which uncover from 2 to 7 feet.   The depths on the remaining portion of the bank vary, some parts are nearly dry, and others have 2 to 3 fathoms over them.

To the westward of La Banche are three patches, named Basse du Turc with 5 fathoms water on it, Basse de l'Astrolabe with 4¾ fathoms, and Basse Michaud with 4½ fathoms, lying respectively S.W. ¼ W. 1¾ miles W. by N. ¼ N. 3¾ miles, and N.W. ¼ N. 5¼ miles from the light-tower on Le Turc.

La Lombarde is from 3¼ to 5 miles E.S.E. from Le Turc light-tower, and there are two patches of 4½ and 5 fathoms in the passage between. This shoal, 1¾ miles long, east and west, and about a mile broad, marked by a bell buoy on the S.E. extreme, has several patches with from 8 to 11 feet on it, and a rock which dries 2 feet at low water, and from which

St. Nazaire church is open a quarter of a point southward of the Tour d'Aiguillon, about E. by N. ¾ N., and Le Turc light-tower bears W.N.W. 3¾ miles.

LIGHTS.—The lighthouse on Le Turc ledge of the Plateau La Banche exhibits at 70 feet above high water a *fixed red* light, visible in clear weather at a distance of 10 miles.

At the extremity of the jetty at port Pouliguen is shewn a fixed *white* light on an iron lamp-post, elevated 23 feet above high water, and visible in clear weather 5 miles, between the bearings of North and N.W.

RIVER LOIRE, one of the principal rivers in France and having the longest course, rises on the west slope of the Cévennes, department Ardèche, about 20 miles W. by N. of Privas, and flows generally north and north-west towards Orleans, where it turns to the south-west and west, a direction it maintains till it falls into the sea, 30 miles below Nantes. Its whole course is about 600 miles. It first becomes navigable at Noirie, but the navigation properly begins 45 miles lower at Roanne, which is 450 miles above its mouth. The river since 1846 has been subject to great inundations, owing to the embankments having given way, and the soil brought down by its waters form islands and shifting banks which materially impede the navigation.*

The entrance is barred by an extensive flat with from 12 to 16 feet on it, at low water, after crossing which the deep water channel, carrying from 5 to 7 fathoms, is along by the northern shore. The Charpentiers bank, just described, is on the northern side of the bar; and on the southern side are, the Vert rock, which uncovers 7½ feet at low springs, and marked by a red buoy, the Jardinets reef, which uncovers 3 feet, and the Truie rock, which uncovers 9 feet, and has a red beacon on it. At 3 miles within the bar, on the south side of the channel, are the Morées rocks, on one of which is a round tower.

NANTES is a flourishing commercial town standing on the summit and ascent of a hill on the right bank of the Loire, 30 miles from its entrance, at the influx into it from the north of the river Erdre, the junction of the two rivers being in the middle of the town. The Sèvre from the south flows into the Loire a little below the town. Commodious quays extend about 2 miles along the Loire, and on both sides the Erdre. The Loire is gradually becoming less navigable, owing to the numerous deposits of sand in various parts forming large banks and rendering the navigation difficult and dangerous, as vessels of less than 100 tons can only arrive at Nantes, and leave, at the time of spring tides.

Nantes has a large shipping trade, and in importance was formerly the

---

* *See* Admiralty plan:—Entrance to Loire river; scale, *m* = 1·5 inches, on chart No. 2,646.

fourth port in the empire. The manufactures comprise cotton yarn, refined sugar, serge, blankets, preserves, &c., and the trade is greatly favoured by a canal which communicates with Brest, and by the railway which connects Paris with the west coast. Ship building is carried on to some extent, and in 1865 upwards of 8,000 tons was constructed.

On an island 5 miles below Nantes is the vast government steam factory of Indret, probably the most extensive establishment of the kind in the world; there is, however, neither coal nor iron in the neighbourhood, and the place is not well situated for shipping the machinery, which is conveyed in barges to St. Nazaire.

During the year 1865, 170 British vessels, of which 140 were laden with 18,424 tons of coals (value 18,424*l.*), 50 with general cargo, and 16 in ballast, arrived at Nantes. But owing to the state of the Loire, the vessels which visit Nantes scarcely average 100 tons each, and all vessels of large tonnage remain at St. Nazaire. The total imports in British vessels to Nantes was 25,863 tons, and exports 27,263 tons.

ST. NAZAIRE stands on the north side of entrance of the Loire; formerly a fortified town, it had relapsed until lately into an insignificant village, but is now (1880) one of the principal commercial ports on the west coast of France.

There is a regular line of steam vessels which leave St. Nazaire twice a month with mails and passengers for the different ports in the West Indies, Central America, Pacific, &c.

During the year 1879, 429 British vessels, amounting to 214,053 tons, discharged cargoes at St. Nazaire.

Docks.*—There is a basin at St. Nazaire capable of admitting vessels of 24 feet draft: it is 634 feet long, 207 yards wide, and has two entrances, one of which is 82 feet and the other 42 feet wide. This basin is in immediate proximity to the railway, and a tram road extends along the quays, so that vessels can discharge cargoes into the trucks.

There is a graving dock 350 feet long, opening into the basin, but it is principally used by the Transatlantic company.

There is a new basin 1,200 yards long, and 280 yards wide, with an average depth of 26 feet; three graving docks open into this basin.

LIGHTS.—Two light-towers, Tour d'Aiguillon, 69 feet high, and Tour du Commerce, 108 feet high, stands on the northern shore of entrance to the Loire, and when in one bear N.E. ¼ E. and S.W. ¾ W. of each other, a long mile apart.

Tour d'Aiguillon, the southern tower, exhibits, at an elevation of 118 feet above high water, a *fixed* white light, visible in clear weather at a distance of 14 miles.

---

* H. P. Sutton, Esq., British Vice-Consul, St. Nazaire, 1880.

Tour du Commerce shows, at 197 feet above high water, a *fixed* white light varied every *two minutes* by a *flash*, also visible at 14 miles. The flash is preceded and followed by eclipses, which are not total within 6 miles.

Ville-es-Martin Point, a *revolving red* light, attaining its greatest brilliancy every *half-minute*, is shown at an elevation of 33 feet above high water, and visible 12 miles ; within a distance of 4 miles the eclipses are not total.

Point de l'Eve.—From a small turret on the summit of point de l'Eve, at a quarter of a mile to the south-west of Tour d'Aiguillon, a *fixed red* light is shown, at an elevation of 102 feet above high water, and visible 9 miles. When within this light, and it becomes masked by Tour d'Aiguillon, a vessel will be in the deep water channel leading to St. Nazaire ; when seen north of that light she will be approaching La Ville-es-Martin ; and when seen south she will be in danger of running on the Morées rocks.

St. Nazaire and Paimbœuf.—Two *fixed* white lights are exhibited within the entrance ; one from a tower on the new mole-head of St. Nazaire, and the other from a tower at the end of the mole of Paimbœuf on the south shore. Both lights are elevated 26 feet, and visible 8 miles.

Pierre à l'Œil, *red* light fixed, visible 8 miles.

St. Nicholas Isle.—*Light proposed.*

Mindin Point.—*Light proposed.*

Brivet.—At the entrance to Brivet, on the northern bank 1¼ miles N.E. of St. Nazaire, are shown two harbour lights,—the first on a lamp-post elevated 18 feet above high water, is a *fixed red* light.

St. Mean.—The other on the tower of the church of St. Mean, 113 yards west of the former, is a *fixed* white light, elevated 36 feet above high water. Both are visible at the distance of 5 miles.

Tides.—It is high water, full and change, at St. Nazaire at 3h. 40m. ; springs rise 15¼ feet, neaps 11 feet. The tide rises 2 feet in the first hour of flood, 3½ feet the second, 4 feet the third, 2½ feet the fourth, 2 feet the fifth, and one foot the sixth hour.

Pilots for the Loire will be found cruizing off Les Cardinaux rocks, and the mouth of the river, weather permitting, and pilots for the navigation of the river up to Nantes may be obtained at St. Nazaire, as well as a steam-tug, by hoisting the pilot flag at the mast head.

Directions are given for entering the Loire, but as changes constantly occur in the depths on the bar and banks at entrance, from floods, winds, or other disturbing causes, a stranger should always avail himself of the assistance of a pilot.

The Chenal du Nord may be entered by passing northward of the Plateau du Four, and then between it and Croisic point; but with southerly winds it will be more convenient to sail between the Four and La Banche. The south-east end of the Four will be avoided by keeping Guérande church open eastward of Croisic church spire; and the north-west end of La Banche, by keeping Guérande church a little open north-west of the spire of Bâts church bearing about N.E. by E. ¼ E.; this latter mark will lead between the Michaud and Astrolabe patches. Continue with either of these marks on, until the Four lighthouse bears N.W. ¼ N., thence with this bearing astern a S.E. ¼ S. course will lead up to the bar marks.

To cross the bar at night, steer in with the Aiguillon (*fixed*) and Commerce (*flashing*) lights in line, until near the bar, when the latter light should be brought a little open eastward of the former. When the *revolving red* light of Ville-es-Martin is in line with the *fixed* white light on the jetty of St. Nazaire, keep on that line until the Aiguillon and *fixed red* light on the Pointe de l'Eve are in line, which latter lights lead just southward of the black Bell buoy on the extremity of the Ville-es-Martin shoal. The mariner will have no difficulty in following these routes during the day, or in reversing them when leaving the river. The Bonne Anse, a shoal with 7 feet water on it, will be left on the port hand in going on; it lies with the pilots' mast in line with Tour d'Aiguillon, and the mill westward of Tour du Commerce in one with the coast-guard station at Portsay point.

BOURGNEUF BAY.—From St. Gildas point on the south side of entrance to the Loire, the coast is moderately high, and trends abruptly to the south-east for 5¼ miles to the small port of Pornic, which dries at low tide, but a considerable trade is carried on, and the place is much frequented for sea bathing.

At 7½ miles farther south is the town of Bourgneuf, at about 1¼ miles inland, which gives its name to the bay; but strangers desirous of running up to this place must have a pilot. Thence the shore trends in a south-westerly direction for 10½ miles to the Goulet de Fromantine. Here Ile de Noirmoutier, almost joining the mainland, trends to the N.N.W., and forms the south-west side of this extensive bay.

DANGERS.—The navigation of Bourgneuf bay is much impeded by rocks and shoals:—the Banc de Kerouars, lying parallel with the northern shore, 1¾ miles southward of St. Gildas point, is 5¾ miles long, half a mile wide, and the general depths on it are from one to 8 fathoms over sandy bottom, but there are several rocky patches of 3 and 4 feet, and a rock which uncovers 7 feet at low water. This latter, named La Couronnée, lies half a mile within the western end of the bank, and 2½ miles west of the south entrance of St. Gildas point, with Pierre Percée rock in line with the most western sand-hills of Escoublac, bearing about N. ¼ E.

At 1¼ miles eastward of the Kerouars bank, and abreast of Pornic harbour, are the Notre Dame and Caillou banks, studded with rocks, many of which dry at low water; each of these banks is marked by a beacon. These rocks range about 1½ miles from the coast, and between them and the shore to the eastward there is no passage, as extensive rocky flats dry some distance from the land, and the Pierre du Chenal, which uncovers 2 feet at low springs, lies about S.W. by S. 2½ miles from Pornic lighthouse. La Pierre Moine rock, lying E.N.E. 2½ miles from Charniers point, the north-east extreme of Noirmoutier, is always uncovered, being 3 feet above high-water springs, and is marked by a beacon coloured red and white. Basse des Pères, with 7 feet water, lies W. by N. ¾ N. 1½ miles from La Pierre Moine rock; a buoy is moored on the northern edge of Basse des Pères. The head of the bay, from a little south-east of Pornic, is bordered with shallow water and rocks, and the southern part dries at low springs, 5 miles from the shore.

The northern coast of Ile de Noirmoutier is surrounded with rocky ledges and other dangers, some of which are 3 miles from the land. A black buoy is moored on the S.E. extreme of a shoal, situated about a mile westward of Pte. de Herbaudierre. At 2¼ miles from its north-west extreme is Pilier islet, with a light-tower on its northern end. At 3 miles E. by S. ¼ S. from Pilier islet, and one mile from the shore lies Martroger rock, which is marked by a beacon; nearly a mile east of this rock lies Roches des Pères, marked by a beacon. Outside Pilier is a rocky ledge, named Les Chevaux, the northern end of which is three-quarters of a mile from the light-tower. [Both this ledge and the Chaussée des Bœufs (having a red bell beacon upon its south-west extremity) to the southward, should be approached with caution, and a vessel should not stand into a less depth than 10 fathoms at low water.

Anchorage.—On the south side of Bourgneuf bay, good anchorage may be obtained in 5 fathoms, sand and mud, with Les Pères rocks beacon in line with Ile du Pilier lighthouse bearing W. by N. ¼ N., and La Pierre Moine rock beacon north. This anchorage is safe except during a north-west gale.

LIGHTS.—The tower on north end of Pilier islet exhibits, at 105 feet above high water, a *fixed* white light, varied by a *flash* every *four minutes*, and visible in clear weather at a distance of 16 miles, except through an arc of 45° to the south-west covering the Chaussée des Bœufs; and in the direction of La Couronnée reef at the south side of entrance to the river Loire, or between the bearings of N. ¾ E. and N.E. ¼ E.; in which directions a *red* sector of light is shown, visible 14 miles; by keeping the *white* light in sight these dangers will be avoided.

o 17801.   E

Pornic.—A *fixed* white light is shown from the west point of entrance of Pornic, on the northern shore of Bourgneuf bay, at an elevation of 52 feet above high water, and visible 10 miles. Signals are made from the lighthouse, which is square, indicating when there are 6½ and 9¾ feet water in the channel.

Dames Point.—On Dames point, at 1¼ miles northward of the entrance to the port of Noirmoutier, is a square tower, which exhibits at 112 feet above high water a *fixed white* and *red* light; the white light is visible at a distance of 13 miles, and the red at a distance of 10 miles. The white light is visible round a great part of the horizon, and the red portion through an arc of 85° between the bearings of S. by W. ½ W. and W. by N., and in the direction of the Chaussée des Bœufs through an arc of 30°, between the bearings of E. ¾ S. and E.N.E.

Directions.—Approaching Bourgneuf bay from the westward, the dangers off the north-west end of Noirmoutier will be avoided by giving the lighthouse on Pilier islet a berth of about 2 miles, or by not standing into less than 10 fathoms water. When the lighthouse bears South about 3¼ miles, steer S.E. by E. till Noirmoutier church bears S. by W., or the ruined abbey La Blanche S.S.W. ¼ W., when the vessel will be eastward of the Blanche bank, on which there are only 2 feet water. The east extreme of this bank lies 2½ miles N. by E. ½ E. from La Blanche (ruined) abbey.

Steer now S.W. by S. for 1½ miles, so as to pass southward of a patch with 11 feet on it; and then for the red and white beacon on Pierre Moine rock, which may be passed on either side, when the vessel may take a pilot for Bourgneuf, or run to the southward for Rade du Bois de la Chaise with this rock bearing North, and when Noirmoutier church bears W.S.W. steer for it, anchoring in 3 fathoms at low water, about a mile off shore or 2 miles from the church; or the vessel may be anchored farther off in deeper water (page 65). Care must be taken to avoid a shoal more than half a mile in extent, in an east and west direction, with one to 3 feet water on it, in the northern part of this anchorage, with its east end bearing about E. by N. ½ N., from La Cobe rock, and S. by W. ½ W. from the Pierre Moine.

Tides.—It is high water, full and change, at Noirmoutier at 3h. 2m.; springs rise 16 feet, and neaps 11¼ feet.

ILE de NOIRMOUTIER is 10 miles long, N.N.W. and S.S.E., irregular in shape, being a quarter of a mile broad in the middle, and 3½ miles broad at its northern part; the shores on all sides are studded with dangers. The town of Noirmoutier, on its eastern side, has a population of about 2,500, and its little tidal harbour will admit vessels of 50 or 60 tons burthen. The south end of the island is separated from the mainland by a narrow channel, the Goulet de Fromantine, which is nearly choked up with sand, and can only be navigated by vessels of light draught with a local pilot. On the northern side of the Goulet is a small fort, and on the southern side the land rises to the Fromantine mountains.*

Life Boat.—There is a life boat stationed at Pointe de l'Herbaudière, the north-west extreme of Ile de Noirmoutier.

ILE D'YEU, lying 10 miles off the coast southward of Noirmoutier, is 5¼ miles long N.W. and S.E. and about 2 miles broad, and the prominent object on it is St. Sauveur church with its pointed steeple. The soil is scanty, the whole island being a mass of granite, on its west side steep, and on its east side low and flat. There are two small harbours, port de la Mule on the south-west shore, and port Breton, the chief port of the island, on the north-east shore, but they dry every tide and will only admit small craft. Port Breton is protected by a fort, and there are several batteries placed on the most prominent points of the island.

The north-west end of the island is encumbered with rocks, the outermost of which, named Chiens Perrins, lies nearly three-quarters of a mile from the land; there are many rocks between these and port Breton, but none farther off than half a mile. From port Breton to Corbeau point, the south-east extreme, the shore is fronted, to the distance of 1¾ miles, with rough uneven ground, upon which the depths are from 1½ to 4½ fathoms. Nearly a mile east of port Breton lies La Sablaire, a shoal three-quarters of a mile long, N.N.E. and S.S.W. and a quarter of a mile broad, with 9 to 15 feet water, the northern edge of this shoal is marked by a black buoy, and the southern edge by a red buoy.

The eastern end of the island is connected in some measure with the mainland, at the village of Notre Dame de Monts, by a bank with 3 to 4 fathoms water on it, sandy and rocky bottom, called Pont d'Yeú, over which, unless in case of necessity, it would be imprudent for a vessel of more than 15 or 16 feet draught to venture at low tide. The deepest water is about one-third over from the island to the shore, and towards the mainland it is very shallow, the depth being only 3 feet at 3¼ miles from the shore.

. **LIGHTS.**—A *fixed* white light is exhibited from a tower standing on an elevated spot nearly a mile within the north-west extreme of Ile d'Yeu. The light is elevated 112 feet above high water, and visible in clear weather at a distance of 18 miles.

On Corbeau point, the south-east extreme of Ile d'Yeu, is a square tower, from which is exhibited a *fixed red* light, at an elevation of 64 feet above high water, and visible at a distance of 8 miles.

---

* *See* Admiralty chart:—France, west coast, sheet 4, Les Sables d'Olonne to Bourgneuf, No. 2,647; scale, m = 0·5 of an inch.

Port Breton.—From a lighthouse, 20 feet high and painted red, on the extremity of the north-west pier at port Breton, is exhibited, at an elevation of 28 feet above high water, a *flashing* light, visible through an arc of 163$\frac{1}{4}$°, showing *white* flashes between the bearings of N.W. by W. and S. $\frac{3}{4}$ E.; and *red* flashes between S. $\frac{3}{4}$ E. and S.E. $\frac{1}{2}$ S. The white light should be seen in clear weather from a distance of 9 miles; the red light from a distance of 6 miles.

With the white light in sight, vessels will be clear of the dangers near point Gautier, and those south-eastward of port Breton; also of du Boite shoal, north-westward of that port.

The south-west limit of the sector of red light leads half a cable seaward of Cantin shoal, so that vessels approaching from the north-westward with the flashing red light in sight, are clear of that danger, but it should be borne in mind that the red light is shown over du Boite shoal.

Also a *fixed red* light is shown from a lamp-post on the wall of the left bank of the entrance to port Breton, 95 yards from the extremity, elevated 26 feet above high water, and visible in clear weather 5 miles.

Life Boat.—A life boat is stationed at port Breton.

Tides.—It is high water, full and change, at Ile d'Yeu at 3h. 6m.; springs rise 14$\frac{1}{4}$ feet, neaps 10 feet.

Anchorage.—The best anchorage off Ile d'Yeu is in about 5$\frac{1}{4}$ fathoms water, with its north-west end bearing West, the east end S. by E., and St. Sauveur church S.S.W. distant 2$\frac{1}{4}$ miles; in this position a vessel will be about 1$\frac{1}{2}$ miles off-shore.

A vessel may also anchor off the south side of the island, but a berth of upwards of half a mile must be given to the shore, as dangers lie nearly that distance from it. The best position is in 13 to 16 fathoms, fine sand, with Corbeau point N.E. by N. distant about 2 miles; or more to the eastward in a similar depth on mud and sand, with the point bearing N.W. by N.

COAST.—The west coast of Noirmoutier island, with the mainland, trends in a general S. by E. direction about 40 miles to Pointe de l'Aiguille. Devin point, the west extreme of Noirmoutier, is bordered by flat rocky ground (Chaussée des Bœufs), the principal ledge of which dries 5 to 10 feet at low springs, and extends off 3$\frac{1}{2}$ miles. The outer or south-west part of this ledge has a beacon on it, with shallow water beyond, as at 7 miles from Devin point the depth is only 4 fathoms.

Between the Goulet de Fromantine and the village of Notre Dame de Monts the sandy shore is low, and fronted by flat rocky ground and shallow water to a distance of 4 miles off. A rocky ledge extends in a W. by S. direction from the shore a little southward of the village, and dries for 1$\frac{1}{4}$ miles off at low water, and at about the same distance farther out is a patch which also uncovers at low water. Les Marguerites lie from one to

2¼ miles off shore, with the church of the village bearing E. by S. ½ S The Basse de l'Aigle, a rocky shoal, three-quarters of a mile in extent, lies N.W. by W. from the church and 5½ miles off shore; there are only 1¼ to 2 fathoms on it, and 8 fathoms between it and the flat bordering the shore; but outside the shoal the water deepens to 6 and 7 fathoms. About 1¼ miles south-west of Basse de l'Aigle a red buoy is moored in 7 fathoms water.

From Notre Dame de Monts the shore for 10½ miles to Gross Terre point is fronted by an extensive shallow flat. A red buoy is moored in 5 fathoms water, at about 5 miles west of Notre Dame de Monts. Gross Terre point and the coast for about 1½ miles north of it is cliffy and rocky.

St. Gilles-sur-Vie is a small tidal harbour close to the southward of Gross Terre point; but it will not admit vessels over 120 tons burthen. The town is in a valley, but it will be recognized by its vicinity to a large wood. Small vessels anchor in 7 to 12 feet at low water in the road outside the harbour, between Pilours rock, 12 feet high, with a beacon on it, and a rocky bank named the Bonneau, which is awash at low tide.

LIGHTS.—On the head of the jetty, at the north side of entrance to the harbour of St. Gilles-sur-Vie, a *fixed* white light is shown at an elevation of 39 feet above high water, and is visible 5 miles in clear weather.

Leading Lights.—The direction for entering the harbour of St. Gilles-sur-Vie is indicated by two lights. The outer light is a fixed *red* light, 22 feet above high water, visible in clear weather from a distance of 9 miles. The lighthouse is a square tower, situated near Croix de Vie quay.

The inner light is a fixed *red* light, 75 feet above high water, visible in clear weather from a distance of 9 miles; it bears N. 57¾° E. from the outer light distant 284 yards. The lighthouse is a square tower, situated at the edge of the enclosed road of Croix de Vie.

POINTE de l'AIGUILLE.—The shore from St. Gilles-sur-Vie continues its southerly direction for about 18 miles to Pointe de l'Aiguille, having no danger farther off than about half a mile from the land; but in approaching the point the lead must be kept going, and the soundings not decreased under 10 or 11 fathoms at low water by day, or 15 fathoms at night, to avoid Les Barges d'Olonne ledges, which extend 2½ miles W.N.W. from the point, and parts of which uncover at low water. From the westernmost danger, a patch of 4 fathoms named Basse Vermenou, the church of Sables d'Olonne is just seen south of Chaume mill, bearing about E.S.E. St. Jean mill open south of La Grange Farm, S.E. by E. ¼ E., will lead clear of the south side of these dangers, and up to the leading mark for entering the harbour of Sables d'Olonne.

LIGHT.—On the Grande Barge d'Olonne is a round tower, from which is exhibited at 75 feet above high water, a *fixed* light, varied every *three minutes* by a *red flash*, visible at a distance of 14 miles. On the Petite Barge d'Olonne, at about two-thirds of a mile southward of the lighthouse, is a bell buoy.

PORT Les SABLES d'OLONNE.—The small tidal harbour dries at the lowest tides, and a stranger should not attempt to enter without a pilot. The entrance is between two piers or breakwaters, both projecting southward ; that on the east side is the larger, and extends from the west end of the town of Sables d'Olonne ; and that on the opposite side from the outer extreme of the harbour, on a ledge of rocks which protects it from the westward. A battery, and a small church with a steeple (St. Nicholas) stand on the point.

The roadstead and approaches to the harbour are eastward of three rocky shoals :—The Noura of 8 feet, the Nouch of one foot, and the Barre Marine of 24 feet water, lying south of St. Nicholas church ; the latter is a mile from the entrance to the port, and nearly three-quarters of a mile from the eastern shore ; but in bad weather the breakers from the two first extend to the middle of the roadstead, making it an unsafe position to be in should the wind blow strongly on shore, when it would be impossible either to make sail or enter the harbour.

Docks.*

LIGHTS.—Two *fixed* white lights are established for entering the harbour of Les Sables d'Olonne, one from a tower on the jetty head at La Chaume, on west side of entrance, and the other from a tower on the head of the great jetty on east side of entrance. The lights are elevated respectively 105 and 36 feet above high water, visible at 10 and 8 miles, and when in line, bearing N. by W. ¾ W., lead through the principal channel to the entrance.

Two lights are exhibited from towers erected to the south-east of the town of Les Sables d'Olonne, as leading lights through the south-west pass of the roadstead,—a *fixed red* light on the river bank, named the Stockade light, elevated 33 feet above the level of high water, and a *fixed red* light, named the Potence light, bearing E. by N. ¾ N., distant 420 yards from the Stockage light, and elevated 93 feet above the level of high water. Both lights, in clear weather, should be seen from a distance of 7 miles ; they will be visible through an arc of about 12° on each side of the line of direction, and the power of the light diminishes as that line is departed from.

DIRECTIONS.—Vessels entering the port of Sables d'Olonne by the south-west pass should keep the Stockade and Potence lights in line

---

* There is a dock at Sables d'Olonne capable of admitting vessels of 16 feet draught, at high-water springs, and about 9 or 10 feet at neaps.—*G. L. Link, Esq., H.M. Consular Agent, Tonnay-Charente,* 1880.

bearing E. by N. ¾ N. until the two lights of La Chaume are in line, which
lead to the channel between the jetties.

Vessels entering by the south-east pass, or Great channel, should keep
the jetty light a little open to the eastward of Chaume lighthouse until the
two red leading lights are in line, and from this point the lights of La
Chaume may be kept in line.

A Life Boat is stationed at La Chaume.

Tides.—It is high water, full and change, at St. Gilles-sur-Vie, and
at Les Sables d'Olonne at about 3h. 26m.; springs rise 14 feet, neaps
10 feet.

The COAST from Sables d'Olonne trends about S.E. by S. 16 miles
to Grouin du Cou point, which is only 30 feet high; the shore is low all
the way, and skirted by many rocky shoals. From thence the shore runs
11½ miles farther to the south-east to Aiguillon point, and forms the
north-east side of the Pertuis Breton or Breton channel.*

LIGHTS.—On Grouin du Cou point, at the north side of entrance to
the Pertuis Breton, is a square tower, which exhibits a *fixed* white light,
at an elevation of 92 feet above high water, visible in clear weather at a
distance of 10 miles.

Aiguillon Point.—On Aiguillon point, in the eastern part of the
Pertuis Breton, a *fixed* white light is shown from a wooden tower, at an
elevation of 43 feet above high water, and visible 10 miles.

ILE de RÉ lies parallel to and about 5½ miles off the coast just
described, and forms the south side of the Pertuis Breton. The island is
rather low, 14 miles long, N.W. and S.E., and its breadth is irregular,
averaging about 3 miles, but near the north-west end it is nearly
separated by a narrow isthmus not more than 170 yards across. The
northern shore is much indented, and there are several good havens,
particularly those of the villages of Ars and La Flotte, and the small town
of St. Martin, which is the principal place. The last is defended by a
citadel of considerable strength, and there are forts on other parts of the
island.

The soil of this island is not fertile, scarcely producing either corn or
pasture, but the vine thrives well, and is cultivated. A considerable
extent of surface is occupied by salt marshes. The population amounts
to about 18,000, whose principal employment is in fishing and the manufacture of salt. There are also several distilleries of brandy.

The island is surrounded by a shallow bank, and from its north-west
end a reef extends N.N.W. 2½ miles, and skirting the south-west side of

* *See* Admiralty chart :—France, west coast, sheet 3, Point de la Coubre to Les
Sables d'Olonne, No. 2,648; scale, m = 0·5 of an inch.

the island, projects nearly the same distance southward from Chanchardon point, at 4 miles to the south-east, thence continuing, at 1½ to three-quarters of a mile from the shore, to Chauveau point, the south-east extreme of the island.

LIGHTS.—On Baleines point, the north-west extreme of the Ile de Rè, is an octagonal tower, which exhibits, at an elevation of 164 feet above high water, a *revolving* white light, attaining its greatest brilliancy every *half minute*, and visible in clear weather at a distance of 24 miles. The eclipses do not appear total within 10 miles. A life boat is stationed at Baleines point.

Haut-banc du Nord.—On the Haut-banc du Nord, at about 1¼ miles N.N.W. from the north-west extreme of the island, is a circular tower, which exhibits, at 75 feet above high water, a *fixed* white light, visible 14 miles. The mariner is warned that dangers extend more than a mile seaward of this light.

Mer du Fief.—Two lights are exhibited on Pointe du Fief, west side of the entrance of the Mer du Fief (Fiers d'Ars).

The upper is a *fixed green* light, exhibited from a window of the keeper's dwelling, at an elevation of 36 feet above the level of high water.

The lower is a *fixed* white light, exhibited from an iron post, bearing E. ¾ S. distant 370 yards from the upper light, and elevated 28 feet above high water. In clear weather both lights should be seen from a distance of 5 miles.

These lights in line indicate the channel into the Mer de Fief.

St. Martin.—Two *fixed* lights are shown at St. Martin; one a *red* light, from a tower standing on the salient angle of the demi-bastion at about 100 yards east of the entrance of St. Martin, at an elevation of 56 feet above high water, visible 7 miles; and the other a *white* light, from a tower on the new mole at La Flotte, at an elevation of 33 feet, and visible 9 miles.

Chauveau Point.—A *fixed* white light is shown from a tower on the outer edge of the reef extending from Chauveau point, the south-east extreme of the island. The light is elevated 59 feet above the sea, and visible 14 miles. There is a red sector shown from this tower, to cover all the rocks along the south coast of Ile de Rè, as far as to the westward of Point de Chanchardon, and by keeping the white light in sight these dangers will be avoided.

PERTUIS BRETON, the passage between Ile de Rè and the coast, is 16 miles in length, and from 5 to 7 miles wide, but banks and shoal water extend a long distance off both shores. Vessels of large draught must keep nearer the island than the main. The eastern part of the passage is encumbered by an extensive mud-flat, over which there are not more than 8 or 9 feet at low-water springs; but the channel over it is clear of danger, and vessels of proper draught cross it and enter Basque road by the narrow channel between the south-east end of the island and the mainland.*

Anchorage.—Vessels can anchor in the Pertuis Breton, and be sheltered from all winds but those from the north-westward, in 9 and 10 fathoms, and clear of the banks that are well defined on the chart. There is good anchorage for small vessels in 2 and 3 fathoms in the roadsteads off St. Martin and La Flotte. Aiguillon bay, on the north-east shore, dries at low water, but it affords shelter for vessels that can take the ground, which is of soft mud, and an excellent place for vessels to run for in the event of losing masts or anchors.

Directions.—To sail into the Pertuis Breton, the light-tower on Aiguillon point bearing S.E. by E. ¼ E. will lead in the deep water channel at the entrance, between the northern extreme of the Baleinas reef and the long narrow bank extending W.N.W. from Grouin du Cou point. When the light-tower on this latter point bears N.N.E., steer S.E. ½ S. until St. Martin church bears S.W. ¼ W., then run towards the church, and anchor in from 5 to 3 fathoms water, sand and mud. Vessels of heavy draught may anchor farther out in 8 or 9 fathoms. If the wind is contrary be careful to avoid the bank extending at least 2¼ miles eastward from Loix point. Only vessels of light draught can enter the little harbour of St. Martin, as the bar at the entrance dries nearly 5 feet at low tide.

But should a vessel be bound into Aiguillon bay, proceed as before until Grouin du Cou western light-tower bears N.N.E., then steer S.E. ½ E. until Aiguillon point light-tower bears E. ¼ N., then steer with this latter tower a point on the port bow, and gradually haul into the bay. The channel is narrow and the water shoals rapidly as the vessel advances.

If bound to Rochelle and the vessel's draught admits, bring Aiguillon light-tower to bear N.E. by E., and St. Martin church W. ¼ N., then steer for St. Marc point, and through the narrow channel between the south-east end of Ile de Rè and the mainland. Having passed the beacon on the ledge of St. Marc point, haul in towards the shore until Plomb point is shut in with Repentie point, then either steer for the harbour, or anchor in about 3 fathoms water, at half a mile E.S.E. from the beacon on the Lavardin, or farther in according to the vessel's draught.

---

* *See* Admiralty chart :—Environs de la Rochelle, Rades des Basques et d'Aix, with plan of La Rochelle, No. 2,746 ; scale, m = 1½ inches.

ILE D'OLERON lies off the coast abreast the mouths of the Charente and Seudre rivers. Its northern part is separated from Ile de Rè by the Pertuis d'Antioche, and its southern part from the mainland by the Pertuis de Maumusson, which communicates with Aix road, but leads more directly into the river Seudre.

The island is 16 miles long, N. by W. and S. by E., and its greatest breadth is about 6 miles. It is of moderate height, the soil very fertile, and on first making it from seaward a peculiar and well-marked saddle will be seen not far from Chassiron point, its north extreme, on which is a light-tower. On its south-east side is the town of Le Chateau, where there are building slips, distilleries, rope walks, &c. St. Pierre, the principal town, stands near the centre of the island. The total population of the island is about 17,000.

Oleron is almost entirely surrounded by flats and rocky reefs, which on the western side extend in places 2 miles off shore, and should not be approached within the depth of 10 or 11 fathoms at low water. The extensive flats of sand and mud bordering the eastern side dry at low water; and between the island and the main are numerous shifting sands making the navigation dangerous. The Antioche rocks, extending N.E. 1¼ miles nearly from the north end of the island, dry in many places. Near the north extreme of these rocks stands a refuge beacon painted red.

LIGHTS.—On Chassiron point, the north extreme of Ile d'Oleron, is a round tower, which exhibits, at 164 feet above high water, a *fixed* white light, visible in clear weather at a distance of 18 miles.

Pérotine.—A *fixed* white light is also shown from an iron post on the jetty head at Pérotine, on east side of Ile d'Oleron, at an elevation of 20 feet, and visible 5 miles.

Port Chateau.—At the east part of port Chateau are two round towers, N.N.W. and S.S.E. of each other, 261 yards apart, elevated respectively 33 and 77 feet above high water; from each is shown a *fixed* white light, visible in clear weather at a distance of 8 miles.

PERTUIS D'ANTIOCHE and BASQUE ROAD.— The Pertuis d'Antioche is the passage between the islands of Oleron and Rè, and leads to Basque and Aix roads, and Rochelle and Rochfort; but the tides in it are strong, and strangers should have the aid of a pilot.

Basque road is bounded on the south-west by the Longe and Boyard banks, and on the east by Ile d'Aix, and flats and other dangers extending some distance off the mainland, which should not be approached by a stranger within the depth of 5 fathoms. Aix is a low, strongly fortified islet, surrounded by ledges and flats, and the road is just to the south-west of the islet, between it and Longe or Boyard bank, and has from 6 to 11 fathoms water. There is no passage, except for boats, between it and the main at low water.'

Anchorage.—There is good anchorage in Basque roads in 6 to 11 fathoms, muddy bottom.

LIGHT.—A *fixed* white light is shown from a tower on the fort at the south end of Ile d'Aix. The light is elevated 66 feet above high water, and visible 10 miles.

Directions.—Vessels entering the Pertuis Antioche must be careful to avoid the Antioche rocks off the north end of Ile d'Oleron, and the ledges running off the south-west side of Ile de Rè, and the Plateau du Lavardin, which is a rocky flat lying 1½ miles off its south-east end. The northern part of this flat is marked by a stone beacon, 33 feet high, painted in *red* and *black* alternate horizontal bands, erected on a rock which dries 8 feet. In entering keep in mid-channel, and do not approach either Ile de Rè or Oleron within the depth of 9 or 10 fathoms, until the Chauveau lighthouse on the ledge off the south-east end of Ile de Rè bears N.N.E.; then steer for Aix island, anchoring either in Basque or Aix road.

At night, the light on the south end of Aix bearing S.E. by S. will clear the shoals off the east side of Ile d'Oleron, and lead to an anchorage in the southern part of Basque road.

LA ROCHELLE, the capital of the department of Charente Inférieure, stands on the shore in a bight to the north-east of Basque road, and is the residence of the principal consular officers of foreign countries, a British consular agent resides at Tonnay-Charente. The port of La Rochelle is well situated for commerce, fully sheltered, and has an inner and outer basin, with two docks and a gridiron. The gate of the outer dock is 55 feet wide, and will admit vessels of 16½ feet draught at neap and 20 to 21 feet draught at spring tides; the gridiron will accommodate a vessel 200 feet long. The Digue du Cardinal, which encloses the port, projects from either side, leaving an opening mid-way to the town. The quay, bordering the port, is planted with trees and forms an agreeable promenade. A steam vessel for training coast pilots is stationed at this port.

The only manufactory of importance is that of coal bricks; there are also ship-building yards. An extensive trade is carried on in wine, brandy, oil, salt, timber, grain, and salt fish. In 1879, 821 vessels, amounting to 157,247 tons, entered inwards.* Water and supplies for shipping are abundant. The population (1879) is about 20,000.

---

* Lieutenant-Colonel J. Hayes Sadler, British Vice-Consul, La Rochelle, 1880.

LIGHTS.—At La Rochelle there are two harbour lights: one a *fixed* white light, shown from a tower on the east quay of the inner floating basin, at 79 feet above high water, and visible 10 miles. This light is obscured from E. ½ N. to E. by N., not visible east of E. ¼ N. The other a *fixed red* light, west of the floating basin and 257 yards W. ¾ S. from the former, at 46 feet above high water, visible 9 miles, from E. ¼ N. to E. by N. ¾ N. These two lights in line lead into the harbour; the lower light is only visible about 15° on either side of the line of direction. The east tower is octagonal and white ; the west tower round and white, the upper part of which is red on the side towards the passage.

RIVER CHARENTE rises on the frontiers of the department to which it gives its name. Its first direction is about north to Civray; it then bends round to the westward and proceeds to the southward to Mansle; here it becomes extremely tortuous, but still keeps its southerly direction till it reaches Angoulême. It now runs westward, passing Cognac and Saintes, when it resumes its original course to the northward, and passing Rochefort, pursues a winding course for about 10 miles to fort de la Pointe on the right and port des Barques on the left bank, below which the shores separate and forms an estuary 5 miles in length to Ile d'Aix.

The whole course of the river is about 200 miles. It is navigable for small vessels as far as Montignac, 60 miles from its mouth ; and for vessels of large draught with the tide to Tonnay-Charente 3½ miles above Rochefort, but at low water, there is only 2 feet of water at the entrance to, and in the river. Flowing generally through a rich and fertile valley it is of great importance, both from the facilities it gives to transport, and the numerous public works upon its banks. A little above Rochefort, two canals, the Brouage and Cherras, lead off, the one from its left and the other from its right bank, intended to drain the salt marshes around Rochefort, which made the whole district very unhealthy.

Time Ball.*

LIGHTS.—From an iron pillar at the end of the pier of Fouras north harbour, a *fixed white* light is exhibited at an elevation of 21 feet above high water, and should be seen from a distance of 7 miles.

On the northern bank, at the entrance of the Charente river, are two white square towers, N.W. and S.E. of each other, and 656 yards apart. The eastern tower exhibits a *fixed red* light at an elevation of 45 feet above high water, and the western tower a *fixed green* light at an elevation of 25 feet; in clear weather these lights are visible 16 and 11 miles.

---

* At Fouras a ball is hoisted close up at 6 minutes before signal, and dropped at 11h. 58m. 27s. Fouras mean time. Signal repeated at 0h. 0m. 27s. p.m. Fouras mean time.

On the southern bank, at the entrance of the same river, are two similar towers, N.N.W. ¼ W. and S.S.E. ¼ E. of each other, 536 yards apart, each showing, at an elevation of 44 and 17 feet respectively above high water, a *fixed red* light, visible in clear weather 9 miles.

Directions.—Vessels entering the Charente by night should keep the *red and green* lights on the north bank in a line, until the two *red* lights on the south bank are in line, which will lead to the anchorage of port des Barques. A ray of *red* light visible from the upper or eastern tower on the north bank will indicate a near approach to the anchorage.

ROCHEFORT stands on the right bank of the Charente, about 10 miles from its entrance. It is built partly on a height, and partly on a low flat, and is surrounded by ramparts, planted with trees which afford a shady promenade. Its streets are wide, well paved, and intersect each other at right angles; the houses are low but neatly built, and the only buildings of consequence are those connected with the naval arsenal. The largest edifice is the Hôpital de la Marine on an eminence outside the town.

Rochefort owes much of its importance to its admirable position, which has made it conspicuous among the naval arsenals of France, the one here being on an extensive scale. The river abreast the town is about three-quarters of a cable wide, and the general depths are 18 to 20 feet at low water; there is a commodious dock with steam cranes for discharging vessels.*

Shipbuilding is the principal branch of industry. The trade is corn, colonial produce, salt, wine, brandy, &c. Water and all supplies for shipping are plentiful. The population is about 24,000. There is railway communication to all parts of France.*

Time Ball.†

Pertuis de Maumusson is a narrow winding channel between the south end of Oleron island and the mainland. It is but little more than a mile wide between Maumusson and Arvert points, at the western entrance, where there is a shifting bar with only 6 feet on it at low water, and on which a heavy sea breaks in bad weather. The entrance has been marked by buoys, the outer buoy with black and red stripes being moored in 4¼ fathoms, 2¼ miles W. by N. ¾ N. from Maumusson point.

Within the bar the water deepens, and there are from 3 to 8 fathoms between the sand-banks for a distance of 2¾ miles, after which there are sandy flats with narrow channels between them leading to Aix road and

---

* G. L. Link, Esq., 1880.
† At St. Louis tower a ball is hoisted close up at 6 minutes before signal, and dropped at 11h. 59m. 0s. a.m., Rochefort mean time. Signal repeated at 0h. 1m. 0s. p.m., Rochefort mean time.

Seudre river. Within this river there is water for vessels of the largest draught; but the sands fronting the entrance frequently shift, and a stranger should not attempt its navigation without a pilot.

LIGHT.—A *fixed* white light is exhibited from a lantern suspended from the gable of the keeper's dwelling, at Pointe de Mus de Loup, entrance of Seudre river. The light is elevated 22 feet above high water, and is visible over an arc of 196°, or between the bearings of N.W. ¼ N., through West to S.S.E. ¼ E.; in clear weather it should be seen from a distance of 8 miles.

Tides.—It is high water, full and change, at Rochelle, at 3h. 31m.; ordinary springs rise 17 feet, and neaps 13 feet. In Basques road, at 3h. 20m.; rise 17 and 12½ feet. At Rochefort, at 4h. 6m.; rise 17 and 18 feet. In the Seudre river, at 3h. 26m.; rise 14 and 10 feet.

PLATEAU de ROCHE BONNE is one of the most dangerous shoals off the west coast of France, particularly to vessels bound to Rochefort, and the neighbouring ports. It is an extensive rocky flat, 9 miles long, N.W. by N. and S.E. by S. nearly, and between 2 and 3 miles broad, lying between the parallels of 46° 9′ and 46° 16′. There are three rocky heads with 10, 18, and 23 feet water on them, marked on the chart, but there may be many others, as the extent of the breakers in bad weather is nearly 6 miles. The rocky head of 18 feet, named Roche du Sud-Est, on the south-east part of the shoal, is in lat. 46° 11′ 25″ N., long. 2° 25′ W. and W. by N. ¼ N., distant 36 miles from the lighthouse on the north-west end of Ile de Rè. The rocky head of 10 feet, named La Congrée, lies about 3 miles N.W. ½ N. of the already described Roche du Sud-Est.

CAUTION.—Considerable caution is necessary when navigating in the vicinity of the Roche Bonne, there being deep water close-to on all sides of it. A little eastward there are from 25 to 33 fathoms, red sand and shells; to the westward the water quickly deepens to 60 fathoms, soft bottom.

The TIDES also run strong over it, about 2 knots at springs; the flood sets N.N.E. It is high water, full and change, between 5h. and 6h., and the rise is about 12 feet.

LIGHT VESSEL.—A light vessel painted red, with two masts surmounted by skeleton balls, is moored on the east side of the Plateau de Roche Bonne, nearly 3 miles E. by S. of the Roche du Sud-Est, and shows two *fixed* white lights, the one being 46 and the other 33 feet above the level of the sea, and in clear weather should be seen from a distance of 10 miles. During foggy weather a compressed air trumpet will be sounded, each blast lasting about *three seconds*, with an interval of *fourteen seconds*;

under favourable circumstances, the trumpet should be heard from a distance of 6 miles.

Mariners are warned against placing too much dependence on the vessel always retaining her position.

RIVER GIRONDE.—From the Pertuis Maumusson a low shore trends S.W. by S. 6 miles, to Coubre point, at the northern side of the estuary of the Gironde, the entrance to which is about 10 miles wide ; but, with the exception of the Passe du Nord and Passe de Grave, it is nearly blocked up by dangerous banks and patches of shallow water. These channels, as well as the banks within the river, are buoyed ; the *black* buoys should be left on the port side in entering and ascending, and the *red* to starboard, as usual. The buoys are liable to be carried away in bad weather.*

The entrance to the Gironde will be readily distinguished by the Cordouan light-tower, a handsome structure 203 feet high, standing on a bed of rocks which dry at low tide, S. ¾ E. 7¼ miles from the lighthouse on Coubre point. This point is low, but there is a white light-tower on it 100 feet high, a beacon close to the northward of the tower, and a black tower called the Tour de Bonne Anse a mile to the eastward. These, together with Terre Nègre fort ; the light-tower on the downs of Pointe de la Palmyre ; Terre Nègre light-tower coloured black and white, and beyond it the church, mill, and village of St. Palais ; the Chay light-tower, and the light-tower and church of Royan, are all conspicuous objects on the north shore of entrance. A light-vessel with two masts is moored in 8 fathoms of water, about 2 miles south of Coubre point.

Opposite Royan is Grave point, the south point of entrance to the river on which is a wooden light-tower 82 feet high, and 3½ miles to the westward of it is the light-tower of St. Nicolas; these in line form the leading mark for the Passe de Grave. Twice a day the names of vessels entering and leaving are announced at Bordeaux from the semaphore at Pointe de Grave ; but in order that the names may be given correctly, vessels must be supplied with the *International Code of Signals,* which, by means of four letters indicated by flags, makes known the name of each vessel in the official list drawn up by the governments of France and England.

There are many towns and villages upon the banks of the Gironde, but the first trading place of consequence is the town of Pauillac, on the left bank 27 miles above Grave point, where vessels of too large draught to ascend to Bordeaux usually discharge, and outward bound vessels provision and water. At about 5 miles farther up, on the opposite bank, is the town of Blaye, remarkable for its citadel and fortress. Between, several islets

* *See* Admiralty chart :—France, west coast, sheet 2, No. 2,664 ; scale, *m* = half an inch.

are formed in the middle of the river, and on one of them is fort Pâté (so called from its round shape), which crosses its fire with that of the fortress of Blaye on the right bank and of fort Médoc on the left, and thus commands the passage of the river, which is here only 1½ miles wide. At 7 miles above Blaye is the conflux of the rivers Garonne and Dordogne; and about 13 miles above this, on the left bank of the Garonne, stands the commercial city of Bordeaux.

The Garonne rises in the central Pyrenees, in the valley of Aran, in Spain. Its whole course is about 300 miles. Of these 45 miles, commencing at the point where it enters France, are sufficiently deep to float timber from the Pyrenees. At Toulouse it is joined by the Languedoc canal, communicating with the Mediterranean, after which it flows through a wide and almost continuous plain; but its channel continues shallow, it is subject to frequent inundations, and brings down so much débris, that it cannot be considered quite clear for navigation higher up than the town of Marmande. The influence of the tide is felt about 25 miles below this town, near Langon. The whole course of the Dordogne is about 290 miles, of which 170 miles, beginning at Mayronnes, are navigable.

BORDEAUX, the capital of the department of Gironde, is one of the largest, handsomest, and most opulent cities in France; as a maritime and commercial place being second only to Marseilles and Havre. The town is built in the form of a crescent (2¼ miles long and a mile broad) on the western bank and along the bend of the Garonne river, 55 miles from the sea, and its extensive quays are generally crowded with shipping up to the handsome stone bridge, 531 yards in length, of 17 arches, which spans the river.

The river abreast the town is one-third of a mile wide, and the general depths are 7 to 12 feet at low water, but there are two deep places for shipping, the Mouillage de Lormont on the right bank, and the Rade de Bordeaux on the left bank, which are three-quarters to a mile in length and a cable wide, and carry from 20 to 30 feet. Besides the immediate access to the sea by the river, Bordeaux has the advantage of a direct communication with the Mediterranean by the Languedoc canal, and is thereby enabled to supply the south of France produce as cheaply as Marseilles, to which it is connected by railway.

There are numerous docks and building-yards for vessels of every size. The trade is extensive, particularly in wines, brandy, plums, almonds, and other fruits. Its manufactures are chiefly tobacco, brandy, sugar, wine, vinegar, iron and steel goods, chemicals, leather, liquers, cottons and woollens, kid gloves, &c. In 1864, 3,132 vessels, amounting to 486,327 tons, entered inwards; of these 121,626 tons were British; and 3,094, equal to 485,307, cleared outwards. Steam navigation between England and Bordeaux is gradually superseding that of sailing vessels, for in 1864 out of 397 vessels arriving from Great Britain, 233 were steam vessels belonging to various established lines, viz., London, Liverpool, Dublin, Glasgow, Bristol, and Hull. Water, coal, and all supplies are abundant. The population in 1872 amounted to 191,240.

LIGHTS.—The following lights are established at the entrance to the Gironde :—

Cordouan Rocks.—The circular tower on the Cordouan rocks, near the middle of the entrance, exhibits, at 194 feet above high water, a *revolving* white light, attaining its greatest brilliancy every *minute*, and visible in clear weather at a distance of 27 miles ; the eclipses do not appear total within 10 miles. The light shows *red* in the Passe du Nord, in an angular space of about 81°, when bearing between S. by W. ¾ W. and W. by N.

Pointe de la Coubre.—At Pointe de la Coubre, the north point of entrance to the Gironde, a *fixed* white light is shown from a black wooden structure, at an elevation of 121 feet, and visible 15 miles.

A light-vessel exhibiting two *fixed* white lights, one on each mast, elevated 34 and 23 feet, visible 10 and 8 miles respectively, is moored on Grand Banc, about 2 miles south of Pointe de la Coubre, and about 6 miles N.N.W. ¼ W. of the Cordouan light-tower, in 8 fathoms of water.

Pointe de la Palmyre.—On the downs of Pointe de la Palmyre, S.E. by E. ¼ E. about 4¼ miles from the light-tower of Pointe de la Coubre, a light-tower constructed on three pillars, exhibits an *alternating red* and *green* light, at an elevation of 167 feet above high water, visible in clear weather 14 miles.

On Falaise, at 4¼ miles N.E. ¾ E. from Cordouan lighthouse, stands a black and white tower from which, at an elevation of 46 feet, is exhibited a fixed *red* light, visible 10 miles.

The Terre Nègre tower, 2¼ miles S. by E. ¾ E. of the Palmyre lighthouse, exhibits, at an elevation of 121 feet above the sea, a *fixed* white light, obscured in the direction of the sea from a line drawn through the N.E. buoy of the Monrevel bank, northward, visible 14 miles.

The tower of Chay is square, the upper part being painted black; situated westward of Royan, and a cable from the edge of the cliff, it exhibits, at an elevation of 88 feet above the sea, a *fixed red* light, visible in clear weather 10 miles. A similar tower, painted in red and white horizontal bands, is situated north of Royan, and bears N.E. by E. ¾ E.

from the ..... tower, it exhibits, at an elevation of 177 feet above the sea, a fixed red light, visible in clear weather 12 miles.

Royan.—At 132 yards within the end of the jetty at Royan, a fixed white light is exhibited from a tower, at an elevation of 44 feet, and visible 12 miles.

Port St. George.—Two fixed red lights are shown, one from the top of a house on the south extreme of Valliere point, at the entrance of the little port of St. George, and the other, about 1½ miles to the south-east, from the top of a house on the hills of Salmac. The light off Valliere point is elevated 46 feet, visible 12 miles, and that on the Salmac hills 121 feet above high water, and visible at a distance of 18 miles.

Grave Point.—The square tower on Grave point, the south point of entrance to the Gironde, exhibits, at an elevation of 85 feet, a *flashing* light with eclipses of short duration, succeeding each other at intervals of *five seconds*, in the direction of Talais light, and in the south channel into the Gironde ; but it is a *fixed* light in the direction of the North channel.

St. Nicolas.—A square tower on the downs of St. Nicholas, bearing W. ¾ S. from Pointe de Grave light-tower, exhibits, at an elevation of 71 feet above high water, a *fixed green* light, visible in clear weather 7 miles.

LIGHTS in the River.—A light-vessel moored in 2¼ fathoms water, on the north-east edge of the Tallais bank, about 4½ miles S.S.E. of Grave point, exhibits, at an elevation of 33 feet above the sea, a *fixed* white light, visible 10 miles. The vessel carries a red ball at mast-head and a bell is sounded in foggy weather, five strokes every half hour.

The Richard is a *fixed red* light shown from a tower on the left or south-west bank of the river, 10 miles above Grave point, and about 5 miles from the Tallais light-vessel. The light is elevated 106 feet above high water, and visible 16 miles.

Two light-vessels are moored farther up the river, off the left bank, one in 13 feet water, nearly abreast the Tour de By, the other in 23 feet between Maréchale and Mapon. They each exhibit, at 34 feet above the sea, a *fixed* white light, visible at about 10 miles. The former vessel is black and red, the latter red.

Near the entrance of Calonge canal a fixed *red* light is exhibited from an iron support, at an elevation of 32 feet, visible 4 miles.

On the north extreme of Patiras isle, in the middle of the river, is a wooden scaffold, about 5 miles above the Mapon light-vessel, from which is exhibited a *flashing* white light with eclipses every *four seconds*. The light is 43 feet above high water, and visible 13 miles.

At the landing-place at Pauillac, on the left or western bank of the river, abreast Patiras isle, a *fixed* white light is shown on an iron post at an elevation of 20 feet, and visible 7 miles.

At Gaët, half a mile north of Pauillac, from a white iron beacon a light shows *white* through the greater portion of the horizon, but *red* towards Gaët, elevated 20 feet above high water, and visible 6 miles in clear weather.

At St. Lambert, half a mile south of Pauillac, a *red* light is exhibited visible 8 miles.

East of the village of Mousset and north of Gaët one mile, on a black wooden structure elevated 67 feet above high water, is a *fixed* white light, showing *red* towards Gaët, visible in clear weather 6 miles. At port de Blaye, on the east bank of the river, about 5 miles above the north end of Patiras island, three lights are shown ; one at the entrance of the port, *red ;* one at the extremity of the discharging place, *yellow ;* and one on a wooden scaffold elevated 16 feet above high water at the landing place *white,* visible in clear weather 4 miles.

At Plagne harbour, on the right bank of Dordogne river, a *red* light is exhibited, visible 4 miles.

Pilots.—No large vessel should attempt to enter the Gironde without a pilot, on account of the shifting banks, and the uncertainty of finding the buoys in their proper positions. The pilots are in general excellent seamen, and worthy of confidence. They will sometimes be met with 25 or 30 miles from the land. When they see that the entrance is impracticable, they run into the Pertuis d'Antioche or the Pertuis Breton.

Steam tugs are always ready, but it is not obligatory to employ them. The expense can be and is frequently avoided without loss of time especially at spring tides.

Tides.—It is high water, full and change, at the entrance of the Gironde, at 3h. 37m. ; ordinary springs rise 18¾ feet, neaps 10½ feet. At St. Seurin, about 20 miles within the entrance, at 4h. 11m. ; rise 14¼ feet and 11 feet. At Bordeaux, at 6h. 50m. ; rise 14 feet, and 12¾ feet. Equinoctial tides rise 17 or 18 feet.

The tides, both ebb and flood, set strong through the channels at the entrance, and great caution is required when approaching the river in thick weather. They follow the direction of the Passe du Nord, and turn at 1¼ hours after high or low water, there being hardly any slack water. In the Passe de Grave, with Cordoun light-tower bearing N.E., they set as follows ;—First of the flood, North; one-third flood, N.E.; half and two-thirds flood, E.N.E. First of the ebb, S.E.; one-third ebb, South ; half and two-thirds, West. In the channel between the Cordouan bank and Grave point, the flood sets generally S.E.; the ebb from West to W.S.W.

The winds have a great influence on the tides; and in general, a favourable tide may be depended upon when the wind blows strongly into the river, and a low one with a strong wind blowing seaward.

Bore.—The Gironde is liable to a *bore* at high spring tides. The crest of it rises 13 to 16 feet above the surface of the river, and this great mass of water moving along with impetuous velocity, often causes serious damage to vessels, not only in the Gironde, but in the Dordogne, which river it ascends for about 20 miles.

Anchorage.—The first anchorage in the Gironde is in front of Royan, on the north shore of the entrance. It is, however, exposed to-seaward, and often there is a heavy sea, which, in a weather tide, causes vessels to ride uneasily.

The holding ground in Verdon roadstead, 2 miles within Grave point, is not good; but as the anchorage in 6 fathoms water is easy to weigh from, vessels often use it in bad weather.

The Rade de Richard, 8 miles higher up the river, is securely sheltered in $3\frac{1}{4}$ to 4 fathoms, muddy bottom.

PASSE du NORD on the northern side of the entrance, carries from 6 to 11 fathoms water; but the soundings within deepen in places to 15 fathoms. It is navigable for large vessels; but as the channel is limited by sand-banks which shift their position, a stranger should not attempt it without a pilot. The channel is bounded on the northern side by the Demi bank at entrance, and the Barre à l'Anglais a little within; and on the southern side by Le Grand Banc and the Plateau de Cordouan.

The Demi bank is a flat extending $3\frac{1}{4}$ miles N.W. by N. from Coubre point; the general depths on it are 3 to $4\frac{3}{4}$ fathoms; but on its southern part, bordering the west side of the point, are some patches with from 3 to 9 feet, which are steep-to. The Barre à l'Anglais runs north-westward more than 3 miles from Palmyre point; there are 3 fathoms on its outer part, but towards the point it shoals from 9 feet to a dry bank.

On the south side of the Passe is the Mauvaise shoal, with $2\frac{1}{4}$ to 3 fathoms water on it,—on the north-west end of Le Grand Banc,—which contracts the channel here to a little more than half a mile in breadth.

Le Grand Banc, with numerous shallow patches of 3 feet to $2\frac{1}{4}$ fathoms water on them, extends to the south-east—fronting the mouth of the Gironde—for about 11 miles to the Passe de Grave. On the northern side of the bank, $2\frac{1}{4}$ miles from Palmyre point, is the Monrevel shoal, with one fathom water on it. From the Monrevel shoal the channel is clear up to the buoy of the Platin at $1\frac{1}{4}$ miles northward of Grave point

Buoys.—The Passe du Nord is indicated by the following buoys :—A large red buoy with bell and prismatic mirror, is moored in 10 fathoms in the fairway outside the bar, with Coubre point lighthouse in one with the lighthouse on the downs of Palmyre S.E. by E. ¼ E. distant 5 miles. The northern side of the channel within the bar is marked by six black buoys, two of which are on the outer edge of the patches off Coubre point, two others, about 1¼ miles from each other, on the outer edge of the Barre à l'Anglais, and two about a mile apart on the outside edge of the St. George bank ; the southern side is marked by four red buoys, two of which are on the outer or north edge of Mauvaise shoal, and two on north-east edge of Monrevel shoal ; there is also a red buoy on the north part of the bank off Grave point.

PASSE de GRAVE, the southern entrance to the Gironde, is narrow and not so deep as the Passe du Nord, but it is occasionally preferred by vessels that cannot procure pilots, because its entrance is well marked by objects on the land. They must, however, be careful not to approach too near the Coast of Medoc in tacking, as the flood sets strong towards it ; and, as not more than 12 feet can be reckoned on in the channel at low water, a vessel of large draught should not attempt its navigation except with a rising tide and fair wind. At all times therefore a preference should be given to Passe du Nord, as the depth is greater, and the ground in all parts good for anchorage.

The leading marks for the Passe de Grave are easily recognized, the outer ones are the light-towers of St. Nicolas and Pointe de Grave, and the inner ones the light-towers of Chay and Royan. The two first of these marks in line lead between the Chevrier bank on the north-west side of the channel and the Olives bank extending from the shore on the south. On the extremity of this latter bank, at 2¾ miles from the shore, the depth is only 2¾ fathoms, and within this distance there are several rocky patches with less than 6 feet water on them. When Royan light-tower and that of Chay are in line, they lead in the deepest water between the shoals into the main channel.

Buoys.—The Passe de Grave is indicated by the following buoys :— The outer large fairway buoy is black and red, with a conical cage, and moored in 9 fathoms water, distant about 5 miles from the land, with St. Nicolas light-tower bearing E. ¼ N. 7½ miles, and Cordouan lighthouse N.E. by E. ¼ E. about 5½ miles. On the south-west end of the Chevrier bank there is a black can buoy in 4¼ fathoms water, with Cordouan light-house bearing N.E. ¼ E., and Vieux Soulac beacon S.E. by E. ¾ E. On the extremity of the Olives bank is a red conical buoy in 3¾ fathoms, with Cordouan lighthouse N.N.E. ¼ E., and Vieux Soulac beacon E.S.E., and about a mile to the north-eastward of this latter buoy is another red buoy with a conical cage, in 4½ fathoms water. A black can buoy lies in 3¼ fathoms on the Matte du Gros-terrier, with Cordouan lighthouse N.W., and Point de Grave lighthouse W. by S. ⅜ S. A red conical buoy lies on the St. Nicolas rock, abreast the St. Nicolas light-tower, a black and white buoy on the southern edge of the Platin shoal, and a black buoy on the Cordouan bank about half a mile N.E. by E. of the Cordouan light-tower.

Directions for Passe du Nord.—Sailing vessels should not attempt to enter the Gironde when the weather is hazy, and there is an appearance of a calm, because at such times a heavy swell frequently arises in an instant. This phenomenon, called by the pilots Le Brume Sèche or the *dry haze*, is a sort of mist, accompanied by a calm, which is invariably followed by a swell in all the channels. Vessels should also be on their guard when approaching the entrance at night, as fog frequently obscures the lights.

To sail into the Gironde by the Passe du Nord, steer for the light-tower on Coubre point,—*fixed white* light—in one with the Palmyre light-house, —*alternate red* and *green* light—S.E. by E ¼ E., which will lead close to the red bell fairway buoy, moored outside the bar. When the Coubre point light vessel,—two *fixed white* lights—is on with Cordouan light-tower—*revolving* white light—S. by E. ¾ E., steer with these two in line, opening the light-vessel a little to the southward, and steering eastward towards the Terre Nègre light tower,—*fixed white* light—until the St. George and Suzac lighthouses—each a *fixed red* light—are in line, bearing S.E., which is the mark to continue upon until the Talais light-vessel,—*fixed white* light—and Richard light-tower,—*fixed red*—are in one, which last is the leading mark up to the anchorage in Verdon road.

By Night the same directions apply, attention being paid to the descriptions of the several lights, and in leaving the river, by reversing the order in which they are here placed.

River Lights.—To facilitate the navigation, the following lights are established indicating the channel up the river ;—on Grave point a *flashing* light,—Talais floating, *fixed* white light,—Richard, *fixed red*,—Tour de By and Mapon floating, *fixed* white lights,—Calonge canal, *fixed red*,—Patiras isle *flashing* light,—Mousset, Gaët Pauillac, *fixed* white lights,—on the east side of the river, three lights at port de Blaye, *red, white,* and *yellow.*

Directions for Passe de Grave.—To sail through this channel, bring the light-tower—*fixed green* light—on the downs of St. Nicolas in line with that on Pointe de Grave—*flashing light*—E. ¼ N., and steer with these on until the Chay light-tower and that of Royan—

each a *fixed red* light—are in line N.E. by E. ¾ E., proceed with these in line until the Talais floating light—*fixed white*—is in line with Richard light-tower—*fixed red* light—which is the leading mark up to the anchorage in Verdon road.

If these marks are followed 12 feet at least will be carried over the shoalest parts at low-water springs; but if they are departed from there must not be a greater depth than 8 feet calculated upon.

In working through do not stand farther westward than to have St. Pierre de Royan church in line with the Chay light-tower ; nor farther towards the shore than to have the church but little open to the eastward of the tower, for the flood stream strikes with such force upon the coast, that in many cases it will be almost impossible to keep the vessel thoroughly under command.

At Night the above directions apply, attention being paid to the different descriptions of lights, bearing in mind that those of Chay, Royan, and St. Nicolas are not visible more than 12° beyond the line of direction. When leaving the river, reverse the order in which they are here placed.

The COAST from the Gironde river trends S.S.W. ¼ W. about 57 miles to the lighthouse of cape Ferret, northward of the entrance to the Bassin d'Arcachon, and consists throughout of low sandy downs with a few clusters of trees. At about midway, a short distance inland, and parallel to the shore, are two remarkable lakes, the northern of which is named Etang de Carcans, the southern, Etang de la Canau. They communicate with each other and with the Arcachon basin.*

LIGHTS.—On the downs between the mouth of the Gironde and cape Ferret, about 220 yards from each other N.N.E. and S.S.W. nearly, are two wooden towers 78 feet high, the southern one being in lat. 45° 8′ N., long. 1° 10′ W. They exhibit, at 177 feet above high water *fixed* white lights, visible in clear weather at a distance of 20 miles.

On the tongue of land bounding the west side of the Bassin d'Arcachon, at about 1½ miles northward of the entrance, is a round tower, which shows at 167 feet above high water a *fixed* white light, visible 20 miles.

BASSIN D'ARCACHON.—This extensive basin, although full of shoals, and its entrance nearly blocked up by sand-banks, is much frequented by vessels for cargoes of resin and pitch, which the neighbouring districts furnish in abundance. The fishing also is good, and gives employment to the inhabitants of the numerous villages along its shore. The largest village, La Teste de Buch, is on the southern shore, and until 1854

---

* *See* Admiralty chart:—France, west coast, sheet 1, No. 2,655 ; scale, = 0·5 of an inch.

consisted only of a few fishermen's huts; but the place being admirably adapted for sea bathing, and connected by railway to Bordeaux, there is now a population of more than 5,000. The basin is bordered by beautiful smooth sands and encircled by sand downs covered with fir woods which shelter it. The river Leyre falls into its south-east angle.

˙ The entrance to this basin is fronted by an extensive flat, through which are two channels, known only to the fishermen and pilots, who are found cruising off the port. The principal channel is from the southward, but its bar so frequently shifts that no chart can be depended on for any length of time. The least water on the bar is 13 feet, and for crossing it two beacons, one of which is moveable, are erected on the shore; from thence the narrow channel leading to the entrance trends in a N.E. direction close to the eastern shore, and carries from 5 to 9 fathoms water. The soundings deepen to 15 and 16 fathoms at the entrance; they then decrease, and at 1½ miles within cape Ferret there is anchorage off Moullo in 5 and 6 fathoms, sand. The only safe anchorage in the basin for large vessels is between Bernet point and the Teich channel, but it is difficult of access, being separated from Moullo roadstead by a bank of fine sand, which frequently shifts.

When approaching from seaward, the position of the basin will be recognized by the circular brick light-tower on the north side of entrance, where the land is low, level, and destitute of trees; whilst on the south the sand downs are somewhat higher and covered with trees. The breakers at the entrance may always be seen, and the soundings decrease gradually towards them; but a heavy sea frequently breaks on the bar, rendering crossing occasionally impossible. The fishermen often prefer keeping at sea for days in rough weather rather than risk crossing the bar, and are frequently obliged to run for Rochefort or the Gironde.

Buoys.—The outer buoy (named Landing), entrance to ˋBassin d'Arcachon, is a red and black spiral buoy moored in 13 fathoms, with the lighthouse north of cape Ferret bearing E. by N. ¼ N., and the semaphore at point d'Arcachon S.S.E. ½ E.

Rastey buoy, conical, red and black, is moored one mile S.E. ½ E. from Landing buoy.

Tides.— It is high water, full and change, in the Bassin d'Arcachon at 4h. 37m.; springs rise 11¾ feet, neaps 2¼ feet. The tide is an hour earlier on the bar than in the basin, at Notre Dame chapel.

Life Boat.—A life boat is stationed at Bassin d'Arcachon.

The Coast from Arcachon basin trends in the same direction as before for 62 miles to Bayonne. The land between is low and level, excepting some little downs covered with trees, which appear to be elevated above the general level; for a distance of about 20 miles northward from Bayonne they are from 120 to 170 feet in height, and extend about a mile inland, but their form is continually changing.

LIGHTS.—On the downs at Contis between the Bassin d'Arcachon and the mouth of the Adour is a round tower, which exhibits, at 164 feet above high water, a *revolving* white light, attaining its greatest brilliancy every *half minute*, and in clear weather should be seen from a distance of 24 miles. The eclipses are not total within the distance of 10 miles.

Beacons.—At Biscarosse, about midway between the lighthouses of Arcachon and Contis, is a beacon 62 feet high, with a black top. On the downs of Huchet, between Contis and Cap Breton, is another beacon, 75 feet high, formed by two triangles one over the other, the upper white, the other black.

FOSSE de CAP BRETON.—The soundings between Arcachon and Bayonne are regular, sand, gravel, and shells, shoaling gradually, from 30 fathoms at 5½ miles off shore, to 10 fathoms at one mile, and 5 fathoms at half a mile, within which are occasional patches of 3 to 6 feet at low water; but 8 miles north of Bayonne, abreast Cap Breton, there is a singular pit or break in the soundings, with deep water, over mud bottom, from seaward nearly up to the beach. This is called the Fosse de Cap Breton, and its general direction is indicated by two beacons, on the sand-hills abreast, which when in one bear about S.E. by E. ¼ E.

At 6 miles from the shore it is about 1¾ miles wide and 172 fathoms deep; at 2¾ miles, three-quarters of a mile wide and 205 fathoms deep; at one mile, a third of a mile wide and 57 fathoms deep; at a quarter of a mile, half a mile wide and 17 fathoms deep; and 8 fathoms deep at less than 2 cables from the beach.

LIGHT.—On the left bank of the entrance to port Cap Breton, a *fixed red* light is exhibited at an elevation of 26 feet, visible 9 miles.

The anchorage at the end of the Fosse is less dangerous than any other part of the coast in the neighbourhood of Bayonne, and it affords to vessels that may have to run on shore the best place in the neighbourhood of Bayonne.

To enter in bad weather, keep at least 5 miles from the shore till the beacons are in one; then run in with these marks on so as to avoid the tremendous sea which breaks on both sides of the Fosse. A vessel near the bar of Bayonne, and endeavouring to steer along shore towards the Fosse, would be in danger of being swamped in crossing the southern edge.

The **RIVER ADOUR,** the mouth of which is 8 miles to the south-west of Cap Breton, has its source in the mountain ridge of Tourmalet, in the department of Hautes Pyrenees. Its course is first North, then West, S.W., and S.S.W., passing St. Lever and Dax, to the former of which it is navigable, and falls into the sea at 3½ miles below Bayonne. Its whole length is about 170 miles. The current is rapid; and sometimes serious inundations are caused by the melting of the snow on the Pyrenees. Timber is brought down the river from the Pyrenees, and pitch, tar, resin, cork, grain, brandy, &c., from Armagnac; but a shifting bar at its mouth renders the passage in and out difficult, and sometimes dangerous, though the employment of steam tugs diminishes the risk.*

The piers in progress on either side of entrance now extend in a straight line more than 500 yards outside low-water mark, and the breadth between them is 170 yards. Within the bar the soundings deepen, but are irregular, varying generally in the deep water channel from about 14 to 35 feet, abreast Bayonne.

The bar is only passable for sailing vessels during daylight and with the flood tide ; but under favourable circumstances in fine weather it may be crossed at the beginning of the ebb. It is not always the depth of water on the bar which prevents a vessel crossing, but the heavy sea caused by the ebb tide. The sea is often smooth in the offing when the bar is impassable. No vessel should enter without the aid of a pilot. With a smooth sea, vessels drawing 14 feet can cross the bar at springs, and those drawing 11 feet at neaps, provided they do so at high water.

BAYONNE stands on the left bank of the Adour, at the confluence of that river with the Nive. The latter divides the town into nearly two equal parts, called Great and Little Bayonne, connected by iron and stone bridges. Both parts are surrounded by ramparts, flanked with bastions and broad deep ditches, which at any time can be filled with water. Abreast Bayonne, on the right bank of the Adour, is the suburb St. Esprit, where, on an eminence, is the citadel, which commands with its formidable batteries the town, both rivers, and the plain. The Adour is here about 250 yards in breadth and spanned by a stone bridge. The dockyard is commodious, and the arsenal of Bayonne is one of the best and most complete in France. The military hospital also is of considerable extent, being capable of accommodating 2,000 invalids.

The shipping trade, however, has been much injured since the connection of this port with the north of France, and, from the difficulties of the

---

* *See* Admiralty plan :—River Adour from its mouth to Bayonne; scale, = 0.7 inches with Bar and Entrance, No. 1,343.

bar, vessels of not more than 360 tons rarely arrive. The chief produce is brandy, liqueurs, chocolate, rope, glass, and refined sugar. The exports are resin, woollen cloths, linen, serges, silks, drugs, wines, brandy, &c. ; the imports are Spanish wool, liquorice root, iron, cocoa, oil, mill-stones, &c. This port is frequented by about 430 vessels annually. Coal, water, and provisions are plentiful. The total population is about 25,000.

LIGHTS.—A round brick tower, 144 feet high, stands on St. Martin point, 2½ miles south-west of the mouth of the Adour, and shows *alternately a white* and *red flash*, at intervals of *twenty seconds*. The light is elevated 240 feet above high water, and visible in clear weather at a distance of 22 miles.

A *fixed* white light is exhibited from the signal tower close to the south jetty at the south side of entrance to the Adour when the passage is considered practicable, and a *fixed red* light when the state of the sea will not allow vessels to enter by night. The light is elevated 56 feet above high water, and in clear weather is visible 6 miles.

When the white light is shown, and the passage practicable, two *green* lights are exhibited, which kept in line, will lead in the direction of the channel between the jetties.

Signals.—A red flag at the mast-head on the tower, at the south shore of entrance, denotes that no vessel can enter the Adour. A white flag with five blue crosses denotes that a tug can get out. The same flag at half-mast denotes that a tug cannot get out. A sailing vessel should not approach the bar nearer than just sufficient to distinguish the signals.

Tides.—It is high water, full and change, on the bar of the Adour at 3h. 45m.; springs rise 12 feet, neap 10¾ feet. But the time of high water is subject to variations from the duration, direction, and force of the winds which may have previously prevailed.

Directions.—Vessels bound to Bayonne from the westward, with the wind from that quarter, should endeavour to make the coast of Spain between cape Machichaco and St. Sebastian, particularly in the winter months; so that, should the weather become unsettled, and crossing the bar be attended with risk, they may enter either port Pasages or San Sebastian, in Spain, or St. Jean de Luz, in France, where they will be sure of obtaining pilots.

The Adour is subject to freshes, or a considerable increase of water, which strengthens the current of the river so much as to retard the flood-side, and prevents its entrance. The stream under these circumstances always runs out, as may be found by the water of the river being met 3 miles or more outside. A vessel should not then attempt to enter the river, because the stream increases the danger of crossing the bar :

nevertheless, if the wind be fresh, and the entering be not interdicted by the usual signal, it may be attempted; but it will be necessary to carry all possible sail, and if the vessel be deeply laden, to have the hatches, boats, &c., well secured, as the sea on the bar is then dangerous : under these circumstances it is necessary to be ready to enter at least an hour and a half before high water.

Vessels entering in bad weather, with the wind aft and a heavy sea, should carry all sail they can bear. The fore and aft sails should be hoisted, particularly the jib and fore stay-sail, and the sheets hauled well aft. This precaution is indispensable; for if the sea broaches the vessel to, either way, the assistance of the head-sails is necessary to regain the course. But, if, from tempestuous weather, a vessel is not able to cross the bar, she should, if the wind permits, make for port Pasage, in Spain.

Care should be taken, when bound for the Adour, to keep to the north-ward of the entrance, if the wind has previously prevailed from N.N.W. to East; but southward of it when the wind has prevailed for five or six days from South to N.N.W. Experience proves that in the former case the current sets to the S.W., and that vessels have sometimes been carried down to the coast of Spain; and in the latter, they have been drifted northward of the bar, where, finding no shelter, and being unable to keep off the land in bad weather, they have been stranded between the Adour and Vieux Boucant.

When the wind is from N.N.W. to N.W., a vessel may steer directly for the mouth of the river, bearing in mind that St. Martin point light is 2¼ miles south-west of it. A vessel bound to the river, with the wind from the westward, and near the coast of Spain, and at such a distance as precludes the hope of entering before dark, should stand off and on under a sufficient press of sail, so as to counteract the effect of the cur-rent, which runs to the north-east, and at times at the rate of 4 or 5 miles an hour, when the wind has been blowing some days between W.N.W. and South. It will be prudent also to strive to keep an anchorage under the lee, into which she may run in the morning, in case the weather obliges her to seek for refuge.

Anchorage.—To the north of the Adour there is no anchorage in bad weather, not even in the Fosse of Cap Breton. A vessel may, how-ever, run for a chance of saving her crew on the beach at the head of the Fosse, page 89, but to gain the entrance in bad weather it is necessary to work off about 6 miles from the coast. To the north and south of the Fosse, the sea breaks heavily on the sandy flats, where it is scarcely passable. There will be less danger in remaining at anchor outside the bar of the Adour, in 12 to 15 fathoms, sand and mud, N.W. a mile from the entrance, which is the best position to run in from, at the first favour·

able moment, and where the ebb tide assists a vessel off the land in the event of a change of wind. It will be better, however, to endeavour if possible to seek refuge in St. Jean de Luz, or Fuenterrabia.

The COAST from the Adour trends round to the S.W. and West for 15 miles to the entrance of the Bidassoa river, the boundary between France and Spain. The mountains of the Pyrennees, as well as those that branch off to the westward, are of considerable height, and will be seen a great distance seaward. At 2¼ miles from the Adour is St. Martin point with its lighthouse, and a mile farther on the little port and village of Biarritz, with a population of about 2,500. This place is much frequented for the sake of its baths and the beautiful scenery in its vicinity. It has a communication with Paris by telegraph. In fine weather there is anchorage at a mile from the shore, in 12 or 13 fathoms water, fine sand and mud, with the village bearing E.S.E.

At 2¾ miles south-west of Biarritz is Bidart village, standing a quarter of a mile northward of a rivulet. From thence the coast consists in general of low rocks, with a few patches of sandy beach; but the country inland is high. This part of the coast is fronted by the Plateau de St. Jean de Luz, with varying depths on it of from 6 to 35 fathoms, rocky bottom, for which the mariner is referred to the chart. A vessel has nothing to fear in crossing this bank when the water is smooth, but the sea breaks heavily on its shallow parts in bad weather, and the shore should not be approached too close.

St. JEAN de LUZ BAY, at 10 miles south-west of the Adour, is three-quarters of a mile wide and half a mile deep, and affords anchorage in 3 to 6 fathoms water, sand and rock; but it is exposed to the northward, and sometimes inaccessible in bad weather from the heavy sea which breaks at the entrance on the Artha rocks; and also on the shoal spots on the Plateau de St. Jean de Luz. The bay of Fuenterrabia is then the only refuge for vessels that cannot work off shore. A breakwater about 20 feet above the sea extends from Socoa across the bay to the eastward.

The river Nivelle falls into the head of the bay, between two quays, 30 yards apart, and at its mouth, on the right bank, is the town of St. Jean de Luz, which is connected to its suburb, Siboure, on the left bank, by a bridge. The bar at the entrance to the river dries 2 feet at springs, at which period there are not more than 3 feet between the quays. The trade is small. A few vessels sail annually for the Newfoundland and other fisheries. The population may be about 2,500.

St. Barbe point, the eastern point of the bay, has a battery on it, and on the rocks at the extreme of the point there is a landing place. These rocks extend more than a cable west and two cables south from the point, and dry at low water, making a close approach to this side of the bay dangerous. At half a mile N.N.E. of the point are two patches of 3 and 4 fathoms, named Les Esquilletac, close outside which the depths are 8 and 9 fathoms.

The western point of the bay is also rocky. Here is the little tidal harbour of Socoa, enclosed within piers, and protected by a fort, but it dries at springs as far as the north jetty. With a smooth sea, the harbour will admit vessels of 11¼ feet draught at springs, and 8¼ feet at neaps. With West or N.W. winds the tide rises a foot higher. A life boat is stationed here.*

LIGHTS.—At Socoa, on the west side of St. Jean de Luz bay, is a square tower painted white with a black vertical stripe, from which is shown a *fixed* white light, at 115 feet above high water, and visible at a distance of 10 miles; through an arc of 17½ degrees this light shows *red*, indicating the point where the leading mark of the two *green* lights, shown from the head of the bay, terminates, being the position to turn to starboard for the anchorage.

On St. Barbe point are two *fixed red* lights, exhibited from brick structures, 411 yards apart, and bearing from each other S.E. by E. ½ E. and N.W by W. ½ W., which during the day serve as leading marks. These lights attain their greatest brilliancy when in line, diminishing their brightness in proportion as that line is receded from, and are only visible through an arc of about 15° on each side of that line of direction.

The high light is elevated 33 feet above the ground, and 166 feet above the level of high water, and should be visible in clear weather from a distance of 13 miles.

The low light is elevated 10 feet above the ground, and 95 feet above the level of high water, and should be visible in clear weather from a distance of 13 miles.

At the head of the bay is a stone tower, which shows, at an elevation of 52 feet above high water, a *fixed green* light, visible 10 degrees on each side of the leading marks to the anchorage, visible in clear weather 7 miles. On the western jetty, N. 8° W. 500 yards from the preceding, is shown another *fixed green* light, which in line with the first is the leading mark to the anchorage.

Signals.—A red or tricoloured flag indicates that a vessel can enter the port; when it is hauled down, and a flag hoisted on the end of the jetty, the vessel should anchor.

Tides.—It is high water, full and change, in St. Jean de Luz bay at 3h. 45m.; springs rise 12¼ feet, neaps 8 feet.

* *See* Admiralty plan :—St. Jean de Luz bay, No. 1,345 ; scale, *m* = 9·8 inches.

Directions.—A vessel's position can be ascertained by cross-bearing of the two mountains, Larhune and Batallera. Mount Larhune, bearing S. ¼ E. 5¼ miles from fort Socoa on the west point of entrance to the bay is lofty and sharp pointed, and has a hermitage on its summit, but when bearing from S.S.E. to S.S.W. it presents a level ridge from the summit to the S.E., which seems to be prolonged when it bears west of S S.W., many ridges will be seen much farther inland. Mount Batallera, bearing S.W. by W. 8 miles from fort Socoa, is high and broad, and, when viewed in the above direction, appears like a crown, set round with a number of small peaks on its summit; when bearing west of S.S.W. it loses this appearance and presents only three irregular peaks.

St. Jean de Luz bay is known by the light-tower, and having made it out, steer in, avoiding the Artha rock, a patch with 20 feet on it at low water, lying midway between the entrance points, and on which the sea often breaks. The steeple of St. Jean de Luz bearing S.S.E. ¼ E., leads through the west channel between the Artha and fort Socoa. Small vessels pass between the Artha and the east point of entrance, but they must be careful to give a good berth to the rocks extending from the point. The usual anchorage is midway between fort Socoa and the entrance to the Nivelle, in 3 to 4 fathoms, sand and rock. Vessels moor with the starboard anchor to the northward, and the port anchor to the south-west, and a hawser to steady them.

If the sea is not too heavy, vessels that are unable to enter the Adour, will be able to reach the tidal harbour of Socoa, but the vessel's draught and the state of the tide should be considered, as it is necessary to avoid being at the entrance before half-tide. The pilot boats can leave at a quarter tide.

At night.—Entering St. Jean de Luz bay by night, bring Socoa *fixed* white light to bear S.S.E., and steer for it: when the two *fixed red* lights on St. Barbe point are in line, alter course and keep them so until the two *fixed green* lights at Siboure are in line; this last course leads between Socoa mole and Artha breakwater; when Socoa light has changed from white to *red*, haul to the south-west for the anchorage.

CHAPTER III.

COAST OF SPAIN.—FUENTERRABIA TO CAPE PEÑAS.

VARIATION in 1881.

Fuenterrabia Bay - 18° 00′ W. | Cape Peñas - 20° 00′ W.

The province of Guipúscoa is bounded on the east by the river Bidassoa, and terminates on the west at Santurraran point. It contains only about 30 miles of a rocky broken but generally clear coast, which trends nearly in an east and west direction, with some slight inflexions to the south. Its capital, San Sebastian, is of some commercial importance. The ports of the province are few and insecure, except Pasages, which alone deserves the name, and where vessels of 15 or 16 feet draught can enter. Visited as the coast of this province is in winter by strong north-westerly gales, the utmost caution is necessary by the navigator, for if the small ports are missed nothing awaits a vessel but a lee shore and probable destruction. For this reason every endeavour should be made to enter port Pasages when running for refuge in a north-west gale, and when neither Santander nor Santoña can be reached.

To avoid disaster the necessity of navigating near the coast is strongly recommended with a view of being able to recognize the land distinctly for the purpose of determining the position of the vessel, as it is more or less obscured during north-west and south-west gales. Should it be necessary to stand off the land to wait for daylight, as much sail as possible should be carried, so as not to lose ground, for with the wind hanging steadily to the north-west the vessel will drift towards the head of the bay. When waiting for daylight during winter with a view of entering a harbour, and high water being from 9h. to 11h. a.m., a vessel should be in with the coast at daylight so as not to lose the opportunity of entering.

Currents.—The navigator must bear in mind that the currents are stronger in proportion as the head of the bay of Biscay is approached, and there they turn to the north-east and north along the French coast. With a north-west gale they are said to run 4 miles an hour, and the local pilots consider that they occasionally attain 5 miles. The strength of the current during the gales of winter, which always haul to the N.W. quarter, accounts for the many losses on the banks of Arcachon and

Cap Breton. In summer and during north-east and south-east winds the current generally sets West and W.N.W. from one to 2 miles an hour.

Galernas is a name applied to those sudden changes of wind to the south or the north-west which blow strong and are common on the coast of this province and that of Vizcaya or Biscay. They generally occur in the months of July, August, and September, after a prevalence of hot southerly winds. It is seldom after a day of excessive heat that a galerna does not blow in the evening, the greatest strength of which will last from ten minutes to half an hour. Sometimes the galerna comes on with the strength of a hurricane without any warning. Many of the wrecks on the coast of Guipúscoa in summer are occasioned by the sudden changes of wind which overtake vessels with all sails set in a calm.

FUENTERRABIA BAY, at 4 miles westward of Socoa, is the most easterly port on the north coast of Spain. At its head is the entrance of the river Bidassoa, a narrow winding stream, which forms the boundary between France and Spain, and the villages of Fuenterrabia and Hendaya; the former with its fortress belonging to Spain, and the latter to France.* At 2¼ miles higher up is the town of Irun, the first town on the Spanish frontier, with about 2,800 inhabitants. It stands on the southern slope of mount Jaisquivel, and the road to France passes through it. Near it, in the middle of the stream, is the ile de Faisans or Pheasants, covered with vegetation, but scarcely above water.

The bay is 1¼ miles wide at the entrance, but not more than three-quarters of a mile deep, for at that distance within is the bar of the Bidassoa, which dries 2 to 3 feet at the lowest tides. The river is shallow and will only admit coasters, which load timber and iron ore for Ferrol. Fuenterrabia, on the western shore of the inlet at about 1¾ miles within cape Higuera, was formerly of considerable strength, but now a miserable dilapidated place. The inhabitants, numbering about 1,000, are chiefly occupied in fishing. The salmon of the Bidassoa are much esteemed.

Cape Higuera, the western point of the bay, is rocky and surrounded by reefs, which uncover at low water. The rocky islet of Amuck lies about a cable north of the cape, is of moderate height, and connected to the shore by a reef which dries at low water. A reef also extends northward from the islet, and it should not be approached too close. St. Anne point, the east extreme of the bay, has close to its west side two round rocks resembling towers, and others of a smaller size lie off its north and north-east sides; these are connected to each other and to the shore by a ledge which dries at low water.

Briquets Reef.—At 4 cables E.N.E. of St. Anne point is La

---

* Beacons and pyramids have recently been erected on the shores of Fuenterrabia bay, to indicate the limits of the French and Spanish jurisdictions. *Paris Annonce Hydro-graphique*, No. 91 of 1880.

Roche Noire (Black Rock), 3 feet above high water springs ; and three-quarters of a mile N.N.E. of the point is a dangerous reef named the Briquets. This reef, half a mile in extent N.W. by W. and S.E. by E., is narrow, has rocky heads on it which dry 2 to 6 feet at low water, and soundings of 3 to 7 fathoms close around, which rapidly increase seaward, the depth being 17 fathoms at less than three-quarters of a mile distant.

LIGHT.—On cape Higuera, the west point of Fuenterrabia bay, a temporary light (fixed and visible in clear weather from a distance of about 10 miles) was re-exhibited on 1st November 1880, and will continue to be shown until 30th April 1881, unless directions are given to exhibit the light from the new lighthouse now approaching completion.

Aspect.—Fuenterrabia bay will be recognized by the high land immediately westward of it, which, beginning at cape Higuera, gradually increases in altitude, until about 4 miles from the cape it rises to mount Jaisquivel, called also Olearzú (or Shoulder of the Mountain, in allusion to its being the last of the Pyrenees towards the sea coast), which reaches 1,940 feet above the sea. It has various inequalities on its summit, and the coast at its base is barren, and in places formed of cliffs. The moun-tains Larrun and Batellera, 6 miles inland, are also good distinguishing marks for the bay.

Directions.—Approaching from the eastward, give St. Anne point a berth of a mile to avoid the Briquets reef. Amuck isle, W. by N., leads north of the reef ; and St. Anne point South, or Fuenterrabia church S.W. ¾ W., leads westward. There are 2¼ to 7 fathoms water between the reef and the Roche Noire, but no vessel should attempt this passage, it being always safer to pass outside. With the exception of a rocky patch with 23 feet water on it, in the middle of the bay, the bottom is clear and the depths gradually decrease towards the river. Give the shore of the cape a berth of a quarter of a mile in passing.

Anchorage.—Vessels will be sheltered from strong south-west winds on the west side of the bay. The best berth is from 2 to 3 cables E.S.E. or S.E. by E. of the fort or castle—which stands on the cliff about 3 cables south of Amuck islet—in from 6¼ to 8 fathoms water, muddy sand and good holding ground. Small vessels anchor farther in. During strong north-west winds this anchorage should not be used, particularly in winter, because if the wind veers to north or N.N.E. a vessel would have no shelter, and none but small vessels could run for Fuenterrabia, and then only at high water.

Tides.—It is high water, full and change, at Fuenterrabia, at 3h. 15m. ; and the rise 12 or 13 feet. The ebb at springs runs out 3 miles an hour.

Winds.—The prevailing winds in this locality in winter are from south-west and north-east, generally with rain. In summer, gales from east and north-east with clear weather are frequent. The currents generally follow the direction of the wind.

PORT PASAGES.—At 3¾ miles westward of cape Higuera is Turrulla point, projecting a short distance from the foot of mount Jaisquivel; the shore between is rocky, with one small sandy beach. Thence a steep rocky coast trends W.S.W. 3¾ miles to the entrance of port Pasages, which is a narrow but safe inlet formed by high steep shores.*

The land on either side of entrance is rugged and from 450 to 550 feet high, but the two points are low, rocky, and project respectively W. by N. and E. by S., thereby narrowing the channel to 180 yards. The eastern point is named Great Arando, the western point, Little Arando or cape La Plata; both are bold and clear of danger, there being 7 fathoms close-to, but at high water a part of each point is covered, and the entrance appears larger than it really is. Within the entrance the shores are craggy and rugged; the eastern shore is fringed with rocks, some of which are uncovered; the western is clearer to 1¼ cables within the point, but from thence to Cruces point (with an iron cross on it) it is bordered by a rocky shoal, named Los Sepes. Many of the rocks on this shoal are uncovered at low water, and between them there are from one to 3 fathoms water. From the eastern extreme of the shoal Cruces point bears S.S.W., distant about 30 yards.

Cruces point derives its name from the mount from which it projects. The mount is called Cruces because at about one-fourth up there were formerly several iron crosses, some of which yet remain. At a cable within Cruces point, on the opposite shore, is Santa Isabel castle, built at the foot of a hill close to the water. From this castle to the high round tower of San Sebastian, standing close to the water at 2½ cables farther in on the opposite shore, is the usual anchorage in 3¼ to 4 fathoms water for vessels of more than 10 feet draught. The channel here is 120 yards across, and within the harbour widens out into an eastern and western arm, but it can only be used for small vessels, as it dries at low water.†

The town is built at the foot of the hills on both shores of the arms. The barrio or district of the town on the western shore is named the pasages de San Pedro, commonly pasages de España: it contains about 500 inhabitants, who mostly follow the fishery. The barrio on the opposite shore is named the pasages de San Juan, or pasages de Francia. It

---

* *See* Admiralty chart:—North coast of Spain, Bayonne to Oporto, No. 2,728; and plan of port Pasages, No. 73; scale, m = 12·5 inches.

† It is reported—1880—that a channel, capable of admitting vessels of 16 feet draught, has been dredged, leading to the railroad between the custom house and the western part of the bay.

is larger than the former, and contains about 950 inhabitants. Communication with each other is kept up by boats. On the west shore is a government dockyard, and on the east a dock belonging to the Phillippine company.

East and West Banks.—Outside the harbour are two rocky patches, one named East bank, lying E.N.E. a cable from the east point of entrance; and the other, West bank, lying North about three-quarters of a cable from the west point. The East bank, not more than half a cable long, has from 3 to 10 feet on it, $3\frac{1}{2}$ to $6\frac{1}{2}$ fathoms between it and the shore, the channel being half a cable wide, and 10 fathoms close-to on its north side. The West bank is of sharp pointed rocks, with 6 feet on it, 6 fathoms close-to, and 6 to 9 fathoms between it and the land. The sea breaks on both these banks when there is any swell.

To clear the West bank, coming from the westward, it will be sufficient to keep 2 cables from the shore in approaching port Pasages, and not stand southward until the chapel of Santa Ana is open of Cruces point. To clear the East bank coming from the eastward, keep rather more than a cable from the shore, until Great Arando point bears S.S.W. or the mouth of the port is open. We believe these banks are now marked by beacons.

LIGHT.—The lighthouse on cape La Plata, close to the west point of entrance to port Pasages, exhibits at 484 feet above high water a *fixed* white light, visible in clear weather at a distance of 10 miles.

Pilots.—At port Pasages and the other harbours on this coast, the activity of the native seamen alleviate the dangers considerably, being ready with their boats in piloting and towing vessels into them. Here and at San Sebastian the regulations ordain that the first boat reaching the vessel must be employed, and then those in the order in which they come alongside. Both men and boats are well qualified for towing, mooring, or warping. In bad weather when they cannot venture out, a lookout man is stationed on the heights near the mouth of the harbour to signalize the approach of vessels, and if necessary a gun is fired to command attention.

When the sea is so heavy as to prevent the pilot boats from going outside the mouth of the port, they remain under the lee of Little Arando point, and signalize to the vessel with a piece of cloth or handkerchief on a staff, which is pointed in the direction the vessel is to steer, or held upright if she is to keep her course, and the pilot boards directly she is within the points. It is compulsory for all classes of vessels to pay pilotage. Those under 50 tons pay 58 reals; from 50 to 100 tons, 144 reals; under 200 tons, 196 reals; and those above, 220 reals. Boats used are paid for besides the pilots, according to a tariff; and in bad weather vessels may depend on a supply of anchors, cables, hawsers, &c.

Tides.—It is high water, full and change, at port Passages, at 3h. 20m.; equinoctial tides rise 15 feet; ordinary springs 12 feet, and neaps 9 feet. The ebb runs 2 miles an hour.

Directions.—The entrance to port Passages from the eastward may be ascertained by a bearing of mount Jaisquivel, the west slope of which extends to the entrance. From the westward it may be recognized by the lighthouse at San Sebastian and castle of La Mota, and when 2 or 3 miles northward of this port the lighthouse at cape La Plata will be seen, which is conspicuous from its whiteness, but if close in shore it will be shut in with the land. From the offing, when the lighthouse cannot be distinguished, mount Urdaburu, which rises about S. by W. 5½ miles from it, is a good mark; and also the mountains of Jaisquivel and Batallera to the eastward; mounts Urgull and Frio, with the buildings on them, to the westward; and finally, the natural opening formed by the port, which when it bears South or S.S.W. may be run for.

Should the weather be thick or foggy, the approach to the harbour is well indicated by the soundings, as at 15 miles northward of the entrance the depths vary from about 90 to 110 fathoms, gradually decreasing until within 2 miles of the land, then 30 and 25 fathoms, in some places on a rocky and in others on a sandy bottom.

A sailing vessel entering the harbour should have a fair fresh wind and a flood tide. A moderate wind outside generally dies away when between Cruces point and Isabel castle, but the tide added to the ship's way, with boats to assist, will keep her clear of danger. The sea also should be moderate, for with a heavy swell outside, the water is so disturbed in the harbour as to prevent the vessel's steerage. The wind from W.N.W., round by north, to E.N.E. is fair for entering. Other winds are apt to take the vessel aback in the windings of the channel, which is too narrow to admit of tacking. With light airs vessels anchor at the entrance, and are warped or towed in by the native boats with the flood tide.

The worst wind for entering is from the West, for although between the entrance and Cruces point it draws to the north-west, yet within this point it veers to the south-west with squalls, placing a vessel in danger, as this is the narrowest part of the harbour. When bound therefore to this port from the westward, with a West wind and bad weather, if possible run into San Sebastian and wait for a change, or if sufficiently to the westward find shelter in Guetaria bay, 9 miles west of San Sebastian, the anchorage there being safe and easily taken.

Steering for the harbour, the first buildings seen will be the castle of Santa Isabel, and about a quarter of a mile within it, on the same shore, the chapel or hermitage of Santa Ana. When about a quarter of a mile from the entrance, the hermitage with the breastwork at its base, open of the iron cross on Cruces point, or the extreme of this point on with the west angle of Santa Isabel castle, will lead to the entrance. When within the points keep towards the eastern shore to avoid the shoal off Cruces point, until the tower of San Sebastian appears midway between Isabel castle and the above point, when steer towards the tower, keeping mid-channel in the deepest water.

Having passed the castle, bring up with a stern anchor in $3\frac{1}{2}$ to 4 fathoms, and run a stout hawser out from each bow to rocks on shore bored through for the purpose. At high water there will be room for the vessel to swing, when moor head and stern, especially in winter, when a sea sets in, and whirling gusts of wind rush down through the breaks in the hills around the harbour. The bottom is mud, and should a vessel's stern touch in swinging, no injury is likely to occur. Small vessels may go farther in and lie secure in all weathers. Steam vessels, from their facility in being able to enter at any time, will find Pasages an excellent port to seek from stress of weather.

COAST.—Arando Chico or Little Arando, the western point of entrance to port Pasages, is low and of rock, but commanded by rugged land 460 feet high, named cape La Plata, and by the fishermen Espejo de Pasages. At $1\frac{1}{4}$ miles westward is Talayero or Atalaya point, which is steep ; and N.N.W. $\frac{1}{4}$ W. from it is the Pequechillá rock, with 8 feet water on it at low springs, and on which the sea breaks when there is a little swell. In case of necessity, coasting vessels may run between this rock and the land. At half a mile further westward is Mompas point. The coast between this point and Arando Chico, high and rugged, is the northern brow of the Sierra de Mirall, generally known as mount Ulia.

Mompas point is low and rocky, and falls in declivities from the high land forming part of mount Ulia, and on the height commanding the point there is a look-out house. At nearly a mile W. by S. $\frac{3}{4}$ S. from it is the north-east point of mount Urgull, and between is the bay of Zurriola, receding to the south-east. It is strewed with rocks and reefs, and partly covered by a wide sandy shore, which dries out considerably at low water. The little river of Urumea runs into the head of the bay. Its bar is dry at low water, and only at high water and during fine weather can boats pass over it, when they can go up to the town of Astigarraya. A wooden bridge crosses the river near the bar.

SAN SEBASTIAN.—The position of this town may be easily known by mount Urgull or Orgullo, which is connected with the mainland by a low sandy isthmus, on which, at the foot of the mount, is the town of San Sebastian, the capital of the province of Guipúscoa. The town is strongly fortified, being defended by outworks on nearly all sides, and commanded by the castle of Santa Cruz de la Mota, 492 feet above the sea. The population may be about 10,000. In 1866, 188 vessels, amounting to 21,414 tons, entered inwards, and 112 vessels, of 71,887 tons, cleared outwards, besides about 36,000 tons of coasting trade. A regular steam communication is kept up with London, Liverpool, and Bordeaux.*

A square tower stands on the north-west side of the mount; it is white, and, contrasting with the dark background, is seen at a great distance. The cliffs of mount Urgull are more conspicuous than those of mount Frio on the west, and the large patches of whitish rock of which they are com-posed are also seen at some distance. At the foot of the mount rocks ex-tend about half a cable in a north-west and northerly direction. Mount Igueldo, on the west side of San Sebastian, terminates to the eastward in a hill 625 feet above the sea, and with a slope of 45° to the north. This height is called mount Frio, and on its summit is a square tower, formerly a lighthouse, and an excellent mark for the bay; the present lighthouse is on the northern slope of the same height. Several rocks with 6 and 7 feet water extend nearly three-quarters of a cable N.N.E. from point Arrincobaja, the northern extremity of mount Igueldo.

Between the above hills is the rocky islet of Santa Clara, 174 feet high, and about 2 cables in length W. by S. and E. by N.; on it is a small white house and a lighthouse. The islet is clear of danger on its south side, foul on the north, and nearly connected with mount Frio by a reef, which uncovers at low water, and on which some stones, formerly deposited to form a port, yet remain.

The bay of San Sebastian between the mounts Frio and Urgull recedes to the south-east, is about half a mile deep, and surrounded by a white sandy beach, of some extent at low water. The bottom is clean, and there are from 3 to 5½ fathoms water at low springs, in the middle of the bay; but it is shallow on the western side. Vessels which cannot enter the tidal basin anchor under the limited shelter of Santa Clara, but where they are exposed to gales from N.W. to N.E., for the sea which sets in east and west off the islet is occasionally so heavy as to occasion the loss of vessels and their crews.

The bay is not adapted in winter for vessels which cannot enter the basin, nor should those in the basin go into the bay if there is any likelihood of a north-west gale, as the little safety it then affords, the impossibility of

* *See* Admiralty plan :—Port and town of San Sebastian, No. 88; scale, $m = 12 \cdot 4$ inches.

entering the basin again, and the difficulties to be overcome in getting well secured in time, are reasons for not doing so.

A basin is formed by two piers extending westward from the town, and two others running eastward from the foot of mount Urgull, which overlap the former, leaving a narrow entrance. At high water vessels of 300 tons can enter, but it is necessary to secure to the piers or other vessels, so as to keep upright when the tide is out, as a great part of the basin is then dry. Vessels intending to enter the basin anchor during fine weather near the entrance, and large vessels should ;have the aid of the country boats, as the men belonging to them are necessary.

Mooring Buoys.—There are eight buoys in the bay for the use of vessels, to which they make fast ; these buoys have large rings secured to heavy moorings, and vessels ride with two cables ahead and two astern, head to N.N.W. The pilots are charged with securing the vessels and to caution their commanders how to act.

La Bancha.—The only danger to be avoided entering San Sebastian bay is a rocky shoal named the Bancha, lying parallel to and 2 cables northward of Santa Clara islet. The shoal covers about the same space as the islet, and the general depths on it are $4\frac{1}{2}$ to 6 fathoms; but there is a patch with 2 and $2\frac{3}{4}$ fathoms water on it, near the east end; and another with 3 fathoms near the west end. The sea breaks on it when there is any swell. Between the shoal and mounts Frio and Urgull, as well as between it and Santa Clara islet, the passages are about 2 cables wide, 9 fathoms deep in mid-channel, and either may be used; the bottom is rocky. This shoal is supposed to be marked by beacons.

LIGHTS.—On the northern slope of mount Frio, at the west side of entrance to port San Sebastian, is a white lighthouse, which exhibits, at 428 feet above the sea, a *fixed* white light varied by a *flash* every *two minutes*, and visible in clear weather at a distance of 15 miles.

On the summit at the eastern part of Santa Clara islet is a round light-house of blue limestone, which shows, at 174 feet above the sea, a *fixed* white light, varied by a *flash* every *minute*, and visible 9 miles.

Pilots.—The port of San Sebastian has an establishment for pilots, and in fine weather vessels are boarded well outside the bay. If the state of the sea prevents boats going out they lie under shelter of the eastern part of Santa Clara islet, and signalize with a flag to the vessel running in. If the flag is held upright the vessel is to keep on her course, or to starboard or port, according as the flag is pointed. It is compulsory for all vessels over 50 tons to take a pilot. Those of 50 to 100 tons pay 120 reals ; 100 to 200 tons, 150 reals ; and those above 200 tons, 180 reals. Anchors, hawsers, &c., are charged for according to a tariff.

Tides and Current.—It is high water, full and change, at the piers of San Sebastian, at about 3h. 0m., but the tide may be accelerated or retarded according to the wind; equinoctial springs rise 14 feet, ordinary springs 12 feet, and neaps about 9 feet. With strong winds from S.W. to N.W. the tide rises 1½ to 2 feet above the usual level, and those from N.E. to S.E. depress it below the ordinary level to the same amount. On the coast in fine weather the flood sets east and ebb west. In strong winds from N.W. to S.W. the current runs strong to the eastward.

Directions.—Vessels should only enter San Sebastian bay during moderate weather, so as to be able to secure to either of the buoys without difficulty. From the westward, during bad weather in winter, vessels should put into Guetaria bay, or other safe port, to the westward. There is a good supply of anchors, cables, and other necessaries for all classes of vessels in a building retained for the purpose on the western pier of the basin. The heavy swell, which runs in during a gale outside, produces so much motion in the small navigable part of the bay that it displaces not only the sandy bottom, but also lifts the anchors, when vessels are exposed to imminent danger, and no assistance can be given from the shore.

The bay may be taken by sailing vessels with all winds, except those from the south-east quarter. With the wind from S.S.W. to West, and blowing hard, there is some difficulty in consequence of the eddy winds from mount Frio, in entering by the channel between the mount and La Bancha. With north-west winds vessels may enter between La Bancha and mount Frio, or by the channel between La Bancha and mount Urgull, as convenient. Should the wind be from the north-east quarter mount Urgull should be neared, and the channel between it and La Bancha used. This passage should always be used if there is much sea, keeping mid-channel.

When strong winds from north-west prevail, the breakers on La Bancha, which show well, will be the best mark; and should the wind be from West to N.W. brace sharp up, as the current and swell set always towards mount Urgull. With a heavy sea it breaks outside La Bancha and also across between the mounts Urgull and Frio, when a vessel should not enter the bay. In winter, and particularly in the months of January and February, when the land is humid and cold, the south-west winds prevail on the coast even when a north-west gale is blowing in the offing. It often happens that a vessel running with a strong north-west wind and a heavy sea, confident of entering San Sebastian bay, as she approaches finds the wind drawing ahead, and even off-shore, or falling calm. This is one of the greatest dangers which the navigator has to contend with in making for this bay, for in a heavy sea, the vessels drift unmanageable towards the land.

Coming from the westward the large tower on mount Frio will be seen ; it is conspicuous, an excellent mark, and cannot be mistaken. The castle of Mota, on mount Urgull, the old lighthouse on the north slope of the same hill, and the present lighthouse on the north slope of mount Frio are equally good marks. Mounts Hernio and Itzarriz may serve as landmarks by which San Sebastian may be identified from a long distance, also that of Urdaburu, which rises S. by E. ½ E., distant 6 miles from the entrance of the bay, remarkable for two peaks on its summit inclining eastward, and lower down, one leaning in the same direction.

Mount Aya or Batallera, is also a good point of recognition; it rises S.E. ¾ E. from mount Urgull distant 9 miles, extends N.E. and S.W., and may be known by its three peaked summit, the south-western being the less pointed, and the three inclining in that direction ; it reaches about 2,780 feet above the sea. In approaching the land the bay will be distinctly made out, and the islet of Santa Clara, with the houses of San Martin at the head of the bay will be seen, and finally the town of San Sebastian.

In approaching the eastern passage to San Sebastian bay, do not bring Santa Clara light to bear southward of S.S.W. The church of San Bartholomew (at the head of the bay on rising ground near the shore) in line with mount Urdaburu, S. by E. ¾ E., leads between La Bancha and mount Urgull; and when the piers of San Sebastian are seen, the vessel may take up a berth in the bay according to her draught.

Mount Hernio, at the back of the high coast land, is seen from the offing, with its three peaks, not very marked, but sufficiently conspicuous to distinguish it from the rest. It rises about S. by W. of the mouth of the Orrio, 7 miles inland, and reaches 3,537 feet above the sea. Farther westward is also seen above the high coast land another peaked mountain called Itzerris, 6 miles inland, and about S.S.W. of the estuary of Sumaya. These mountains are good distinct marks for the estuaries of Sumaya and Orrio, and the bay of Guetaria.

The COAST from mount Frio, at the west side of entrance of San Sebastian, is high and precipitous, and trends westward 5½ miles to the river Orrio. The high land immediately over this part of the coast is named mount Igueldo, and the village of the same name stands on its summit, on its eastern part. The most remarkable rise in the mount is the peak of El Agudo, a little east of Tierra Blanca point. The cliffs which distinguish this part of the coast are of a slate rock, which when wet, reflect the sun's rays and appear in large white patches ; but in cloudy weather they lose that whiteness which has obtained for them the name of Tierra Blanca, and show a greyish colour which contrasts with the green appearance of the background.

A series of these white cliffs mark the eastern limit of Orrio bay, and form a point which projects somewhat to the north, but only discerned when the sun shines on the cliffs. They are backed by mount Mendizorroz or Agudo, 1,514 feet above the sea, by which this part of the coast may be known. Galera point, to the eastward, is more prominent, and a reef projects from it northward a considerable distance, to which a berth should be given. Between the east extreme of mount Igueldo and Galera point is the small bay of the latter name, with a narrow sandy beach in the middle of it. The bay is clear of danger. A rock, named Arribaton, lies near Tierra Blanca point ; it is about the size of a large boat, and covered at high water. Small vessels may pass between it and the land. Further westward, at about a third of a mile eastward of the mouth of the Orrio, is the islet or rock Aranarri, low, and about 35 yards in length ; in fine weather and a smooth sea, boats pass inside it.

The RIO ORRIO rises in the Pyrenees, passes Tolosa, and runs over a course of about 33 miles ; it is somewhat larger than the Deva, and its freshes are so strong that vessels in the river are obliged to be additionally secured. The town of Orrio, containing about 1,035 inhabitants, with its shipbuilding establishments, &c., stands on the eastern bank, more than half a mile within the bar. The river empties itself in the bay of the same name between Tierra Blanca point and Malla-arria point, 3½ miles westward. The bay recedes to the south and the coast is high and rocky. The mouth of the Orrio is nearly in the middle of it, and the bar, which has 2 feet on it at low water springs, can be crossed by vessels of moderate size, but only at high water with a smooth sea.

The entrance has high land on either side, is very narrow, and open to the N.N.W. Within the bar the river soon trends to the eastwards, widens, and the water deepens. The bar is of shifting sand, which extends from the eastern nearly to the western point of entrance ; a vessel should therefore keep close to the west side, and then steer for, and in, the middle of the channel as far as the town. The island of Guetaria or San Anton and the beach of Saraus are good marks for vessels bound to Orrio from the westward ; the old and present lighthouses of San Sebastian, the town of the same name, mount Agudo rising from that of Igueldo, &c., are good marks from the eastward ; and mount Hernio, which rises 7 miles inland about S. by W. of the mouth of the river, is a good distant mark from the northward.

Pilots.—In consequence of the bar of the Orrio being of shifting sand, it is requisite to have the aid of a pilot, and it is compulsory to take one.

Very fine weather is necessary for a vessel of moderate size to cross the bar, and when the state of the sea does not admit of entering the river, vessels wait an opportunity in Guetaria bay.

Tides.—It is high water full and change at the mouth of the river Orrio, 3h.; and the rise is about 11 feet.

MALLA-ARRIA POINT.—This point projects from the foot of a hill named Talayamendi, at the east side of the bay and plain of Saraus. The point is surrounded by rocks always above water, and the most remarkable of them is named Malla-arria, pointed, not large, but isolated at high water. A heavy sea sets in on the point, and it should be carefully avoided. At half a mile northward of the rock there is a depth of 31 fathoms, sand.

SARAUS, a town at present in a flourishing condition from the great resort of strangers in summer, and the manufacture of textures, stands on a plain near the beach in the western part of Saraus bay, and contains 1,864 inhabitants. A small pier for landing extends from the middle of the town, and a rivulet runs into the sea at the east end of the beach. At a short distance south of Itegui point is Allé point, which projects from the foot of mount Santa Bárbara, on the summit of which is a hermitage. This point forms the western extreme of the bay of which Malla-arria point is the eastern. The bay is bounded by a clear level beach nearly 1¼ miles in length, but entirely exposed to the worst winds of the coast.

Alzacoarria Point, the southern extreme of Guetaria bay, is low, surrounded by rocks, and overlooked by high rugged land. Between the point and town of Guetaria there is a small sandy beach named Malcrobre. With the exception of this beach, the shore is rocky and commanded by rugged cliffs more than 90 feet high. Itegui point, at half a mile south-east of the former point, is a tongue of land which projects from the foot of a cliff, and a cable farther on is the Antimon-arria rock, with a passage inside it carrying from 5 to 8 fathoms, and about three-quarters of cable wide; this rock only shows at low-water springs, and appears like a buoy.

GUETARIA BAY.—The island of San Anton or Piedra Alzada is about three-quarters of a mile in circumference, rugged, with steep rocky cliffs on its north-west; the highest part is 360 feet above the sea, terminating in two peaks, the higher being to the northward, and on which are the remains of a hermitage and a lighthouse. It lies north and south, and is connected with the mainland by a ridge of rocks, upon which a pier is erected in a N.E. and S.W. direction, about 145 yards. The island

and the main land to which it is united forms Guetaria bay, open to the
E.N.E.*

The bay affords anchorage in from 3 to 8 fathoms at low water, sand
and mud, good holding ground, and sheltered from the westward as far
round as N.N.W., but not farther north, as at N.N.E. vessels are exposed
to wind and sea. A heavy north-west sea is inconvenient, but does not
risk a vessel's safety; that from North to N.N.E. is terrific; it seldom
occurs, but when it does come from this quarter the seamen must use his
own judgment and prepare for the worst. The best anchorage is in
5 fathoms at low water, sand, at a long cable S.E. of the pier. Small
vessels may go nearer the shore with a cable fast to the pier. There is a
warping buoy at which vessels may lie temporarily, and it is intended to
lay down others.

It is proposed to make a port of refuge in this bay, as it is considered
the outport of San Sebastian and Pasages, and navigators will act prudently
in putting in here, when bound to either of the above ports in a gale from
south-west, which would render their entrance difficult. It is also a good
port of call for vessels bound to Orrio when the bar cannot be crossed, or
to Sumaya. At the southern part of San Anton island is the little port of
Guetaria, a small space between two piers, with the entrance to the south-
west and about 30 feet wide. It is dry at low water, and fishing boats and
such craft alone can enter. The bottom is rock, and the craft suffer from
the swell when there is any sea. The town of Guetaria is on the point
of the main land, between two cliffs from 90 to 160 feet high, inclining
towards the port. It is a walled town, with a population of about 1,000,
and small supplies may be obtained.

LIGHT.—On the north peak of San Anton island, and a cable inland,
is a blue octagonal tower, with a white lantern, which exhibits, at 295 feet
above the sea, a *fixed* white light, visible in clear weather at a distance of
10 miles.

Tides.—It is high water, full and change, in Guetaria bay, at 3 h.; and
the rise is about 12 feet.

Directions.—San Anton island from the westward will be known
by its somewhat saddle-like appearance, and the ruins of the hermitage on
the northern summit. The tower of the church and some of the roofs of
the houses will first be seen, the rest of the town being concealed by the
western cliff. At some distance to the northward San Anton island will
appear in a conical form, and somewhat blended with the high land from
which it projects; but the whitish sand, forming the Playa de Saraus to

* *See* Admiralty plan :—Guetaria bay, No. 725 ; scale, ᴍ = 14 inches.

the east of it, will indicate the position of the bay. A berth of a quarter of a mile should be given to the north point of San Anton; the rocks of Itegui and those of Antimon-arria should also be avoided; and the swell and eddy wind from the high land should be considered. If the westerly wind be too strong for working in the bay, a vessel may anchor as soon as 8 or 9 fathoms water are obtained, when she will be sheltered.

COAST.—Next westward of San Anton island is the bay of Gasteatape, with a sandy beach and nearly throughout skirted by rocks, some of which uncover at low water. The bay terminates in Bizcarraya point, which is also foul, and between it and Isustarri point, a short distance to N.W., there is a break in the land through which a small river runs into the sea. Isustarri point is low and salient; a reef extends from it, which in part uncovers at low water; the sea breaks a considerable distance outside it, and a berth of a mile should be given to it. Then follows Orruaga bay, with a small sandy beach and a rivulet running through it. A factory stands near the shore.

SUMAYA INLET.—San Telmo point is low, rocky, surrounded by reefs; the hermitage of the same name stands on the heights above it. To the eastward of the point is the estuary of Sumaya, which recedes to the S.W. to the entrance of the river Urola. The river is only a small volume during summer, but in times of rainy weather strong freshes set down, for which it is necessary for vessels to be prepared. The bar of Sumaya has from 3 to 4 feet on it at low-water springs. The channel is narrow, and can only be taken at high water; it lies along by the western shore, with the sands of Santiago on the west.

The town of Sumaya, with about 1,200 inhabitants, stands on the western shore of a small peninsula named mount Santa Clara. It is seen from seaward when it bears S.W., and there is a mole close to it for mercantile operations. Vessels of 120 tons frequent the estuary of Sumaya for wrought iron, grain, &c. carrying thither iron ore; and there is sufficient depth at low water for them in the immediate vicinity of the town.

Land marks.—The Piedra Blanca on the west, and the island of San Anton de Guetaria a short distance on the east, are good marks for the Sumaya inlet; on nearing the land, the hermitage of San Telmo will be seen on the height over the west point of entrance, when a vessel should steer for it and make the signal for a pilot. Vessels bound to Guetaria bay during a strong breeze from the N.W. should keep 4 or 5 miles from Deva bay.

LIGHT.—On mount Atalaya, at the west side of entrance to Sumaya inlet, is an octagonal tower, 37 feet high, which exhibits, at an elevation of 295 feet above the level of the sea, a *fixed* white light; visible in clear weather 9 miles.

Pilots.—No vessel should attempt to enter the inlet without a pilot and the assistance of one or more boats, in consequence of the narrowness of the channel, which scarcely admits of their winding. The expenses are the same as at Deva.

Tide.—It is high water, full and change, at Sumaya, at 3h.; and the greatest rise is 11 feet.

ACHURI or PIEDRA BLANCA POINT.—From San Telmo point, the coast, which is of moderate height, runs westward in a series of rocky cliffs to Achuri point; the most salient part is Elorriaga point, 2 miles east of the latter. It is all along skirted by rocks, and should not be approached too close. Achuri point, called also Piedras Blancas, lies in the middle of a rocky bay; the point is surrounded by rocks, and the bottom is very irregular, which causes much sea in blowing weather. A berth of 2 miles should be given to it. Piedra Blanca is the name given to some whitish fissures in the land over Achuri point, which in some parts are 415 feet above the sea, and being visible at the distance of about 20 miles form an excellent mark for this part of the coast.

RIVER DEVA.—Santa Catalina point, at a long mile westward of Achuri point, extends from a hill on which there is a hermitage of the same name. This point forms the eastern extreme of the Deva inlet, and is surrounded by rocks which uncover at low water. The sea often breaks on the extremity of the rocks, and a berth of a mile should be given to them. Arrangasié point forms the western extreme of Deva inlet, projects to the north-east from the rugged coast, is surrounded by rocks, and on its eastern side is an indentation with a smooth sandy beach, for which boats usually run when from the swell or the tide being out they cannot reach port Motrico or the Deva inlet.

To the southward of the sandy beach is the bar of the Deva, over which there are 11 to 12 feet at high-water springs. The Deva rises in mount Aramo, but is of little service to navigation, as the bar shifts and nearly dries at low water, leaving only a small channel, and the sea often breaks on it even at high water. The channel is very narrow, and there is much swell in it when there is a sea outside; it is partly formed by two piers parallel to each other, which nearly reach the bar. Beyond the narrow part of the channel the inlet widens, and on its eastern shore on the north-west slope of mount Andúz is the town of Deva, containing about 1,200 inhabitants, most of whom are employed in the fisheries. Coasting vessels are built here.

The entrance to the Deva will be known by the objects east and west of it, by mount Andúz, 2 miles south-east of the town, and by the conspicuous hermitage of Santa Catalina, eastward of the bar, and on the high land over the point of the same name.

Pilots.—Vessels bound to the Deva should have the aid of a pilot, whom it is compulsory to take, and one will generally be found off the coast.

Tide.—It is high water, full and change, at the Deva, at 3 h.; and the rise is 11 feet.

PORT MOTRICO.—At about 1½ miles westward of Arrangasiá point, and a little southward of Atalaya point, is a small cove with rocky shores receding to the south-west. Here between two small piers is the little port of Motrico, where coasting and fishing vessels find refuge; but the bottom is rocky, and it dries at low water springs. The mouth is narrow and open to the south-east, and when there is much sea small craft are unable to enter.

Outside the entrance, there is a small space with a depth of 4 or 4½ fathoms water, muddy sand, where vessels can lie in moderate weather; but they risk being wrecked on the cliffs of the cove if bad weather should suddenly come on, and prevent them entering the port. It should only be resorted to by small vessels in summer, for during winter there is nearly always a heavy north-west sea on the coast.

The town of Motrico, with about 2,200 inhabitants, stands on rather a sudden slope of the land commanding the port. It is seen from a great distance, owing to the whiteness of the houses; but it is necessary to have Cardal point bearing westward of south in order to see it well. Besides the town of Motrico, Atalaya point, and mount Arnó known as Alturas de Arnó, are good marks for it. This mountain is about 2,080 feet above the level of the sea, and bears S.W. 2 miles from Motrico; it extends towards the inlet of Ondárroa, and terminates to the north-west with another mountain not so remarkable, called mount Arnosate.

Tides.—It is high water, full and change, at Motrico, at 3h.; and the rise is 10 feet.

SANTURRARÁN POINT.—Atalaya or San Nicolás point is barren, and rocky, and on its highest part is a small lookout house. Cardál point is the next westward, salient, with a reef extending from it to the north-east, on which in fresh breezes there is a heavy sea. In a north-west gale, a berth of 3 or 4 miles should be given to it, when a vessel bound to Guetaria should keep cape Ogoño well open of Santa Catalina de Lequeitio. At more than 1½ miles westward of Cardál point is Santurrarán point, being the east extreme of Ondárroa bay. This point is rocky, and a reef extends some distance from it ; it is commanded by high rugged land terminating that called mount San Nicolain, and also the coast of the province of Guipúscoa. On its west side is a sandy beach, much exposed to north-west winds.

ONDÁRROA.—At 2½ miles N.W. of Atalaya point is Santa Clara or Peña Mayor point, which is foul, as an extensive reef extends from it to the south-east. It will be known by the hermitage of Santa Clara, the only building and white, standing on the slope of the land forming the point. To the southward of the point the shore recedes to the south-west and forms Ondárroa bay, about 3 cables wide and surrounded by a sandy beach, but the reefs at either point narrow the entrance.

In this bay, the inlet of the same name trends a short distance southward and then westward to the river Artibas. The bar shifts, but is considered the safest between Machichaco and San Sebastian, and is taken when no others can be approached, as it is protected from the north-west sea by the point and reef of Santa Clara, which enables vessels nearly always to cross it at high water. There are from 12 to 13 feet water on the bar at high-water springs, and one to 2 feet at low water ; but the channel is narrow, and within the bar the whole inlet dries at low-water springs.

It is frequented by coasters drawing 7 to 9 feet, and those of the latter draught should enter at high water and in fine weather. At a long half mile inside the bar is the pier or landing place, where coasters load and discharge, but they lie dry at low water, and the pier is covered at high water. The town of Ondárroa stands on the western shore of the inlet, faces the south, and has about 1,800 inhabitants, most of whom are employed in the fisheries. Small vessels are built here. A bridge connects the two shores.

Vessels from the westward will find Alto de Lequeitio, together with the point and hermitage of Santa Clara, good marks for Ondárroa, bearing in mind that the hermitage is the only building of the kind seen between it and Lequeitio. In entering the inlet keep along the western shore, where the channel generally lies in a S.W. and N.E. direction. Strangers should not, however, enter without a pilot. If from the eastward, a vessel's position will be known by San Anton island.

Tides.—It is high water, full and change, at Ondárroa, at 3h. ; the rise is 11 feet, and neaps about 6 feet.

———————————

The province of Vizcaya or Biscay commences on the east at Santurrarán point, the east extreme of Ondárroa bay, and terminates on the west at the river Sabiote or Onton. It contains about 40 miles of bold coast, without a port or shelter for large vessels, with the exception of Bilbao, which may be entered by vessels of 14 feet draught, in fine weather at spring tides. The small inlets and ports which it contains are fit only for fishing craft, &c., which enter them at high water and in fine weather. In the bay on the east side of cape Machichaco is the only place where temporary anchorage may be obtained for large vessels with west and south-west winds; but here they will be exposed to great danger should the wind suddenly shift to the opposite quarter.

The stormy north-west winds blow with great force on the coast of Biscay, and the heavy sea prevents any mercantile operations in its small ports. The coast is, however, clear of any outlying dangers, and it may be approached to a prudent distance. In the interior the land is generally mountainous and broken. From a distance are seen the lofty and rugged crests of the Pyrenees, the remarkable peaks of Gorbea and Amboto rising above the sea 5,115 and 4,526 feet respectively. The spurs of the chain, which descend in declivities to the coast, presenting a series of mountain peaks, many of which as seen from the north-west appear in the form of perfect cones. On the coast the land is rocky and barren, with cliffs and ravines. In places the sand appears washed up by the force of the north-west sea, and these are only approachable in fine weather.

Winds.—During summer, the winds from north-east and east prevail on this coast, alternately with those from the north-west and west, and generally fall in the evening, when they are succeeded by the land wind. In the autumn, southerly winds blow hard for two or three days, and at times for eight or nine days; but as soon as they haul to the S.S.W. the sky begins to cover with scud, south-west and west winds follow, and after some days veer to north-west, with heavy squalls. This wind, which causes a heavy sea on the coast, continues for about a fortnight, being interrupted by two or three days of moderate weather; it may bring heavy rain, with intervals of fine weather, enabling mariners to make the land.

The North and N.N.E. winds are dead on shore, and completely obscure the coast by clouds and continual rain and hail; but they are not of long duration, and generally blow between the middle of December and the end of February or beginning of March. Some winters pass with only two or three hard northers, but in others they predominate very much. North-east winds are not frequent in winter, but sometimes they come with heavy clouds, when they last two or three days and are called *nordeste pardo* or dry north-easters. As they go down they veer to the east, and are then preludes to southerly winds.

When the wind changes from N.E. to East and S.E. a vessel should close the coast, as a southerly wind will soon follow. But after two or three

days of southerly wind if it veers to S.W., it will not be long before it shifts
to N.W. In the spring the winds are moderate, but nearly always from
the S.W. or N.W. quarters, accompanied by rain; and in some years they
are as late as July.

The north-west sea having a range of the whole distance from North
America causes the most destruction. There is no shore it reaches that
does not feel its effects, and it is only in the interior of the inlets at low
water that a vessel is not exposed. It is felt from the middle of September
or beginning of October, and continues with slight interruption for two-
thirds of the year. It is nearly always the prelude of the wind which
causes it and at times precedes it 24 hours. In the winter, a heavy sea
gets up during a calm, rolling in on the coast, breaking in from 20 to 28
fathoms water, and closing the ports and estuaries.

In the month of August, heavy squalls and sudden changes of wind
called *galernas* are experienced on the coast of Biscay. They gather over
the land during the heat of the sun, and rise in the south-west, when the
horizon becomes obscure, and by the time the wind reaches West the
weather becomes thick. The wind soon veers to the north-west and bursts
violently; so that a vessel should be prepared to receive it, as it does
considerable damage. It lasts generally 3 or 4 hours in full force,
accompanied with rain, after which it subsides and the weather becomes
clear and the wind moderate from the north-west, and at nightfall it is
calm. At times, particularly in summer, the galerna shifts suddenly from
South to N.W. without any warning, and then blows with much force. It
is also common to see these two winds striving for the mastery, being
separated by a belt of calm, and both of them curling up the sea on
their borders. A vessel in this calm belt should be under easy sail for the
result.

A southerly wind is foretold by the clearness of the atmosphere, which
admits of the peaks of the most distant mountains being clearly seen, and
the remotest objects appearing as distinct as if they were only a short
distance off. When the wind is easterly, or in a calm, and the high land
appears clear, and the summits of the mountains well defined and greyish,
the southerly wind is near.

Lightning is frequent at the beginning or termination of bad weather
and also during the gathering of the galerna. The distinctness with which
the report of guns is heard, may be taken as an indication of the wind
coming from the direction whence they were heard.

The Barometer rises with winds from the West round by North to
N.E., and falls with those from the opposite quarter.

The Currents in the winter set East and N.E., and with greater strength off shore than near the land. On this part of the coast the navigator should be on his guard. It is not easy to determine the velocity of these currents, but in a westerly or north-west gale it may be estimated at 3 miles an hour. In summer, the current is scarcely perceptible, and there are occasions when it runs West and N.W.

Directions.—Vessels not bound to Bilbao or any of the ports in Spain eastward, would do well to keep clear of the coast of Biscay; but those bound to any of the above ports should approach it as near as prudent. As the prevailing winds are from the S.W. and N.W. quarters, it will be fair along the coast, and by keeping it aboard, the lights, towns, and remarkable objects are seen by which a vessel's position may be ascertained. The north-west gales in winter lose much of their force near the coast, and the current is not so strong as at a distance from the land. Many wrecks have occurred on the banks of Arcachon, from vessels not having been navigated near, and in sight of the Spanish coast.

Vessels at a distance from the coast are exposed to the worst state of the weather, and the full force of the currents which sets towards the coast of France. The dark and cloudy weather, and the distance off, do not admit of sighting any point by day, nor the lights at night, and when, according to his reckoning, the mariner believes himself clear of all danger, he finds himself in a dangerous bight, and on a dead lee shore on the coast of France. The navigator in winter time bound to Bilbao, San Sebastian, &c., should run along the coast from Santoña until the port of destination is sighted.

SAUSATEN BAY.—At about 3½ miles N.W. by N. nearly of Santa Clara point in San Nicolás islet, the coast between—forming a bay named Sausaten—continuing high, broken, and rocky, but clear and bold, as at 2 cables from it there are 18 to 23 fathoms, mud and sand, except between the point and that of Mocoa, a short distance westward, where the bottom is rocky. In the bay are to be seen the houses of Endaidi and Mendeja, and two guardhouses. The north-west sea does not prevail much in this bay, and in the opinion of the local pilots it affords good anchorage for large vessels, with the winds from S.E. round by south to W.N.W.

The holding ground is good, the anchors sink in deep, and the best berth is between the two guardhouses at about a mile from the shore, in 23 to to 27 fathoms water. The only places approachable for small vessels are the coves of Endaidi, Chantarreca, and Barurdo, and the loading places of Portuchiqui and Portuandi; but these places can only be used in fine weather. The squadron under Sir Home Popham in the summer of 1812 used to anchor off the cove of Endaidi.

San Nicolás Islet is a quarter of a mile in length N.E. and S.W., 140 feet high, with the ruins of a battery on its summit, and two houses on the southern slope. It is rocky on its north-west and north sides, and lies east of Lequeitio, forming two entrances to that bay; the one on the north-west is the principal, the other, about a cable wide, is nearly dry at low water.

LEQUEITIO.—Between San Nicolás islet and Amandarri point at 1¼ cables N.W. by W. of it, is the entrance to Lequeitio bay, which recedes about 2 cables S.S.W. to a clean sandy shore, extending from the town to the mouth of the river Lequeitio. The sands are shifting. The depth of water in the bay is from 4 to 18 feet, but there are rocky heads in all parts of it, and 26 to 36 feet at the entrance. It may be taken with facility with the wind from S.W. round by North to S.E. With a south-west wind, close with Santa Catalina point, and keep the coast aboard. The port of Lequeitio is a name given to an irregular mole open to the south-east. At low water it is nearly all dry, the rocky bottom being covered by a thin layer of sand. It is frequented by coasters, but when there is much sea outside the swell is considerable, and they suffer accordingly. In moderate weather vessels may lie in the bay, but if a sea gets up they must run into the port. Small vessels winter in the river, which runs into the south-east angle of the bay.

The town of Lequeitio, with a population of about 2,500, is scattered round the bay, and near the beach, south of the entrance, is the palace of Ulibarren.*

LIGHT.—On the extremity of the cliffs terminating Santa Catalina de Lequeitio point N.N.W. ¼ W., distant nearly 1¼ miles from the entrance to Lequeitio bay, is a conical light-coloured lighthouse, which exhibits at 148 feet above the sea, a *fixed* white light, visible in clear weather at a distance of 10 miles.

Tides.—It is high water, full and change, at Lequeitio, at 3h.; springs rise 10¾ feet, and neaps 8 feet. The flood is scarcely perceptible, but the ebb is felt in the channel formed by San Nicolás islet, and the swell at times is inconvenient.

Directions.—Mount Otoyo or Alto de Lequeitio, and the hermitage of Santa Catalina, are good marks for a vessel bound to Lequeitio from the north-west or north; and San Nicolás islet, the town of Lequeitio, and palace of Ulibarren, seen at some distance, and also the conical hill of Calvario, 288 feet above the sea, a short distance southward of the town, are good marks from the north-east or eastward. To enter the bay it is

---

* *See* Admiralty plan of port Lequeitio, on sheet of plans, No. 75.

sufficient to steer for the palace, which is conspicuous, giving Amandarri point a berth of about 30 yards. In the extreme case of a vessel having to run ashore on this part of the coast, the beach of Lequeitio may be chosen, being well adapted for saving the lives of the crew. The vessel should be reached as far westward of the castle as possible, and the soft nature of the sand will secure the safety of the hull, especially if she is grounded at, or near, high water.

SANTA CATALINA de LEQUEITIO POINT.—From Amandarri point at the west side of entrance to Lequeitio, a small reef extends off, which partly dries at low water. The coast which follows is cliffy, bends a little to the south-west, and trends northward to Santa Catalina point. This latter point projects from the base of the Alto de Lequeitio to the north-east, terminates on all sides in cliffs about 140 feet high, and having a hermitage on it is very conspicuous; it is clear of danger, and in fine weather may be passed within a moderate distance.

MONTE OTOYO or ALTO de LEQUEITIO.—From Santa Catalina point the land suddenly rises, and about a mile westward reaches 1,792 feet above the sea. It is called Monte Otoyo, but more generally Alto de Lequeitio, and presents some remarkable features seaward, terminating in peaks so clear and distinct, as to be easily recognized from the neighbouring land, and is consequently a good mark for this part of this coast.

OGUELLA BAY.—From Santa Catalina de Lequeitio point the coast trends north-west, forming a tolerably deep bay with a rocky shore terminating in Apiquel or Ea point, which bears N.W. ½ W. distant 2 long miles from the former point. There is but one place accessible to boats in summer, which embark fuel and the product of a neighbouring factory. The whole bay is strewed with rocks and some sandy patches; the bottom is irregular, and a heavy sea sets in. Apiquel or Ea point, named also cape Montenegro, is salient, rocky, and the reef extends a cable from it. It separates Aguella and Ea bays, and as with much sea the breakers extend some distance off, it should be avoided.

EA BAY is formed between Apiquel or Ea point and Nachitúa point at 3 miles N.W. ½ W. of it. The shore of this bay is nearly everywhere of rock, and in the middle of it is a ravine which extends southward. It has a small sandy beach where the river Ea runs into the sea. The Ea can only be entered by small fishing vessels, which find shelter in the little pier harbour within the bar. The entrance is not only narrow but dangerous even with a gentle swell, and the bar dries at low water. The town of Ea contains about 1,200 inhabitants and is divided by the estuary, into which a small stream falls.

There are numerous rocks in the vicinity of the entrance to the Ea, the most conspicuous is half a mile eastward and a little off shore. At a mile farther east, and about a cable N.W. of Apiquel point, is Cacharri islet, hilly and rocky, having within it a channel about 55 yards across, fit for boats. The whole coast, as far westward as cape Machichaco, is high and broken by fissures and ravines which terminate at the sea in cliffs, some of which are of a considerable height. The coast is generally rocky, although the rocks do not extend far from the shore.

OGOÑO ANCHORAGE.—Nachitúa point is steep and surrounded by rocks, and on the heights above it are the houses of the same name. At about 1¼ miles farther in is cape Ogoño, and on its east side there is good summer anchorage with south-west and west winds in 12 to 15 fathoms water, gravel bottom, at about a cable S.E. of Monte de Ogoño, Apiquel point on with Santa Catalina de Lequeitio point, and the church of Elanchove open of the cape is the usual berth.

As it is necessary to be so near the shore in order to obtain shelter, it would be difficult to get away quickly in the event of a vessel being surprised with an onshore wind; the anchorage should not therefore be used by large sailing vessels. In anchoring with strong westerly winds care must be taken against the strong eddies which come down from monte de Ogoño.

On the east side of the cape some table land extends towards the sea, terminating in tolerably high cliffs with a bend to the south-west. Here the port of Elanchove is formed by two solid moles, but only capable of sheltering a few small vessels, and it dries at low water. At high water, when there is much sea from north-west, there is a heavy swell in it. The town of Elanchove is scattered along the heights over the port, some of the houses being 460 feet above the sea. It contains about 1,000 inhabitants, most of whom are seamen and fishermen.

Isaro Islet.—At 2 miles N.W. by W. of cape Ogoño is Isaro islet, a third of a mile in length, N.W. and S.E., the latter part being 150 feet high. It is rugged and surrounded by reefs, which extend off a considerable distance, and it should not be approached nearer than a mile. The islet is rocky on all sides, with some vegetation on its summit, and the remains of a convent. The round islet of Arriederra lies a short distance to the N.E., leaving between them a boat channel about half a cable wide.

Between the reefs of Isaro islet and Uguerray point on the west, the passage is 1⅓ miles in breadth, and between it and Santa Catalina de Mundaca is another passage 6 cables in breadth. The depth in both channels varies from 5¼ to 13 fathoms, sand, and some rocky places. When there is any sea it runs high in both channels, and often breaks.

Las Lobos.—Two rocks nearly united and uncovered at low water lie between Isaro islet and Anzora point, and are named Las Lobos. They may be passed on either side; but the north channel, which is the better, is a quarter of a mile wide, and carries 25 feet at low water. In using this channel, when the rocks are seen pass about 30 yards from them. The southern channel, between the rocks and Anzora point, is not so good, and but little used, there being sunken dangers; it is only 50 yards across, and 17 feet deep. These channels should only be used with a smooth sea.

CAPE OGOÑO.—The land of this cape is of a reddish colour salient, nearly perpendicular on all sides, and rises suddenly to an elevation named monte de Ogoño, having a watch tower on its summit—nearly 1,000 feet above the sea. It is an excellent mark, and there is no other like it on the coast. The cape is bold and may be approached to 6 or 7 fathoms water. The rugged islet of Arguesto lies at about half a cable S.W. of it.

Between cape Ogoño and Anzora or Lara point, a mile westward, is the bay and beach of Anzora, visible at some distance. A reef extends from the latter point and partly uncovers at low water. Off the point the bottom is sand with patches of rocks. The houses of Anzora are seen on the slope of the land over the point.

The River Mundaca runs into the sea, southward of Isaro islet, between Santa Catalina de Mundaca point on the west, and the sandy point of Laida on the east. The former point is rugged and rocky, and on it is a hermitage and the remains of a fort. The navigable channel into the river is about 12 yards wide, and 14 to 17 feet deep at low water; but on passing the bar the depth decreases to 4 or 5 feet. The river is choked with sand-banks, which dry at low water; but at high tide there is a navigable channel along by the western shore for vessels of about 7 feet draught up to Arteagu, and for boats as far as Quernica, two towns in the interior.

The town of Mundaca, with about 2,000 inhabitants, stands on the west shore at about 1½ cables within the bar; it is visible from seaward, and its church is conspicuous. Here is a small pier harbour which affords accommodation to a few coasters and fishing craft. With northerly winds a vessel may easily enter the river; but very generally, and especially in winter, the wind blows off the land; no stranger should enter without the aid of a pilot.

Tides.—It is high water, full and change, at Mundaca bar, at 3h.; and the rise is about 11 feet. The water which enters the river on the flood, and that from the river and its tributaries, cause a stream on the ebb at the rate of not less than 3 miles an hour at springs. The sea at times breaks a great distance from the bar.

UGUERRAY POINT.—Trompon Mayor is the name given to the highest part of the land commanding Uguerray point, on which are the ruins of a battery, which may be recognized by the roof of a house still standing. The Trompon Menor is another small height farther west. The two points of Uguerray and Atalaya terminate from a plain extending eastward and northward from the base of mount Sollube ; they are similar in appearance and surrounded by reefs. Atalaya point has the ruins of a battery on it, and a rock, which barely uncovers at low water, lies a short distance from it.

From the latter point, the cliffs continue southward as far as the mole of Santa Clara of Bermeo, here being the cove and little port of the same name. Outside the mole there are some large rocks, dry at low water, and which partly protect it from the sea. At a little distance to the eastward of these rocks is another group called Las Laisuas, two heads of which uncover at low water. They are dangerous, and should be carefully avoided. It is in contemplation to place a beacon on these rocks. At a long mile eastward of Bermeo is the entrance to the Mundaca, the coast between being high, rugged, and rocky.

CAPE MACHICHACO bearing N.W. ¼ N., distant 3¼ miles from Isaro islet, extends from high land, and terminates northward in a salient point ; the western extreme of which is of cliffs, while the eastern descends in a gentle slope to the sea. The cape is a continuation of a spur from mount Sollube, which lies north and south, and from which rises a remarkable peak named Burgon; when seen from the westward or eastward it will be known by its projecting northward, and by a slight saddle-like appearance before its termination.

When on with the high land, from which it proceeds, it is difficult to recognize from any distance, but if not far off, the white lighthouse and buildings connected with it, standing on some table land about a cable from the point, is a sufficient mark. Some authorities say, "within the point the land gradually rises at an inclination of about 20°, and forms at last a high broad wooded hill. At about half way up the slope is a sudden break in the face of the hill, which is conspicuous when bearing from W.S.W. round by South to E.S.E."

DANGERS.—Two rocks above water lie a short distance from the cape, and a reef extends from it on which there is often a heavy sea. A vessel should not approach it nearer than a mile.

LIGHT.—The round white tower on cape Machichaco shows a *fixed* white light, varied every *four minutes* by a *flash*. The light is elevated

268 feet above high water, and visible in clear weather at a distance of 20 miles.

MACHICHACO BAY.—Between Uguerray point and Potorroarri point, at about half a mile south-east of cape Machichaco, is the bay of the latter name, about half a mile deep, with good holding ground, and affords shelter from the S.W. quarter, and partly from the N.W.; but the winds from this latter quarter send in much sea, when vessels should leave. It is surrounded by rocks to a short distance from the shore, which is generally cliffy. Potorroarri point is rocky, with an islet near it, scarcely separated from the shore. The only part of the bay which can be approached with a moderate sea, is the little beach of Gibela or Arichachú, westward of Uguerray point, which is commanded by some high cliffs.

The Anchorage is dangerous during winter, as it would be difficult to obtain an offing with a fresh North and N.N.E. wind. A sailing vessel should always be ready to leave and to stand to the eastward, as the coast trends to the S.E., and if her draught permitted she might enter San Sebastian or Pasages, as a N.E. wind is right on shore. The best berth for leaving is in 14 fathoms water, sand, and mud, between Potorroarri point and the ruins of fort Valdés, with Arriederra islet (north-east of Isaro), in line with the hermitage of Santa Catalina de Lequeitio, and the Trompon Mayor on with the trees of the Atalaya de Bermeo, or the centre of Isaro), in line with the peak of Burgon S.E. ¼ S. In the above position a vessel will only be half a mile from the shore, but in good holding ground. The depths are from 12 to 17 fathoms, and the bottom all over the bay of a sandy nature, but near the shore it is rocky.

Bermeo, at 1¼ miles westward of Isaro islet, is a small cove a cable wide, 2 cables deep, and open to the north-east. The town stands on the slope of a ridge, facing south. It is not seen coming from the north-westward, but is partly seen coming from the north-east and east; and the chief occupation of its inhabitants, which number about 4,000, is agriculture, fishing, and salting and drying fish for exportation. It has a small harbour formed by two piers for fishing and coasting vessels, of which a great number belong to the place, but is nearly dry at low water, the bottom being rocky, covered with mud and gravel.*

CAPE VILLANO.—From cape Machichaco the coast trends in a W. by N. direction for about 6¼ miles to cape Villano, which is high, broad, precipitous, and foul. At two-thirds of a mile W. ¼ N. from the former cape is Aquech islet, round, steep, and clean all round, except towards the land, from which it is distant about a cable; and 1¼ miles

* *See* Admiralty plan of port Bermeo, on sheet of plans, No. 75.

westward of the cape is another islet, high, rugged, and connected to the land by a bridge, and having on it a chapel dedicated to San Juan de la Peña, which is reached by an ascent of 372 steps. The building and islet can be seen at some distance; on its north side are two rocks above water, and to the south-east of it is a small rocky islet near the shore. The land behind it is high and rugged. In this space are two indentations of beach, in each of which there is a fishing village, seen from seaward, the first named Baquio, the other Armenza ; there is also midway between the capes a hill, named mount Jata, or Alto de Plencia, which rises about 2 miles inland, and being the most elevated ground in this locality serves to point out the positions of the capes. As this coast is exposed to northerly winds, vessels should give it a berth of 2 or 3 miles in passing.

At half a mile W.N.W. from cape Villano is a small low islet close to the land, and on its south-west side is the point of the same name. A reef extends northward from the islet, and in bad weather the sea breaks nearly a mile outside it, when a berth of 2 miles should be given to it.

The large promontory projecting to the north-west, named cape Villano, has a look-out house on its summit, about 900 feet above the sea. The land slopes to the west, and terminates in Villano or Ormenza point, which is low and foul, a reef extending seaward. Between this point and Gorliz point are two sunken rocks, known by the breakers, about half a cable from the shore, and the same distance apart.

RIO de PLENCIA.—The estuary of this river extends in a S.S.W. direction to the bridge of the town, under which boats pass to the mills above. At high-water springs there are 9 or 10 feet water on the bar, but at low water the estuary is dry, except a small pool with about 4 feet water in it. The entrance is between a large high rock named San Valentin on the west, and the sandy point of Gorliz on the east. In the middle is another rock about the size of a boat that uncovers at half tide. The passage is between the two rocks, but nearer to San Valentin. The course of the river is about 20 miles ; it is visited only in summer by some coasting craft and boats, as the mouth is open to the north-west. The town stands at the foot of a hill, on the east side of the estuary, about half a mile in, and contains about 1,000 inhabitants. It is not seen from seaward, but the houses of Gorliz, on the sands of this name, are easily made out. It is high water here at the same time as the last-mentioned place.

The COAST from Villano point trends to the southward for a mile to the estuary of the river Plencia, thence W.S.W. 5 miles to Galea point, the eastern point of entrance of Bilbao bay, and is bordered with rocks. The shore is moderately high and even, but precipitous, and being of a whitish colour, appears at a distance like a tract of sand-hill. It is exposed to the full force of the north-west sea, and a wide berth should be given to it. In the extreme case of a vessel near this dangerous coast, from any accident, being obliged to run ashore, the sand of Gorliz is a good place to save the crew. The extreme northern part should be selected, where the point forms an elbow and affords shelter from the north-west sea. A small pier at the foot of a hill, and at the extremity of the sand may serve as a guide, and it will be sufficient to beach at half a cable southward of it.

MOUNT LUCERO or LUZUERO, on the west side of entrance to Bilbao bay, extends N.W. and S.E., with a smooth slope to the sea. It is 1,011 feet high, and when seen from seaward resembles the peak of Montaño westward of it. When in one with mount Serantes, the two appear conical like one mountain. When Lucero bears about S.W. by S., Serantes appears a little open to the left of it. The coast at its foot is cliffy and broken until it joins the sands of Somorrostro on the south-west. Its N.W. extreme is Lucero point, and surrounded by rocks. The peak of Montaño rises 1,122 feet high from the eastern shore of Somorrostro estuary, and is remarkable for its perfectly conical form, when seen from the north-west.

Mount Serantes extends N.W. and S.E., like Lucero, and reaches at rather more than half a mile from the shore of Bilbao bay, 1,414 feet above the sea; it presents a conical shape, and is a good mark.

BILBAO BAY is an inlet running about 3 miles into the land in a south-east direction, between points Galea and Lucero or Luzuero, which bear W. by N. and E. by S. from each other, and are three miles apart. From its entrance, where the depths are 14 and 15 fathoms, sands, the bay gradually narrows and shoals to its head, where the river Nervion disembogues.* The eastern coast of the bay trends S. by E. $\frac{1}{4}$ E. from Galea point, and continues steep, abrupt, and of a light colour for nearly 1$\frac{1}{4}$ miles to Ignacio point, which is red and has a battery on it. About half a mile within Galea point, on a height, stands the castle of Galea.

A cluster of rocks, some of which are under water, extends N.N.W. a quarter of a mile from San Ignacio point; and at half a mile in the same direction from the point, and 2 cables off shore, is the Piedra del Piloto rock, so named from its having, at low water, the appearance of a buoy. About half a mile southward of San Ignacio point is the village of Algorta, containing about 1,500 inhabitants, with a small pier; the houses are scattered along the height and seen at a great distance. A little farther on

---

* *See* Admiralty plan:—Portugalete and Bilbao, with the channel of the river Nervion, No. 74; scale, m = 5 inches.

is Begoña point, with a battery on it. From thence a low sandy shore runs south-west, nearly a mile, to the entrance of the Nervion.

Lucero point is high, barren, and bordered by rocks, which skirt the coast along the west side of the bay. Nearly half a mile eastward is the Savella point ; thence the shore takes a S.E. ¼ S. direction, and at the distance of a mile is the village of Ciérvana or Siérvana, in a deep valley on the shore of a small creek used only by fishing boats. Los Nogales is the name given to the valley between mounts Lucero and Serantes, on account of its being covered with trees of the above name. To the north-east of it, in 14 or 15 fathoms water, is the anchorage called Nogales. At 2½ miles south-east of Ciérvana is the village of Santurce, with about 300 inhabitants ; and on the coast between are three batteries at about equal distances apart, named Xebiles, Cuertas, and Campillo. From the former battery, signals are made to the pilots at the bar. Santurce has a small circular pier harbour, which dries at two-thirds ebb, rocky bottom. Here reside the pilots for the bar and river ; thence to the entrance the distance is half a mile.

Winds.—In the bay during the fine season there is a good breeze nearly every day, and the land wind at night ; but in the winter, the West and N.E. winds blow strong and cause a heavy sea.

LIGHTS.—A *fixed* white light is shown from Galea castle, half a mile to the southward of Galea point, the east point of entrance of Bilbao bay. It is elevated 401 feet above high water, and visible in clear weather at a distance of 10 miles. A white light is also shown from the round white pilot tower at the end of the S.W. mole or sea wall, when the bar is passable ; but should the light appear and disappear several times suddenly, vessels should not approach the bar. A light is also used at the foot of the tower for the purpose of signalizing to the pilots.

PORTUGALETE.—The entrance of the river Nervion is formed by two seawalls or piers, about three-quarters of a cable apart, which are continued along each bank of the river to Bilbao, a distance of 7½ miles. On the west side of the entrance at a quarter of a mile within the piers is the town of Portugalete, off which is the best anchorage for vessels, as the river here is deep, and they can make fast to the guns or stone pillars on the quays. The town numbers about 1,500 inhabitants, whose occupation is chiefly that of loading and discharging vessels of too large a draught to ascend the river.

Between Portugalete and Olaviaga, a distance of 4½ miles up the river, there are several muddy flats which dry at low water, stretching out from both banks ; and a little above Olaviaga a flat of shingle, which also dries at low water, extends from the left bank nearly across the river.

The breadth of the channel varies between a cable and 40 fathoms, and the depth is continually decreasing from the silt and gravel brought down the Nervion and its tributaries. Between Portugalete and Olaviaga there are from 4 to 18 feet at low-water springs.

Vessels of 9 feet draught can proceed up to Bilbao at high-water springs, and of 7 feet at neaps; but in all cases they discharge and load on the ground. At the railway quay, opposite the town, the ground is bad, and no vessel drawing 7 feet can lie alongside. A path runs along the right bank of the river, by which vessels with contrary winds are tracked by bullocks from its mouth to the city.

Beacons.—The southernmost rock extending from the right bank of the river, abreast monte Aspe, about 1¾ miles from the entrance, is marked with a white ball beacon 6 feet high, a quarter of a mile east of which, on the right bank, are two red and white vertical striped beacons. Nearly abreast these beacons, on the mud bank extending from the convent gardens; there is a beacon surmounted by a triangle and painted green and white vertical stripes, and a similar beacon on the opposite side of the river a few yards within the sea wall, between mounts Aspe and Erandis.

The Bar of the river is dangerous, and its position and depth varies with every fresh of the Nervion, and with every gale, so that the pilots have to sound and examine it often. In the winter season a heavy sea sometimes sets into the bay, preventing the pilot boats coming out. Generally the bar is found along by the western shore, about 4 cables outside the mole heads, with depths of 14 and 15 feet at high-water springs. The north-west gales affect it most, and at times close it completely. At low water extraordinary spring tides it is left nearly dry, with only about a foot water over it. No vessel drawing more than 8 feet water should attempt to enter without the aid of a pilot. No vessel of more than 14 feet draught should engage on a voyage to Bilbao, for although vessels of larger draught may have entered under favourable circumstances, the pilots do not as a rule undertake to cross the bar with vessels of more than 15 feet draught ;* in this case it must be at the top of high-water springs, the sea smooth, and for a sailing vessel a commanding breeze. If there is any sea the bar breaks even at high water.

BILBAO, the capital of the province of Vizcaya or Biscay, stands on a fertile plain on the right bank of the river Nervion, 7 miles from its mouth. The town is surrounded by hills on all sides, except towards the sea, and when viewed from any of these heights is exceedingly picturesque. It is connected with old Bilbao, on the opposite bank, by three bridges,

---

* Navigating Lieutenant E. J. T. Behenna, H.M.S *Lively*, remarks, that he observed three or four vessels of 15 feet draught in the river, in May 1872.

one of which is an iron suspension bridge. The trade is important, and shipbuilding is carried on to a large extent. There are four building yards on the river, and in 1855 twenty-one vessels were built, the aggregate tonnage being 2,735 tons.

The chief manufactures are woollen and linen goods, silks, iron, copper ware, hats, paper, and soap. English cod is imported, but one of the chief imports is dried cod. In 1866, 1,582 vessels of an aggregate tonnage of 98,856 tons entered inwards, and 1,495 vessels of 98,084 tons cleared outwards. Water and other supplies are plentiful. A British consul resides at the old town; there is communication by electric telegraph, as well as a regular steam communication with England and other European states, also a railroad communicates with the interior. The population of both towns, including the suburbs, in 1873 may amount to about 18,000.

Telegraph.—At Bilbao, the terminus of the cable is on playa de las Arenas (playa de Guecho), close to the telegraph station house; it is thence laid in a N. by W. ¼ W. direction for 2 miles, and after a slight westerly bend, N.W. by W. ¼ W. for 7 cables, passes out of Bilbao bay in a N. by W. ¾ W. direction.

Mariners are cautioned not to anchor in the vicinity.

Olaviaga, about 2 miles below Bilbao, contains about 1,000 inhabitants; it extends along both banks of the river; large vessels lie secured along the south-west sea wall, with their heads up the river. Here there is a dry dock, and all kinds of stores and provisions may be obtained, this being the usual place for loading and discharging vessels, as any vessel that can cross the bar can proceed as far as this, and discharge and load afloat by lighters.

Freshes.—The province of Biscay is proverbially rainy, and in the winter months one incessant fall of rain lasts throughout, notwithstanding which the freshes of the river are capricious in their visitations. In May, 1850, the river at Bilbao suddenly rose 18 feet above the average high-water mark, and the loss of property in consequence was immense. The destructive freshes occur mostly on a continuous fall of heavy rain after dry weather.

Tides.—It is high water, full and change, on the bar of the Nervion, at 3h., springs rise 13 feet, and neaps 7 feet; at Olaviaga, at 3h. 15m., springs rise 12 feet; and at Bilbao, at 3h. 20m., spring rise 9 feet. With fresh N.W. winds the tide rises nearly 2 feet higher at the bar, and the time of high water is half an hour later; whilst the contrary effect takes place with strong winds from N.E. to South, which should be taken into consideration. The stream of the ebb runs 3 knots at springs, and 1½ at neaps.

Caution.—It is necessary to be particular in calculating exactly the time of high water on the bar of the Nervion river, if intending to enter, so as to be delayed in the bay as short a time as possible.

Pilots.—As many as 40 pilots are registered between Portugalete, Santurce, and Algorta, and vessels bound to Bilbao, in fine weather, will generally find one a short distance from the land to the westward. Many of the fishermen living within the vicinity of the river are pilots. They seldom await vessels eastward of Bilbao, as the land is generally made to the westward. A chief pilot, whose duty is to guide vessels across the bar, is always in attendance outside, and his boat will be known by a *red* flag, by which he directs the vessel's course by pointing to starboard or port, and holding the flag vertically, if going well; and it should be remembered that the flag is to direct the vessel's head, and not the helm.

Signals.—If the state of the weather does not permit the pilot to go out, the signal is made from the small tower at the end of the south-west mole or sea wall, where the signal from the boat is always repeated. A battery in ruins, called Xebiles, stands on the cliffs at the foot of mount Serantes at 1¼ miles S.E. of Ciérvana. The signals of the pilot at the bar are also repeated here by a white flag. When there is sufficient water on the bar, the flags at both places are shown, and no vessel should approach the bar without having sight of the flags. In doubtful weather, a *red* flag indicates that the bar is passable, a *white* flag the contrary.

Directions.—The bay of Bilbao will be easily recognized, when approaching it from the eastward, by cape Machichaco, as well as that of Vallane (remarkable by the islet near it), and by the deep opening of the bay itself. From the westward it will be known by mount Santoña, the town of Castro-Urdiales, and the peaks of Lucero, Montaño, and Serantes. If from the north-west the mountain of Amboto, 4,526 feet above the sea, with its head inclining westward, is an excellent mark, and with it bearing about S.E. by E. leads to the bay; on nearing which, the white and reddish sands of Algorta and Guecho will be successively seen, the light-tower on the highest part of the cliffs of Galea, the town of Algorta, that of Portugalete, the church of which is visible at a great distance, the buildings near the end of the north-east mole, and finally the little white circular pilot tower at the end of the south-west mole. With a fresh westerly breeze vessels should wait off Castro-Urdiales for the favourable moment to enter the bay. In fine weather there is no difficulty in entering the bay at any time, and anchoring off Nogales, or nearer the bar in 8 or 9 fathoms water, to await either daylight or high water.

As the worst gales are those from North round by west to S.W., a vessel should, particularly in winter, close the coast about Santander or Santoña, so as to be able to enter these ports in case of bad weather, or to keep to windward of Bilbao in the event of having to heave-to; besides the chance of meeting with a pilot, as they seldom or ever fail being on that part of the coast. It would not be prudent in a large vessel to enter the bay during bad weather without a pilot; but if embayed at neap tides, and on-shore winds, and unable to get out without a press of sail, the anchorage of Nogales would be the best, where the holding ground is good. The best berth is at half a mile from the shore, in 14 or 15 fathoms water, sand, with Galea point on with cape Villano; a second anchor should be ready to let go.

Should a vessel of light draught get into the bay during a gale, and the tide favourable for crossing the bar, attention should be given to the signals made from the shore. Sail should be kept on the vessel so as to keep before the sea, and the head sheets aft to pay her off in case of broaching-to ; also care should be taken that the men are not washed off the deck, as two or three heavy seas may probably break over the vessel. In a heavy gale the sea begins to break in a direction between Galea point and Ciérvana cove, and therefore a vessel will be in the breakers long before her arrival at the bar, but inshore the sea is smoother.

The bar is taken in all winds, excepting those from S.E. to S.S.W., which are off-shore. Those from the south predominate much in October and November, and are very strong at the entrance of the bay. The wind comes down in squalls and eddies from the high land on the west coast, and in working for the bar the vessel should keep between the east coast and the middle of the bay, so as to avoid the eddies. For vessels of large draught the high tide from 2h. to 5h. p.m. is the best, and they should be at the bar an hour and half before high water. The bar may be taken even an hour after high water, if the vessel can make headway against the current.

A vessel should leave the river before the flood is done, and the best tides are those between 5h. and 7h. a.m., so as to have the land-wind, which scarcely ever fails, if it does not blow hard outside. Departure should never be attempted with the ebb tide, or with a sea on the bar.* The assistance of a steam tug may always be obtained.

In moderate weather, during the summer months, the land and sea breezes prevail on this coast with tolerable regularity. During the winter north-west gales are frequent, and invariably accompanied with rain; if

---

* In November 1868 H.M.S. *Terrible* found a very heavy ground swell on the bar, with the ebb tide.

also with lightning, they may be expected to blow hard. Southerly winds prevail about the vernal and autumnal equinoxes. They blow at times with great force, are generally dry and warm, though when veering to the south-west they are accompanied with rain. The barometer generally gives warning of their approach by a sudden fall of 0·25 or 0·30, and perhaps more; and, though these are off-shore winds, the bar frequently becomes impassable when they blow strong.

During the summer season, sailing vessels waiting tide to enter the river should stand off and on, keeping outside the bay and well to the westward, in order to avoid being driven on cape Villano by the north-west swell should the wind fail.

The general mark for approaching the bar, for small vessels (say those drawing 8 feet), is the churches of Portugalete and Sestao in line, S. by E. Steer in this direction until the vessel is midway between Campillo point and Santurce; the western pier at the entrance of the river will then be end on S. by E. ⅜ E., which is the leading-mark over the bar. When abreast the house named Casa del Campo Grande, which stands alone about one-third the distance from Santurce toward the pier-head, haul over for the middle of the river, to avoid a ridge of loose stones, with only 4 feet over it at low water, extending upwards of a cable from, and in line with, the western pier-head. There is a similar ridge, dry at low water, extending 2 cables from eastern pier-head.

Then steer midway between the piers until abreast of Portugalete, where there is good anchorage in the middle of the river, nearly as far as the bridge named las Siete Ojos, which is three-quarters of a mile up the river on the opposite shore. From Portugalete the two green and white beacons in line will lead to abreast the white ball beacon on the rocks near monte Aspe, thence the two vertically striped red and white beacons, on the right bank of the river, in line bearing E. by S. ½ S. will lead clear of the mud-bank extending from the convent gardens at St. Nicholas. Should the wind be unfavourable for proceeding up the river, vessels may be towed or tracked from the right bank all the way to Bilbao.

RIVER SOMORROSTRO.—From the west point of entrance of Bilbao bay the coast trends to the south-west, and forms a bay; and at a mile from the point is the entrance to the Somorrostro, the bar of which is dry at low water. At high-water springs there are 8 feet on it, so that it can be crossed only in fine weather, by vessels of light draught, which visit the inlet for iron ore, rich mines of which are worked in the neighbour-hood. The village of Muzquiz and various houses are scattered along the western shore of the river. Between the mouth of the river and the western slope of mount Lucero is the sand of Somorrostro, which is seen

15 miles off. The hermitage of Nuestra Señora del Socorro is seen on the western side of entrance.

Directions.—In standing for the river Somorrostro keep under the west shore of the bay. Muzquiz point, on the west side of the entrance to Somorrostro, is low and rocky, thence˙the coast westward, for 2 miles to the town and small bay of Onton, is moderately high and bold, with elevated land in the interior. The bay being full of rocks cannot be used even by small vessels. The river Onton here separates the provinces of Vizcaya or Biscay and Santander.

The COAST from Onton river trends N.N.W. $\frac{1}{2}$ W. 3 miles to the Peña de Santa Ana, near the town of Castro-Urdiales; in this latter space is the town of Mogoño with its bay, too shallow even at high water to admit any but small vessels which load with iron ore.

The province of Santander is bounded on the east by the river Onton or Sabiote, and on the west by the river Deva. It contains about 65 miles of coast, somewhat indented, but deficient of harbours capable of receiving large vessels. Santander, the most capacious, often presents great difficulties in entering with gales from the N.W. and S.W. quarters, which so frequently happen during winter and spring. The land of this part of the coast is high, but of less variety than that of the province of Astúrias which follows to the westward. The cliffs are not so remarkable or uniform, nor does the shore present the level land which characterizes the coast of Astúrias, and the mountains of the interior, although high, are more gentle in their acclivities, and their offshoots towards the sea are more gradual, and without those rugged summits which distinguish the high land of Astúrias.

The higher parts of the Pyrenees are concealed from the view of the mariner when near the coast; but at a sufficient distance from it, the remarkable peaks known generally by the name of Urrieles, extending some distance east and west, and embracing parts of the provinces of Oviedo, Santander, and Leon, are excellent marks for correcting a vessel's position when the state of the atmosphere admits of their being seen. The highest of these elevations, and conspicuous from its pyramidical form, is that called Torre de Cerredo, which rises in the province of Leon, and reaches about 8,903 feet above the level of the sea.

More remarkable, however, from its outline and the facility with which it is distinguished, is that called Naranjo de Bulnes, 8,504 feet above the sea. Its isolated position, its figure like the portion of a column standing vertically above all, and its barren and red appearance, prevent its being

I 2

taken for any other peak; besides which it is nearer the sea. The summits of the mountains are covered with snow during a great part of the year, and to vessels making the coast between cape Peñas and cape Mayor, particularly between Rivadesella and Barquera, they are very distinct.

Winds.—The prevailing winds on the coast of the province of Santander during winter are southerly, which veer to south-west and north-west. The southerly wind during its first days preserves a clear atmosphere, and is considered by navigators as the precursor of a north-west wind. It begins to set in during October, and ends in February. Should it become cloudy with rain the wind veers to S.W. and soon after to West, and nearly always with dark cloudy weather, which terminates in a north-west gale and heavy showers. When the wind is north-westerly it is clear between the showers, enabling the mariner to recognize the land.

Heavy gales generally begin from the southward by blowing hard, and the harder it blows the more clear is the weather. When the sky becomes entirely overcast the wind may be expected to haul to the north-west with heavy showers. If the wind changes from N.W. to North or N.N.E. it becomes very severe, admits of no canvas being shown, closes all the ports, and makes the coast a dead lee shore. If a northerly gale, after lasting two or three days, changes to N.W., the gale will freshen up again ; but should it veer to N.E. the weather moderates and some fine days follow. But should the wind veer to the east and S.E. it will continue on to South, and all the bad weather will come over again.

In autumn these changes of the wind are generally attended with fine weather, particularly after the gales of the equinox. The spring is nearly always a continuation of winter, during which the *vendavales* (westerly winds) predominate, if not with as much strength of wind certainly with as much rain. In summer, here considered as commencing in July, winds from the north-east quarter prevail, which on the coast become more northerly during the heat of the sun, and from the land at night.

The Barometer rises with westerly winds round by north to N.E., and falls with all others.

Currents.—During winter the currents generally set to the eastward, caused by the continual winds from the S.W. and N.W. quarters. In a north-west gale their rate may be considered more than 3 miles an hour. A strong current to the eastward in fine weather is generally a prelude to a north-west gale. A considerable rise of the water above the usual level in the different ports is also a prelude to similar weather. In summer, currents may be found setting west and W.N.W., but not strong; so that it may be considered as a general rule that there is a constant easterly current at some distance from the coast, especially from off cape Peñas.

CASTRO-URDIALES CASTLE.—At about half a mile S. ¼ E. from a point named Rabanal is the Atalaya de Castro-Urdiales, which is a perpendicular mass of rock about 68 feet high, and on which are the remains of a look-out house. A little to the N.W. of it there are several detached rocks, and an islet close to the shore. Close to, S.E. of the Atalaya, and upon another rocky eminence of greater height, stands the castle of Castro-Urdiales, an ancient fortification with four large circular towers, one at each angle. The castle is white towards the sea, and visible at a great distance. On the south-east side of the castle is the Peña de Santa Ana, another rock 63 feet high, scarped on all sides except the west, where it has some slope ; on its summit is a chapel dedicated to Santa Ana. Between this rock and the castle there are two others, one larger than the other, the whole connected by bridges to communicate with the chapel. In 1861 walls were being raised for the purpose of connecting these rocks, and sufficiently high above water to impede the entrance of the tide, and to protect the bay of Castro-Urdiales.*

LIGHT.—On the south-eastern of the above towers is a circular light-tower, which shows at 148 feet above the sea a *fixed* white light, with *red flashes* every *three minutes*, and visible at a distance of 7 miles.

Cotolino Point.—At about half a mile south-eastward of the Peña de Santa Ana is Cotolino point, low, rocky, and · forming the south-east extreme of Castro-Urdiales bay. At a third of a mile farther to the south-east is Mioño point, which is high, steep, and clear; both points extend from the Cueto de Mioño, a height with an oval base, and appearing of a conical form when seen from the westward. A sandy beach of some extent at low water lies between Castro-Urdiales and Cotolino point ; it is scattered with rocks, and the river Brazonar runs over them into the sea, from which the beach takes its name.

To the eastward of Mioño point is the beach and the river of the same name. Here is the small port of Mioño or Dicido, available for vessels of light draught at high water in fine weather, which convey iron ore to Oriñon and places on the coast of Biscay. The village of Mioño, containing about 300 inhabitants, stands close to the shore inside the port. At the eastern extreme of Mioño sand is a high rocky point named Salta-Caballo. The land in the interior is high and mountainous.

CAUTION.—Between the Villano islet and point La Castra, at 13¼ miles westward, the coast forms a bight 4 miles deep, and in the

---

* *See* Admiralty plan :—Port Castro-Urdiales and adjacent bays, on sheet of plans, No. 710.

middle of it is Bilbao bay forming a cod, which recedes 3 miles to the S.E. This deep bight is dangerous with in-shore winds, for with much sea it would be difficult for a vessel to get out of it. It would, therefore, be prudent to avoid it, unless bound for Bilbao, and at a time when the bar is practicable. A heavy sea sets in on the coast with strong winds from N.E. to West, and, with the exception of Castro-Urdiales, there is no refuge for vessels whatever. Southerly winds acquire a terrific force in this bight, and from vessels being unable to carry sail they are blown off the coast.

CASTRO-URDIALES BAY is limited, and only convenient for vessels of light draught. It affords shelter from North round by West to S.E.; but when there is a heavy sea from N.W. vessels lie very uneasy. It is open to the eastward, and should only be considered as a temporary anchorage; the bottom is nearly everywhere rock, covered with a thin layer of sand. The depth in the bay is from 3 to 4½ fathoms at low water. Vessels of 9 to 11 feet draught may remain in the bay during bad weather, or for the tide to cross the bar for Bilbao. The southerly wind is the most convenient in winter from its violence, and it is necessary to have good anchors to prevent driving on the Santa Ana rock.

What is termed the port of Castro-Urdiales is formed by two moles, with the mouth, 45 feet wide, open to the southward; but a heavy swell runs into it with a N.W. or northerly sea, and causes much damage to small craft in it. The bottom is rock, with a slight layer of sand and mud, and at low-water springs the whole port is nearly dry, excepting near the mouth, where there are 5 to 8 feet. It has sufficient room for 130 fishing boats and 15 to 20 coasters, which are secured in tiers. The town is surrounded by walls, and contains about 4,000 inhabitants; it faces the port, and extends north and south, so that seen from the east it presents a pleasing and imposing appearance. Its principal trade is in fish, and 500 to 600 men are employed in the fishery. A small river falls into the bay south of the port.

The town is seen from a great distance, particularly the church, which stands on elevated ground, a little west of the castle and lighthouse. The number of rocks which surround the bay are detached from the main land. At a great distance, when the town cannot be seen, the peak of Cerredo is a good mark. To enter the bay from the westward with winds from that quarter, Rabanal point should have a berth of at least a mile, then continue on for the castle and cliffs of the Peña de Santa Ana, which may be closed to a distance of a third of a cable, as they are steep-to. The bay should only be frequented by vessels that can enter the port.

Tides.—It is high water, full and change, at Castro-Urdiales, at 3h. ; springs rise 12 feet.

COAST.—The land between Castro-Urdiales and Santoña, 8 miles westward, is high and mountainous in the interior, but the shore is low and generally clear of danger. Rabanal point is foul, and a good berth should be given to it when there is any sea ; between it and Castro-Urdiales is a bay about 3 cables deep, but open to the north-east. At 8¼ miles N.E. by N. of the point there is a small bank, named Castro-Verde, with 25 to 30 fathoms water on it, on which there is a considerable sea, which sometimes breaks. Between the point and bank, the depths are from 55 to 65 fathoms. In bad weather care should be taken to pass well outside, or well inside this bank.

The bank lies with Monte Cabarga de Santander in line with the highest part of mount Brusco, and with a hummock on Castro, on which is a chapel, in line with the peak—not very prominent—of monte Cerredo, named the Verde. The Verde peak is westward of the highest peak of Cerredo.

MOUNT CERREDO.—This mountain is rugged and broken to the westward, and extends east to the town of Castro-Urdiales. Its northern side slopes gradually, and terminates in low land at the coast, which appears in large patches of slate rock. At its base is the river Oriñon. Towards the western side of the mountain, and in the vicinity of Islares, the peak of Cerredo reaches an elevation of 1,813 feet above the level of the sea, and on it there is a landmark. This peak is a good mark for Santoña and Castro-Urdiales.

A similar high mountain, visible only at a distance seaward, rises 5½ miles inland, S.W. of the Cerredo and South of the Candina. There is a very conspicuous hummock on its summit named Castro, crowned by a chapel. The mount is the most elevated in the valley of Guriezo, and is a good mark for Santoña and much used by fishermen.

The shore eastward of Islares point is low, with slight bends, and appears in large whitish patches. It terminates eastward in a large high cliff named La Castra point, which is 3 miles eastward of Oriñon point, and about a third of a mile S.E. of it is Rabanal point, low and rocky. The Cerdigo rock is a low dark islet close to the point of the same name, between Islares and Castra points, and connected to the shore by a reef. In a strong breeze the sea washes over the islet.

MOUNT CANDIÑA rises on the coast a mile eastward of the headland of Ahorcado to about 1,390 feet above the sea, and is remarkable from the white patches which are conspicuous in the midst of the dark woody land. The mountain is of calcareous rock, which appears here and there, and terminates in peaks, but these are not so conspicuous as those of mount Santoña westward. Between the mount and the bay of Yesera westward there is an islet close to the shore, leaving a passage for boats. Several other rocks lie close to the shore between Ahorcado and Laredo.

ORIÑON or SONABIA POINT.—From the foot of mount Candiña, a narrow, low arm of land projects to the north-east, named Oriñon or Sonabia point. A ridge rises from its middle, and is connected to the main by a narrow low neck, which is partly covered at high water, and entirely when there is a high sea. Seen from 'a distance this tongue of land appears like an island at a good distance from the shore. Its extremity is rocky, and with any sea it should not be approached nearer than half a mile.

To the south and east of the above point is that named Ilares, and the town of the same name is near it. The point is low, a little salient, with rocks off it; it forms the east extreme of Oriñon bay, the sands of which extend to the foot of mount Candiña and some way up its eastern slope.

ORIÑON INLET.—Near the western extremity of the above beach is the mouth of the Oriñon inlet, which recedes southward to the valley of Guriezo, and receives the river of this name. Small coasting vessels enter the inlet with iron ore for the foundries in some of the towns of the above valley. The river winds along on the eastern side of mount Candiña, it has a shifting bar, which at low water is nearly dry. The village of Oriñon contains about 200 inhabitants, and stands on a sandy plain on the western shore of the inlet, which reaches up the slope of the mount. On the opposite shore is the village of Islares, of little more importance.

At a distance seaward, the inlet of Oriñon may be recognized by the great ravine which the land forms between mounts Cerredo and Candiña. The white sand of Oriñon may also be seen at a great distance, and the point of the same name appears like an island.

LAREDO.—At a mile westward of the foot of mount Candiña there is a high, steep, and rugged headland, named Ahorcado. On its east side is the little bay of Yesera, having pits of a chalky substance in its neighbourhood, and in fine weather small vessels resort here for it. The coast thence is steep and clear for 2 miles westward to Rastrillar point, which slightly projects, is surrounded by rocks, a battery stands on the cliffs, and on its west side is the walled town of Laredo, with about 3,200 inhabitants who are chiefly employed in the fisheries. The mole is choked with sand and the boats have to be beached. From Rastrillar point the shore forms a bay on the south, and then trends northward to the Passage point;

between the points the shore all along for about 3 miles is sand, and named the sand of Laredo, or *Salvé* in the language of the country.

MOUNT SANTOÑA is of an irregular form, 5¼ miles in circuit, and 1,322 feet above the sea. It is nearly isolated, being merely connected to mount Brusco on the west by the sandy plain or isthmus of Berria. It is formed of calcareous rock, broken towards the sea, and covered with fertile soil. It has several peaks, Escalara or Canzo being the highest. The peak of Nespral is conical, 943 feet high, and on its summit is the atalaya or look-out tower, which is circular. The mount at a distance appears like an island, which in reality it is, as the heavy seas break through the dyke which joins it to the main land, and the waters unite with those of the lagoons which surround Santoña.

It will be known by its height, peaks, look-out tower, its white and reddish cliffs, and by the white rocky land near its summit, which contrasts well with the dark wood beyond it; mount Brusco, on the west, is also a good mark for it. It is possible without attention to mistake it for mount Candiña, which rises on the coast S.E. by S. of it; but the latter has not so many peaks, and no look-out tower. On nearing it from the westward the fort of Mazo, standing on a height 495 feet high, the battery of Cueva and guard-house close to it, at a short distance from Atalaya point, and the village of Dueso on the north-west slope of the mount, will be successively seen.

From a long distance the mount of Neustra Señora de las Nieves will be seen, with the chapel on its summit. It is some 2,516 feet above the sea, and when in line with mount Santoña bears about S. ¾ E. From the eastward mount Santoña appears somewhat open and isolated. When running for the inlet in a N.W. gale, care should be taken not to approach the coast too near on the north side of the mount, so as to avoid the breakers on the Doble bank, which is 2 miles from the shore.

LIGHTS.—On Pescador point, the north-east extreme of mount Santoña, is a conical lighthouse with a circular tower of white stone, which exhibits, at 126 feet above the sea, a *fixed* white light varied by a *flash* every *three minutes*, and in clear weather should be seen at a distance of 17 miles.

On Caballo point, the east extreme of mount Santoña, and nearly three-quarters of a mile S.S.E. of the former, is a circular tower, which exhibits, at 85 feet above the sea, a *fixed red* light, seen from seaward, when bearing from S. by W., round by West, to N. by E. ¼ E., at a distance of 7 miles.

A *fixed* light is exhibited from St. Martin castle, visible 5 miles.

SANTOÑA INLET.—The entrance to this islet is formed between the shore of mount Santoña and the adjoining beach on the north, and the beach of Passage point, and bank of Pitorro (which extends from the sands of Laredo) on the south. The inlet is divided into various channels, the principal being that of Colindres on the south, after passing Passage point. This channel trends southward for more than 4 miles to the town of Rada, where it joins the little stream of this name. It is navigable for small vessels as far as the town of Colindres, about 2¼ miles up, and carries 8 to 14 feet at low water; but at the entrance of the Cicero there is a rocky bank with only 4 feet water on it.*

At rather more than 2¼ miles within the principal channel is that of Limpias, which runs eastward nearly a mile to the town of that name, when it trends southward about the same distance to the villages of Marron and Ampuero; here it receives the Marron, a small stream in summer, but swollen by the freshes in winter.

The most important town of the inlet, commercially considered, is Limpias from its communication with Castile. It has about 1,400 inhabitants including the suburbs. Vessels of 11 to 13 feet draught load here with grain and flower; those about 13 feet draught complete their cargoes lower down, abreast the tower of Treto. The town of Santoña, is entirely military, and stands at the foot of the mount of the same name, on a level sandy plain, with marshes to the northward of it and creeks on the west. It is surrounded by trees and gardens, and has about 1,800 inhabitants, but neither commerce nor industry.

The port affords shelter and safety to vessels that frequent it. The best anchorage is in 6 or 7 fathoms water, off the battery of Isabel II., which is on the beach south of the town, partly covered with trees, and northward of Passage point. The breadth of the channel is here a quarter of a mile across, and the depth 3¾ to 4½ fathoms, which continues well within the Ano channel westward. The latter channel is another branch of the inlet, which, leaving the Colindres on the south, continues westward to the towns of Bárcena and Escalahte, but has little depth at low water.

Mount Ano, 574 feet high, is of conical form, like the peak of Cavada de Santander, and covered with a thick wood. It is on the north bank of the above channel, and isolated by a small channel or dyke which surrounds it. A convent stands at the foot of the mount on its south-east side, and is the only building in the vicinity. Passage point is the north extreme of an extensive sand named Laredo, which terminates at the town of the same name, S.S.E. of the battery of Isabel II., distant 2¼ miles. The point is remarkable for its bareness, projects N.N.E., and on it may be seen the

---

* See Admiralty plan :—Port Santoña, No. 75 ; scale m = 3 inches ; the bar of which has considerably changed since Tofiño's survey.

ruins of a castle, one of the marks for entering, but which is rather difficult at first to make out.

Bar.—The Pitorro bank extends from Passage point in an E.S.E. direction for more than a mile, when its edge trends to the southward. At low water there are 3 to 10 feet water on it. The above bank and that of San Carlos, north of it, form the entrance to the inlet. The bar or navigable part of the entrance is between the eastern extreme of this bank and Fraile point. It is here 1¼ cables across. The least water on the bar at low-water springs is 9 to 12 feet. Farther in the depth increases from 3 to 8 fathoms, to the anchorage. A buoy with staff and ball lies on the south edge of San Carlos bank, and a similar buoy about 3 cables S.E. of it; there are also two buoys on the south side of the channel near Passage point. The positions of these buoys cannot be depended on.

San Carlos Bank.—At 2 cables S.W. of Fraile point is the Redonda rock, connected with the shore. At half a mile farther on is San Carlos point, which is steep, and on it is a strong castle of the same name. From the Redonda a beach appears at low water, along the shore of the mount inwards to the port; and between Redonda rock and San Carlos point the bank extends 2 cables to the S.S.E., with 6 to 8 feet water on it, named San Carlos bank, and requires in a large vessel care in entering.

Directions.—The inlet of Santoña being open to the south-east cannot be entered during north-west winds, which are the most stormy on this part of the coast, and blow down over the mount in heavy squalls, for which a sailing vessel should be 'prepared. The most favourable winds for entering the inlet are those from N.E. round by East to W.S.W. With moderate winds from other points a vessel will have to work in, or back, and fill, with the flood. With north-west winds a vessel may run down as far as Fraile point, when it will be necessary to tow or steam as the wind draws ahead. With a northerly wind a vessel may reach Redonda rock, but southward of it the wind here draws out, and renders entering under sail impossible.

There is anchorage also in 4½ fathoms about 3 cables S. by W. ¾ W. from Fraile point, whence with steam or a tug a vessel may get into the inlet. With a fair wind bring the castle of San Carlos—the most southern fortification on a high cliff at the foot of mount Santoña—in line with mount Ano, until Fraile point comes in line with Caballo point north of it about N.N.E.; then steer W.S.W. until the convent under mount Ano is in line with the ruins of the castle on Passage point—the remains of a wall, which will be seen between the small downs at the termination of the point, and the seaweed which partly covers it—and then steer for the battery of Isabel II., and anchor off it in 6 or 7 fathoms water, at 1½ cables from the beach at Santoña.

In a large sailing vessel with a scant, or foul wind, a pilot should be taken, as the edges of the Pitorro and San Carlos banks are subject to change, and the channel only known to those frequenting it. Vessels of more than 50 tons are charged pilotage. A steam vessel may, however, enter by attending to the directions given. Vessels moor N.E. and S.W. Between fort Isabel II. and Cruz point, the bottom is stiff clay and good holding. The worst winds are those from South to West, which blow strong, when it is necessary to drop another anchor, as accidents often happen. The southerly winds blowing with great force down the Colindres channel cause much sea; on this account, in winter, vessels should anchor near the Ano channel. Vessels bound to Limpias, anchor at Santoña to deliver the papers. The pilotage from here to Limpias is 90 reals for vessels of 50 to 150 tons, and 120 reals for those of larger tonnage.

Tides.—It is high water, full and change, in Santoña islet at 3 h.; springs rise 12¼ feet, neaps 10½ feet. The ebb is always much stronger than the flood, running about three miles an hour at springs, which much facilitates leaving the port during north-east or easterly winds. When much rain has fallen, and the river Marron has heavy freshes, the ebb acquires considerable strength, and the current of the Celindres channel disturbs the beach of Santoña. Vessels should then anchor farther westward, so as to be clear of the mouth of the above channel. In winter it is prudent to lie near the channel of Ano.

The ebb tide on leaving the mouth of the inlet sets to the S.S.E. over the Pitorro bank and into Laredo bay. Vessels becalmed are liable to be set on Rastrillar point, if precautionary measures are not used. The flood tide in entering the inlet sets strong on Passage point and into the channel of Colindres.

Fraile Anchorage.—Vessels will find shelter off Fraile point, mount Santoña, from a north-west gale when unable from any cause to get into Bilbao. The anchorage is good with winds from the S.W. to N.W., but vessels ride uneasy if there be much swell. Caballo point, the north-east extreme of the mount, may be passed at the distance of 2 cables; anchor at about a quarter of a mile E.N.E. of Fraile point, in 7½ or 8 fathoms at low water, sand. A good berth will be in 7½ fathoms, with Fraile point bearing W. by S. ½ S., and Caballo point N. ¾ W., 2 cables from the Merana bank, which is near the shore.

Vessels should lie here at single anchor, and be ready to slip or get under way either for the inlet or to stand eastward, should the wind suddenly shift to N.E. Fraile point is 140 feet high, rugged, perpendicular, cannot be mistaken, and is seen the moment Caballo point is passed. This latter point is low, rocky, slightly projecting, commanded by high precipices, and is known by the circular lighthouse and keeper's dwelling.

Doble Bank, named by the fishermen Ganzanilla, is dangerous in a heavy sea, and lies about $2\frac{1}{4}$ miles off the beach of Bérria. There are 10 and 11 fathoms water on it, 16 and 18 fathoms close around, and between it and mount Santoña 15 to $16\frac{1}{2}$ fathoms. From the least depth on the bank the battery of Cueva bears S. by W. $\frac{1}{4}$ W., Pescador point S. $\frac{1}{2}$ E., cape Machichaco S.E. by E. $\frac{3}{4}$ E., and cape Queio W.N.W. northerly : mount Ano appears a little open west of mount Brusco, and cape Ajo a little open of cape Queio. Vessels bound to Santoña inlet in a north-west gale should be careful to avoid this bank, as there is not only a heavy sea in its neighbourhood, but at times it breaks.

Playa de Berria.—Between mount Santoña and Brusco point, a mile westward, is the isthmus or playa de Berrier, a low, flat, sandy plain . The beach is clean, but near Brusco, rocks appear above water ; the inhabitants of Santoña communicate with the country by means of a road over the sand.

Mount Brusco is a dark looking mountain, from being covered with wood, rising at the south end of Noja bay ; it terminates at the sea on its east side in the point of the same name. The point is rocky and foul, and near it ends the reefs which skirt Noja bay.

NOJA BAY is formed between Brusco point and Garfanta point, 2 miles northward of it. Its shore is low and rugged, with a level beach scattered with rocks, the latter at low water appearing above the sand ; the shore throughout is skirted with rocks, which extend off half a mile, and the water is shallow outside them. When there is any sea, the breakers extend to a considerable distance from the shore ; hence the bay should be carefully avoided. The church of the town of Noja, south of Garfanta point, is conspicuous from seaward ; it stands in the middle of a plain, and not far from the shore. The population is about 750. Garfanta point, commonly called Mesa de Noja, is level, rocky, arid on the summit, projects to the north-east, and terminates in rocky points and reefs ; the latter extend out some distance, and should be avoided.

CAPE QUEIO, at $1\frac{1}{4}$ miles from Garfanta point, terminates in broken cliffs, and on its summit is an old watch tower. On the east side of the cape the shore is low, and interspersed by a rock beach ; and some isolated rocks lie near the shore, the largest of which is named Isla, and affords shelter from westerly winds.   There is an hermitage on Isla, and a short distance outside is an islet.   Between the cape and cape Ajo, 3 miles N.W. of it, the coast is low, rocky, arid, and of a reddish colour.   The capes Quintres, Ajo, and Queio, seen from the westward or eastward, present an even projecting surface.   The town of Isla has about 700 inhabitants, and is seen south of cape Queio, not far from the shore, in the midst of trees and cultivation.

CAPE AJO, 3 miles westward of cape Queio, and 7½ miles E. by S. of the lighthouse of cape Mayor, is the most salient point of all this coast. It is clear of danger, and may be approached to a prudent distance.   When seen from the east or west it appears in cliffs to the northward similar to steps.   It resembles Queio, and is not so high as Quintres.   At a small beach eastward of cape Ajo is the mouth of the inlet of the same name, a narrow arm of the sea, which admits boats at high water to go as far as the village of Ajo, a mile from the sea; this place stands in a plain inland south of the cape, and contains about 700 inhabitants.

From cape Ajo the coast is bold, and trends S.W. with a bend to the south-east for 2 miles to cape Quintres.   The land forming this cape is high and level, and the ruins of a look-out house are seen on its summits, and to the south-west the ruins of a tower.   When seen from the west and north-east the cape appears vertical, as if cut down.

CAPE GALIZANO, at 2 miles S.W. of cape Quintres, is formed of cliffs terminating in steps, and a small remarkable peak known to navigators as the Pico de Galizano.   To the eastward of the cape is the sand of the same name; here fishing vessels find shelter from S.W. and westerly winds.   The river Galizano falls into the sea between capes Galizano and Langre, after passing near the town of Galizano; it flows from the south, and boats can only cross the bar at high water in fine weather.   The coast eastward of the river is of cliffs of little elevation, but in the interior the land is high and mountainous.   At a mile westward of the cape is the rocky point of Langre, and about the same distance farther on the island of Santa Marina, on the east side of entrance to Santander.

The PORT of SANTANDER is the best on the north coast of Spain, eastward of cape Ortegal, but it should not be attempted by a stranger, as the tides are strong, and the banks within, formed of the deposits brought down by the streams which discharge into it, frequently shift.   Neither should it be attempted in a north-west gale if the vessel can keep the sea; and even after the gale, for a day or so, it should be approached by a sailing vessel with caution, in order not to get so far embayed as to be unable to haul out again, should the bar (as it is termed) be up; for at this time from Mouro islet to Puerto point, and across to the Puntal sands, is one confused sea breaking in 7 and 8 fathoms water.*

The entrance to the port is between Santa Marina island and cape Mayor, which bears N.W. 2¼ miles from it. From Santa Marina island the east shore of the inlet trends to the south-west, and is fronted by extensive flats, which reach three-quarters of a mile to the northward, dry at low water, and are then intersected by numerous channels; but at high tide the inlet shows a large extent of water. Cape Mayor, the west point of entrance, is about 200 feet high, steep, and has near it a lighthouse 103 feet high. Cape Menor, at half a mile to the S.S.E., is lower than the former cape, has a battery on its summit, and terminates in a low flat point, with a small reef, on which the sea occasionally breaks, and at some distance outside it.

At 1¼ miles S. by E. of cape Menor is Puerto point, which is low, and has on it a square brick light tower, 45 feet high. On the high ground over it is the remains of a fort; between is a bay with a beach named Playa del Sardinero, in which vessels anchor when the wind and tide are adverse for entering the harbour. The best position is in 9 fathoms, sand, at 3 cables south of cape Menor, farther south the bottom is rock and stone. There are three batteries on the shore of the bay; and N. by W., 2 cables from Puerto point, stands Ano castle and semaphore, on a precipice. From Puerto point the shore trends to the westward, and at a short distance is Cerda battery; thence round to the north and west to Promontorio point, forming a bight 6½ cables wide, and full of rocks.

Close to the shore of the bight, and joined to it at low water, is Torre islet, low and divided into two parts but united by a natural bridge. At three-quarters of a cable south-west of it is a rocky bank with 8 feet water. At a little more than a cable S.E. of Torre islet is a smaller one, named Horadada, from its being pierced through so as to resemble two rocks connected by a bridge; this islet has a beacon on it. San Martin point, situated nearly three-quarters of a mile westward of Horadada islet, has a battery on a precipice, and a number of rocks, named Las Hermanas, on its west side. At half a mile westward of San Martin point is the town of Santander; thence the shore trends round to the south and east, the whole being fronted by extensive sand-flats, dry at low water, and leaving a navigable channel throughout the whole extent between them and the shore of from 1½ to 3 cables wide.

At 2 miles westward of the Darsena, the elevation named Peña Castillo

_____

* See Admiralty plan :—Port Santander, No. 76; scale, m = 5·25 inches.

rises from the shore, 396 feet high, seen from the westward it appears conical.

The Town of Santander, and capital of the province of the same name, is well built, and extends northward and westward on the sides of two small hills crowned with trees, which contribute to its picturesque effect. The cathedral stands on the summit of the hill which runs along the shore of the inlet, at the foot of which commences the line of rail leading to Castile. It has a population of about 30,000 (in 1874), and is a place of considerable commercial activity. In 1866, 468 vessels amounting to 63,293 tons entered inwards, and 315 vessels of 49,638 tons cleared outwards, besides 99,480 tons of coasting trade. A steam communication is kept up with England. A little more than half a mile west of San Martin point, is the east end of a good solid and well-paved mole; it extends westward in front of the town for more than 3 cables, terminating in a recess named the Dársena.

Vessels here lie aground at low water alongside the mole and jetty. A handsome line of houses runs along in the rear of the mole facing the south. The captain of the port's residence, the health office, and custom house are situated on the mole. Here will be found all the resources looked for in a commercial port. Water is obtained alongside from tanks, and from fountains at the mole.

Telegraph.—There is a sub-marine cable at Santander, communicating with northern Europe.

Mouro Islet, commonly called Mogro, lying at the entrance of the port, bears E. ¼ S. from Caballo point, distant about 4 cables from the shore. The islet is rugged, nearly circular, less than a cable in diameter, and about 90 feet above the sea, with a light tower on it of white stone, 56 feet high. A rock above water, named the Corbera, lies half a cable from the east side of the islet, with a rock on its south-west side which uncovers at one-third ebb; a bank with 2½ fathoms water on it lies three-quarters of a cable from the west side of the islet. In a gale from the north or north-west the islet is enveloped in spray.

Pico de la Cavada—or Cudio of the pilots—is a conical hill 830 feet high, and rises about S. by W. ¼ W. 5⅝ miles from Mouro islet. It is easily known by its peculiar form, and the woods upon it, which give it a dark appearance, and when in line with the Alto de Ruballo leads through the western passage. A mountain named Cabarga, ranging east and west, about 1,970 feet above the sea, a short distance westward of the above, is another mark for Santander.

Alto de Ruballo is a hill sloping east and west entirely covered with wood, and rises about S.S.W. ¼ W. 1¼ miles from Mouro islet.

Arenal del Puntal.—The extensive sands of this name, which border the shore west of Santa Marina island and form the southern boundary of the channel to the port of Santander, extend northward from the Alto de Ruballo for nearly a mile, and are dry at low water.

Banco de las Quebrantas.—This is a dangerous shoal, with 6 to 15 feet water on it, stretching northward 4 cables from the Arenal del Puntal in the direction of Mouro islet. Its extremity lies with the castle of San Martin open south of Horadada islet, and Capes Mayor and Menor in line. The channel between it and the islet is half a mile wide, with 3¼ to 7 fathoms water.

LIGHTS.—The tower on cape Mayor, 1¾ miles westward of the entrance to Santander, exhibits at 298 feet above high water a white light, which *revolves* every *minute*, and is visible in clear weather at a distance of 20 miles; the eclipses are not total within 8 miles.

A blue flag by day indicates that the steam tug cannot put to sea.

A square brick tower on Puerto point, the north point of entrance to Santander, exhibits, at an elevation of 79 feet above the level of the sea, a *fixed green* light, obscured westward, of a S. ¼ W. bearing, and having a sector of 5 degrees of white light covering Horadada islet. The light is visible in clear weather at a distance of 4 miles.

The tower on Mouro islet shows, at 136 feet above high water, a *fixed* white light, visible through an arc of 270° between the bearings of E. by S. through South to N. by E. at a distance of 12 miles. Through the remainder of the circle, a faint light will be seen, when 4½ cables from the lighthouse.

A *fixed red* light, at an elevation of 30 feet above the sea, is shown from the south-west angle of the Capitania at 2 yards from the edge of the pier, visible 3 miles.

Pilots wait in adverse weather under the lee of Puerto point, and it is compulsory for all vessels above 50 tons to take one; too much reliance cannot, however, be placed upon their knowledge.*

Tides.—It is high water, full and change, at the bar of Santander, at about 3h. 20m.; springs rise 12 feet. The ebb stream is stronger than the flood, and attains the rate of 4 miles an hour at spring tides, during which there is very little slack water.* In the mouth of the harbour a branch of the ebb stream turns to the S.E. towards the bay south of Santa Marina island, which should be carefully guarded against. In the rainy

---

* Navigating Lieutenant A. J. Burniston, H.M.S. *Terrible*, November 1868.

o 17301.   K

season the strength of the ebb is considerably increased, making the
entrance difficult for a sailing vessel without a strong fair wind. Gales
from south-west and north-west cause the tide to rise from one to 2 feet,
and those from north-east and south-east depress it.

Buoys.—A black mooring buoy lies in 5 fathoms, about 4 cables west
of Horadada islet; a conical red buoy is moored on the edge of the bank,
on south side of channel abreast Horadada islet; at three-quarters of a
mile west of this buoy lies another conical red buoy on south side of the
channel abreast St. Martin's castle; there are also three red buoys on
north side of Banco del Bergantin.

The positions of these buoys cannot always be depended on.

Directions.—The position of Santander will be recognized when
approaching it from the westward by the reddish white sandy tract on the
west slope of Liencres hill (page 148), which rises 7 miles westward of
the entrance, the island of Cabrera or Suances, and Ballota point; and if
from the eastward mount Santoña, and capes Ajo and Quintres. Cape
Mayor, the west point of entrance, may be known by being rather more
elevated than the line of coast, terminating abruptly, and having a light
tower on its summit. The town cannot be seen from seaward.

It is of the utmost importance that a vessel from the westward with a
fresh breeze from that quarter should close the coast and make out the
land, so as to be certain of the vessel's position. With any sea, if near
the coast, the San Pedro del Mar (page 148), a rocky bank on which the
sea often breaks, should be avoided. During southerly winds the coast is
clear, but with those from S.W. or N.W. when blowing hard it is
generally obscured. With the wind from the eastward between N.N.E.
and S.E. a vessel may pass on either side of Mouro islet, but large
vessels from the westward with the wind from N.N.W. to N.E. should
enter by the western channel, called the bar, which should be taken at
half flood.

Steer in with the peak of Cavada in line with the middle of the
Alto de Ruballo, southward of Mouro islet, past Puerto point, until
Horadala islet is in line with Promontorio point; then steer for Peña
Castillo, passing half a cable from Horadada islet, and a cable from San
Martin point. But if at the time of low water, and the vessel's draught is
13 or 14 feet, stand on with the Capitania of the port in line with San
Martin point until westward of Torre islet, and the Polvorin (the powder
magazine in the bay eastward of Promontorio point) bears N.N.E., when
the rock S.W. of Torre islet will be cleared.

Promentorio and San Martin points and the Hermanas should be passed
at the distance of about half a cable, and the line of coast followed to the

anchorage within the Capitania del Puerto, or vessels may anchor south-ward of Promontorio point, or if necessary in any part of the channel westward of Puerto point. Moor with open hawse to the southward during winter, with a long scope on the starboard anchor, as the wind from that quarter blows with much violence. Should the wind be from the westward, and the tide flood, when the Peña Castillo is well open of Horadada islet, a vessel may back and fill up to the anchorage with her head to the northward, bearing in mind that two-thirds of the way across the channel the tide sets to the south-west.

With an ebb tide it will be better for a sailing vessel to anchor off Sardinero beach. In a north-west gale it would not be prudent for a large vessel to run for Santander, if she can keep the sea. It will be better to remain outside and to windward of the port, bearing in mind that the easterly current sometimes attains the rate of 5 miles an hour. A vessel unable to keep the sea may try the anchorage of Sardinero beach, attempt the entrance of Santander, or run for the port of Santoña. A heavy swell rolls into Sardinero bay during a north-west gale. As during a heavy north-west sea it breaks on the bar, the latter cannot be taken until 4 or 5 hours flood, and then with a fresh and fair wind.

Vessels generally leave the port with the land wind in the morning, even with a flood tide; but a vessel may leave with a foul wind and ebb tide by backing and filling. To ensure getting well out, it will be prudent to drop down previously to one of the outer anchorages.

Anchorage may be obtained in 4¾ fathoms, sandy bottom, with Horadada islet bearing E. ¼ N., and Promontorio point N.N.W. ¼ W.; in rather deeper water, with the north point of Santa Marina on with Cerda castle, or in fact anywhere within Puerto point. The Alto de Miranda is a hill about 278 feet high, commanding San Martin point. The anchorage for small vessels is higher up, within the Capitania del Puerto.

The COAST from cape Mayor is steep and rocky, and trends westward one mile to a headland of lower elevation, named cape Lata, with an islet named Ansion on its north-west side; thence follows a lower but still rocky shore for three-quarters of a mile to Cornuda point, when it turns more to the south for two-thirds of a mile to a small open bay with a sandy beach named San Pedro del Mar, with a battery on its east point. On the west side of the bay a narrow inlet runs westward, in which fishing vessels find shelter in north-east and easterly winds; but if there be any sea from the north-west it cannot be entered, for the sea always breaks on the bar, which is of rock. There is a water mill in the inlet, and at high tide launches go up to it, where they lie in safety.

At 1¾ miles westward of San Pedro del Mar is the islet of Nuestra Señora del Mar, with a hermitage on it; the islet is rocky, low, steep, and joined to the land by a bridge. At one mile farther on is the point and watch-tower of San Juan del Canal, high and precipitous, and between is a small bay with a sandy beach receding to the south-westward and useful for boats in westerly wind and a smooth sea.

A bank named Cabezo de San Pedro del Mar, and of some extent in an east and west direction, lies 1½ miles from the shore off San Pedro del Mar. It has 10 or 12 fathoms water on it at low tide, and 20 fathoms between it and the shore. The sea often breaks on it, and even near it. A vessel should either give it a berth or pass inside it. From the depth of 10 fathoms on it cape Mayor light-tower bears S.E. easterly, Hermitage of N. Señora del Mar S.W. by W., and the west point of Cabrera islet W. ¼ N. The roof of the Hermitage of Virgen del Mar is on with the middle of the road to Santander, both objects being a little west of the peak of Viérnoles ; and Cabrera islet appears within Ballota point.

The above part of the coast is low and rugged, but higher towards the interior, forming a long and even range as far as cape Mayor. An inner range running east and west, which is the Alameda Alta de Santander, and the village of Cueto with numerous houses and buildings are seen, and above these ridges the Peña Castillo, 396 feet high, rises from the shore of Santander inlet.

Between San Juan del Canal point and Somocueva point, at 2½ miles south westward, the coast is broken, low, and cliffy, with sandy beaches. It is fronted at a short distance from the shore by a chain of rocks above water, known by the name of Urros de Liencres. There is a channel between the rocks and also between them and the shore for small craft in fine weather. But outside them the bottom is foul, and no vessel of any size should approach them. Somocueva point, called also Liencres, is rather low, rugged, and projects westward. The low coast following for 2½ miles to Cuerno point forms a bay, and as far as Aquila point 1¼ miles on, is a clean flat sandy shore, off which breakers extend a long distance out.

A small islet lies off Aquila point, and eastward of it the river Mogro or Pas falls into the sea, passing on the western side and at the foot of the hill of the same name. The bar can only be crossed by boats at high water and in fine weather, for at low water it is dry. In the river there is sufficient water for small craft, and in the winter it is swollen by freshes.

The **LIENCRES HEIGHTS** rise between Somocueva point and Mogro peak ; they are of a dark colour, extend 1½ miles N.N.E. and S.S.W., and on the southern part there are two well-defined peaks resembling a saddle ; the southern peak being the higher, and 695 feet above the sea. The town of Liencres, remarkable by its high church tower, is seen at the northern part at the foot of the heights. Extensive sands of a light red colour, named Val-deiarena or Liencres, between Somocueva and Aquila points, extend in from the shore and about 165 feet up the slope of the heights, and can be seen at a distance of 15 miles. It is the only elevated land on the coast between Suances and Santander, and is a good mark for vessels from the westward for the latter port, and cannot be mistaken.

PICO de MOGRO is a small isolated conical hill about 535 feet above the sea, and the village of the same name, with about 400 inhabitants, stands on its north side. The peak is conspicuous, and used as a mark for San Martin de la Arena. The mariner is warned not to mistake this peak for that of Cavada, nor the sand of Val-de-Arena for that of Puntal (page 145).

CUERNO POINT, the east point of entrance to San Martin de la Arena, projects northward, and terminates in a reef which connects it to Demetria islet, nearly a cable distant. On the western side of the point are several rocks which only show at low water, the outermost of which are called Joaquina and Jarillo ; the latter is 1¼ cables W. by S. from the point.

SUANCES ISLANDS.—A group of five islands, denominated the Suances, lie off Cuerno point. The northern and largest, named Cabrera or Conejos, is 2 cables in length, and half a cable in breadth. It is bounded all round by cliffs, difficult of access, and its east end is 175 feet high. When seen from the westward it appears small and square from its being end on. It may be approached to a short distance, as it is bold and clear of danger ; the rocks on the south side are connected to its shore. The west end of the island is 3 cables distant from Cuerno point.

Between Cabrera island and Cuerno point is Demetria island, low and surrounded by reefs. There is a clear narrow channel between the islands, carrying 4¼ and 5¼ fathoms water, but no passage betweeen Demetria and the point, except for small craft at high water. The three other islands, Casilda, Segunda, and Solita, lie eastward of Demetria, with channels between them for small craft. At about three-quarters of a mile W.S.W., of Cuerno point is Afuera, the inner point of entrance to the inlet of San Martin de la Arena ; the coast between forms two smalls bays separated by Umbrera point. The western bay is the larger, and contains a small beach named Playa del Patrocinio ; the shore of the other is steep rock. Whilst Cuerno point and the islands off it bound the east side of entrance to San Martin de la Arena, Dichoso, and Torco de Afuera points are on the western side.

SAN MARTIN de la ARENA or SUANCES.—This inlet, although nearly 3¼ cables wide at the entrance proper, is narrowed within by sand banks on either side which dry at low water, leaving a channel from about a half to a cable wide. The entrance is entirely open to the north, and the points of Dichoso and Torco de Afuera afford only slight shelter from north-west and westerly winds. The bar is constantly shifting; every gale and every fresh of the river changes it. When the latter is strong the water forces itself through the sand and leaves a channel 6 or 7 feet deep; but a gale from the northward causes the sand to accumulate, and to dry at low water.*

The average depth on the bar may be about 2 feet at low water springs, and the channel within carries from 3 to 20 feet; the nature of the bottom is mud or muddy sand nearly throughout, and in places the latter depth is found close to the shore at low water. Vessels intended for this inlet should not draw more than 9 or 10 feet, for although vessels of 11 to 12 feet draught can enter under favourable circumstances, much time is lost in waiting for spring tides, which are not always accompanied with moderate winds and a smooth sea, and thus two or three months may be lost. A small lift of the sea always prevails on the bar, and 4 or 5 feet should be allowed for the descent of the vessel.

The bar may be taken in all winds, except those from S.E. to S.W., whenever the state of the tide and sea admits. At the time of a great fresh, which will be known by the colour of the water some distance outside, the entrance should not be attempted on account of the strength of the stream. The land on either side of the inlet is covered with wood and meadow, and scattered with villages and farm houses. The principal village of the inlet is Suances, containing about 550 inhabitants. It stands on a height on the western side, is the first village on entering, and here the pilots, the marine authorities, and the health officer reside.

Requejada is a small village with large granaries, which give it an imposing appearance, about 5 miles up by the bend of the inlet, on the eastern bank, near the high road from Santander to the interior. At low water there are 12 to 13 feet, mud, near the landing place of the village, and foreign vessels having cargoes of grain and material for the railways proceed here to discharge. No other description of merchandise is allowed to be disembarked; vessels arriving in ballast discharge it at Suances. This port, as well as those of Comillas and San Vicente de la Barquera, are in the vice-consulate of Santander.

The rivers Saja and Besaya during the rainy season discharge so much

---

* See Admiralty plan :—Bar and entrance of San Martin de la Arena ; scale m = 5 inches, on chart of Spain, North and West coasts, No. 2,728.

water into the inlet that it overcomes the stream of flood tide, and renders it difficult for a vessel to make way against it.

LIGHTS.—On Torco de Afuera point is a white tower, which exhibits, at 118 feet above the sea, a *fixed* white light, visible at a distance of 7 miles.

Tides.—It is high water, full and change, at the bar of San Martin de la Arena, at 3h. 30m.; springs rise 15 feet. The stream runs in the direction of the channel 4 miles an hour between Atalaya and Marsan points, and increases considerably in the freshes. The swell generally rolls in heavily with north-west winds; and with fresh winds from S.W. to N.W. the water rises from one to 2 feet above the usual level of high tide, but winds from the opposite quarter depress it from one to 2 feet. The entrance should be approached by the larger vessels that enter, on the flood.

Pilots.—Pilots are indispensable for this river. When unable to go out, they wait inside the breakers, and the vessel is then guided by the signals made from a green hillock about 55 feet high, called the Atalaya, on the first point on the western side within the entrance. From the Atalaya the bar and channel are distinctly seen, and a white flag is held in the direction the vessel should steer. When the bar is passable the flag is kept in a vertical position; when impassable it is waved to and fro.

Directions.—When bound to San Martin de la Arena, the light-tower on cape Mayor, the heights and sand of Liencres, the peak of Mogro, and Cabrera island, are good marks on the east; whilst on the west are Ballota point high and steep, the Meseta de Cortiguera, and the heights 400 feet high, on which stands the town and church of Suances on the west side of the inlet, and the white lighthouse on Torco de Afuera point, at the entrance to the inlet. If the low coast land cannot be made out, and that in the interior is clear, the peak of Viérnoles, 1,600 feet above the sea, which rises S.S.E. ¼ E. from the entrance of the inlet, is a good distant mark. In closing with the inlet the rocks west of Cuerno point should be avoided.

Pilot Signals.—If the bar be passable, and a pilot unable to come out, it will be requisite in entering to observe strictly the direction the flag is waved from the Atalaya within the entrance. While the flag is held upright the vessel is to keep on her course, but if pointed to port or starboard, steer in that direction until the flag is again held upright. When within the bar the pilot will board and take charge of the vessel. If too much sea or little water, the flag will be waved from side to side, and the vessel should stand off. If on returning to the entrance the flag is held stationary, the bar may be taken, but the mariner must consider the tide and vessel's draught.

Dichoso Point, the west point at entrance to San Martin de la Arena, is low, rocky, and of a light colour, with a rounded hill on it named the Alto del Dichoso. A narrow low neck separates it from the inner land, which makes it appear at a long distance from the westward like an island. A bank about 20 yards in extent, with 15 and 16 fathoms water on it, lies N. by W. ¼ W. 2 miles from Dichoso point. Between it and the point there are from 25 to 28 fathoms, decreasing to 18 fathoms near the point; and at a short distance outside it 36 to 55 fathoms. It is named the Canto, and in strong winds there is a heavy sea on it, and a wide berth should be given to it. When the Luaña and Torriente banks break, this does also and it probably forms part of the same (page 153).

BALLOTA POINT is a remarkable salient steep black point. It lies 1¼ miles north-east of Santa Justa, and is sometimes called Negra point. Reefs extend from it, and the Percebera rock, about the size of a ship's launch, dries at low water a short distance from its extremity. The rock is steep-to, and there is a passage inside it for small craft. The coast between this point and Dichoso eastward forms the bay of Garrera. Outside the bay the bottom is clean, and water deep.

CALDERON POINT is low, rocky, projecting. The point is sub-divided into two; one point projects to the N.E., the other to the N.W., and respectively afford shelter for boats from east and west winds, on sandy bottom, but the shore is rocky. At a short distance from the coast the depth is from 13 to 22 fathoms. The coast N.E. of the point is higher, in places covered with vegetation, but generally bare, showing the light-coloured rock of which it is formed. The beach of Santa Justa is at the head of a bay, and a chapel of the same name stands on the shore close to the rocks on the western part of the beach. At a short distance eastward of Santa Justa beach, separated by a rocky ridge, is a more extensive beach, but foul with a heavy sea on it.

The coast between the heights of Santa Justa and Calderon point is foul and rocky. At 2 miles west of Calderon point is Carrastrada point, with outlying rocks, the coast between being cliffy with ravines. At a moderate distance from the shore the church of San Pedro is seen standing between the points on a hill near the shore, conspicuous on account of its tower and isolation.

SAN VINCENTE de LUAÑA.—The bay of Luaña is choked with sand, and has a clean extensive beach. A small river descends through a ravine over the beach to the sea. On Ruiloba or Luaña point, at the west extremity of the bay, is the hermitage of San Vicente, and on the heights above and a little inland stands the town of Ruiloba. To the eastward of the point and the rocks which surround it, fishing craft find shelter from westerly winds. A vessel under the necessity of running ashore to save the crew should, if possible, select the middle of Luaña beach, and at high water. It is seen at a long distance, and is the only beach of any extent between San Martin de la Arena and Comillas. The coast between Carrastrada point and San Vicente de Luaña at 2 miles to the south-west is low, but higher near the former point.

REMEDIOS POINT.—At a mile westward of Ruiloba point is Remedios point, salient, with a reef extending a short distance from it. Two large and remarkable caverns from their dark colour appear in the cliff east of the point. The church of Nuestra Señora de los Remedios, conspicuous from its size and isolated position, stands on a hill above the point a short distance from the shore. It is a good mark for the port of Comillas.

A little south-west of Remedios point is Miradorio point, which is rocky and of moderate height, with reefs extending some distance from it. Between this point and Puerto Comillas, west of it, there is a bay with a narrow beach fronted with reefs. A small stream of water falls into the bay, and east of it, close to the shore and the base of the cliffs of Miradorio, is a calcinating establishment, from which the mines are but a short distance.

TORRIENTE and LUAÑA BANKS.—To the northward of the above points, and at 3½ to 4 miles from the coast, are two rocky banks, which are dangerous when there is much sea. The eastern bank, named the Torriente, is about a cable in length N.W. and S.E., with 10 to 12 fathoms least water on it, 45 to 55 fathoms mud on its north edge, and 27 to 37 fathoms between it and the shore. It lies 4 miles from the coast, and from the least depth on it Cabrera island bears S.E. by E. ¾ E.; the beach of Luaña, S. by W. ¾ W.; cape Oyhambre, W. by S. ¼ S.; and mount San Cosme, W. ¼ S.

The westernmost bank, called the Luaña, 2 miles W.S.W. of the former, is of small extent, with 11 to 17 fathoms water on it, and on its outer edge 35 to 45 fathoms, increasing to 55 fathoms, muddy bottom; between the bank and the coast there are from 27 to 32 fathoms, sand and rock. From it Cabrera island bears E.S.E.; the beach of Luaña, S. ¼ E.; and mount San Cosme, W. ¼ S. It breaks with much sea from the north-west, and the breakers are very heavy. The Torriente is equally dangerous; but a vessel may pass over either bank in fine weather.

PORT COMILLAS.—The small port of this name is in a little bay on the east side of Castillo point, which is rugged with a reef extending to the N.E., affording some shelter to the bay. The point derives its name from the fortress which still remains 'on it. The village of Comillas, containing about 1,300 inhabitants, stands on a hill about a mile S. by E. of the point. A small port is formed in the bay by two piers, enclosing a space sufficient only for fishing craft of the neighbouring coast. It is entirely dry at low water, and the bottom is muddy sand; the entrance is open to the N.N.E. and about 8 yards wide.*

The channel to the port is 'narrow, tortuous, shallow, bordered by reefs, and can only be taken in moderate weather with the assistance of a pilot and boats. Vessels as large as 120 tons burthen enter the port for minerals, but it is inconvenient for those of more than 70 or 80 tons, ten only of which are admitted at the same time. There is much swell in the port when there is any sea outside, although the entrance is somewhat protected by a kind of half gate formed of strong wooden bars. Two white conical pillars are placed on the heights, and when in line lead to the middle of the bar. At night when the weather is bad, each pillar is lighted, and also a temporary fire is made as a guide for the fishing craft.

At a moderate distance from the shore the establishment for calcinating minerals, standing 6 cables E.S.E. of the mouth, is easily seen, the chimneys of which, and surrounding worksheds, render it conspicuous, and are the only buildings of the kind to be seen on the whole coast. At the same time the walls of the mole, the masts of the vessels inside, and the village scattered over a hill will be observed. To the westward of the port, cape Oyhambre, the sands of Meron and Rábia, and the heights over the inlet of San Vicente de la Barquera are good marks; whilst to the eastward are the islands at the mouth of San Martin de la Arena, the sands of Luaña, the town of Suances, and the white lighthouse on Torco de Afuera point.

The mariner will observe that the village of Comillas is to the eastward of the extensive sands of Meron and Rábia, and that San Vicente de la Barquera is westward of the sands.

MORIA POINT, at a short distance west of Castillo point, is low and cliffy, and surrounded by reefs at a considerable distance off. The most dangerous of these is called the Moro, and the breakers on it are extensive. Between this point and the islet of Rábia, west of it, the shore is of sand, broken by rocky points. The coast westward to San Vicente de la Barquera is low and undulating, but high in the interior.

CAPE OYHAMBRE, at 2¼ miles westward of Moria point, presents to the N.N.W. a face of a mile in extent, with small hills and whitish cliffs; the former are from 150 to 170 feet above the sea. It is

---

* *See* Admiralty plan :—Comillas anchorage, on sheet of plans, No. 710.

also known by the sands of Meron on the west, and the sands of Rábia on the east. Nowhere on the coast, from San Martin de la Arena to cape Prieto, are the sands so extensive and so close together.

From the western extreme of the cape reefs extends in a N.W. direction for a distance of about three-quarters of a mile; and from the eastern side others of no less importance extend in an E.N.E. direction. From the face of the cape several rocks and reefs extend off, on the outer of which at times there is a considerable north-west sea. There are 17 and 18 fathoms water at 2 miles from the cape. In bad weather a berth of 3 or 4 miles should be given to it.

La Molar.—On the eastern reef there is a conical rock of this name, on which the sea frequently breaks, and when it does it breaks also on Comillas bar. The fishermen watch for the breakers on La Molar to know the state of Comillas bar.

RÁBIA BAY.—On the east side of the cape Oyhambre the coast bends in to the south-west, forming the bay of Rábia, which is surrounded by a beach of nearly the same extent, whiteness, and elevation as that of Meron, west of the cape. The bay is so encumbered with rocks that there is only one part of it clear, which is near the cape, and for which the fishing boats make in strong winds from N.W. to S.W. when they cannot approach their own ports. But for a stranger to go between the reefs it would be necessary to have the aid of a pilot.

An inlet named Rábia is formed at the eastern extreme of the sandy beach. Its bar is changeable and dry at low water, but within, small craft lie afloat. A long low islet lying east and west fronts the bar, and at low water is surrounded by sand. Vessels enter the inlet to load with building wood for La Barquera. It should be approached at the west end of the islet at high water and in fine weather, for the bar breaks with the least sea on; vessels go up to the bridge of Rábia, which crosses the inlet, for the road to Comillas. There is no village, but a house or two close to the bridge. To the eastward of the islet is Cabrero point, steep, with a reef extending to the north-west.

Meron Sand.—From the west side of cape Oyhambre, the extensive white sands of Meron (sable de Meron) extend 1¾ miles westward fronting mount Braña, and terminating within and nearly choking up the inlet of Barquera.

SAN VICENTE de la BARQUERA is a large inlet on the south-west side of cape Oyhambre. It runs to the south-west, and is divided by a rocky height into two arms; the western called Ria del Peral, and the southern that of Villegas or Barcenal. The first extends more than 1½ miles inland, and leads past the bridge of Nuevo or Tras

San Vicente with its nine arches to the barrio or district of Entram-bosrios; whilst the other arm runs about 3 miles in, and leads to the barrio of Barcenal. By the latter arm, flat-bottomed craft go up to the factories with iron, under the bridge of Maza with its 32 arches, and 1,594 feet in length.*

The town of San Vicente de la Barquera contains only about 850 inhabitants; it consists of two parts, an old and a modern. The old houses stand on the crest of the rocky height which divides the inlet into two arms, and the modern part stands on the eastern slope, extending to the edge of the sand, and so close that the sea occasionally reaches the doors of the houses. On the highest part, where the old town stands, is a handsome conspicuous white church, 230 feet above the sea, and the remains of a castle.

Point de la Silla, a low rocky point with a stone light-tower upon it, 140 feet high, lies on the west side of entrance, and between it and another point named Castillo, a cable southward of it, there are isolated rocks which cover at high water. At half a cable off Castillo point is the rocky islet of Callo or Peña Mayor, 50 feet high, 160 yards in length, and in bad weather the sea washes over it. The islet is connected with the point by a reef with only 3 feet on it at low water, which however forms the western passage into the islet, and is used with north-west winds by passing close to the west end of the inlet. Another islet called Peña Menor lies N.E. of Callo, the space between being dry at low water ; and at half a cable north of the latter islet is the Plancha rock, awash at low water springs.

Between the above islets and rocks on the north, and the sands of Meron, bordering mount Braña on the south, is the eastern passage into the inlet, which is used with north-east winds. The sands of Meron are dry at low water springs, and form various banks with channels between them; the sand is gradually drawing towards Callo islet, and threatens at no distant period to unite with it. The depth of water east of the islet is therefore constantly lessening, and requires frequent examination. The inlet in former times was resorted to by vessels of large draught, but as it is now almost choked up with sand, it is frequented only by vessels of 9 to 11 feet draught.

The western or Peral channel is the one most frequently used, and at high water there is sufficient depth for vessels of 11 to 14 feet draught to proceed as far as Nuevo bridge, where there is a hole or well large enough for two or three vessels to lie afloat, secured head and stern. The only inconvenience is the swell when it blows hard from north-west. In

---

* See Admiralty plan :—San Vicente de la Barquera, No. 725 ; scale, m ~ 8 inches.

entering the inlet, whether passing east or west of Callo, it is necessary to keep the islet aboard. The long mark given for steering in eastward of Callo islet is the church of San Vicente de la Barquera, in line with the south side of the islet. The long mark for going in westward of Callo is the ruins of an old house called Maza, in one with the west end of the islet A stranger should have the aid of a pilot.

The breaks in the Tinas, page 159, are good marks for vessels from the westward for San Vicente de la Barquera, and also mount San Cosme or Rabo del Cabo, as it is called by the country seaman. To the eastward of the Tinas the land declines, and terminates in the low rocky point. of Silla and Castillo. The inlet may be entered with the wind from any quarter but the south-west. It should not be attempted till half flood or nearly high water, according to the vessel's draught, and never on the ebb. When the state of the weather prevents the pilots from going outside they remain under the lee of Callo islet, and direct the course of the vessel as usual by means of a flag.

Mounts Escudo and Burgon.—The mountain of Escudo, rugged and barren, running east and west, rises inland southward of Barquera to a peak 3,288 feet above the sea, and bears S. by W. ¼ W. from the summit of mount Boria. Mount Burgon, forming a cone 1,051 feet high, 3 miles southward of Barquera, will also be recognized.

These mountains are good distant marks for vessels coming from sea for Barquera, and as the land is approached, the islets of Callo and Peña Menor, and the white sands of Meron will be seen. There are no other sands of large extent but to the eastward.

LIGHT.—On point de la Silla, at the west side of entrance to San Vicente de la Barquera, a white stone tower shows, at an elevation of 142 feet above the sea level, a *fixed red* light, visible in clear weather at a distance of 9 miles.

Tides.—It is high water, full and change, at San Vicente de la Barquera, at 3 h. ; springs rise 12 feet. With strong winds from S.W. round by West to North, the water rises 2 feet above the ordinary level, and the winds from N.E. to S.E. cause a depression to the same amount. The ebb stream runs 3 knots per hour at springs, and 2 knots at neaps.

PELLEREZO POINT.—Between Silla point at the entrance to Barquera, and Linera point, a third of a mile westward, the coast is bordered at the distance of a quarter of a mile by a ledge of rocks with one to 2 feet water on them, and which uncover at low springs ; there are 5 fathoms close to them, and 2½ to 3½ fathoms between the ledge and the shore. Linera point projects to the N.W. from mount Boria, a ridge of some 350 feet high. Pellerezo point at about 2¼ miles westward of Silla point is low and steep; the land eastward of this point descends in gentle declivities to a low undulating coast, but to the westward the part intersected by the Tinas inlets is high and level, and specially marks this part of the coast. The high land in the interior, to the eastward, is not so rugged, nor have the mountains so many peaks as those to the westward.

Between San Vicente de la Barquera and Llanes there is a large extent of level coast some 650 feet high, with three breaks or ravines nearly equidistant from each other, the middle and most conspicuous one being the Tina Mayor. Between it and Tina del Oeste or Santiuste, over the table land of the coast, is the village of Pimiango, and on a slope of the hill not far from the shore is the hermitage of San Emeterio. The False Tinas is a name given to some breaks in the bay of San Antolin, ria de Niebro, and the bays of Celorio and Póo, which appear like the real Tinas. The land of the coast about these points has much the same appearance, and in bad weather the higher land of the interior cannot be seen, but the Tina Mayor at a moderate distance will be known by the light-tower on San Emeterio point.

TINA MENOR or del ESTE.—At two-thirds of a mile westward of Pellerezo point is the entrance to the inlet of Tina Menor or del Este, which trends with high land on either side north and south through a channel 1¼ cables in breadth, and three-quarters of a mile in length, when the inlet widens out, and at high water appears of considerable extent; but at low water it is nearly dry, with a shallow winding stream about 40 yards in breadth between the banks of mud and weeds. The bar is dry at low water, and the inlet is only used by boats. The small village of Pesués, containing about 320 inhabitants, stands on the western side a short distance within the mouth.

Pechon point.—To the westward of Vigia point, on the west side of entrance to Tina Menor, is a rugged islet, off the east end of a small bay, with a shingle beach. The steep point of Pechon follows, and the village of the same name stands on the north slope of a hill midway between the Tinas Menor and Mayor. The land over the shore is high and level, like that between Tina Mayor and Santiuste, but as it descends it becomes uneven, and terminates in cliffs. Close to the entrance of Tina Mayor there is a beach of white sand, and at the western part of it is the east point of entrance to the inlet, with rocks off it, several of which uncover at low water. The bottom is rocky, and there are about 25 fathoms water, at 2 miles from the shore.

TINA MAYOR.—The entrance to this inlet, about 2¼ miles westward of Tina Menor, is open to the north, less than three-quarters of a cable in breadth, and formed by high steep hills on either side. At about three-quarters of a mile within the entrance the elevated land recedes on both sides, leaving between a spacious cultivated plain, through which the river Deva runs into the inlet. The village of Bústio, with about 200 inhabitants, stands on the western side of the Deva, at about 1½ miles within the entrance of the inlet. Beyond the high land closes and forms a narrow valley, through which the river runs.*

Vessels of only 9 to 11 feet draught frequent the inlet, although those of 13 to 14 feet can enter under favourable circumstances; they lie aground at low water on soft mud, about half a mile from the entrance. Small vessels go as far as Bústio, where there is a well or hole with 6 feet in it at low water, but it can only be reached at high water, for a shingle bank in the channel dries at low tide. The exports are iron and timber. There are no supplies.

After a north-west gale the inlet is often closed by sand-banks, but the pent up water of the Deva soon forces the usual passage. The freshes of the river, however, cause in some places an accumulation of gravel, which uncovers at low water, narrows the channel through which vessels have to pass, and at about a quarter of a mile within the entrance, between the gravel and western shore, it is only about 30 yards in breadth. From the east point of entrance rocks extend northward 1½ cables, and those nearest the shore dry at low water. With strong north-east and north-west winds flaws and eddies blow over the high land which forms the entrance, making it difficult to enter ; and on these occasions the sea breaks heavily on the bar. It should not be attempted when the freshes are strong, which will be known by the discolouration of the water.

It is easy to leave the Tina Mayor, for the land wind never fails about daylight, and enables a vessel to get clear of the coast.

LIGHT.—On San Emeterio point, at 1½ miles westward of the entrance to Tina Mayor, is a light blue tower with a white lantern, which exhibits at 223 feet above the sea a *fixed* white light, seen in clear weather at a distance of 15 miles.

Tides.—It is high water, full and change, at the entrance to Tina Mayor, at 3 h. ; springs rise 11 feet. The tide is felt as far up as Molleda, a village on the eastern bank of the Deva, a little above Bústio, and where the flood tide only lasts for 2 hours, being overcome by the river stream. The ebb stream runs from 3 to 4 miles an hour at Bústio, whilst the flood is scarcely perceptible.

The Deva and its tributary, the Cares, discharges a considerable quantity of water into the sea, the stream running at not less than 7 or 8

* *See* Admiralty plan :—Ria de Tina Mayor, No. 723 ; scale, m = 5·8 inches.

miles an hour during the freshes, and between 2 and 3 miles on ordinary occasions. In the spring and until the month of July, if the snow during winter has been heavy, the freshes are strong.

Water from the Deva may be used by shipping in any part of the river at low tide, as it is fresh nearly to the entrance.

TINA del OESTE.—The coast westward as far as the west Tina is formed of cliffs and small shingle beaches. The last of the Tinas or great bays is called Tina del Oeste or Santiuste. It extends to the S.W., but is completely choked with sand and gravel, so that only small craft and boats can cross the bar at high water. The little river Cabra falls into the sea at the west end of the beach. The islet of Castron de Santiuste lies in the entrance of this Tina, but nearer the western coast; it is connected with the shore by reefs which scarcely cover at high water. When the islet bears about S.W. ½ S. the bay is open and an extensive sandy beach is seen, conspicuous from its whiteness in contrast to the dark rocky shore.

BALLOTA POINT, at nearly 5 miles westward of Tina del Oeste, is level, and projects to the N.N.E., forming a sandy bay on either side of it. At about a cable off it is an islet of the same name, nearly the same height and appearance as the point, flat and steep on all sides, with a passage between it and the point for small craft. When in one with the point bearing S.W. ½ S. the two sandy beaches are visible, the larger being to the eastward. A mile eastward of the islet is the little bay of Puron, and a rivulet of the same name runs into it. At a mile farther east is Vidiago point and the village near it. To the eastward of it is a small shingle beach, and next to it is Pendueles point, steep and rocky. There are one or two small islets and rocks close off this part of the coast, and a wide berth should be given to it.

SANTA CLARA POINT.—The coast immediately east of Llanes is formed of cliffs, which are washed by the sea, the interior being high, mountainous, and barren. The point Santa Clara projects northward, and is 1¼ miles distant from Llanes. Close westward of the point and near the shore there are three islets called Canales. Another islet, called Toro or Manuela, lies westward of them, and is connected to the shore.

LLANES.—This small port admits coasters of about 6 feet draught. Its mouth is open to the eastward, and formed between Calaverojondo and Caballo points. At about 65 yards eastward of the latter point is a rock named Osa, which uncovers at low water springs. Between it and the point there are 2¾ fathoms water, sand; and between it and the opposite shore 3 to 3½ fathoms, but the interior of the harbour is dry at low water. A vessel may enter on either side of the Osa; the eastern channel is the wider, but not so easy to navigate. To enter by the western channel, bring a chapel standing on the south side of the entrance of the port in line with another chapel seen on a height bearing S.W. ¼ S. nearly. A beacon is to be placed on the Osa. The port should be entered with a smooth sea, and a stranger should have the aid of a pilot and the assistance of a boat, as the channel is narrow and winding. The town of Llanes contains about 1,250 inhabitants. The little river Carrocedo empties itself in the port.

LIGHT.—On San Antonio point, on the southern shore of the mouth of the port, is an octagonal white lighthouse, which exhibits, at 64 feet above the sea, a *fixed* white light visible 9 miles.

Aspect.—The peaks of the mountains named Urrieles de Llanes rise 8,900 feet above the sea, 12 miles south of the town, and are good distant marks for it. That named Naranjo de Bulnes, 8,622 feet high, is one of the most remarkable points of the chain, from its isolation, barren, and pyramidical form. Between the Urrieles and the coast there is another chain, not so high, named Sierra de Cuera, extending east and west, with a remarkable peak rising above the middle of it called Mojon, which is about 3,060 feet high, and less than 5 miles south of Llanes. The Mojon and Naranjo de Bulnes in line lead to the entrance of Llanes.

On approaching the coast the town of Jarri will be seen on a height, and the pilots' watchhouse, round and white, on San Pedro point, west-ward of the town, the church of Guia on a height eastward of the town, and the white lighthouse of the port.

PALO de PÓO ISLET.—The bay of Póo, next west of Llanes, is somewhat larger than that of Celorio, from which it is a mile eastward. It has a beach through which the rivulet Guera runs into the sea, the mouth of which is entered by small coasters at high water. The town of this latter name, with a population of about 500, is a little inland and visible from seaward. Off the eastern part of Póo bay there are some islets, the outermost and most remarkable is called Palo de Póo. It has the form of a pyramid, and seen either from east or west appears like a ship under sail. It may be approached to a short but prudent distance.

NIEMBRO INLET, on the east side of cape Prieto, runs south and south-west for 3 cables to a beautiful fine sandy basin on the N.W., and another to the S.E. The entrance is about two-thirds of a cable wide between Cueva Ladrona point on the east, and Borizo point on the west. The channel varies from about 45 to 110 yards in breadth, with only 8 feet at the entrance at low water, when the interior is dry. The bottom is a muddy sand, on which coasters of about 7 feet draught ground, having entered the inlet at high water. The best berth is to the south-east, near

o   17801.   L the church; the passage is in between the islets. Keep mid-channel and steer by the light colour of the bottom; the rocks on either side show by their dark colour.

The village of Niembro, which contains about 300 inhabitants, is in the N.W. angle of the basin. The belfry of the church alone is seen outside when north of the entrance. The little river of the above name discharges itself between the two basins, and the water is good for drinking.

Tides.—It is high water, full and change, at Niembro inlet at 3h.; springs rise about 11 feet. The interior of the inlet dries at three-quarters ebb, so that the greatest rise of water above the ground is from 8 to 9 feet within the basin, and a little more in the channel leading to it. The stream is said to run out about $1\frac{1}{2}$ miles an hour.

Borizo Island, at a short mile eastward of the Niembro, is nearly circular, steep on all sides, flat, and about the same height as the point to which it is connected by reefs, over which there is scarcely water for a boat. There are two small islets on its western side. To the eastward of Borizo is the little bay and islets of Celorio. The town of this name, with 500 inhabitants, stands a little way back in the interior, but a convent only is seen from the sea, and near it an old Benedictine college on a cliff of the coast. Two islets like Borizo lie a short distance from the shore east of Celorio.

CAPE PRIETO.—Jarri point, west of Llanes, is salient and steep, with a look-out house on it and a small bay on the eastern side. Cape Prieto, 4 miles to the westward, is of moderate height, with a gentle slope to the sea, terminating in steep rugged rocks, which are only seen when near, and east or west of the cape. The north face of the coast forming the cape rises from the east end of San Antolin beach, and terminates to the E.N.E. in a projecting rocky point, which is the real cape. On a hill over it are the remains of a look-out tower. In the front of the cape there is a strip of clean beach at the head of a small bay, and some rocks, which appear isolated at high water, lie along the shore of the cape.

A rock named Vaca lies E.N.E. distant, $1\frac{1}{2}$ cables from the cape, and uncovers at low water. It is dangerous when covered with smooth water, but when there is any sea it breaks. There are $4\frac{1}{2}$ to $5\frac{1}{2}$ fathoms between the rock and cape, and coasters use the channel in fine weather. At a cable south of the Vaca is a small islet called Peyes, and from it a reef extends westward, showing a head at low water, which then appears like an islet; there are $4\frac{1}{2}$ to $5\frac{1}{2}$ fathoms water between it and the Vaca. There are several other islets and rocks to the south-west or inshore of the latter, with channels between them for boats; and a clean sandy beach named Toranda between cape Prieto and the mouth of the Niembro, sheltered from the north and north-west seas by the above rocks, and which serves as a refuge for fishing craft.

SAN ANTOLIN BEACH.—To the westward of cape Prieto and eastward of Huelga point, which projects a little, there is a small islet ; the shore in this latter direction is low and rocky as far as San Antolin beach, which is about a mile in extent, and terminates at Pistaña point, a short distance off which there is an islet. The beach is of shingle and sand of remarkable whiteness, and conspicuous at a distance. It is scattered with rocks at either end, which extend 2 cables from the shore, and uncover at low water, having a beach of 2 cables between them. The river Bedon or San Antolin falls into the sea near the west end of the beach, and in winter is a large stream. The ravine through which it descends may be seen at a great distance.

Many navigators in a gale have sought this beach for safety, and have lost their lives in consequence of not being aware of the above rocks. The convent of San Antolin, the only building near the beach and east of the river, in line with the road on the summit of a ridge, leads between the rocks ; the beach of San Antonio, near cape Mar, should, however, be preferred, being less flat, clean, and of fine sand, and off which vessels may anchor under favourable circumstances, and be sheltered from north-west and westerly winds. The winds from north to east blow on it, but life may be saved.

CAPE de MAR is low, steep, and projects to the N.E. It is easily recognized in running along the land, but difficult to make out from seaward, as it then appears blended with the cliffs near it. It is bold, and may be approached to a moderate distance, but there is much sea off it in bad weather. On the east side of the cape the shore forms an angle with a little beach named San Antonio del Mar, where fishing craft resort to when surprised by a westerly or north-west gale. The land near the coast eastward of the cape becomes higher, and the rugged peaks in the interior are covered with snow.

NUEVA RIVER.—The coast from cape de Mar forms a slight bay westward for about 2¼ miles to the Nueva river, which passes near the town of the same name; it falls into the sea through a small clean sandy beach named Cuevas de Mar. Fishing boats find refuge in the . river during bad weather, entering at high water ; it is easily distinguished by the ravine and white beach, being the only one between cape de Mar and Rivadesella. A little westward of it is the islet of Orcado de

Cuevas a short distance from the shore, but the channel between is foul and rocky.

At about 2 miles westward of the Nueva is the mouth of the little river Aguamia; its eastern point is a high, bold cliff, and the southern low. Between the two rivers is a small cape called Villanueva, and the village of the same name is near it.

RIVADESELLA HARBOUR.—The entrance to this harbour is 4 cables wide, and lies between mount Guia or Corbero on the east, and monte Somos somewhat higher, on the west. Between these two hills the shore is of white sand, called Santa Marina, which in the form of a crescent nearly connects them. A narrow channel, varying in breadth from about 55 to 90 yards, and carrying from 8 to 21 feet at low water, runs along by a mole on the southern side of mount Guia to the town, and which is bounded on the west by the Santa Marina, and other detached banks. As the north shore of mount Guia is rocky, and a reef with 5 feet on it at low water, extends from Caballo point, its north-east extreme ; in entering the port with an easterly wind, a berth should be given to it.*

The only part of the mole seen from seaward is its high solid head, with the flagstaff ; it abuts against the cliffs which descend from the heights, on which stands the temple of Guia, and is therefore easily recognized. Between the mole head and the edge of Santa Marina sands is the bar of the inlet, with about 8 feet at low water springs, and 20 feet at high water ; at neaps there are 11 feet at low water, and about 17 feet at high water.

When there is much sea from the north-west it breaks between Caballo point and the mole head, and renders the entrance almost impassable. In case it should be absolutely necessary to enter, good way should be kept on the vessel so as to keep before the sea. About 3 cables within the bar there is ample security in 21 feet at low water, where vessels generally moor or secure to the mole. Small vessels go further in, and should they take the ground at low water the bottom is soft. Within the north part of the town different channels are formed through the banks of mud and sand.

The town of Rivadesella contains about 1,000 inhabitants. The trade is small, the chief exports being staves and nuts.

Directions.—In entering the harbour steer midway between the points at entrance, and then direct for the flagstaff, passing about 35 yards from the mole head, and then along by the mole. When the freshes are running strong the water is discoloured, and a sailing vessel should not enter without a commanding breeze. In winter moor head and stern with

---

* See Admiralty plan :—Harbour of Rivadesella, No. 735 ; scale, m = 7 inches.

the vessel's head up the harbour, and cables fast to the mole so as to be better secured against the freshes. In summer, vessels can lie with their heads out. The swell caused by a north-west gale is inconvenient to vessels moored in the outer part of the port.

Tides.—It is high water, full and change, in Rivadesella harbour, at 2 h. 54 m., being somewhat retarded or accelerated according to north-west or north-east winds; springs rise 12 feet. The ebb stream runs 2 miles an hour at springs, and increases to 5 or 6 miles with the freshes from the Sella; at neaps it runs 1¼ miles an hour.

LIGHT.—On mount Somos, at the western side of entrance to Rivadesella harbour, is a white rectangular lighthouse, with a square tower, which exhibits, at an elevation of 370 feet above the sea, a *fixed* white light, varied by a *flash* every *four minutes*, and visible in clear weather at a distance of 15 miles.

MOUNT GUIA, named also Corbero, is 323 feet high, and is easily recognized by its isolated 'position (being connected to the main by a narrow neck of land), dark colour, and by the white chapel of Guia, situated on a height of 175 feet, over the mole head of Rivadesella. To the eastward of the mount the coast is low, with broken cliffs rising to high land in the interior. The islet of Palo Vorde, of moderate height, in the form of a pyramid, is about three-quarters of a mile eastward of the mount, 55 yards from the shore, and the passage between carries from 7 to 9 fathoms, rock.

Mount Carrandi, 8 miles W.S.W. of Guia, is remarkable from its peaks, and its eastern slope terminates near Rivadesella, so that when bound to this port it will be sufficient to steer for the lowest visible part of the slope of the mountain. Another rugged mountain, with its peaks covered with snow the greater part of the year, will be seen terminating S.S.E. of Rivadesella, it is called Peña Santa, and its summits reach 8,670 feet above the sea; seen from the northward it has the same appearance, from its rugged resemblance, as the mountain of Monserrate.

MOUNT SOMOS.—An arm of land extends eastward from Carreros of Sierra point, and terminates by a rapid descent in the entrance to Rivadesella. Its north-east extreme is named Somos or Berguiz point, and the whole of it forms mount Somos. On the north it presents reddish cliffs, and its available ground for cultivation is of the same colour; it is 343 feet above the sea, and on one of its heights, close to the entrance of Rivadesella, is the lighthouse.

CARREROS POINT and REEFS.—Carreros point is steep, projects northward, and in the same direction, at the distance of 1¼ miles, there are several reefs with 3¾ to 5¼ fathoms water on them. There is a channel between the reefs and the point, which admits coasters. With a strong north-west wind the sea breaks heavily on these reefs, and a berth of at least 2 miles should be given to the point.

SERROPIO BANK is about half a cable in extent east and west, with 8 and 9 fathoms water on it, lying rather more than a mile north of mount Guia, and when there is any sea the breakers on it are extensive. Between it and the shore there are from 14 to 18 fathoms, rock, and the same depth a short distance outside it, deepening rapidly seaward. Although the water inshore of it may not break, vessels should pass seaward of it when there is any sea. From its west end cape Lastres bears N.W. ¾ W., and the chapel of Guia S.W.'

MOUNT CARRANDI.—A high and rugged mountain, named monte de Carrandi, with a town on its northern slope, rises S. by W. from Lastres, 5 miles inland. It extends E.N.E. and W.S.W., with well defined declivities towards these points, and it slopes to the sea shore between Penote and Carrèros point. Its summit is a series of conical peaks, the largest of which, called Pico de Sueve, is more than 3,709 feet above the level of the sea ; and its form and dark colour render it conspicuous at a distance. Spurs from this mountain take a northerly direction, and descend gradually to the sea, terminating in Carreros, Atalayas, and Arrobado points.

Between the two former points there is a beach, called Arenal de Vega, occupying a large portion of an extensive bay, and between the points Arrobado and Atalaya is the Arenal de Moriz. The coast here is much indented, and the shore foul ; it may, however, be approached to a moderate distance. To the eastward and inland of mount Carrandi are rugged and broken mountains interspersed in great confusion, and with them the peaked crests of the Pyrenean chain, almost always covered with snow, are seen for more than 60 miles at sea.

The point of Atalaya with that of Isla, about a mile westward, forms the entrance of a bay which recedes to the south, at the head of which are the extensive sands of Espasa. The village of the latter name is a short distance from the sea on the bank of the river, which runs through the middle of the sands. In summer coasting vessels embark charcoal.

CAPE LASTRES projects northward and is known by its level surface, and by its sudden slope to the sea. Its north face is of reddish cliffs, and at its foot about half a cable off is a rock called Vaca, which uncovers at low water. Small craft may pass inside the rock. Reefs extend some distance from the cape, and in north-west gales the sea breaks more than a mile from the coast. At 1½ miles south-east of the cape is

Misiera point, and a cable off it is the Plancha rock with 5 fathoms water on it; the rest of the coast is of cliffs, and clear of danger.

The little bay of Lastres, south of the point, is sheltered from northwest and westerly gales. The village contains about 760 inhabitants, and a small indifferent mole affords some little shelter to the fishing boats. Vessels occasionally take shelter here from north-west winds, and when unable to enter Rivadesella on account of the sea or want of water.

Anchorage.—The best anchorage is in 6 and 7 fathoms water, mud, with cape Lastres in line with Misiera point, and the Pico del Medio seen to the south-west in line with the hermitage of San Telmo, south of the village, and half-way up the slope of a hill. A vessel from this anchorage would probably clear cape Lastres if caught in a north-east gale.

Colunga River.—At about two-thirds of a mile southward of Lastres, the little river Colunga runs into the sea over a small sandy beach. At high water small coasters enter, and proceed as far as the bridge of Luz, half-way to Colunga, were they load with wood and other produce. The coast southward of Lastres becomes lower, but to the east of the river Colunga is a height named Penote; its base is washed by the sea, and it descends eastward and terminates in a cliffy point of little elevation called Isla, from which a reef extends off, and some of the rocks appear above water.

TAZONES BAY, between Rodiles and Tazones points, bends to S.E., and is backed by high land, which descends rapidly to the sea, and in the middle of it is a break and the village of Tazones, containing about 170 inhabitants. To the north of the village is a conspicuous white chapel, and below the village near the sea is an acient tower. The shore of the bay is rocky, and in the middle of it is a small shingle beach, on which the fishermen haul up their boats, being the only craft belonging to the place. In the middle of the bay and in an easterly direction seaward the bottom is clean sand, and good holding ground.

Anchorage.—Vessels of about 300 tons may anchor here in 6 to 10 fathoms water, with winds from N.W. round by west to S.E., as soon as the chapel and village is open of the land of Tazones point. A vessel taking the anchorage in a north-west gale should give the point a wide berth.

LIGHT.—On Tazones point is a yellow rectangular lighthouse, having a square tower with white lantern, which exhibits a *fixed* white light at an elevation of 220 feet above the level of the sea, visible at a distance of 7 miles.

VILLAVICIOSA INLET, which falls into Tazones bay, presents the appearance of an extensive lake, at high water, forming here and there bays and gullies, bounded by hills covered with trees, vegetation, and scattered villas. But at low water the extensive banks of sand and rushes extend from the eastern to nearly the opposite shore, leaving narrow channels between the numerous marshy islets. The passage over the bar is about 14 yards wide at low water, and 6 to 7 feet deep. The channel within lies along by the western shore, but a pilot is necessary, and one will be found at Tazones.

On the western shore and about 4 cables from the bar is Piedora point which forms the north extreme of the bay and anchorage called Barquero. The shore of this bay is composed of a shingle beach, and beyond San Telmo (its south point), there is another bay larger than the former, named Puntal, frequented by vessels on account of the bottom being soft, and those drawing 9 to 11 feet water, being able to lie afloat at all times. From puntal the channel of the inlet becomes tortuous and shallow, and admits only vessels of 9 feet draught going a mile further up, but those of a lighter draught go on to Espuncia, a loading place from whence merchandise is conveyed by carriage to the town of Villaviciosa, which contains about 750 inhabitants, and stands on the eastern side of the inlet about 3 miles from the sea. The river Viacaba falls into the inlet a little south of the town. The exports are filberts, chesnuts, citron, coal, and lime; and grain is imported.

Tides.—It is high water, full and change, at the bar of Villaviciosa, at 3 h.; and the rise is about 13 feet. In strong north-west winds the tide rises about 2 feet above the usual level of high water, and an hour or more later; whilst north-east and south-east winds depress it to the same amount. The stream at springs runs about 3 miles an hour, but more during the freshes.

RODILES POINT.—From the bar of Villaviciosa the sand of Rodiles extend eastward to the foot of the mount of the same name. The mount is high, isolated, connected to the main by a neck of low land, and a rocky point projects to the N.W. from its foot. Between the point and cape Lastres is the bay of Conejera, and the coast is foul. During fine weather vessels usually anchor off the beach of Rodiles to await the tide for Villaviciosa.

COAST.—Tazones point, about 4-miles westward of cape Lastres, is high, and slopes suddenly to the sea. A wide rocky ledge, which at low water uncovers a cable off, extends some distance from it, which should not be approached too close. Olivo point at 1½ miles westward of the above is high, salient, and appears the same east or west, but from the offing is blended with the other land. A reef extends off a considerable distance, and in a heavy sea should have a wide berth, as in a north-west gale the breakers are more than three-quarters of a mile from the shore. At a mile north of it there are 15 fathoms water, rock. The coast between the point and Barqueta or Meron bay, is covered with vegetation to the edge of the water, but here and there it is of cliffs. It is clear of danger, and may be approached to the distance of a mile.

Entornada point, the western extreme of Barqueta bay, is high, round, and projects seaward. Barqueta bay is small with a sandy beach. Coin point, which is high and steep, forms its eastern extreme, and the coast is similar to it. Small villages and extensive cultivated land with scattered houses are seen on the heights. The coast westward to the high land over cape San Lorenzo is of a regular height, terminating in cliffs, and skirted at the distance of half a cable by large detached rocks, which uncover at low water. At 2 cables outside the rocks there are 8 and 10 fathoms water, at a mile from 15 to 23 fathoms; and at 2 miles 30 fathoms, rocky bottom.

España bay, between Entornada and Peña Rubio points is a mile wide, and rather less than a mile deep; its shores are rocky, and in the middle of it there is sandy beach, through which the little river España falls into the sea. Peña Rubio is high, steep, and a little salient, and at 3½ miles westward is cape Lorenzo, which projects northward, and terminates at the sea in a small dark steep hill. The extremity of the cape seen at high water east or west appears like an island. The land over the cape is high, and on one of the heights is a chapel in ruins, which, with another building on the higher part of the land, are good marks.

On the east side of the cape there are three low black rocks, named Estaño; they are half a mile from the shore, with 3½ to 4½ fathoms water between them, and 7 fathoms between them and the cape. Small vessels at high tide and in fine weather pass between and within them. Pedro bay, westward of Lorenzo point, is obstructed by rocky beds covered with sand, and there is no anchorage. The low marshy land at the head of the bay terminates in a sandy beach, which shows largely at low water, and a reef extends a long distance from Cervigon point on the east side of the bay.

BAY of GIJON, between the hill of Santa Catalina on the west side of San Pedro bay and cape Torres, is 2 miles wide, N.N.W. and S.S.E., about a mile deep, and its western part affords shelter from westerly winds; but being quite open to the north-east a vessel should be prepared to leave in case the wind veers to the northward and blows hard, which it frequently does even in summer. These heavy onshore winds commonly last 2 or 3 days, and prevail from the north-east. Small vessels run for the basin of Gijon. Fishing vessels, when they cannot from the heavy sea take the bar, run for a little creek with a shingle beach, and protected by a reef, on the western shore of the bay, a mile from the cape and about 1½ cables south of Arnao castle.*

Anchorage.—The greatest depth in the bay is 11 fathoms, which is at the entrance, the water thence gradually shoaling to the shore, over a rocky bottom, but near the cape patches of sand predominate. A good berth for large vessels is in 10 or 11 fathoms, sand, with the town of Candas (about 4 miles north-west of the cape) just shut in with Orrio islet, at the foot of cape Torres, and distant about 4 cables from the islet. Small vessels anchor in 8 or 9 fathoms, good holding ground, about a quarter of a mile off shore between a cove near the cape and Arnao castle ; but at all times keep Olivo point well open of cape San Lorenzo, for shutting that point in with the cape will place a vessel on rocky bottom.

Buoys.—At the anchorage for large vessels, a red buoy is moored in 11 fathoms, with Arnao castle bearing S.W. by W. ½ W., and Santa Catalina lighthouse S.S.E. At the anchorage for small vessels a red buoy is moored in about 7 fathoms, with Arnao castle W. by S. ½ S. and Santa Catalina lighthouse S.E. by S. There are three red mooring buoys in the outer port of Gijon and a conical red buoy with a white stripe north of the southern mole, in progress (1876).

Dangers.—Nearly all Gijon bay is bordered by a rocky flat, and its southern part is filled with rocky patches, which make the access to the basin difficult to a stranger.

The westernmost of these patches, named Osa, lies N.W. ⅞ W. from the light-tower on the hill of Santa Catalina, and distant a mile nearly from Santa Catalina point. It only shows at low water, when the weed is seen, and the sea breaks on it. The Serrapio de Mar, or outer Serrapio, is a rocky ledge with 10 feet on it at low water springs, from the middle of which the same light-tower bears S. ¾ E.; there are 6 fathoms between it and Santa Catalina point, from which it is distant 3¼ cables. When the sea breaks on this danger it also breaks on the bar, so that the pilots watch the surface of the water over it for taking the bar. The San Justo, the next patch to the south-west, and lying N.W. ¼ W. 3 cables from Santa Catalina point, has 12 feet on it, and is dangerous with a heavy sea.

The Serrapio de Tierra or Inner Serrapio, is a rocky ledge which shows at half tide, and on which the sea always breaks. It lies N.W. by W. 3 cables from the mouth of the basin, and, in connection with the reef extending from the mole at Bocal point, forms the bar. Another rocky shoal, the Vendavel, no less dangerous than the preceding, but not so extensive, lies a short distance westward of it, the two forming the Carrero

* *See* Admiralty plan :—Bay of Gijon, No. 77 ; scale, m = 5 inches.

channel. Separated from the beach in the southern part of the bay is a rocky height, nearly isolated and of small elevation, Coroño, between which and the town numerous rocks of all sizes uncover at low water, some of them a quarter of a mile from the beach.

Town of Gijon.—The small hill of Santa Catalina, with an old chapel on its summit, is 148 feet high, and joined to the main land by a low isthmus. Its sides are precipitous, and on its southern slope stands the town of Gijon, with a population of about 10,500, the importance of which is daily increasing. On the north-west part of the hill is the castle of Santa Catalina and the light-tower. The battery of San Pedro and its magazine stands on the east part of the hill. The Darsena or Basin, on the western side of the hill, is 1¾ cables long, N.N.W. and S.S.E., and half a cable broad, and will contain from 80 to 100 vessels of 50 to 200 tons burthen. It is surrounded by a stone wall, with an entrance 55 feet wide, open to the south-west. The basin dries at low tide, but will admit vessels of about 13 feet draught at high water springs; at high water neaps there are not more than 11 feet at entrance.

It is recommended that vessels trading here should be strongly built, capable of taking the ground, and their keels plated with iron, for the bottom is rocky, and a swell sometimes sets in. The bottom is also rock outside the entrance, and some dangerous pinnacles show themselves at low water on the south of the bay. Repairs of all kinds can be effected. A branch line from the Langreo railway is brought to this port for the conveyance of charcoal to vessels loading with it.

Water and Supplies are plentiful; the former is excellent, and conveniently obtained from a fountain.

Pilots.—As no leading marks, easily recognized, can be given for crossing the bar, a stranger should always avail himself of the services of a pilot, especially if his vessel draws much water. Directly a vessel arrives off the port a pilot goes out, and if the sea be such that he cannot cross the bar, he remains in the best place for receiving the vessel, and signals are made from the staff at the extremity of the mole for the direction she is to steer.

LIGHTS.—The light-tower on the hill of Santa Catalina shows, at an elevation of 167 feet above high water, a *fixed* white light, visible in clear weather at a distance of 10 miles.

A *fixed red* light is exhibited from an iron column at the extremity of the mole, extending from Bocal point, elevated 28 feet above the sea, and visible in clear weather 7 miles. A small *red* light is also seen on the north mole of the basin when within the bar.

The Bar.—From Bocal point, the west extreme of Santa Catalina hill, a mole extends in a west direction, and between the shallow water off it at the Inner Serrapio, is the principal passage over the bar. This passage is much contracted by the Bar rock, which has 5 feet water on it, lying nearly in mid channel, and by the Juan Sancho, a pinnacle rock dry at low water springs, which is a little detached from the north part of the Inner Serrapio. The greatest depth on the bar is 23 feet at high water springs, and being narrow, vessels if they have good way on, do not receive more than one wash or heave of the sea when crossing. None, however, should attempt it without being certain that there is water enough for them at the entrance of the basin.

Tides.—It is high water, full and change, at Gijon, at 3h.; springs rise 14 feet, and neaps 11 feet. With south-west and north-west winds, an excess of 2 feet may be expected above the usual rise, and the reverse with opposite winds. The streams are weak, but when there is a heavy sea the eddies are strong in the channel and at the entrance.

Directions.—Vessels bound to Gijon from the westward, should in bad weather give cape Peñas, a berth of 5 or 6 miles, to avoid the heavy sea off it. With south-west winds they may pass between the cape and the Somos Llungo shoal, or even borrow on the Romanella rock if the water be smooth, for as soon as the cape is doubled the wind will become scant. If waiting for the springs or for daylight to enter Gijon, with south-west winds they will be well sheltered between this cape and cape Torres, taking care to keep 2½ or 3 miles off shore, which at night may be done by bearings of cape Peñas or Gijon lights.

From the eastward, keep at least half a mile from Santa Catalina point in passing, especially if there be any sea, to clear the Outer Serrapio; taking care, with the wind from the eastward, not to run too far to leeward before receiving a pilot. The hawser and lashings should be ready on deck before entering the basin, and, if the weather be bad, and much sea on, preparation should be made for all sail to be taken off smartly as the vessel enters, or serious injury may be done by collision with other vessels.

Fishermen and coasters, when the sea is too heavy to cross the bar, take the Carrero channel, between the Inner Serrapio and the Vendavel shoals. There is more water in it than on the bar, but when the sea is high it is very narrow, having scarcely room for a large boat.

Beacons.—The two conical beacons, easily seen on the shore abreast, near the chapel of San Stephen, kept in line lead through the Carrero channel.

CAPE TORRES.—The name of this cape appears to be derived from the land terminating on its sea face in steep, rugged, rocky pinnacles, formed in the shape of towers. A craggy islet, named Orrio, is detached from its north-west point, leaving a passage inside it for boats. The only dangers to be avoided in entering Gijon bay are a reef which only breaks in a heavy sea, extending N.E. a short distance from the cape, and a rocky bank, named the Figar, which forms the northern termination of the rocky bottom in the bay. This bank has 8 fathoms on it, and breaks when there is a heavy sea, at which time all the other dangers show themselves by the breakers; it will, however, be avoided by anchoring before Olivo point comes on with cape San Lorenzo.

RIVER ABOÑO.—The coast from cape Torres trends to the south-west, and continues high, steep, and of a reddish appearance, to the eastern termination of an elevated sandy plain of some extent, named the Aboño, which commences at the mouth of the river of that name, and from its whiteness is visible some distance off. The Aboño enters the sea by a steep beach about three-quarters of a mile from the cape, and in fine weather is frequented by boats at high water. From thence the coast trends in a north-west direction, and continues steep, with rocky points and small patches of beach, for about 2¼ miles to Peran point, a low rugged projection with a little river on its west side.

CANDÁS BAY.—San Antonio point, a mile north-west of Perran point, is high, steep, of a triangular form, with a hermitage on its summit. Between these points is the bay of Candás, capable of receiving small vessels, but in a heavy sea the whole neighbourhood is in a most disturbed state. Outside the bay are the following dangers :—

The Covanin, a rocky head of small extent, with 6 feet on it, and 6 to 10 fathoms around it, lies E. by N. a short half mile from San Antonio point. Another, called Sierra de Santa Olalla, larger than the former, and lying 1¼ miles E.S.E. of the point, has 2¼ fathoms water on it, the lead falling at once into 8 and 9 fathoms, which depth continues to the shore; the sea breaks heavily on it. The Castañar, with 2¼ fathoms on it, the most dangerous of all on account of its distance off shore and its heavy breakers, lies 2 miles E.S.E. of the point; it is not so extensive as either of the others, but more steep-to. There is another of small extent, with 1¾ fathoms on it, named the Sierra, lying S.E. ½ S. about a mile from the point; and farther eastward a rock, named Peton de Entrellusa, which only breaks in heavy seas. The bottom is sandy between all these dangers.

In the western part of this bay, between San Antonio point and that of San Sebastian, which is higher, of the same rugged nature and colour, and 2 cables southward, there is a rocky height which recedes to the west, and on which stands the town of Candas. A small semicircular sandy beach, surrounded by two curved moles, each about 120 yards long, and with an opening 65 feet wide facing the south-east, forms the little port of Candas, which shelters 30 to 40 fishing boats at high water. It dries at low tide, and in bad weather the approach is difficult, being beset by rocks known only to the fishermen.

A short distance north of San Antonio point is that of Cuerno de Candas, and between is a small bight with reddish cliffs, and full of rocks. This latter point is high, steep, and projecting to the north-east, and on its outer part is a battery and guard-house in ruins. Between it and Cabrito point, the next projection to the north-west, is a bay with a beach, called San Pedro, in which fishermen find shelter from westerly winds. Cabrito point is low with a small islet off it, and fringed with rocks, the most dangerous of which is the Cabrito, covered at high water, and with a passage inside it for boats.

PORT LUANCO.—Vaca point, about 1¼ miles northward of Cabrito point, is a high promontory, projecting to the north-east, with cliffs of rugged rocks. At half a cable northward of it is the Chato rock, covered at high water, steep-to, and between it and the shore there is a passage for boats. Between these points the coast forms a bay, at the head of which is the town and port of Luanco. The so-called port is formed by a little mole which curves to the south-west, but the space enclosed by it is so limited that it will only berth a few small vessels. It dries at low water, but vessels are not injured by grounding, the bottom being soft mud. A north-west sea sends a swell in at high water. Excellent water is obtained from a fountain north of the church. Supplies of all kinds are plentiful. The principal exports are grain, timber, and salt provisions. The population is about 1,700.*

Directions.—To enter the port, a vessel will have to pass between the shoal of Juan de Melao, with 2¾ fathoms water on it, on the north, and the rocks of Espiga, &c., on the south. Steer in with the north side of the palace, a conspicuous building, in line with the mole head about W. ¼ N., and anchor in about 2½ fathoms water, sand, and if necessary wait for the tide to enter the harbour.

Tides.—It is high water, full, and change, at Port Luanco, at 3h.; springs rise 13 feet, neaps 10 feet, varying according to the direction of the wind.

BANUGUES BAY.—The coast westward of Vaca point is high and precipitous for above a mile, as far as Aguillon point, which is smooth

---

* See Admiralty plan :—Port Luanco, No. 726 ; scale, m = 8·3 inches : also, plan on chart Bayonne to Oporto on chart No. 2738.

and projects to the eastward, and at a short distance from it is a rock
which takes the name of the point.   Between these points there is an intermediate point which, with Vaca point, forms Moniello bay, more than half
a mile across, and at its head is a rivulet of the same name.   At half a mile
to the north-west of Aguillon point is Sabugo point, and between, the
coast recedes a mile to the southward and forms Bañugues bay, bounded
by a sand, through which the little river Bañugues runs into the sea.
The whole bay is scattered with rocks, and is only used by a few fishing
boats.

Sabugo point, 2 miles S.E. ½ S. from cape Peñas, is low and rugged, with
a reef extending off it which terminates in the Cordero rock, always above
water, and within which boats may pass in fine weather.   From thence the
coast is rugged and fringed with rocks to Narvata point, the south-east
extreme of Llumeres point.

LLUMERES BAY.—The coast on the east side of cape Peñas
trends to the south-east, continuing in steep cliffs and forming a bight
terminated by a high round islet, named Castro, which is separated from
the land by a channel full of rocks.   To the east of the islet is a spacious
bay, named Llumeres, with a clean beach of coarse dark sand, terminated
to the south-east by Narvata point, steep, and of moderate height, from the
foot of which projects a rocky reef; above the point is the ruin of a castle.
The southern shore of the bay is high, steep, and bold, but the northern is
beset with rocks.

Llumeres bay is sheltered by cape Peñas from the heavy north-west seas;
it is also a good place of refuge against south-west winds, and in case of
necessity lives may be saved by running the boats into the smooth water
between the Castro rock and the beach.   Coasting vessels frequent it for
the iron ore which falls from the cliffs, and anchor near the shore in 8 to
10 fathoms, sand; being, however, open to the north-east it should be left
the moment the wind threatens to blow in.

CHAPTER IV.

COAST OF SPAIN.—CAPE PEÑAS TO THE RIVER MIÑO.

VARIATION in 1881.

Cape Peñas	- 20° 0′ W.	Cape Ortegal	- 20° 30′ W.
	River Miño -	- 20° 20′ W.	

CAPE PEÑAS is the name given to the easternmost point of a headland which projects to the northward from the general line of coast, and is named by the natives Pedregal, from the numerous rocks by which it is surrounded. Its northern face is about a mile in extent, east and west, and 340 feet above the sea level, and presents three rugged precipitous points. At the west extreme of this headland is a pinnacle rock, named Agudo de Sabin or Peñas, which may be visited on foot from the mainland; it has on its north-west side a large deep cave, which from a distance has the appearance of a chapel, and the fishermen name it the Capilla or Canalon del Sabin. The islet of Gaviera lies off the east extreme of the cape, with a channel between for boats. On the first plain surface of the cape, a short distance from the edge of the cliff, stands a light-tower, with the keeper's dwelling on its northern side.

LIGHT.—The round tower on cape Peñas exhibits a white light, which *revolves* every *half-minute*, at an elevation of 338 feet above the mean level of the sea, and visible in clear weather at a distance of 21 miles.

The following are the principal dangers by which the headland is surrounded :—

Somos Llungo Bank, lying E. by N. from the light-tower on cape Peñas, and distant 3¼ miles from Gaviera islet, has 13 to 16 fathoms water on it, the lead falling immediately into 30, 40, and 45 fathoms, in a direction principally N.E., towards which the bank seems to be nearly vertical. Towards the land the bottom is more inclined, there being 30 fathoms near the bank, 23 fathoms about mid-channel, and 16 fathoms near the Merendálvarez. In bad weather the sea breaks on it heavily. From the least water the Agudo del Sabin is in line with Deva isle, page 181, and the western peak of monte Ventoso or Peral, is in line with the field of Narvata. This hill, about 5 miles south-west of Avilés, will be known by its three peaks, the highest being to the west, and the lowest and most pointed to the east. The field of Narvata terminates at the sea in a cliff on the south shore of Llumeres bay, and is known by the ruins of a castle.

Merendálvarez Reefs.—Several sharp rocky heads extend in about a N.E. by E. direction from cape Peñas ; and a chain of reefs, named the Merendálvarez, but with little water over them at high tide, extend northward from Gaviera islet in line with the cape, and terminate in a rocky head, the Romanella, which dries at low water, and from which the middle of Erbosa isle bears W. by N. Between this head and the Merendálvarez there is a narrow channel occasionally used by coasters, and there are channels between the reefs for boats. The Romanella is dangerous by night when the sea is smooth.

Erbosa Isle, lying off the western part of this headland, at 1½ cables N. by E. ½ E. from the Agudo del Sabin, is of moderate height, steep to the north-east, and slanting down rapidly to the south-west, on which side there is a natural arch, through which boats pass in moderate weather. The channel between the islet and the Agudo del Sabin, is 7 fathoms deep, but full of rocks, through which coasters thread their way ; but it can only be taken by those locally acquainted, and that in moderate weather, for however little the sea, the whole passage abounds with breakers, and the currents are strong.

A rugged islet of conical form, named the Bravo, lies N.E. ½ E. half a cable from the Erbosa ; another, the Monista, a short distance to the northward of it ; and to the west are numerous minor rocks, five of which, named Corberas, are always above water. There are also three sunken rocks, named the Conos, the most dangerous of which is Noroeste (north-wester, from its lying in that direction) distant half a mile from Bravo, has less than 4 fathoms water on it, but its position is pointed out in fine weather by the ripple over it, and in bad weather by the breakers. Between the Noroeste and Bravo there are 20 fathoms water.

Directions.—Cape Peñas, being one of the most salient points of this coast, is easily made from either direction, either by its light by night or appearance by day. Besides projecting considerably to the northward, the surface of this promontory is level to the foot of the high land which continues along the whole coast of Astúrias at 3 or 4 miles from the shore. In formation it is like capes Busto and Bidio (page 184) and of the same colour, for its cliffs present the same whitish hue of quartz, of which it is partly composed : seen from the east or west it presents the same level down to the cliffs, and only differs from them in having some few groves of trees and houses on its surface.

Vessels from the westward may in fine weather, or with south-west winds, run between the Somos Llungo and the cape, and may borrow towards the Romanella, passing a mile outside the Gaviera and Bravo, in 30 to 40 fathoms water; but in bad weather the cape should be given a berth of 5 or 6 miles, not only to avoid the breakers on the Somos Llungo, but also the heavy sea over the uneven bottom, which extends a considerable distance off the land. To clear the Conos when coming from the westward, the Vaca de Luanco should be kept open of the Merendálvarez rocks; and from the eastward keep well northward until Erbosa is open of Gaviera, then continue westward.

WINDS and CURRENT.—Contrary winds frequently occur in the vicinity of cape Peñas. A vessel will sometimes make the cape with a strong north-east or east wind, and find the contrary in with the land; the same thing occurring with west or south-west winds. In summer the prevailing winds are easterly, with some few interruptions of westerly, accompanied with rain. In winter the winds are between the south-west and west; these bring dirty weather, blowing strong for three or more days, with rain, until in a heavy squall the wind veers to the north-west and the weather clears up. These southerly winds, when they blow hard, make great havoc among the coasters; and the heavy sea thrown in upon the coast by the north-westers completely closes the ports.

The northers, called Travesías, do not last over three days, and only blow between December and March. A vessel caught in one on this part of the coast had better stand to the eastward, as the trend of the land on the east side of the cape is southward of east, and the wind generally ends at north-east.

The general direction of the current off the cape is to the eastward, particularly in the winter. In summer it sometimes runs to the westward, especially should north-east winds prevail. The flood stream sets to the south-east, the ebb to the south-west.

The COAST from the west extreme of cape Peñas trends about a mile to the southward to Arcas or Ratin point, which is low, rugged, and foul. From thence commences an extensive beach, which terminates to the westward abreast Bermea islet. The beach is named Arenal de Berdicio, and in the bay which it forms, coasting vessels anchor for shelter from north-east winds in any convenient depth, but generally in about 14 fathoms, fine sand, a position from which they can make sail and clear the land. The whole bay is clean, and can be navigated by the lead; but be careful not to be caught in it with an on-shore wind.

Bermea islet, so named from its reddish appearance, is rugged, and lies a cable from the beach, with a clear channel of 7 fathoms water between it and the shore. To the westward of this islet, on the east side of Llampero point, is a small cove, named Peurto del Llampero, sheltered from the sea by a point and some rocks, and for which the fishermen of Luanco, Candás, and Avilés run for shelter in bad weather, and haul their boats up on a small shingle beach.

Llampero point is low and craggy, with an islet and some rocks off it. From thence a bold coast, which may be navigated by the lead, trends to the westward, forming a bight to cape Negro, or del Cornorio. This cape is high, precipitous, and like that of Peñas. At its foot are some rocks, which uncover at low water, and a shoal of small extent, but a vessel may pass it safely at half a mile.

From cape Negro a steep and sinuous coast runs to the southward to a rocky projection, named Home point, between which and Forcada point, bearing about S.W. by W. ½ W. 2 miles from the cape, is Chaon bay, bounded by an extensive beach, interspersed with rocks. Forcada point is bold, rocky, and projects to the north-west; and 1¼ cables south-east of it is Castillo point and the bar and mouth of the river Avilés.

RIVER AVILÉS.—Vessels drawing 13 feet can cross the bar of this river in favourable weather at high water springs, but it is so obstructed by shifting sandbanks that only those of about 7 feet draught can proceed up to the town of Avilés, standing on the western bank, 3 miles within the entrance, and even then the channel should be buoyed. Vessels lie alongside the mole at the town, on a mud bottom; but in taking the ground in any other part of the river, take care that the vessel's head is placed to the stream of tide. The deepest water is near San Juan, a collection of houses on the north bank, three-quarters of a mile within the bar. Here there is a hole with 8 feet at low water, where small vessels may lie afloat. Above San Juan the banks dry, and near Avilés the river may be crossed dry-footed.

On the west side of the entrance begins the extensive sandy plain of Espartal, which, from its height and whiteness, is seen from a considerable distance. It terminates to the westward in a low rocky point, named Requexo, the extreme of a steep height. To the westward of this point is the beach of Arnao, on which are hauled up the boats that embark coal obtained from the adjacent mines. The town of Arnao is on a hill near the sea. On the above plain, and near the shore, is the rail by which the manufactures of Arnao are conveyed to the mole formed opposite San Juan.*

The Bar extends from the point on which stands the castle of Avilés, to the north extreme of the plain of Espartal, and the depths on it vary from 4 to 8 feet at low water springs, according to the weather in the

---

* *See* Admiralty plan of river Avilés, on sheet, No. 710.

M 2

offing; the deep water channel, not more than 50 yards wide, lies close to the north point.

LIGHT.—On Castillo point at the north side of entrance to the inlet of Avilés, is an octagonal light yellow coloured tower, which exhibits, at 116 feet above the level of the sea, a *fixed* white light, visible in clear weather at a distance of 10 miles.

Tides.—It is high water, full and change, on the bar of the river Avilés at 3h., and an hour later at the town of Avilés; ordinary springs rise 12 feet. The rise is about 2 feet more with south-west and north-west winds, according to their strength, and the contrary with winds from the opposite quarter. Opposite the town the ebb runs $8\frac{1}{2}$ hours, the flood 4 hours. The river is not subject to freshes, and the greatest rate of the current does not exceed 4 knots.

Directions.—The pilots go out of the Avilés in favourable weather when a vessel is seen in the offing. The channel into the river lying in an easterly and westerly direction, has the advantage of being accessible with south-west and north-west winds; but when these latter blow strong and raise much sea, the bar is impracticable, and a vessel should keep out of the deep bight between cape Negro and Deva isle, or she will be in great danger, and amongst the numerous rocky banks with which the bight is encumbered. With other winds a vessel may anchor to await a tide, in 8 to 10 fathoms, sand, at 2 cables off shore between Forcada point and Avilés castle $1\frac{1}{4}$ cables south of it; but it would not be prudent to pass a night here, for fear the wind should veer to the north-west.

As a general rule, a sailing vessel bound from the westward, with westerly winds, should not stand for the river except at a favourable time for crossing the bar, for, besides the strong current setting towards cape Peñas, she may have to encounter a chopping sea occasioned by the uneven rocky bottom in the bight. Steering for the entrance, keep the land abroad between Forcada point and Avilés castle, and bear in mind that the deepest water over the bar is close to the point of the castle, and that it will be necessary to approach the point almost to the rocks. After crossing the bar keep on the northern shore, the only danger being the Arañon rock, marked by a buoy, a quarter of a mile within the entrance.

AVILÉS BAY.—The deep bight between cape Negro and Deva islet is dangerous with north-west winds when they blow strong, for the sea gets up on the numerous rocky banks within it, and a vessel would be in great danger of being embayed, there being no other means of shelter than to take the bar of Avilés if the tide admit. This bar, too, is dangerous at this time, but being narrow, a vessel may only run the risk of being struck by the sea.

The most dangerous of the banks is the Anuales reef, but, as it breaks with the least sea on, it forms a useful mark.   East of this is the Peton, a rocky head with 5 fathoms water on it, and breaks when there is much sea, and from which the chapel of Espíritu Santo (in the Právia inlet) is in line with the inshore slope of Deva islet, and the Storehouse of San Juan (a white house, and farthest south in the inlet of Avilés) is seen a little open of Avilés castle point; a vessel therefore approaching the Avilés river from the westward should keep the storehouse in line with the point until the line of the Deva with the chapel is passed.

Another bank, with 8 to 9 fathoms water, extends some distance westward from Forcada point inclining towards the above rocks, so that all these are but the summits of a rocky bed, having unequal depths of 15 to 20 fathoms.

RAYO or VIDRIAS POINT, 4¼ miles westward of the Avilés, is high and steep, with a rock off it, named Moro, awash at high water.   A reef named the Anuales, on which the sea breaks heavily, stretches nearly a mile in a north-east direction from the point, with channels between the rocks.   On its outer end are 7 fathoms water, and 16 to 22 fathoms around it; several heads show themselves at low water.

On the east side of Rayo point the coast runs to the southward, forming a bay called Correal, at the head of which is a sandy beach.   Santa Maria del Mar bay, named from the hamlet on the high land of the coast, follows this to the eastward, and off the west part of its eastern point is an islet named Ladrona.   In running along the coast, the houses and chimneys of the factories of Arnao are seen, and a little to the eastward of them those of the zinc works near the shore.

DEVA ISLE.—From Rayo or Vidrias point a high precipitous coast, with patches of sandy beach bordered with rocks, runs in a westerly direction for a mile to Cogollo point, off which, N.E. ¼ N. distant 2 cables, is Deva islet, high, and surrounded with rocks.   There is a navigable channel for small craft between it and the main, but a pilot is necessary, as there are several rocks.   Deva islet is a good mark for Právia inlet.

Cogollo point projects to the north-west, and forms with that of Espíritu Santo the bight in which are the beaches named Bayes and Quebrantes; the former beach has some scattered rocks off it, and terminates at Cogollo point.   This point has also some rocks off it, but they are sufficiently bold to enable coasters to pass them at a short distance.

RIVER PRÁVIA.—This beautiful estuary, of so much importance from the large exports of timber that come down the Nalon, is accessible at high water to vessels of 15 feet draught, with the advantage

of their always lying afloat abreast the village of San Estéban, which
stands on the western shore of the river, three-quarters of a mile within
the bar. Here vessels are secured four abreast in 20 to 30 feet water,
good holding ground, sheltered from westerly winds by the Sierra del
Espíritu Santo. The village stands on the projection of the sierra, and
contains about 250 inhabitants.*

Fresh water is obtained from a fountain at the village, not far from the
ruins of the mole. Provisions are scarce, and they can only be procured
in any quantity at Múros, 1½ miles distant, where the marine superinten-
dent of the district resides.

The Bar is impassable with heavy seas, notwithstanding it is somewhat sheltered by the reefs which extend in a northerly direction from the
west point of entrance. The outermost of these are two rocks called
Lladrona, lying N.E. distant 1½ cables from the hermitage on the point.
The bar, which is of sand, frequently shifts, but always keeps over on the
western side towards these rocks. There are generally 7 feet over it at
low, and 20 feet at high water springs.

Tides.—It is high water, full and change, on the bar of the river
Právia at 3h.; springs rise 12 to 13 feet, neaps about 10 feet. With
westerly winds the rise is 3 to 4 feet higher, there being with these winds
frequently 22 feet on the bar, while with easterly winds there is sometimes not 14 feet. The mean rate of the current over the bar is about
4 knots, increasing to 5 knots, and even more, on the ebb at the time of
the freshes.

Directions.—Vessels of large draught should take a pilot both for
entering and leaving the Právia inlet. If the bar can be crossed, the pilots
go out directly they see a vessel approaching. The best time to enter is
about 2 hours before high water. The only danger in the channel is the
Lamparon rock, about the size of a large boat, lying just within the bar.
It dries at low water springs, and leaves a passage 35 yards wide on its
western side, and another 80 yards wide between it and the edge of the
banks on the eastern shore ; this latter is generally used.

As before stated, the bar is impassable with heavy seas, and it is only
with winds from S.E. round by North, to N.W., that it should be taken by
a sailing vessel. With a north-west wind it must be crossed on the flood,
for the wind will be scant and squally as the land is neared, and on the ebb,
with this wind, a vessel would run the risk of being set on the Lamparon
rock. Having passed this rock, keep 30 to 40 yards from the west shore
of the river, in from 10 to 22 feet at low water, anchoring abreast the
village.

---

* *See* Admiralty plan :—Ria de Právia, No. 726; scale, *m* = 1·8 inches.

PORT CUDILLERO.—About 3 miles W.N.W. from the entrance of the Právia, is the lighthouse on Revallera point which forms the eastern side of the little port of Cudillero. There are several rocks lying a short distance off this part of the coast, the outermost and most dangerous of which, called the Señorío, with 4 feet on it at low water, is 3 cables northward of Furada point, with 3½ to 4 fathoms between it and the point. To pass clear outside, keep Erbosa islet open north of Deva islet.

Port Cudillero is nothing more than an opening in the cliffs, sheltered on the west by a chain of dark islets called Colinas, which run out some distance to the northward. A mole extending east and west with a narrow entrance close to the rocks, is all that affords shelter. The port dries at low water, and is only adapted for fishing vessels, which, on the approach of bad weather, are run upon the beach. The town contains about 2,000 inhabitants, nearly all of whom are employed in the fishery.

LIGHT.—The lighthouse on the east point of entrance to port Cudillero, is a rectangular building, with a white tower rising from it, the whole being 14 feet high. It exhibits, at 93 feet above high water, a *fixed* white light, visible in clear weather at a distance of 10 miles.

ARTEDO BAY, at 1½ miles westward of Cudillero, is nearly a mile wide at entrance, and half a mile deep, and affords a good summer anchorage for all classes of vessels, in 8 to 10 fathoms, sandy bottom, sheltered from south-west and north-west winds ; but in the winter months a vessel would be exposed to a north-west gale, and also to the sea that rolls in from the north-west. A large vessel will find a good berth in 10 fathoms, off a white mark in the cliffs on the west side of the bay, with the hermitage of Santa Ana S. by W. ¼ W., distant 1½ cables from the shore. There is a clean beach at the head of the bay.

Vessels bound to this bay from the westward, will recognize its position by Rabion islet, and by Monte Santa Ana, or Montales, which latter is south of the bay, and will be known by the above hermitage, which is white and stands on its eastern slope. Rabion islet, high and rocky, lies half a mile westward of the west point of Artedo bay. It is connected to the coast by a chain of dry rocks, and several rocks extend from it to the E.N.E., all of which contribute to shelter Artedo bay from the north-west. The extreme end of the rocks extending from the islet is called Rabion point, and in bad weather a berth of at least a mile should be given to it, for the sea there runs high, and even half across the mouth of the bay.

The COAST westward of Rabion islet, between it and cape Bidio, forms two bays, named Oteiro and San Pedro, separated by a high headland, off which are rocks and detached dangers. San Pedro, the western bay, is the larger, and has a clean beach. Cape Bidio or Vidio is of moderate height, and much the same in character as cape Busto, which is nearly 10 miles to the westward. At 30 to 40 yards off it, is a high conical islet named Chouzano or Lozano, with a passage between for boats. The islet, and also the cape, is composed of white stratified rocks ; a cable outside the outlet is a sunken rock called Chouzanin.

The coast between the above capes may be passed at a mile distance in fine weather without risk, in 20 to 30 fathoms, rocky bottom. The cliffs are 230 to 280 feet high, the land rising at 2 or 3 miles in the interior to the mountain range. There are breaks in the cliff more or less deep, with small beaches, which boats can only approach under favourable circumstances. A few rocks lie off the coast ; the most remarkable and farthest out are the Negras, so called from their dark appearance. They are low, have a passage for fishing boats between them and the shore, and are the most prominent of an extensive reef $1\frac{1}{2}$ miles S.W. of cape Bidio.

Cape Busto, having a village on it, is rather higher than cape Bidio, and will be known by its level appearance, by the cliffs in which it terminates, and by its lighthouse, which is an angular white building, with the tower rising from it. A reef, on which the sea generally breaks, extends N.W. from the cape ; it is always covered, excepting a rock, La Moura, which lies a cable from the cape, and dries at low water. An islet of moderate height and conical form, called Serron, lies East from the cape, and is connected with it by a reef which shows at low water ; there are detached rocks off the islet and the cape, but being bold they may be passed at a short distance.

A rocky bank, named the Serron, with 23 to 27 fathoms water on it, deepening to 55 fathoms on the north side, and 45 fathoms on the south, lies E.N.E. from cape Busto, and 4 to 5 miles off the coast. It is only dangerous in bad weather, when the heavy seas have been seen to break. Another rocky bank of small extent, with 27 to 30 fathoms water on it, lies north of cape Busto, distant $2\frac{1}{2}$ miles ; there is a heavy sea over it in bad weather. From cape Busto the coast, high, steep, and reddish, trends to the southward to the river Esba, called also Caneiro, the bar of which dries at low water. Inside the bar is the little port of Cueva, which is annually visited by coasters to embark timber. The bar has a rock in the middle of it, and can only be crossed at high water under favourable circumstances. From thence the coast takes a westerly direction to the entrance of Luarca ; and has some off-lying rocks.

LIGHT.—The lighthouse on cape Busto exhibits, at an elevation of 307 feet above high water, a *fixed* white light, varied every *two minutes* by a *red flash*, and visible in clear weather at a distance of 12 miles.

PORT LUARCA, formed at the head of a small bay of the same name, 3½ miles westward of cape Busto, is only frequented during the summer months by small craft that can take the ground. The bar nearly dries, and vessels drawing 12 feet require spring tides and a smooth sea to cross it, but a pilot is indispensable. The bay has anchorage in 5 to 6 fathoms, sand, but the clean ground is very limited, and vessels should only remain in it during fine weather, or to wait for tide to enter the port.*

The port is very small, in fact it is nearly blocked up by a bed of shingle, leaving only a narrow winding channel, the outlet of the river Negro which dries at low water, and follows the walls of a circular mole or wharf on the eastern side of the port. The town is built in the form of an amphitheatre, the principal part being on the eastern side of the port, and contains a population of about 2,500. Water and provisions are plentiful, and the assistance of shipwrights might be obtained.

LIGHT.—On la Blanca point, and a little north of the chapel, is a square tower which exhibits, at 204 feet above the level of the sea, a *fixed* white light, visible at a distance of 7 miles.

Tides.—It is high water, full and change, at Luarca, at 3h.; the rise is 12 feet at ordinary springs, and 14 to 15 feet when it blows fresh from N.W. to S.W.

Directions.—The position of Luarca will be easily recognized by the lighthouses on cape Busto and la Blanca point, and by the chapel on the latter being the extreme of a small peninsula forming the eastern side of the bay. The chapel has a high belfry, and is conspicuous from a good distance. This point has some rocks off it, the outer one of which, called the Moura, is a cable north of the point, and nearly awash at low water. A vessel should pass outside it, for between it and the point is another rock, with 11 feet water on it. Mugeres point, the west extreme of the bay, is low and rocky, and may be passed at the distance of from 1 to 2 cables in fine weather, but much farther off in bad weather, for the foul ground off it produces much sea; and when it breaks on the rocks off this point, it also breaks on the bar.

The COAST takes a N.W. by W. direction from Luarca, and at the distance of 3 miles is Cuerno de Barayo point, a rocky projection with reddish coloured crags, one of which forms a curve to the south in the form of a horn. The point is clear of danger, and westward of it is a large opening in the rocks by which the river Barayo discharges itself into the sea, but fishing boats can scarcely cross the bar at its entrance at high water. Romanellas point, a mile to the westward, has off it, in a north direction,

---

* *See* Admiralty plan :—Luarca, No. 726 ; scale, *m* = 1·8 inches.

two dark islets, with a passage between them for boats, and nearer the coast there is a larger islet; they are called the Romanellas, and may be passed pretty close, as they are free from rocks.

At a mile westward of the Romanellas is-the Atalaya* de Vega, with a small chapel on it. This chapel may be known from the hermitage on cape San Agustin, bearing from the chapel N.W. by W. ¼ W. 3½ miles, by its being larger and standing east and west, while the hermitage is north and south. It is on the level land, about 90 feet above the sea, and the point which terminates the Atalaya is called Barroco. A short distance eastward of the chapel is the entrance of a tortuous channel between reefs dry at low tide, leading into port Vega. This port dries at low tide, and is very confined, but it is without a bar, and will admit vessels drawing 8 to 9 feet at high water. Coasters run into it when they cannot get into Návia. The population of the village may be about 500.

At three-quarters of a mile westward of the Atalaya de Vega, is Vega island, and a short distance N.E. of it is a rock which dries at low water. The island lies north and south, forming a high round head, and reefs extend a short distance from it in all directions. On its western side near the coast is a dark rocky islet, named Corberon. The coast on the west side of the island is composed of cliffs, broken at short intervals, as far as an extensive sandy beach of a darkish colour, called Freijulfe; the beach is steep and scattered with rocks. Corbera point, about a mile westward of Vega island, is low and rocky, and a short distance outside it is a rock always above water. Between this latter point, and Campbell point at the east side of entrance to the Návia inlet, in a low projection of the coast called Hocico de fuera, dangerous from a sunken rock with less than 2 fathoms water on it, lying a cable outside it, which breaks with the least sea.

RIVER NÁVIA.—The mouth of this estuary is half a mile S.E. of cape San Agustin, and being nearly midway between the lighthouse on cape Busto and that on Tapia isle, they will readily indicate its position. Cape San Agustin, 111 feet high, has a chapel on it. Monte Jarrio, 1,056 feet high, bearing S.W. ¼ W. nearly 2 miles from the cape, is also a good mark for the river.

The Návia is of considerable importance from the abundance of oak timber which comes down it, and from its rich salmon fishery. The entrance is about a third of a mile in breadth, but the channel is narrowed within by marshy ground, and abreast the town it is only half a cable across. It will admit vessels of 9 to 11 feet draught at high water springs, but as its bar, which has a rock lying nearly in mid-channel, is constantly

---

* Atalaya signifies any elevation from which a considerable view may be obtained.

shifting, and always breaks, however little sea there may be on, no vessel
should attempt to cross it without a pilot. Having passed the bar, the
vessel will be well sheltered, and can lie afloat in 11 to 17 feet at low
water.

The village of Návia stands on the eastern bank, nearly a mile within
the bar, and has a population of about 800. There are no pilots residing
in the river; this duty is performed by the fishermen of the town of
Ortiguera, which stands along the craggy declivities surrounding a small
cove on the west side of cape San Agustin.

The COAST between cape Agustin and cape Blanco, which is
5¼ miles westward, is composed of steep cliffs fringed with numerous rocks,
and forms several openings and bays. Lamosas point, 1¾ miles from the
former cape, has some islets off it, named Gavieros, and N. by W. ¼ W.
upwards of a cable from the outer island is an extensive reef lying N.W.
and S.E., a great part of which dries at low water. It always breaks, and,
when there is much sea on, the breakers extend out a considerable distance.
Between the reef and islets there is a channel of 9 to 11 fathoms water,
which coasters use in fine weather.

Acebros point, the next projection to the westward, has a reef off it
which dries at low water. This point forms the east point of entrance to
Torbas bay, which is open to the northward and surrounded by cliffs,
but it has a small beach, and coasters find shelter in it during the summer.
Off Viaveles, about a mile from the shore, there are 11 to 14 fathoms, rocky
ground, which breaks in a heavy sea. Beyond this there are banks with
more or less water, one of which, called the Cabezo, lying 2½ miles from
the coast and N.E. from the entrance of Viaveles, has 23 fathoms on it.
The sea runs high upon this bank, and it would be dangerous to pass over
it in bad weather. Cape Blanco, (so named from its white appearance,) to
the westward, is about 130 feet above the sea, and terminates in a pro
jecting rugged point; some rocks lie a short distance off its western side.

At a mile eastward of Viaveles, is the church and village of Caridad at
the termination of a group of poplar trees, and is a good mark for Viaveles ;
the coast varies from about 90 to 140 feet in height.

PORT VIAVELES, on the east side and half a mile southward of
cape Blanco, hardly deserves the name of a port, but many vessels have
been constructed here of late years, one of which was 640 tons burden, but
was got out with much difficulty. The entrance, lying N.W. and S.E., is
scarcely 40 yards in breadth at low water. About a cable within is a pool
about half a cable across, and in its north-west angle there is an opening
running in a cable to the south-west, with an entrance 18 yards wide. So
much of this, as well as part of the pool, is dry at low water, that even

vessels of the lightest draught cannot lie afloat at low water. Coasters frequent it, and are well sheltered in all weathers.

The mouth of this port is closed in heavy seas, for breakers extend a considerable distance outside it. Water is easily procured from the spring that supplies the town. Provisions are scarce.

Tides.—It is high water, full and change, at port Viaveles, at 3h.; and the rise at springs is 13 feet.

PORCIA BAY.—Between cape Blanco and Porcia bay, westward, the coast is rocky, steep, and of a whitish aspect. At the head of this deep bay the river Porcia runs through the sand. Coasters visit this river to load wood and grain, but they must take advantage of the tide, as the channel nearly dries at low water. The bay is bounded on the west by Forcada point, and on the east by a high whitish headland, called the Atalaya de Porcia and also the Olga Mourina. Outside it there is an islet named Corbero. To enter the river it will be necessary to pass near two large islets, which must be left on the port hand in taking the bar.

CAPE SAN SEBASTIAN, on which stands the chapel of that saint and the village of Tapia, is a small promontory 2¾ miles westward of Forcada point, having off it two islets named Tapia and Orrio de Tapia. The former, lying half a cable northward of the cape, and connected to it by a reef which dries at low water, is 165 yards long, 100 yards wide, and 60 feet high, having on its summit an octagonal granite light-tower. Orrio de Tapia, lying northward and within a cable of Tapia islet, and connected to it by reefs which nearly dry at low water, is round, conical, and much lower than the latter islet. Reefs extend a great distance from Orrio in a N.E. direction; they dry at low water, with the exception of two isolated rocks called Porcegosas, which from a distance resemble boats. The water deepens outside the reefs, and a vessel may pass a mile northward of them without risk.

From cape San Sebastian a bold coast trends westward 4 miles to Rumeles point. Santa Gadia point, about 2 miles westward of the cape, has the two Pantorgas islets off it, and a short distance outside them are two rocks, which dry at low tide. The next point to the westward is named Rubia, steep and of moderate height, off which are some islets; and between one and two miles in a north direction from it is the Castro bank, with 11 to 13 fathoms on it, and 25 to 30 fathoms on all sides. The water breaks on this bank only in heavy seas, which is a sign that the bar of Rivadeo is not passable. Rumeles point, the next westward, is low and rocky, and 3 cables W.S.W. of it is Cruz point. An extensive reef encircles these two latter points and stretches 2 cables off. The latter point descends in declivities from a tongue of land which forms the eastern side of entrance to Rivadeo, and terminates at the sea in cliffs of steep rock.

LIGHT.—The white granite light-tower on Tapia islet, cape San Sebastian, exhibits at an elevation of 77 feet above high water, a *fixed* white light varied by a *flash* every *two minutes*, and visible at a distance of 15 miles.

GULF of FOZ.—The coast from Tapia islet trends W.N.W. 13 miles to the entrance of Foz, then in a N.W. by N. direction for 24 miles to Estaca point, the north extreme of Spain. It is much indented and high, the ridges of the lofty mountains in the interior reaching the shore, especially between cape Morás and Barquero; from thence eastward the mountain slopes become less abrupt, leaving between them and the sea high level ground, terminating in points at the shore. Storm beaten as this coast is by northerly gales, its navigation would be dangerous were it not for the inlets of Rivadeo, Vivero, and Barquero, which afford refuge from those winds, the two latter, free from bars and easily taken. There is also the little port of San Ciprian and other places of shelter for small craft.

The large indentation of the coast between Tapia islet and Burela point is called the gulf of Foz or Masma, after the river of this name, which falls into Foz inlet. Its shores are foul, and the soundings irregular, over generally rocky bottom, which raises a high sea with onshore gales, when a vessel should give it a wide berth, not only for fear of being embayed, but to avoid the breakers, which in some places are then 4 miles from the land. The prevailing south-west gales of winter blow in tremendous squalls in the gulf, their strength sometimes extending 12 to 15 miles off shore, but outside this distance a manageable and regular wind prevails.

RIVADEO INLET, the entrance to which is about half a mile wide, between Cruz point and Pancha islet, was at one time an excellent port from the facility of taking it, but is now so obstructed by sands that there is a difficulty in entering with scant winds. A bank called the Curabela, which extends in a northerly direction from Pasada point on the east side of the inlet towards the Carrayas rocks at half a mile within the entrance, is daily increasing, and threatens to close the entrance of the channel leading to the port, by joining itself to the above rocks; it has from 6 to 14 feet on it at low water, and at present the channel for large vessels between it and the rocks is not more than a cable across.*

The soundings decrease gradually from 10 fathoms between the entrance points, to 5 fathoms abreast the Carrayas rocks, after passing which the

---

* *See* Admiralty plan :—Port of Rivadeo, No. 78 ; scale, m = ' alf an inch.

deepest water is on the west shore, the depth varying in the middle of the channel from 25 to 15 feet, and then decreasing to 10 feet abreast Rivadeo, where the greater part of the vessels remain dry at low water. The interior of the inlet at low water is scarcely more than a shallow bank of sand with a small channel. In moderate weather vessels anchor to wait tide for entering, or when they are ready for sea, in Arnao bay, on the eastern side of entrance, between Cruz and Pasada points; it is 3½ cables deep, and has 6 and 7 fathoms over a clean bottom of sand.

Pancha islet, which has a light-tower on its summit, is separated from the west point of entrance by a space of 55 yards, which dries at low water. The islet is about 275 yards in length; it is steep on all sides, with a level surface 54 feet above the sea, and a reef extends from it to the N.W. At about 1¼ cables N.W. ¼ N. from the lighthouse is a dangerous rock called Panchorro, about the size of a boat, and having only 13 feet on it at low water springs, nearly always breaks.

At half a mile S.S.E. ¾ E. from Pancha islet is the north part of the Carrayas rocks, which extend from Castrelius point in a northerly direction, and are nearly all dry at low water. Nearly 2 cables south of the point stands the castle of San Damian on a high steep point, and a little south of it, and less than 60 yards from the shore, is the Carballo rock, which dries at low water. There is another rock, named Viga, a little farther northward, but not more than 20 yards off shore. A short distance south of the castle is the town and port of Rivadeo. There are 69 vessels of all sizes belonging to the port, and numerous fishing boats, which united measure about 5,946. Population about 3,000.

Vessels are careened and built in a little bay 4 cables southward of the town, but the greater part of the building and careening takes place in the interior of the spacious but shallow bay of Figueras, in the eastern part of the inlet. The river Eo runs into the inlet, and separates the province of Oviedo from that of Lugo.

Pilots.—The village of Figueras, standing nearly opposite Rivadeo, is the residence of the best informed pilots, who look out from a tower 172 feet above the sea on Boy point on the east side of the inlet, and come off to vessels when the colours are hoisted.

Supplies.—Abundance of provisions can be procured at Rivadeo at reasonable rates. The best and most plentiful supply of water is at Castropol, a village on the eastern shore, about three-quarters of a mile south of Rivadeo. It is obtained from a covered fountain, which will load a boat in a very short time, but the watering place can only be reached at high water.

LIGHT.—The white coloured light-tower on Pancha islet exhibits, at 79 feet above the level of the sea, a *fixed* white light, visible in clear weather at a distance of 9 miles.

Tides.—It is high water, full and change, in Rivadeo inlet at 3h.; and the ordinary rise of springs is 15 feet, which is increased by 2 or 3 feet with westerly, and diminished as much by easterly winds. The mean rate of the stream is about 3 knots.

Directions.—The channel into Rivadeo, lying nearly north and south, and being narrow, a sailing vessel has great difficuly in taking it with southerly winds, and at all times the services of a pilot are indispensable to a stranger. The pilot service is well organized, and they go out of the inlet whenever they are required, it being only necessary for a vessel to show her colours. Monte Mondigo, 1,942 feet high, from its conical form, its solitary appearance, and the jagged rocks which crown its summit, is an excellent mark for vessels bound to Rivadeo from the northward, for directly it is seen it will be sufficient to steer for its eastern slope, which terminates in the inlet.

It frequently happens that a vessel coming towards the port with a north-west wind will find a southerly wind at the entrance. If there is any sea at the time, and the wind blows strong out, which is generally the case in winter, care should be taken to avoid missing stays in the vicinity of the Carabela bank, as there is no room to anchor, and the flood tide sets directly on to the bank, which nearly always breaks when there is any sea. With gales from north or north-west, which are sometimes so heavy as to close the port, a heavy sea sets upon the coast, and nearly the whole space between the entrance points is covered with breakers. The entrance is easy with north-east winds, as they do not send in so much sea.

If from the westward, the Farallones de San Ciprian should be made, and from thence, if autumn, or winter, and the wind inclines to the southwest, it will be prudent to run along the coast at 3 or 4 miles distance, for in this season a south-west wind outside draws to the southward in proportion as the vessel advances across the gulf of Foz, which is 19 miles in breadth between Tapia islet and Burela point, and 5 miles deep. When abreast San Miguel point, near the coast to 2 miles if the water be smooth, or 3 miles should there be any sea, until clear of the Longas off Piñeira point, when endeavour to make out the chapel of Santa Cruz, a white quadrangular building on the eastern slope of monte Mondigo, about W.S.W. from the mouth of the inlet.

Keep this chapel in sight above the cliffs until abreast Pancha islet, when steer into the inlet towards the middle of Arnao bay, until Cabanela point, the most projecting point south of the town of Rivadeo, is on with the middle of the fork or saddle formed by two elevations of a mountain in the interior, called Cotos de Balboa, bearing S.W. by S., which is the leading mark through the narrow channel to the anchorage, a short distance inside the castle of San Damian, if the vessel draws 15 to 17 feet, or farther in according to her draught. If the tide is high, the western shore may be kept aboard as soon as the Carrayas rocks are passed, giving them a berth of 60 yards to clear outlying rocks. Vessels moor head and stern, with their heads to the southward, to guard against the south wind, which blows with great violence.

The lighthouse on Tapia islet is a good landfall to make when bound to Rivadeo with north-east winds. From thence steer towards the entrance, keeping 2 miles off the coast if there is any sea, to avoid the breakers off it. The foul ground off Rumeles and Cruz points must also be guarded against.

The COAST from Pancha islet takes a westerly direction 9 miles to Prado point, the eastern extreme of the inlet of Foz. Nearly 2 miles westward of the islet is Piñeira point, surrounded by sunken rocks called the Longas, and the ground outside of them is foul, requiring in heavy seas a berth of 3 miles. From thence to Foz the most projecting points are those called Corbeira and Promontorio, both terminating in sunken reefs, which extend a considerable distance from them. Between the points, the shore forms slight bends with small beaches, nearly all scattered with rocks; between points Corbeira and Promontorio, and close to the shore, are two high islets, called Portelas, from which a short reef projects.

Escairo or Cairos point, the north-west extreme of Foz inlet, is low and even, forming a plain three-quarters of a mile across, extending to the west, and terminating at the foot of a small hill 220 feet high, called Coto de Castro, the pine trees on which are an excellent mark for the inlet. A rock, named Escairo, 46 feet high, with a steep black face to the north, is off the point, and there are two islets of equal height a short distance N.N.W. of the point.

Foz Inlet.—To the southward of Escairo point is an opening 4½ cables wide into the inlet of Foz, which is spacious, but choked up with sand, and nearly all dry at low water, excepting some channels and small holes with one and two fathoms water. A few coasters visit it during the summer months for corn and wood, but as the bar at its mouth is shifting and shallow, vessels of not more than 10 feet draught can enter at high water springs, which rise about 11 feet; high water, full, and change taking place at 3h. The village of Foz, standing on the western shore, contains about 220 inhabitants. The river Masma falls into the interior of the inlet.

The Coast from Escairo point trends nearly N. by W. $\frac{1}{2}$ W. $7\frac{1}{2}$ miles to Burela point, forming several projections, between which are sandy beaches. The shore from Escairo point to Villarmea point is low, sandy, and scattered with rocks. The latter point and Fazouro point, which follows it about a mile to the north-west, are low and rocky, and between them the river Oro or Fazouro falls into the sea by the houses of the village of that name ; the bar at its mouth is practicable at high water for vessels of light draught. Nois point presents a steep, bold, black front to the north-east, and fishing vessels take shelter in the elbow on its south side during south-west winds ; the village of Nois is scattered on the plain from which the point projects. A rocky coast follows Nois point for a mile as far as Areoura point, which, although like the former, does not project so far to the north-east ; between them, close to the shore, is a rocky islet, called Orjal.

Burela Point projects to the north-east, and is the termination of a high mountain named Ronadoira, with rather a flat summit. The point, which is low, rocky, steep, and of a reddish colour, may be passed at the distance of a mile when the sea is smooth, but it must be given a wide berth in bad weather, for there is then a heavy sea on the irregular rocky bottom which extends from it. Less than a cable north of the point are the Chacineiras, appearing as three islets at high water, but as one at low water, and surrounded by reefs. Another, named Piedra de Burela, lies S.S.E. $\frac{1}{2}$ E. about 3 cables from the point, to which it is connected by sunken reefs ; at high water the islet looks like a boat, and a short distance outside it are 7 and 8 fathoms water, sand and rock. The bay which follows the point to the south-east is named port Burela, from the village of that name which is scattered about it ; coasters visit it in the summer.

From Burela point the coast takes a north-west direction, and at nearly 4 miles is a small peninsula, on the north end of which is an Atalaya or look-out, and on the west side the little port of San Ciprian ; on the east side is a little bay called Caosa, off which are some rocks, the outer and most dangerous of which, called the Leixon del Nordeste, nearly always breaks. It lies S.E. $\frac{1}{2}$ E. half a mile from the Atalaya, and will be avoided by not passing south of the parallel of the north extreme of the peninsula.

The coast is backed by high mountainous land, the peak of Gistral being 3,395 feet above the level of the sea. The peak of Tres mujeres, 3 miles W.S.W. of Areoura point, rises 1,635 feet high ; and Cabaleiros, $3\frac{1}{4}$ miles W.S.W. of Burela, 1,670 feet high.

Currents.—During summer, westerly and north-west currents are constantly experienced, according to the contour of the coast and distance from it. The tides reach but a short distance off; the ebb running west, and the flood east. From June to September the currents set to the W.N.W. about 2 miles an hour, especially off Orrio de Tapia and Burela point, if the wind is steady at N.E. In winter, on the contrary, the currents set eastward, and off Burela point to the south-east, towards the head of the gulf of Foz about 2 miles an hour when north-west winds prevail. In unsettled weather the mariner should be cautious when navigating in this vicinity.

Fogs are frequent in June and July; they continue for three or four days, and are almost always preceded by a fresh north-east breeze. In Rivadeo, when Monte Mondigo is covered with fog or haze and the coast westward about San Ciprian obscured, it is a sign of a north-east wind; but when Mondigo and the coast is clear, a westerly wind may be expected.

FARALLONES de SAN CIPRIAN.—At one mile N. by E. $\frac{1}{4}$ E. from the Atalaya of San Ciprian, are three rocky islets, named Sombriza, Baja, and Pié. Sombriza, the largest and westernmost, is nearly a quarter of a mile long, east and west, narrow, and of moderate height. Baja at half a cable to the south-east of Sombriza, is about the same length E.S.E. and W.S.W., and half a cable across. The Pié, the most remarkable of the three, is a nearly circular inaccessible rock, 83 feet high, of a reddish colour; it is distant 70 yards E. $\frac{1}{4}$ N. from Sombriza, being separated by a passage, in which there are rocks that are scarcely covered at low tide, but with $5\frac{1}{2}$ to $6\frac{1}{2}$ fathoms water between. The passage is not navigable between Sombriza and Baja; around both these islets, at a short distance, are $4\frac{1}{2}$ and $5\frac{1}{2}$ fathoms, sand bottom, and there are $6\frac{1}{2}$ to 13 fathoms, sand and rock, in the channel between them and the peninsula of San Ciprian. A rocky bank with 11 to 13 fathoms water on it, dangerous only in heavy seas, lies 3 cables N.E. of Sombriza.

Between Sombriza and cape Morás, which is $1\frac{7}{10}$ miles to the N.W., is a rocky ridge or chain of reefs named San Clemente, which inclines to the southward, with $4\frac{1}{2}$ to $6\frac{1}{2}$ fathoms on it at low water, and the sea breaks on it in north and north-west gales. When there is much sea the best channel lies close to Sombriza, and to use it a vessel must pass 2 cables distant from the west point of the islet. There is another channel, not so good as the former, between the above reefs and the cape, which may be used by passing a cable from the cape.

The principal passage to the anchorage within the Farallones, is between them and the peninsula of San Ciprian, but when there is much sea it breaks S.S.E. 2 cables from Baja; care must be taken to avoid a reef, lying S.E., about half a mile from the Atalaya. These dangers are only to be feared in heavy seas, and between them there is a deep wide channel for vessels of the largest draught.   Anzuela islet, lying about half a cable from the north-west side of the peninsula, is low, rocky, 1¼ cables long east and west, and nearly covered at high water springs; about a cable from its northern side are the Leixon du Vendanbal rocks, which uncovers at half tide.

PORT SAN CIPRIAN is the name given to the anchorage in the little bight on the west side of the above peninsula, between it and Anzuela islet.   It will not accommodate more than 5 vessels of about 100 tons burthen conveniently, and they must secure themselves to the rocks of the islet, and to anchors laid out to the southward.   The depth is from 3 to 3½ fathoms, sand and weed, but in fresh north-west winds it is only protected from half ebb to half flood, as at high water a considerable sea runs over the islet.   Vessels of 200 tons load in the port during the summer season.

A river falls into the south-west corner of the bight, but owing to the little depth on its shifting bar, it is only available, at high water springs, for vessels under 8 feet draught.   A vessel once inside is secure from all winds, with the only inconvenience of lying aground at low water on a bottom of soft mud.   The iron works of Sargadelos are 3 miles up the river.

On the east side of the peninsula is the village of Figueiras, containing about 400 inhabitants.   From thence a neck of sand, about a cable long, and half a cable wide, extends to the north-east, forming the isthmus of the peninsula, which is a mass of granite rock, with a covering of sand, terminating to the northward in level ground, on which is the height called the Atalaya or look-out, 83 feet high.   The village of San Ciprian stands on rocky ground on the west side of the peninsula.   In north-west gales the isthmus is overflowed, and the communication is then cut off between the villages.   Water is obtained in the river.   Provisions are scarce.*

LIGHT.—On the north extreme of San Ciprian peninsula is a light gray coloured granite tower, which exhibits, at 121 feet above the level of the sea, a *fixed* white light, visible in clear weather at a distance of 9 miles.

Tides.—It is high water, full and change, in port Ciprian, at 3 h.; springs rise about 10 feet, but more or less according to the direction of the wind.

Directions.—A vessel bound to San Ciprian from the eastward should pass between the Farallones and the peninsula; if from the wes'

* *See* Admiralty plans :—San Ciprian bay, and port, on sheet of plans, No. 77

ward, between cape Morá and San Clemente reefs if the water is smooth ; or between the reefs and the Farallones when there is much sea. There are two channels into the port, one on the east, the other on the west side of Anzuela islet. The former, although the smaller, is generally adopted, being clear of rocks ; the mark through, is the Baja un with the Pié, astern. If a pilot is required, one will come out immediately the signal is made, and boats are always ready to render assistance.

When running for the port with a heavy sea from the north-west sail should be carried to get quickly through it at the narrow entrance ; but the sail must be taken in and the anchor let go the moment the vessel is inside, as the space is very limited.

LAGO BAY.—The coast between San Ciprian and cape Morás, at $2\frac{1}{4}$ miles to the N.N.W., forms a large bight, within which are four bays, with beaches. The smallest, which is nearest the cape, is named, Portiño ; and the next Lago, from a village on its shore. Lago bay is clean and navigable, with good holding ground and shelters from south-west and north-west winds. It is much frequented by coasters, and by vessels that cannot get into Barquero or Vivero during south-west gales, for there is no difficulty in entering it, and it is free from the heavy gusts of wind encountered in those inlets.

The best position for a large vessel to anchor, is with the cape bearing N.N.E. and Pié islet (Farallones) E. $\frac{3}{4}$ S., in 11 fathoms, fine sand ; outside this there are patches of rock. Should a northerly gale come on, there will be no risk, provided the vessel has good ground tackle, for the rocky bottom with $4\frac{1}{2}$ to $6\frac{1}{2}$ fathoms water on it between the cape and the Farallones breaks the sea considerably. If obliged to abandon the vessel the crew will be saved by running the boat under the lee of a salient point. If surprised here with a north-east gale, get under sail on the port tack, so as to weather the cape on the other board. There will be no difficulty in passing between the Farallones and San Ciprian in depths of 11 to 13 fathoms.

CAPE MORÁS, steep, rocky, and 85 feet high, projects to the north-east, and is commanded by elevated land which reaches 1,250 feet above the sea. On its west side is the village of Morás. There is a farallon at its foot, and N.N.W. half a mile from it is a bank with 13 fathoms water on it, called the Cangrejeiro. Anzaron island, at $1\frac{1}{2}$ miles N.W. $\frac{1}{4}$ W. from the cape, is high, rugged, and arid, presenting to the northward, whitish cliffs. It lies so close to the coast that at a distance it is blended with it, and difficult to distinguish. It is clean and bold, having 8 fathoms close to, and 20 fathoms at a short distance. The coast between Anzaron and Roncadoira point, rather more than a mile to the

N.W. by W., recedes to the southward, forming Reboira bay, at the head of which is the mouth of the river Portocelo, admitting only boats at high water, and on its west side are two islets.

From Rohcadoira point, a high and rocky coast, with 23 fathoms water within half a mile of it, trends a mile westward to a point close off which are two islets, named Los Netos, the shore between the points forming a bay, at the head of which there is a small islet close to the shore. The Netos, one high, the other low, may be passed at a prudent distance, there being 28 fathoms at 2 cables from them, rocky bottom. From thence a steep and rocky coast runs west three-quarters of a mile to Saiñas point, which is low at its extreme, but clean, and can be passed at a distance of 2 cables. From it Faro point bears W.S.W. 2 miles, and between is a deep bay, named Esteiro, the whole of which is rocky and foul, and when there is much sea the breakers reach a long distance from the shore.

VIVERO INLET, the entrance to which is a mile wide, between Faro point on the east, and Socastro point on the west, is chiefly resorted to by vessels which in north-west or south-west gales have been driven to leeward of Barquero, or have been unable to gain an anchorage there on account of the violence of the wind. It extends inland 2½ miles in a S.S.W. direction, has good holding-ground, and affords shelter from south-west and north-west winds on its western shore, and from those from north-east and east on its eastern shore. A heavy sea, however, tumbles in with northerly gales, and a vessel using it during the winter months should be provided with good ground tackling.[*]

Both shores are high, bold, and clean, all dangers off them showing above water. The depths decrease gradually from 10 fathoms at entrance to 3 fathoms near the head of the inlet, which by degrees is shoaling with sand. Vessels under 11 feet draught can proceed at high water as far in as the bridge at the town of Vivero, through a channel kept open by the tidal currents of the river Landrove, which here falls into the sea; but they lie aground when the tide is out. Large boats can get to Landrove village, about 3 miles up the river.

On the east side of the entrance is monte Faro, a round hill with the ruins of a watch-tower on its summit, 664 feet high, the slope of which descends seaward to Faro point; and on the west side of entrance is Socastro point, called Testa de Castro, of moderate height, with rocks at its base. Gabeira islet, a little within the point, is of moderate height, and between it and the shore there is 5½ to 6½ fathoms water in the middle of the channel, which is half a cable across. Between this islet and Caballo

---

[*] *See* Admiralty plan.—Port Vivero, No. 78; scale, m—3½ inches.

point, distant 6 cables to the southward, is a spacious bay with two beaches, the southern of which, called Abrela, is exposed to the north-east, but coasters anchor off it with south-west winds when they cannot get farther up the inlet. The beach is clean, the depth gradually increasing from it to 10 fathoms.

From Caballo point the shore runs S.S.W. a quarter of a mile to Queimada islet, which is close to the land ; it then bends to the westward, forming the bay of San Juan, which has several rocks or small islets near its shore, and is limited to the southward by one named Insua, and by some steep rocks called the Castelos del Grallal. Thence commences a sandy flat, which continues about 6 cables southward, and 8 cables eastward, as far as Lavandeiras bay, choking up the head of the inlet ; the flat is nearly dry at low water, its breakers in bad weather reaching nearly as far out as the parallel of Cillero village. The town of Vivero stands on the eastern shore at the head of the inlet, at the foot of Monte de San Roque, 1,140 feet high, with a population of about 2,600. It communicates with the opposite shore by a bridge of 12 arches, which is continued farther by a causeway 2 cables long. Small vessels are built here, and some coasting and numerous fishing vessels belong to the town.

From the town a high, winding, and in some parts a precipitous shore runs in a northerly direction one mile to Cillero village, which is built on an eminence jutting out into the sea, having on its south side the bay of Lavandeiras, so obstructed by sand as to be nearly dry at low water, and on its north a little bight called port Cillero. The bar at the entrance of the channel leading to Vivero, is at the extremity of the most projecting point of the cliff on which Cillero village stands ; and as it shifts, to cross it in a vessel of 9 or 11 feet draught it is necessary to employ the services of a fisherman of the village. The greatest depth in the Channel at high water ordinary springs is 11 feet.

From port Cillero a high and precipitous shore trends to the northward, and bending eastward forms the bay of Area, with its beach called San Julian. In the northern part of this bay is Area islet, somewhat larger and higher than Gabeira islet ; it is a cable from the shore, and the space between is full of rocks.

Water and Supplies.—Good water is plentiful in the inlet. Provisions can be obtained at Vivero at reasonable prices, and workmen, should a vessel require repairs.

Tides.—It is high water, full and change, at the bar of Vivero, at 2h. 30m. ; springs rise 15 feet, neaps 8 or 9 feet. With strong south-west and north-west winds, the water rises between 4 and 5 feet above its usual level, whilst with those from north-east and south-east it is depressed 3 feet below it.   The stream runs 3 miles an hour in the river, and 1½ miles in the middle of the inlet.

Directions.—Estaca point, cape Vares, and Conejera island, are remarkable, and will successively present themselves when approaching Vivero inlet from the westward ; while the Farallones de San Ciprian, Anzaron islet, and monte Faro, will be known when approaching it from the eastward.   Running for shelter either in this inlet or in Barquero in a south-west gale, keep the coast close aboard, and be prepared for heavy squalls and eddy winds off the land.   If unable to gain Barquero, endeavour to pass inside Conejera island ; for if a large vessel in distress misses Vivero, there are no ports to the eastward but what are barred and difficult to take.   In rounding Socastro point, keep at a prudent distance, but so as to get into Vivero if possible without a tack.   Anchor directly the vessel is in 7 or 8 fathoms water, and give her a good scope of cable.

Socastro point cannot be rounded close-to in a north-west gale, for off it is a rocky bank with 6½ fathoms water on it, called the Có, which breaks when there is a heavy sea, and the whole extent between it and the point being uneven ground is then covered with breakers.   The Có lies 3 cables from the point, and nearly N.N.E. from Gabeira islet, with the Castelos de Laguete rocks (off the beach of San Roman), on with Socastro point, and the Castelos del Grallal rocks in line with the west side of the inlet.   To pass outside the bank, keep the summit of the hill forming cape Vares, in the middle of the passage between Conejera islet and the main, until the Castelos del Grallal opens clear of the west shore of the inlet.   There are 13 fathoms a short distance outside the bank.   Another bank, called the Lage, but with more water on it and less dangerous than the Có, lies W.S.W. a cable from Faro point, which otherwise is bold-to.

If unable to enter Vivero in easterly or south-easterly gales, keep the land abroad and endeavour to enter Barquero.   Sometimes vessels prevented by strong southerly winds from taking Vivero, anchor in 12 to 14 fathoms off the beach of San Roman to await a change   or they run to the eastward towards cape Morás, and keep under sail between Saiñas point and San Ciprian, where they find less wind ; or they anchor in the bay of Lago.

Anchorage.—The best anchorage in Vivero inlet during winter, is on its western side in San Juan bay, the bottom there being muddy sand. A good berth is 2 cables off shore, in 4½ to 5 fathoms water, with Gabiera islet in line with Caballo point.   Southerly winds are frequent, and a heavy sea runs in with northerly gales.   In summer, vessels anchor more in the middle of the inlet, in 5 to 5½ fathoms.   It will be necessary to lift the anchor occasionally, for the bottom is a muddy clay, and there is great difficulty in breaking it out of the ground if long down.

The COAST from the west point of entrance of Vivero trends a short distance westward to the beach of San Roman, it then takes a northerly direction for 2 miles to Ventosa point, half a mile northward of which is Conejera or Coelleira island. The above beach is of small extent, fronted with some conical rocks, named Los Castelos de Laguete; vessels anchor off it in 12 to 14 fathoms in south-west winds, but they must be prepared to leave with the first change.

Conejera or Coelleira Island is a mile in circuit, high and steep to the north and north-east, but lower to the south. It is clothed with vegetation, and on its west side is a small cove used as a landing-place. At half a cable off its north extreme is a rock, which breaks when there is much sea from the north-west. The channel between the island and the main is a quarter of a mile wide, and has $9\frac{1}{4}$ fathoms water in the middle, but with onshore gales the sea breaks the whole way across it.

BARQUERO INLET, running in 3 miles to the south-west between Conejera island and cape Vares, is $1\frac{1}{4}$ miles wide at entrance, easy of access, clear of danger, with good holding ground, sandy bottom, and sheltered from all winds except those from the eastward, but these are not accompanied by any sea to endanger a ship if she has good ground tackling. It is sufficiently spacious to contain a large fleet, and has three excellent watering-places, where boats may water with great convenience. The superiority of this inlet consists in the facility of taking it in bad weather, and being the only refuge for vessels of large draught from all winds, except those from about N.E. to S.E. on the whole Cantabrian coast. The worst wind is a gale from south-west, from the difficulty there is then of gaining an anchorage, as the wind blows out with much force, but in such cases an effort should be made to reach Vares bay south-west of the cape, or Vivero inlet the next eastward.*

Although as a harbour it is not equal to Ferrol or Coruña, it is easier to make in thick weather, the coast is clean and bold, and in approaching it in westerly gales, a vessel does not, as at Ferrol and Coruña, run down on a lee shore. The soundings gradually decrease from 17 fathoms at entrance, to $3\frac{1}{2}$ fathoms at 2 miles within, between points Santa and Castro, where the inlet narrows to half a mile; thence the depths decrease more rapidly, the whole of the inner part being nearly dry at low water

---

* *See* Admiralty plan :—Entrance of Barquero, No. 77 ; scale, *m* = 3·4 inches.

springs, excepting some little channels kept open by the streams of tide. The coasts of the inlet are high, clean, and in many parts approachable to a short distance, but on the western shore between Santa and Campelo points, it is bordered at about a cable off by a bank with 2 fathoms water on it.

Within Santa point is the little port of Barquero, but it is choked with sand, which increases every year, and at present there are not more than 6 to 8 feet at low water, in a narrow channel towards the northern shore, and this is obstructed by a bar which nearly dries. Vessels of 11 feet draught can get up to the town at high water springs; but with north-east winds, however little sea there may be, the sea on the bar breaks, and the entrance is impracticable. The town stands in an elbow on the northern shore, at the foot of a cliff, commanded by high land, about 904 feet above the sea, but it has but few resources. The population may amount to about 900.

Between the town and monte Furado on the opposite shore, is the entrance to an inlet called the river Sor, which separates the provinces of Lugo and Coruña, and extends 4 miles in a southerly and south-west direction. There are some deep spots in it with 7 and 8 feet at low water, while in other parts there is scarcely sufficient depth at half tide for large boats over the banks of fine sand and mud, by which it is obstructed. Small vessels resort to it for cargoes of white earth. Monte Furado is a small hill covered with sand, and terminating in a point to the north-east. Between the hill and Castrelos point is a long sandy beach, from which runs an extensive shallow flat. The bay on the east side of the inlet, between Castrelos and Videiros points, is called Puerto del Vale; it is 4 cables wide and 2 deep, but being shallow the fishing vessels are hauled up on a clean beach at its head.

At a quarter of a mile farther northward, between points Castro and Congrera, is a small bight, 2 cables wide, named Puerto de Vicedo, off which is considered the best anchorage of the inlet in north-east and east winds. Cuevabaja point, 2 cables N.E. of Congrera point, is high and rocky; thence the coast to Conejera island is high, steep, and safe to approach, but exposed to northerly winds. On the norther shore, about half a mile westward of cape Vares, is the little bay of Vares, in the north-east part of which coasters are sheltered by a ridge of rocks extending upwards of a cable in a westerly direction from Bufato point. There is here a clean beach, and the village of Vares, containing about 640 inhabitants.

Water and Supplies.—Water may be obtained at many places in the inlet. The best place is on the south-east shore, close to Congrera point, under Vicedo village. There is, however, an excellent run on the opposi shore, near Campelo point, where two or three boats can water at the same time, even at low tide. In Vares bay it may also be had, although not so good as at the others. Barquero has good water, and here, as well as at Vares, some supplies may be purchased; but provisions in any quantity must be procured from Vivero, 6 miles inland.

LIGHT.—On Conejera island, at the east side of entrance to Barquero, is a light gray coloured granite tower, which exhibits, at 273 feet above the level of the sea, a *fixed* white light, seen in clear weather at a distance of 9 miles.

Tides.—It is high water, full and change, at the mole of Barquero, at 3 h. 15 m.; springs rise 10¾ feet. The rise is from 3 to 4 feet above the ordinary level with strong north-west winds, and the contrary with those from the north-east. The current in the channel runs 3 miles an hour at springs.

Directions.—The inlet of Barquero is easily recognized from the northward and westward, by cape Ortegal and Estaca point; the cape is known by the Aguillones islets lying well out, and Estaca point runs down rugged to the sea, with a lighthouse on it and some conical islets off it. The coast between this point and cape Vares is high and steep, and a vessel from the westward with south-west winds should keep sufficiently near to recognise it, as the land is generally then much obscured. If the water is smooth, the outer islet off Estaca point may be passed at about a mile or less; but in a heavy sea from the west or north-west, a berth of 2 or 3 miles or more must be given it according to circumstances. Cape Vares is bold, and may be kept close aboard, but with strong winds from west to south-west heavy gusts rush down it endangering a vessel's masts.

With strong southerly winds, the coast should be approached as near as the dangers off it will allow. If unable to gain an anchorage in Barquero inlet, endeavour to gain that of Vivero, which is equally good with these winds, passing if possible inside the island of Conejera. In choosing an anchorage in Barquero inlet, attention should be paid to the time of year and the prevailing winds. A vessel will be sheltered from north-west gales when cape Vares is eastward of N.N.E.; but a good berth will be found at about 3 cables of Almeiro point, with cape Vares N.E. ¾ E. and Conejera island S.E. ¼ E.; in this position a vessel will be well sheltered, and have room to veer or get under way if desired.

During a heavy sea in the offing, the swell comes in round cape Vares, when the smoothest water will be found between Cuevabaja and Castro Grande points; it was here that 29 sail of merchant vessels rode out the heavy gales of 1839-40. Large vessels should anchor in 6 or 7 fathoms water, with Conejera island open nearly its own breadth of the main land.

Sobrepuesta and Santa points are under a high mountain, from whence heavy squalls come down; there is, however, good winter anchorage in their vicinity from south-west and north-west winds for vessels of not more than 11 feet draught; but if there is any appearance of a north-east wind they must shift to the opposite shore.

The coast between Estaca point and cape Prior is composed nearly throughout of steep inaccessible rugged rocks, especially from cape Ortegal to Cedeira, and is dangerous to be on in winter with north-west and northerly winds. With north-west and north-east gales, cape Prior and the coast eastward of it should have a berth of at least 6 or 7 miles, to avoid the heavy sea in the neighbourhood of the rocky banks alluded to in page 211, or in case of being becalmed. The same caution should be observed in reference to cape Ortegal and Estaca point, to avoid the calms which sometimes occur in their vicinity, and near the land, with easterly and north-east winds.

With south-west winds these points may be passed at a short distance, for the sake of shelter, but it will always be prudent to keep a good offing if the weather is doubtful, or if there is a chance of its being a dead lee shore.

ESTACA POINT, the northernmost of the coast of Spain, is the west extreme of the northern face of the rocky promontory forming the west side of the inlet of Barquero; the other extreme, $1\frac{1}{2}$ miles to the east-ward, being cape Vares, which is high, round, bold, and steep to seaward. The point extends in a north-west direction in a gentle declivity from the conical hill, 694 feet high, which forms cape Vares, narrowing as it advances into the sea, where it terminates in rugged pointed rocks.

A short distance off the point are two conical rocky islets; the outer being the smaller, and named Estaquin, is half a cable distant from the inner; and a little outside of Estaquin are two rocks scarcely covered at low water. The depth gradually increases seaward, there being 14 fathoms at a cable, and 22 fathoms, rocky bottom, at 3 cables from the Estaquin. In a gale from the north-west, the sea breaks some distance outside the point, which at that time should be carefully avoided.

Between cape Vares and Estaca point, the coast presents a steep and nearly inaccessible front to the northward, and nearly midway is Moiños point, a rocky projection with rocks some distance off it, which should be given a good berth when there is any sea, or by vessels running along the land at night in fine weather.

LIGHT.—On Estaca point is a round gray-coloured granite light-tower which exhibits, at an elevation of 306 feet above the sea level, *a revolving* white light, attaining its greatest brilliancy every *minute*, at visible in clear weather at a distance of 23 miles. The tower, which is 46 feet high, and adjoins the keeper's dwelling, stands on an eminence 4½ cables S. by E. ½ E. from the outer islet off the point.

The COAST from Estaca point, formed of steep whitish rocks broken by small beaches, takes a W. by S. direction 5 miles to a rocky projection called Baneja point, towards which it gradually becomes high and hilly. The Piedra Mea are two rocks lying close together N.N.W. from this latter point, and nearly 2 miles from the coast, with 3½ to 13 fathoms water between; they are awash at high water, and the sea always breaks. A vessel should only pass inside them in fine weather, and then close to, for when there is any sea, the whole channel between the rocks and the point is covered with breakers; in passing outside give them a berth of at least 2 cables.

At half a mile south-west of Baneja point is a high steep headland, with a watch-tower on its summit, the shore between forming a small bight with a beach, named San Antonio bay. Carnero or Espante point, at a mile westward of this headland, is the extreme of a long tongue of land separating two bays, the northern of which, named Espasante, after the village in the north-east part of it, is spacious and bordered by a beach, but open to the north-west. The southern bay extends 1½ miles eastward, and nearly dries at low water.

CARIÑO INLET.—The Piedra Mea rocks with Marbeira island N.W. ½ N. distant 2½ miles from them, form the entrance of Cariño inlet, and from a line between the two the coast forms a bight about 5 miles deep, with arms of the sea running east and west; the larger and more important being that to the eastward, which leads to the town of Santa Marta, at the most inland part of it. The inlet is navigable as far as Fraile and Carnero points in mid-channel, with depths gradually decreasing from 18 to 20 fathoms at the entrance, to 4 fathoms near the bar formed between the two points.

The western coast of the inlet between Marbeira island and Cariño point forms a bay, with a somewhat steep shore, which may be navigated at the distance of half a mile in 10 fathoms water, sand. Cariño point is the north extreme of Cariño bay, about three-quarters of a mile in extent, which is frequented by coasters, but only affords shelter from south-west winds when not strong, for then the sea renders it a bad anchorage. In the middle of the bay are 3 to 4 fathoms, sand, the depth gradually decreasing to the sandy shore. The town of Cariño stands on the beach in the north part of the bay, and contains about 1,670 inhabitants.

Vessels bound to Santa Marta anchor in 10 to 12 fathoms, east of Cariño point in fine weather, to wait tide for crossing the bar, or to obtain a pilot from Cariño. Mentaron point, the south extreme of Cariño bay, has two rocks off it which are uncovered at high water ordinary tides ; the outer one is steep-to, and may be passed at a short distance in 7 fathoms, sand. From thence the coast continues of moderate height, but high in the interior, to Fraile point, which has a conical islet off it. About a mile to the eastward, off the eastern shore, is San Vicente islet, large, round and covered with vegetation, having a passage inside it at high water.

PORT SANTA MARTA.—The bar of this port is entirely of sand and has two openings, one with 15 feet at high water springs, near Fraile point, and the other near San Vicente islet. The latter channel is the deeper, but the former is preferred, because the channels from it to Sismundi are straighter and more navigable. Within the bar a large sand-bank extends to the south, east, and west, which is for the most part dry at low water, leaving channels for boats and flat-bottomed small craft. There are, however, some holes of 5 to 8 fathoms water, especially near Sismundi, in which vessels anchor rather than lie aground.

Anchorage.—The anchorage off the village of Sismundi is at the mouth of the port abreast of a bend of the western shore. The village, numbering about 200 inhabitants, stands on a hill half a mile inland. Within this anchorage is the port of Santa Marta, 3 miles long and 2 miles wide, but, being obstructed with sands, will only admit vessels of 11 feet draught at high water springs, and 9 feet at neaps. This draught may go up to the town, off which they can lie afloat if they keep in the channel. The town of Santa Marta, called also Ortigueira, is on the north side of the port, and contains about 1,050 inhabitants; it supplies provisions and good water.

Tides.—It is high water, full and change, at port Santa Marta, at 3h., and half an hour sooner at Sismundi; springs rise 11 feet, and neaps 9 feet. With strong winds outside, the rise is 3 to 4 feet higher.

Directions.—The inlet of Cariño can only be frequented with safety during the summer months. In winter there are but few days that a vessel can enter or depart, in consequence of the heavy seas, whether from N.E. North, or N.W., which are felt in the inlet. A vessel bound to port Santa Marta should touch at Cariño for a pilot, for the mouths of the channels over the bar are constantly changing ; but no vessel should attempt to enter except with smooth water, as the bar breaks with the least sea. Having crossed the bar and anchored in one of the deep holes off Sismundi, she will be secure from all winds.

CAPE AGUILLONES, bearing W. by N. ¼ N. 7 miles distant from Estaca point, is precipitous and much broken, terminating in numerous sharp peaks, which rise above each other, and attain a considerable altitude. The cape presents a triangular steep front to the north-east, half a mile in extent, rising to a considerable height, and terminating to the south-east in a point, off which is a rocky islet, named Marbeira, with a passage inside it for boats. At a short distance outside the islet are 10 fathoms water, sand, which depth continues for a mile to the southward, as far as Cariño point.

A chain of high steep sharp-pointed black rocky islets, called the Aguillones extend in a northerly direction from the cape. The outer one, which is about a mile from the cape, is called Caballo Juan; the next inshore of it, Tres Hermanos, from having three sharp peaks of the same size; the third, Insua Mayor, from being the largest of all; the fourth, Rodicio, is like a pyramid; and that nearest the shore is named the Longa. A sunken rock, the Rocemada, on which the sea always breaks, lies a short distance outside them. There are clear passages between the islets, the least water being 10 fathoms; a mile to the north-east the depth is 28 to 32 fathoms, coarse shells.

CAPE ORTEGAL* or Alto del Limo, nearly 2 miles westward of cape Aguillones, is high, round, and precipitous to seaward, and, when seen from the north west, it will be recognized by table-land of different elevations gradually rising to the summit, on the central point of which is the little tower of Limo, 930 feet above the level of the sea. From the fall of the cape a small tongue of low land projects, called Limo point, surrounded to the distance of half a cable by sunken rocks, on which the sea always breaks. At half a mile northward of the point is a dangerous rock, with 2½ fathoms water on it, named the Leé; there are 13 to 16 fathoms between it and the point. The point is not easily distinguished when coming from the northward, in consequence of the high land behind it, but it may be known by a black cliff of a triangular shape in its vicinity; seen from the north-east it appears rounded. At 2 miles off the cape the soundings are about 40 fathoms, sand and shells, gradually decreasing to the shore.

Between cape Ortegal and cape Aguillones the coast is high, steep, inaccessible, and dangerous to be near in bad weather. Large sailing vessels should give it a wide berth, when there is much swell or in light winds, and still more so in gales, for the sea is heavier and the currents stronger here than on any other part of the coast.

Current.—In its normal condition and near the land, the flood sets N.E. and the ebb S.W.; but in the offing the direction of the current is

---

* This cape is known to the local mariners as the Altodel Limo, and cape Agulliones as the real cape Ortegal.

regulated by the prevailing winds, running strong when they are fresh from north-east or south-west. The current, however, sometimes runs against the wind, and even indicates the direction from which it is about to blow. In fine weather a strong current has been observed by the fishermen setting eastward, previous to a north-east wind, which has been stronger in proportion to the strength of the current that preceded it.

The COAST between cape Ortegal and Cedeira may be passed by any vessel at the distance of a mile without risk, but it would be prudent to give it a berth of 3 or 4 miles, and in bad weather 5 or 6 miles, and still farther off in the winter season, when there is an appearence of a gale Cuadro point, 2¼ miles W.S.W. of the cape, stretches out to the north-west with steep prongs to the sea. It descends in declivities from monte Capelada, which has a watch-tower on one of its prominent parts, elevated 2,081 feet above the sea. A rocky islet is detached a good distance from the point, and 3 miles outside it are 40 fathoms water, rocky bottom.

Between Cuadro point and Candelaria point, which bears W. ¾ S. 4¼ miles from it, the steep coast forms a bend about 1¼ miles deep, at the head of which are some high islets named Gabeiras. They lie near the shore which in the whole of this bight is rocky, without any sand. Dominigo point, 1¼ miles westward of the Gabeiras, has some rocky islets a little distance from it, the largest being precipitous, like the rest of the coast.

Candelaria point is dark and steep, being the termination of a conical mountain which descends with abrupt declivities to the shore. It may be recognised by the peaks which are formed by the rugged and broken land, and which terminate in isolated rocky pinnacles that decrease in size as they approach the sea. A reef, with two of its rocky heads above water, lies off the point in a north-west direction, and in fine weather fishing vessels pass inside them; from a distance these rocks have the appearance of two fishing vessels some distance apart, by which Candelaria point may also be known. The tower of Candelaria stands on a mountain of considerable height, but from its dark colour and ruinous condition it is scarcely distinguishable. At about 2 miles farther on is Faucño point, steep, rocky, and salient, with large boulder rocks at its base; the coast being high and precipitous to Cedeira.

Chirlateira or Pantin point, the western point of entrance of port Cedeira, projects northward, and descends in declivities from a hill 673 feet high, named monte Borneira, the foot of which is washed by the waters of the port. This hill, seen from the north-east, assumes the form of a sugar-loaf, and near its summit is a small detached look-out house. A reef extends northward from the point, which should be given a wide

Two of the rocky heads are awash at high water; the outer, named the Meixon, is a cable from the point. At a cable N.E. by E. from the Meixon is the Lage rock, with less than 2 fathoms on it, and which breaks with the least sea; and about 2 cables N.W. ½ W. from the Lage is an equally dangerous rock, with 2 fathoms on it, named the Nieto.

Another rock, called the Peton, lies 5½ cables N.W. of the Lage, but it has 7½ fathoms on it, and is only dangerous in heavy seas. From it Sarridal point, in port Cedeira, is in line with the Meixon; and between it and the Nieto are 15 to 23 fathoms water, and outside, a short distance, 18 to 23 fathoms. There are 13 and 15 fathoms between the Meixon and Lage, and the same depth between the Lage and Nieto. About a cable inshore of the Nieto is the Badaxeira rock, with 4½ fathoms on it; and S.S.E. of this, distant another cable, is the Punxallo rock, with only 1½ fathoms, and the first to show its breakers; between the two latter rocks there are 11 and 13 fathoms, and the same depth between them and the shore.

PORT CEDEIRA is only adapted for vessels drawing 11 to 13 feet, for in the most sheltered part the depths are small. It is a port of refuge, and conveniently situated for small craft which, in strong north-east winds, cannot round cape Ortegal. In these winds it is easily entered, and shelter from the sea is gained directly the entrance is reached. The anchorage is well sheltered from north and north-west winds, if they do not blow hard, but in a gale the swell is inconvenient; the holding ground of sand, however, is excellent, and with good ground tackling there is no risk. Large vessels can find outer berths, but necessarily exposed; if drawing more than 11 feet, they should under similar circumstances run for Coruña in preference to this port.*

The entrance, 6 cables wide, and open to the north, is between the rocks off Chirlateira or Fautin point and the Blancas, which are a group of white rocks above water, lying a cable from the eastern shore. Escaleiron islet, lying to the northward of the Blancas, is clear and connected with the shore. A rocky shoal, with 2¾ fathoms water on it, is said to lie 1¼ miles N.E. of Chirlateira point. There are 12 to 17 fathoms, rocky bottom, at the entrance, the depth decreasing gradually inside to 3, 2½, and 2 fathoms, over sand.

The Medio Mar or Half-tide rocks, lying nearly in the middle of the port, three-quarters of a mile within the entrance, have always breakers on them; when uncovered they show three heads. There are 4 fathoms in the channel on their western side, and 5 fathoms in that on their eastern side. The latter channel is preferred, between the rocks and

_____

* See Admiralty plan : —Port Cedeira, No. 78; scale, m = 4 inches.

Sarridal point, on the heights of which are the ruins of a battery. This point may be passed at a short distance, as well as the shore trending S.E. from it, until the ruined fort of Concepcion appears standing on a high precipitous point. A small bay will then open out, with a beach, called Arena-longa, off which is the best anchorage.

From this shore the bay continues eastward for half a mile, when it turns northward to the town of Cedeira, which stands at the foot of monte Eigil, which is 820 feet high. The town is not seen from the anchorage; its principal front being to the north-east. It can only be approached at high water, for the eastern part of the port is encumbered with an extensive flat which dries at low tide. A small rivulet runs past the town, and the inhabitants, numbering about 850, communicate with the opposite bank by a bridge of 6 arches and a causeway. Excellent water may be had in abundance, but provisions are scarce.

LIGHT.—A *fixed* white light is exhibited from a town erected on Robaleira point, in the inner part of the port and south-west of the town of Cedeira. The light is elevated 89 feet above the mean level of the sea, and visible at the distance of 9 miles, but it will only be seen from seaward when the mouth of the port is open.

Tides.—It is high water, full and change, in port Cedeira at 3h.; springs rise 15 feet, and neaps 9 feet. The rise is 4 feet higher with north-westerly gales, and 4 feet lower with those from the eastward. The greatest strength of the stream is a mile an hour.

Directions.—This port is easily recognized at a distance by monte Borneira; by the chapel of San Antonio, which is half-way up a hill on the eastern shore, and being white shows out distinctly from the dark ground; and by monte Eigil, which rises from the eastern part of the port, and has on its summit the ruins of a tower. A vessel from the westward should not approach Chirlateira point nearer than 2 miles until the entrance of the port is open, and the whole of the white sand of Loira at the head of the port is seen, when she may run in, keeping the eastern shore aboard, giving the Blanca rocks a berth, and passing midway between the Medio Mar and Sarridal point. Vessels generally take up a berth in 2½ fathoms with the castle on this point in line with Chirlateira point, and moor north and south. Small craft run farther in.

The port is easily entered with north-west and north-east winds, but it would not be prudent for a square-rigged vessel to attempt it when they blow strong from the opposite quarters, especially from south-west, for on nearing the entrance the wind draws ahead and comes down in hard squalls. Candelaria point open of Eiras point southward of it, leads outside the rocks off Chirlateira point.

FROUXEIRA POINT is 4½ miles westward of Chirlateira point; low, round, and with several rocks off it, some under water and others uncovered. Between Chirlateira point and Prados point, which is 2½ miles to the south-west of it, the coast is high, dark, and precipitous, with several small projections, forming bays with sandy beaches. The largest and easternmost of the bays is that of Pantin, and the village of the same name stands a short distance inland.

On the east side of Frouxeira point commences the beach of the same name, which extends in an E.N.E. direction for 2 miles, the sands of which become higher towards the interior. The beach is clear of danger, and may be approached, especially at its eastern end; and a vessel driven towards it in bad weather may entertain the hope of saving the crew by making for this end, which is not so shallow as the other part. The sand is recognized at a considerable distance, from its height and whiteness. At the eastern end of the beach is the entrance of the Frouxeira lake, which is shallow, and the channel into it will only admit fishing vessels at high water.

The shore south-west of Frouxeira point is low, backed by high land, with small bays as far as the slope of monte Campelo, which rises from the sea. The largest and most useful of these bays is that called Portonovo, which is resorted to by coasters for shelter in north-east winds, and is even used in northerly winds, but it must be left the moment there is an appearance of the wind becoming north-westerly, for should it freshen from this quarter the loss of the vessel is nearly certain. There are 5 to 6 fathoms water in the bay, sand bottom, and it is terminated by a beach. The entrance is at the extreme of the eastern slope of monte Campelo, which is high, and when seen from the north-west presents the form of a large saddle, but from the north-east it appears conical; the eastern point of entrance is high, appears like an island, and may be recognized by a conical rock near it.

There are 12 to 15 fathoms water at a mile off the coast between Cedeira and cape Prior, and 55 fathoms at 4 miles off, but in strong north-west winds a berth of 8 or 9 miles should be given to Frouxeira point, as a heavy sea gets up in that locality.

CAPE PRIOR, 7 miles W. by S. from Frouxeira point, is the western extreme of a rocky peninsula of moderate height, which presents a steep front of 1½ miles to the north-west. The beach of Cobas bay on the east side of this peninsula, and that of San Jorge on the south, both low, and being separated by a narrow strip of land, give to it the appearance of an island when approaching it either from the south-east or north-east. From the north-west it is backed by the high land of the interior, but it will be recognized by the several small peaks on its summit, one in particular being prominent and conspicuous.   Some islets and rocks, named Cabalo, extend half a mile from the north-east extreme of the peninsula. The islets are small, with the exception of one which is high, but the sea breaks on the rocks with the least swell.

The beach of Cobas bay on the east side of the peninsula is bold, and terminates in the plain of the same name.   Between the bay and monte Campelo to the north-east the coast is steep, and of moderate height.   The bay and beach of San George (called also Do-rios), on the south side of the peninsula, is formed between Cela point on the north, and Erbosa point on the south.   This bay is 1½ miles wide, and a mile deep, and shelters from north-east and south-east winds, but be careful not to be caught in it with on-shore winds.   Cela point is rocky, and the steep dark land rises from it to the cape.   Erbosa point is low and steep, and off its north-west extreme is an islet of the same name, with a channel inside it for small vessels in moderate weather.

About a mile south-west of Erbosa point is Levadizo point, off which distant about 2 cables are two barren rocky islets, named Gabeiras, connected by a reef over which boats can pass at high water.   Between them and the shore is a channel, which although narrow, is sufficiently deep for coasters in case of necessity.   A rocky bank with 9 to 18 fathoms water on it, runs in a north-west direction from the islets, and from its outer end Candelaria point is just open of cape Prior.   Between Levadizo point and a rocky projection called Serantes or Golfin point, 1½ miles to the southward, is the sandy plain of Doniños, off the beach of which vessels may anchor in 8 to 12 fathoms, fine sandy bottom, with winds between N.E. and S.E.

Inland and not far from the sea is the Doniños lagoon, and in the neighbourhood the town of the same name.   The lake is of an oval form, east and west, and carries 39 feet water.   It has no visible communication with the sea, and its margin is lined with reeds.

LIGHT.—In the middle of the slope of the cape, and on the cliff which projects to the north-west, is the light-tower of cape Prior, which exhibits, at 446 feet above the sea, a *fixed* white light, visible in clear weather at a distance of 15 miles.   The building is white, octagonal, and the tower rises from its centre.

The BERMEO BANK, lying about N.N.W. ¼ W. 8½ miles from Frouxiera point, and N.E. 7 miles from cape Prior, is a mile in extent and steep-to, its rocky sides declining suddenly from 16¼ to 40 fathoms water.   It is generally considered that from 9 to 12 fathoms is the least water, but the position of these depths has not been ascertained; it is, however, possible that rocky heads of even less depths exist, for, with strong north-west winds, breakers have been seen on the bank. Another small bank, with 18 fathoms on it, is said to lie a mile north of the Bermeo.

The Currents off cape Prior are generally produced by the wind. In passing the cape, therefore, with a north-west wind and much sea, it should be done with caution, as the current is then strong and sets towards the shore. With moderate winds and smooth water, a small vessel may approach the cape, and avail herself of the tidal stream, but a large ship should give it a berth of 2 or 3 miles. In the bend of the coast between cape Prior and the Sisargas islands to the south-west, and generally on the whole north-west face of the peninsula, the currents are very strong, especially when combined with the heavy sea from that quarter. In moderate weather the current follows the course of the wind, except near the coast under the influence of the tides, where the flood sets eastward and ebb westward, forming eddies in the bays and off the salient points, but it is difficult to ascertain the exact limit of its range.

CAPE PRIORIÑO.—Cape Prioriño chico is the south, and cape Prioriño grande the west extreme of a tongue of land projecting in a south-west direction from monte Ventoso, and which from its resemblance to cape Prior has received the name of cape Prioriño. Cape Prioriño chico, forming the north-west point of the entrance to Ferrol, is of moderate height, rocky, dark, and may be approached by vessels of any size to the distance of a cable : about half way up its southern face is a quadrangular building with a light-tower rising from its centre, and at the foot of it the ruins of a battery, scarcely visible from its dark colour. Cape Prioriño grande, about half a mile to the north-west is of the same height, somewhat similar in appearance, but more bluff ; a reef projects less than half a .cable from its southern part, and the coast between the capes is beset with rocks.*

Monte Ventoso, rising to the height of 795 feet, about 1¼ miles north-east of the cape, is easily recognized from a distance from its isolated position, and from the watch-tower on its summit, from which signals are made. Its western and northern slopes terminate at the sea, and at the beach of Doniños.

LIGHT.—The light-tower on cape Prioriño chico exhibits, at 89 feet above high water, a *fixed* white light, varied every *two minutes* by a *red flash*. The light is visible in clear weather at a distance of 12 miles.

---

* See Admiralty chart :—Ferrol harbour to cape Finisterre, No. 1,755 ; scale, m = 0·5 of an inch ; Ferrol harbour, No. 80 ; scale, m = 3·9 inches ; and Ferrol, Coruña, and Betanzos inlets, No. 79 ; scale, m = 1·6 inches.

A vessel coming from the northward will see it directly it opens of cape Prioriño grande, and will keep sight of it as far as the middle of the mouth of the Ferrol estuary.

FERROL HARBOUR.—From cape Prioriño the coast recedes to the south-east, and forms a large bight, about 6 miles wide, in which are the inlets of Ferrol, Ares, Betanzos, and Coruña. Ferrol, the northern inlet, running eastward about 8 miles, is the best of the four, as it shelters from all winds, being enclosed by high land on all sides. From its mouth between cape Prioriño chico and Coitelada point, which bear N.N.W. ½ W. and S.S.E. ½ E. from each other, distant nearly 1¼ miles, the two shores incline towards each other, and about 1¼ miles within, they form a narrow entrance channel or strait, 1½ miles long and in some parts barely 2 cables wide, within which is a spacious harbour capable of sheltering a fleet, and numerous small vessels in the indentations of its shores. Its great capacity, convenient depth, excellent holding ground, and more especially its arsenal and basin, constitute it one of the best and safest military ports of Spain.

The town of Ferrol, about half a mile eastward of La Graña, is divided into three parts—the old town, the modern, and the part named Esteiro. The old town, forming the western part, occupies the summit and slope of a hill about 260 feet high, the new town extends east and west from the foot of this hill to near Esteiro, which occupies the eastern part; the whole containing a population of about 18,500, and surrounded by a strong wall and numerous batteries. On the south side of, and lying parallel to the new town, is the spacious basin, a magnificent work, half a mile long and a quarter of a mile wide, with its opening to the south. It is surrounded by the workshops and other buildings which together compose a considerable arsenal—commenced in 1726—and on its eastern side, facing Caranza cove, is a building with twelve slipways. Between the building yard and the new town are the soldiers' barracks, a large handsome square building, which serves as a mark for vessels entering the harbour. Timber is at times imported from Havaña, but the greater portion comes from the neighbouring province of Astúrias.

Docks.—In the arsenal at Ferrol there is a dry dock 474 feet long, 78 feet wide, and 39 feet deep. The depth of water on the blocks at ordinary high tides is 31 feet.

Water and Supplies.—Ferrol has abundance of water, and excellent provisions at reasonable prices. It contains ample supplies of all kinds, both for sailing and steam vessels.

Anchorage.—The most available part of the harbour is on the northern shore between the town of Ferrol and that of La Graña. This space, named Serantes bay from the river of that name which runs through the beach at its head, may be considered as the port, from the excellent shelter it affords from all winds. Large vessels anchor in the middle of the bay, in 7 to 9 fathoms, good holding ground ; small vessels, to have more complete shelter, lie nearer La Graña, and merchant vessels nearer to Ferrol, to be convenient to the wharves. At the west end of the town of Ferrol, there is a mole for the use of merchant vessels. La Graña possesses two ship yards, in which merchant vessels are built, and all kinds of repairs carried on.

Jubia Bay.—After passing Ferrol, the shores of the harbour gradually approach each other and trend in a north-east direction $2\frac{1}{2}$ miles to its head, which is called the bay of Jubia, from the river of that name which falls into it. This river is navigable at high water as far as the bridge, and its waters serve the works of a copper factory. It is observed that the depth increases every year in this bay, while it diminishes in that of Malata or Serantes, owing probably to the eddy the tide makes in turning the angle of the arsenal. On the south shore of the harbour, are the village of Seixo and the town of Mugardos, the latter with about 2,200 inhabitants, most of whom are employed in fisheries.

Cariño Bay, on the northern shore of entrance to Ferrol, is $1\frac{1}{2}$ miles wide, 6 cables deep, with depths of 8 to 12 fathoms over sandy bottom, and is much resorted to in north-east or south-east winds by vessels that have not sufficient daylight to work into the harbour. The bay is sheltered from north-west and north-east winds, and is considered tolerably secure from all others, for those from the southward do not blow home, and bring no sea with them.

Anchorage.—The best berth is in 8 to 12 fathoms, a quarter of a mile off the beach at the head of the bay ; but a vessel intending to enter the harbour should anchor farther out, with the channel open.

CHANNEL to FERROL.—The two shores of the channel are rocky and barren, excepting some patches of cultivation on the northern shore in Leusada bay, where there are several magazines and other buildings. The land on either side is high, monte San Cristóbal, on the northern side, being 466 feet, and monte Faro, on the southern, 871 feet above the level of the sea. The general depths in the channel are 8 to 10 fathoms, sand, gravel, stones, and shells, but there are holes of 13 to 15 fathoms in the narrows between the castles of San Martin and San Felipe. A vessel may anchor in any part of it where the lead gives sand and gravel, but avoid the southern shore, where the bottom is not good, and there are several rocks.

San Carlos point, on the north shore, is rocky, shelving, and crowned by a fort, which, with fort Segaño on the opposite shore, commands the channel, which is here only 3 cables across.   At three-quarters of a mile east of fort San Carlos, and on the same shore, is the castle of San Felipe, one of the principal defences of the entrance.   It projects a little distance from the shore, and parts of the walls are washed by the sea, but the water is shallow in its vicinity, especially on its western side, and a reef with 14 feet water on it projects about a third of a cable from its south side. From thence the shore recedes to the northward, forming Leusada bay, in which, at 80 yards from the northern shore, and W. by N. from Bispon point, is the Pereiro rock, which shows at low water ; it is marked by a buoy.*   Bispon point has some rocks lying a short distance off it, and forms, with Redonda point on the opposite shore, the eastern mouth of the channel.

Coitelada and Segaño points, the south points of entrance, are rocky and of moderate height, and between them is Chanteiro bay, with a beach of sand and a hermitage at its head.   Segaño point is commanded by a. hill, on the western side of which is a fort, and on its summit a little watch-house, having a mast with two yards to repeat signals from the station on monte Ventoso.   This point must be given a good berth in scant winds, for besides the rocks bordering it, some of which are above water, there is the Muela rock, with 6 feet water on it, off its north side, half a cable outside the rocks above water.   The Muela is about 20 yards in extent, the weeds on it generally show its position ; it is marked by a red beacon buoy.

Bispon point, just shut in with the point of mount Cristóbal, being the next west of the castle of San Felipe, leads in 5¼ fathoms north of the Muela rock, and no vessel should approach nearer ; and the same point just shut in with the south-west angle of the barracks at Ferrol (a large square building seen in the direction of the channel), leads well clear in 7 fathoms. From Segaño point the south shore of the channel runs eastward 8¼ miles to the point and castle of San Martin, between which and the point of monte San Cristóbal the distance is only 2 cables, but both points are bold, and free from danger.

At 6 cables eastward of Segaño point is the Batel rock, which dries one foot at low water springs.   It lies about a third of a cable off shore, and from its summit San Cárlos castle bears about N.N.E. ¼ E., and San Martin castle nearly East.   Farther eastward, lying a short distance from

---

* The buoyage of Ferrol is not to be depended upon.

the shore, are two rocks named Cabaliño and Cabalo, about 70 yards apart. The Cabaliño, the westernmost rock, lies 80 yards from the shore, and from its round summit, which is awash at low water springs, the south angle of San Cárlos castle bears N. by W. ⅛ W., and the south-east angle of San Felipe castle E. by N. ¾ N. The Cabalo has three heads, which dry 8 feet at low water.

Palma Shoal.—Palma castle has a reef projecting N.W. a third of a cable from it ; and lying parallel to the shore at the distance of one cable is the Palma shoal, about a cable in extent east and west, formed by three pinnacles of rock, with deep water between. The least depth of 24 feet is upon the central pinnacle; from it the south point of San Felipe castle bears W. ¾ N., Palma castle S.S.W. ⅛ W., and Bispon point N.E. ¾ N.

There is a narrow channel, having 6 fathoms of water, between Palma shoal and the reef extending from Palma castle. Vessels of more than 23 feet draught should pass to the northward of the Palma shoal; when midway between Palma and San Felipe castles, steering N.N.E., until the north extreme of San Felipe castle comes in line with monte San Cristóbal bearing W. by N. ⅛ N.; which mark appears from the chart, to take a vessel on a mid-channel course, until Bispon point is passed.*

Another reef extends a third of a cable in a N.E. direction from Redonda point, so called from its round form, between which and Bispon point on the opposite shore the distance is a little more than 2 cables, but the channel is still farther narrowed by the short reefs projecting from both of them.

LIGHTS.—At the salient point 110 yards east of Palma castle, on the south side of the channel, about 1¾ miles within the entrance, is a granite tower, which exhibits, at 38 feet above the mean level of the sea, a *fixed red* light, visible 8 miles. There is also exhibited from the mercantile mole at Ferrol a *fixed* white light, visible 4 or 5 miles.

Tides.—It is high water, full and change, in the harbour of Ferrol at 3h.; ordinary springs rise 15 feet, neaps 9½ feet. The rise is one or 2 feet higher at the equinoxes, and also with strong south-west winds. The tidal stream runs 2¼ miles an hour at springs, and about a mile at neaps; but it is much stronger in the channel, where there is an eddy close to both shores. The flood sets towards Segaño point, which must be guarded against with scant winds.

Winds.—The prevailing winds at Ferrol are north-east in summer, and the opposite in winter. The north-east wind is attended with clear

* This leading mark is from inspection of Admiralty chart No. 80, and not from actual observation.

weather, and is only interrupted by south-west or west winds of short duration. It sets in regularly at 10h. a.m., and dies away in the evening. If it should happen to prevail in the winter, it will be attended with thick cloudy weather and rain.

South-west winds blow with great strength, and bring dirty weather. They come down in heavy squalls, and a vessel should be provided with good ground tackling. Even in summer they are attended with bad weather, and the whole coast outside is obscured. Westerly and north-west winds clear the sky, and although they blow strong and throw in a heavy sea, they are fair for taking the harbour.

Southerly winds are the most disliked, for besides the thick weather with which they are attended, they blow with such violence that they do not admit of the port being gained if the vessel falls to leeward of it.

Directions.—Cape Prior is a good landfall to make when bound to Ferrol from the north or north-east; and from the westward the inlet may be recognized from a considerable distance by the break formed by mounts Ventoso and Faro, which rise abruptly from the shore. The best winds for a sailing vessel to enter with are those from S.W., round westerly, to North. Cape Prioriño may be rounded at the distance of half a mile or less, as there are 11 and 12 fathoms water at a cable from it. From thence steer to the eastward for the entrance channel, keeping in the middle of it or borrowing on either side according to the wind. Take care to avoid the rocks and ledges bordering the shores of the channel, especially the Muela rock—which is marked by a buoy—off Segaño point; and should the vessel draw more than 23 feet, it will be requisite to keep to the north of the Palma shoal, page 216. If blowing fresh from the south-west or south, be prepared for the heavy squalls which come down from monte Faro.

Having passed Bispon point, haul to the north-east for an anchorage, which may be chosen as convenient. Merchant vessels anchor between La Graña and Ferrol. Vessels of war requiring repair enter the basin, and those ready for sea anchor off it; but this is an uneasy berth, especially in winter, when with southerly and south-west winds the squalls come down with much fury. There is a rocky patch with 5 fathoms water on it, some 24 yards in extent, lying S.S.E. 4 cables from the entrance of the basin, with the east point of entrance touching the house of a windmill, a remarkable building in the highest part of the town.

With adverse winds the harbour should be entered on the flood, in consequence of the many boards the vessel would have to make in turning through the narrows; but it will be prudent for a stranger to take a pilot, who will come out as soon as the signal is made, but if the weather is such as to prevent it, one will remain at Segaño point. If the wind be too strong to work to windward, the vessel will find excellent shelter in Cariño bay, or she can bear up either for Ares or Coruña, and wait for a favourable wind.

In fine weather and a fair wind there will be no difficulty in entering Ferrol, or gaining an anchorage in Cariño bay, as the entrance is well pointed out by the *fixed* white light, varied every *two minutes* by a *red flash*, on cape Prioriño chico, and by the *fixed red* light near Palma castle on the south side of the channel.

CAUTION.—It is not prudent to approach Ferrol or Coruña, by night with thick weather from the south-west, as the lights on the coast cannot be seen, the position of the vessel may be affected by currents, and these winds are nearly always accompanied by stormy weather. It will be better then to wait for daylight off the Sisargas islands. Should a vessel fall to leeward of the port, the only alternative would be, if unable to carry sail and work to windward, to make for Barquero or Vivera.

ARES and BETANZOS INLETS, formed in the deep bight between Ferrol and Coruña, have depth sufficient for vessels of all sizes; but as the deep-water space is exposed to north-west and west winds, they are only frequented by vessels whose draught will allow of their running farther in for shelter. Ares inlet occupies the north-eastern portion of the bight, and Betanzos inlet the southern portion. Both have good holding ground, and are free from rocks, with the exception of the dangerous Miranda bank, lying nearly in the middle of the entrance of the bight, and the Serron de la Torrella, lying on the opposite shore at 4 cables E.N.E. of Torrella point and marked by a buoy; these, however, are to a certain extent useful in sheltering the anchorage from the heavy north-west seas.

Anchorage.—If with strong north-west winds a vessel finds herself off the entrance of this bight, and unable to get either into Ferrol or Coruña, anchorage may be taken directly the vessel is eastward of the Miranda bank, with the certainty that, if the ground tackling is good, the anchor clear, and a hundred fathoms of chain given, however hard it may blow, there will be no risk of dragging.

Beween Coitelada point south of the entrance to Ferrol, and Avarenta point is a small bay called Oreoso, in which fishing boats take refuge in north-east winds. On the south-east side of the Avarenta point is a cove, which shelters coasters from the north-east. Thence to Miranda point the coast forms a bay with 4 to 12 fathoms water in it, sand and stones.

Marola Islet, lying on the opposite shore, about 4 cables N.W. ¼ N. from Deixo point, is of moderate height, and steep, with a small islet a

short distance off its north-west side. There is a channel with 6 to 7
fathoms water, rocky bottom, for small vessels, between them and the land.
Another islet, named Corbal or Marobiña, lies about a cable from the
point, with a passage inside for small craft.

Torella Point, at three-quarters of a mile eastward, is of moderate
height, with rocks at its foot. At 4 cables to the E.N.E. of the point is
the Serron de la Torrella, with 3 fathoms water on it, rocky bottom, and to
which a good berth must be given with heavy north-west seas, as it is then
covered with breakers. The reef is marked by a buoy. From thence the
coast trends in a south-east direction nearly 2 miles to San Amade point
forming a bay, at the head of which are the two small beaches of San Pedro
and Cerno.

Miranda Point and Islets.—Miranda point is low and rocky,
and off it are the Miranda islets, connected with the shore by a reef of rocks
which dry at low water. The largest islet, which is the outer one, is 45 feet
high and nearly circular ; the next, called Mirandita, is smaller and of a
conical form ; the others are bare rocks, and their greatest extent is 3 cables
in a west direction from the point.

Miranda Bank, lying about W. by S. half a mile from the outer
islet, is a dangerous rocky reef, 4 to 5 cables in extent E.N.E. and W.S.W.,
with three heads on which there are not more than 6 feet at low water,
with 4 to 6 fathoms between, but in bad weather the whole extent is
covered with breakers. The channel between it and the islet has
$7\frac{1}{2}$ fathoms water, sand and rock, and is sufficiently wide for any vessel in
moderate weather, but when there is much sea it would be dangerous even
for a small vessel to attempt it. With smooth water the bank is indicated
by the eddies over it.

The marks of the shoalest water on the bank are, cape Prioriño
grande in line with Coitelada point, and the tower of Hercules at Coruña
in line with Deixo point. To pass between the bank and the islets, keep
the above cape shut in with Coitelada point ; and to pass outside the bank,
keep cape Prioriño chico well open of the point, or the chapel on monte
Breamo a little eastward of S.E. by E., until the beach of Raso opens of
Ares point.

ARES BAY is formed on the north side of Ares inlet, between
Ares point and castle on the west, and Mauron or Camoco islet on the
east. It is somewhat less than a mile wide, half a mile deep, and affords
good shelter to small vessels from north-west and north-east winds ; but the
want of deep water obliges those of large draught to keep well out, and consequently exposed from south-west and north-west ; with strong north-
west winds a heavy sea sets into the bay, when vessels in the outer

anchorage, if their draught will admit, should run to the eastward and anchor off Redes in 2½ fathoms, over a bottom of soft mud, where there is better shelter.

The bay is bordered by a beach, but there are some rocks off Raso and Ciscada points, between which is the sandy plain of Raso. The town of Ares stands on the western shore, and contains about 2,000 inhabitants.

Ares castle stands on the heights of Ares point, 85 feet above the sea. South-west winds throw in some sea, but with good ground tackling there will be no risk. A vessel and her crew may be saved by running her on the beach between Peña Ciscada point and the outskirts of the town. Water may be obtained from a fountain, a short distance from the beach to the eastward of the town. Supplies are scarce, and must be brought from Ferrol. There is no pier, and mercantile operations are carried on in boats.

Mauron or Camoco islet, off the east point of the bay, is about 60 feet high, and covered with vegetation. It is so close to the shore that the smallest vessel can scarcely pass inside it at high water. Its south and west sides are clean, but there are some rocks nearly a cable off the shore to the eastward of it.

Anchorage.—Coasting vessels anchor off the town, but the water here is so shallow that it is necessary to be some distance from the shore to be in 9 or 10 feet. The bottom of the bay is mostly fine sand. The regular traders anchor with the guard-house on with the castle, at 2 cables from the point, in 2½ fathoms, good holding ground. Larger vessels anchor farther out in 4 to 4½ fathoms.

In entering the bay, give Paella point a berth of 2 cables, and Ares point a berth of a cable in passing.

Tides.—It is high water, full and change, in Ares bay, at 2h. 30m.; springs rise 12 feet, but the rise is affected by the prevailing winds, being one or 2 feet more with south-west winds, and one or 2 feet less with those from the north-east.

REDES BAY, at the head of Ares islet, between Mauron islet and Leusado point, is about 6 cables wide and 1¼ miles deep, and, although open to westerly winds, affords shelter to small vessels, and safety to others from its excellent holding ground. The depth is not more than 14 or 15 feet eastward of the meridian of Redes castle, which stands on the heights of Redes point on the northern shore; but the bottom being soft mud, a vessel may ground without risk. If drawing 12 to 14 feet, the town of Redes may be brought to bear N. by W. and Terella point just open of Mauron islet about W. by N.; if of lighter draught nearer the shore.

Larger vessels will obtain some shelter by anchoring in 3½ to 4½ fathoms mud bottom, in the middle of the bay between Mauron islet and Redes castle. This berth is exposed to the westward, but no injury will occur if the vessel's head is kept to the sea by a small anchor to the eastward, to prevent the ebb stream from the Eume swinging her broadside on. With the castle and church in one, there are 3¼ fathoms at low water. The town is small, and built on a declivity of the land, in a small bight on the north side of Redes point. The church is conspicuous, and stands on a height to the north-east of the town.

The head of Redes bay is filled with sand-banks, which are nearly covered at high water. The two shores trend in a south-east direction to the bridge across the mouth of the river Eume, which here flows into the sea. The bridge communicates with the town of Puentedeume, which stands on the south-west shore, and contains about 2,000 inhabitants. Coasting vessels can get up to the bridge at high water. Monte Breamo, rising to the height of 968 feet above the sea, to the south-west of the town, is an excellent mark for approaching the inlet, and easily recognized. It has a chapel on its summit dedicated to San Miguel.

BETANZOS INLET is 2 miles wide at the entrance between San Amade and Curbeiroa points; from thence it takes a south direction 3 miles to its head, which is nearly choked with sand, and into which fall the rivers Mandeo and Mendo. At 4 miles up these rivers is the town of Betanzos, standing on the declivity of a hill, the base of which is washed on the east by the Mandeo and on the west by the Mendo. Boats can get up to the landing place at high water springs, but at low water the sands remain dry. The population may be about 6,000. The depth gradually decreases from 7 fathoms at entrance of the inlet to one fathom at 2 miles within; thence upwards it is all dry at low water springs, excepting the channels into the rivers.

From San Amade point the west shore of the inlet runs S. by E. 1½ miles to Fontá point, on which is a castle in ruins. At a cable from the point is the islet of Carcabeiro, the channel between being used by small craft. The islet is surrounded with rocks, and at about half a cable south-east of it, is a rocky shoal called Piedra Do-Porto, with 6 feet water on it, and marked by a buoy. Another similar shoal named Pulgueiro shows at low water springs 2 cables S.S.W. of the former; both these shoals are about a cable from the shore.

The village of Fontá stands in an elbow of the shore, a short distance south-west of Fontá point. About a mile S. by W. from Fontá castle is another castle in ruins, on Curbeiroa point, and on the beach of the bay between, is the town of Sada, containing 1,200 inhabitants. Coasters only can approach the town, as the bay is daily becoming more shallow. Opposite Fontá castle, on the eastern shore, is a shallow bay, called

Bañobre, at the head of which a river of the same name falls in the midst of a sandy beach.

Anchorage.—Vessels of moderate draught will find good shelter from south-west winds by anchoring in 3 to 6 fathoms, sand, East or E.S.E. of the castle on Fontá point. Small vessels, by standing farther up the inlet, according to the draught, will be sheltered from west and even north-west winds.

CORUÑA BAY, the entrance to which, between Seixo Blanco point and the north-east extreme of the peninsula of Coruña, is nearly 2 miles wide and 3 miles deep, but being open to northerly and north-west winds, shelter can only be had on its western shore, at the port and town of Coruña. The northern shore of the peninsula is foul and rocky, and near its north end is the light-tower of Hercules, standing on an elevation 290 feet above the sea. Seixo Blanco point on the east side of entrance is high, steep, free from rocks, and distinguished by a vein of white stone up and down its face, appearing from a distance like a road.

The depths decrease gradually from 20 to 22 fathoms at the entrance, to the shores of the bay which are fringed with rocks. The eastern shore is foul, as well as the southern part, in which is the mouth of the river Burgo. Various islets and rocks are scattered along shore at a short distance ; the most remarkable of which are, Canabal between Seixo Blanco and Mera points ; Santa Cruz on which there is a fort, and Judios near St. Lucia. Mera point, in the north-east part of the bay,' is higher than Seixo Blanco point, and has a battery on it. On its south side is a tolerably spacious bay, bordered by a beach, in which shelter may be had from north-east and south-east winds, in 8 to 10 fathoms, sand ; but it should only be adopted in fine weather, and then the Tonina bank, lying outside the entrance, must be carefully avoided, for although there are 10 fathoms on it, the water sometimes breaks.

The entrance to the port is half a mile wide, between an islet, on which is the castle of San Antonio, to the north-east, and San Diego point and castle to the south-west. The port takes the form of a horse-shoe, nearly three-quarters of a mile deep in a north-west direction, and at its head is a narrow isthmus, which unites the peninsula to the main land. On the southern part of the peninsula is the town of Coruña, which with its suburb contains about 30,000 inhabitants. The suburb, named Pescaderia, adjoins the south side of the city, and occupies a great part of the isthmus. There is a great want of jetties. Goods are landed and embarked in front of the custom-house, until half-ebb, when the water alongside the quay becomes shallow.

The manufactures are, glass, soap, starch, common cottons, iron, oilcloth, hats, and the salting of provisions. It has also considerable fisheries, particularly of sardines. A large dock is in course of construction; but at present vessels requiring repair must proceed to Ferrol. There is steam communication with Liverpool, Bordeaux, Santander, Vigo, and Lisbon.

Anchorage.—The port of Coruña will only completely shelter vessels of moderate draught, as the deep water space is limited. There are 4 fathoms in the middle of it, good holding ground, which depth rapidly decreases towards the town and the suburb. The best berth is towards the south-west shore, in 4½ or 5 fathoms, mud, abreast the Palloza, a large cigar manufactory in the district of Santa Lucia. Vessels of heavy draught anchor eastward of the meridian of the castle of San Antonio, and consequently exposed to the sea with northerly winds.

Winds.—Southerly and south-west winds are the most dangerous, and vessels should be prepared for the wind from those directions. When it blows strong either from the north or south, there is an uneasy sea in the port, and mercantile operations are interrupted.

Water and Supplies.—Water may be obtained from the watering place in the Playa de la Palloza, or from a floating tank. Provisions are abundant, and ships' stores readily obtained.

LIGHTS.—The tower of Hercules, on the north end of the peninsula of Coruña, exhibits, at 332 feet above high water, a *fixed* white light, varied by a *flash* every *three minutes*, and visible in clear weather at a distance of 16 miles; the flash is seen in clear weather 20 miles.

To facilitate the entrance of the port at night, a *fixed* white light is shown from an hexagonal tower on the east side of the castle of San Antonio, 56 feet above high water, and visible in clear weather 10 miles.

From the extremity of the embarkation mole, a *fixed red* harbour light is shown from a wooden octagonal lighthouse, elevated 23 feet above high water, and visible in clear weather at a distance of 6 miles.

DANGERS in Coruña Bay.—The entrance of this bay is obstructed in bad weather by a rocky bank, named the Jacentes, a mile in extent E.N.E. and W.S.W., with depths on it varying from 5½ to 18 fathoms. From the middle of the bank Seixo Blanco point bears S.E. by E. 1¼ miles, and the tower of Hercules W. by S. ¾ S. about the same distance. The most dangerous part is a tolerably extensive patch with 5½ to 9 fathoms on it, named the Basuril, at the southern end of the bank. When there is much sea the whole bank is covered with breakers, and in heavy gales the breakers extend as far as Seixo Blanco point, and occasionally also, across the passage between the west side of the bank and Hermino point, in which case the entrance must not be attempted.

The eastern shore of the peninsula, from Pradeiras point, on which is a battery, to San Antonio castle is foul and rocky, with reefs projecting from it, of which the Pedrido is the most dangerous. This reef extends in an E.N.E. direction from the Peña de las Animas, which is a small rugged rock 18 feet above high water, lying N.E. 1¼ cables from the castle, and having a channel a cable wide, obstructed with rocks, between it and the north-east angle of the city. At 2 cables farther to the north-east is the Mouron rock, with 2 fathoms water on it, being the continuation of the reef projecting from the Peña, and on which the sea always breaks.

The Cabanes bank, lying N.E. ¼ E. a long three-quarters of a mile from San Antonio castle, is about 3 cables in extent, N.E. and S.W., has 8¼ fathoms least water on it, rocky bottom, and like the Jacentes is covered with breakers when there is much sea. There are 11 to 13 fathoms between it and the Pedrido reef, and 17 to 19 fathoms between it and Pradeiras point.

There are also two dangers in the entrance of the port, one a small patch with 5 feet on it, named the Gancho, lying 20 yards S.S.E. of the castle of San Antonio ; and the other a round rock with 12 feet on it, called the Laja de Monelos, lying about half a cable from the west shore of the port, off the mouth of the Monelos, a small stream which runs through the sand near Judios islet. A small patch of 6 feet lies one cable N.N.E. from San Diego castle.

Buoys.—On the south side of the harbour of Coruña and in the fairway, three large wooden buoys are sometimes moored, having iron supports for lanterns; they are moved at night to rocks and broken ground, as guides to the fishermen in hauling their nets.

Pilots.—All vessels above 50 tons are compelled to employ a pilot in entering Coruña. A vessel requiring one should make the usual signal at the fore.

Tides.—It is high water, full and change, in the port of Coruña, at 3h. ; springs rise 15 feet, and neaps 9 feet, but the rise is affected by the prevailing wind.

CAUTION.—The coast between capes Ortegal and Finisterre is dangerous to approach at night, especially in the winter season, or in thick foggy weather, which is frequent here, for not only does a powerful current at times set towards the land from the north-west, but the streams of flood and ebb often draws vessels out of their computed position. In the dark gloomy weather of winter the land is often concealed, but the beaches at the foot of the hills may sometimes be seen, when the latter are obscured in mist and haze. The most prudent course to adopt by vessels bound to Ferrol or Coruña from the westward, and not having sufficient daylight to enter the port, is not to advance farther eastward than the meridian of the Sisargas isles (8° 50′ W.), where they should stand off and on during the night, according to the state of the wind, bearing in mind that there is always a slight indraft towards the land.

With fresh south-west winds, the current sets with great strength to the north-east between the Sisargas islets and cape Ortegal, and vessels have often been carried by it to leeward of their port ; this must be carefully guarded against, for if they be driven eastward of Ferrol there is no place of shelter or safety on the whole coast, except the inlets of Barquero and Vivero. The lead should be frequently hove, especially in hazy weather, for the soundings will be a warning before the surf on the shore can be heard.

Directions.—The bay of Coruña should not be attempted when the breakers extend across the entrance, which they occasionally do when the sea is heavy from the north-west. In smooth water, and fine weather the Jacentes and Cabanes banks may be crossed, but when there is any swell they should be avoided, and the channel used between them and the shore.

In entering the bay with a fair wind and smooth water, run towards the land between Seixo Blanco and Mera points, until San Diego castle opens of San Antonio castle ; then steer towards San Diego castle, keeping it its own breadth open of San Antonio castle to clear the Pedrido reef, which should be given a berth of a quarter of a mile in passing. San Antonio castle may be rounded at the distance of a cable, and anchorage taken up between the two castles as convenient. A good berth for a vessel of large draught is with San Antonio castle N.E. by E., but if drawing less than 3 fathoms, she may stand farther in until Seixo Blanco point is between the castle and the city. Before dropping the anchor the nature of the bottom should be ascertained, for in many places there is much sea weed, on which the anchors come home in bad weather.

If attempting the bay in a heavy gale between North and West, the best channel is between the Jacentes and Herminio point, under the tower of Hercules. To do this, run along north-east of the tower, at such a distance from the coast as to see the base of the tower, which in no case should be hidden when approaching Herminio point, which may be neared if requisite to 2 cables. From thence steer S.E. towards the battery on Mera point, until San Diego castle opens of San Antonio castle, when proceed as before.

If wishing to run between the Jacentes and Sexio Blanco point, which is not so good a channel as the other, approach the entrance of Ferrol until cape Priorifio grande bears N.N.E., and Segaño point is in line with the hermitage of San Cristóbal, which is eastward of the cape in the bay of Cariño. Then steer about S.W. by W., with this latter mark on, until Seixo Blanco point is E.S.E., then S.W. by S., and proceed as before. In working into or out of the bay, when within Mera point, do not stand farther eastward than to have Seixo Blanco point in line with monte Ventoso; in making the western board, keep San Diego castle well open of San Antonio castle, to avoid the Pedrido reef.

Sailing vessels leaving the port should do so, if possible, with the land wind early in the morning, so as to be clear of the bay before the breeze comes from seaward.

The COAST from the north end of Coruña peninsula takes a westerly direction, and at the distance of 19 miles is San Adrain point, close off which are the Sisargas islands; the shore between forming a bight more than 3 miles deep. Orzan bay, on the west side of the peninsula, is nearly a mile deep and half a mile wide, open to the north, foul, shallow, and terminates in the beach of the isthmus of Coruña. At 1½ miles W. by N. ½ N. from Hercules tower is Peña Boa point, moderately high and rocky, descending in declivities from monte Peña Boa, more generally known as San Pedro. The mount is 732 feet high, and on its summit is a tower from which signals are made to vessels coming to Coruña, and is an excellent mark. Close off the west side of the point are three small islets, named San Pedro, parallel to the shore.

Langosteira point, nearly 3 miles W. ¾ S. from monte San Pedro, is moderately high, and has on each side of it a bay with low shores. A rocky patch with 2¼ fathoms water on it, named Pego, lies W. ¾ N. 2 miles from Langosteira point, and 1½ miles from the nearest shore; the tower of Hercules kept open of the land leads outside it. There is also a rock named Ferbedoira, marked in the chart at two-thirds of a mile W. ¼ N. from the San Pedro isle, and another, the Curbina, at about a mile N.W. by W. ¼ W. from Cayon tower. At 5 miles from Langosteira point in the same direction, is the small harbour of Cayon, used only by fishing vessels; it is formed at the foot of monte Samon, which is high and flat on the summit.

About 4 miles farther westward, is a small rocky islet lying close to the beach of the low shore of Baldayo. To the northward of this islet lies the dangerous rocky bank of Baldayo, several heads of which are visible at low water, but at high tide only the middle rock shows itself. The bank is about 8½ miles long, north and south, and half a mile wide, with south-west winds vessels pass between it and the land.*

From Razo point at the west end of Baldayo beach, which is about 3 miles in extent, the course is N.W. by N. 5¼ miles to San Adrian point, and clear of danger, with the exception of some rocks close to the shore, and a rocky ledge extending a third of a mile from San Bartolomé point. At 1¾ miles S.S.E. from San Adrian point, is the Atalaya de Malpica, a point of high land projecting eastward about 2 cables, and having on its south side a cove named port Malpica, fit only for fishing craft, and on its north side, a spot of low beach visible from seaward; here rises monte San Adrian, extending north and south, its north extreme being San Adrian point.

SISARGAS ISLANDS are separated from San Adrian point by a narrow passage which may be used in a case of emergency. Their north extreme is 1¼ miles N.N.E. from the point, and at high water the two appear as three islands, of which the western, called Mayor, is the larger, of moderate height, steep sides, round, with flat summit, and a third of a mile in diameter; its north end is a little higher than the south, and on the second northern peak is a lighthouse. On the east side of the larger island lies the second, called Malante, so close to the first at the north end, as only to admit small craft to pass through at high water. Malante is steep on the north side, but low on the south, and in the middle of it is a depression, through which the sea passes at high water, dividing into two parts. The ground around the group is almost wholly rock, the few patches of sand interspersed being of small extent.

At about a third of a mile W.S.W. from the south-west end of the western or large island, is a depth of 2¾ fathoms on the north part of a rocky reef called Carreira, on which the sea breaks even with a moderate swell; and about a quarter of a mile N.N.W. from the north-west point of the same island, is the Campana shoal nearly awash. At a long mile N.N.E. from the north point of the island, lies a rocky shoal with 5½ fathoms water on it, called the Cuervo. A reef of rocks extends a cable eastward from Malante; and another 5 cables from its south point towards San Adrian point. The narrowest part of the passage between the islands and San Adrian point, is between the south extreme of this latter reef and

---

* Tofiño mentions "the southern part of this bank as being one mile from the shore, and the channel between half a mile wide, with 15 fathoms water in it, so that in a case of necessity vessels of large draught might run through;" in the chart by Don Juan De Dios Sotelo, published at Madrid in 1847, the channel is about 1¼ miles wide, and the outer rock full 3 miles about N.E. ½ N. from Razo point at the west end of Baldayo beach. The *Solway* steam vessel was wrecked on this bank 7th April 1843.

the large rocks under the point, the channel here being not more than 1½ cables across.

LIGHT.—On the second northern peak of Mayor island, the larger of the Sisargas islands, is a lighthouse, which exhibits, at 351 feet above high water, a *fixed* white light varied every *four minutes* by a *red flash*, visible in clear weather at a distance of 12 miles.

Directions.—In case of emergency a vessel may run between the Sisargas islands and the land, observing that in this passage the tides are strong, the flood to the east, the ebb to the west, and that with any swell there is broken water all over it.

If coming from the westward, steer for the south point of the western or larger island on a S.E. bearing, until within half a cable of it; the vessel will be then clear of the Carreira and Campana reefs, and have a depth of 14 and 15 fathoms. From thence stand for the east part of San Adrian point, carrying the same depth until within half a cable of the point, where it shoals to 8 fathoms; then steer East, passing between the point and the extreme of the reef extending from the south point of Malante. When bound through the passage from the eastward, steer for San Adrian point until at the distance of half a cable from it, and when abreast the point, steer for the same distance from the south end of the large island, and then N.W. until clear of all dangers.

The Coast takes a W. by S. direction from San Adrian point, and is much broken and indented with bays. Nairja point, at 3½ miles west of San Adrian point, is of moderate height, steep, with reefs, 1¼ cables off it. About a mile eastward of this point, is a small bend of the coast called port Avarizo, frequented by coasters; a reef of rocks lies in the middle of the entrance, but the western shore is clean, and should be kept aboard in entering.

From Nairja point the coast runs southward 2 miles, and then westward 3½ miles to Roncudo point, forming a bay open to the north-west, and in which are several rocks. Roncudo point is of moderate height and forms the base of a lofty mountain which has a number of small eminences on it resembling buildings at a distance; a reef extends W. by N. 3 cables from the point, the outer part of which is uncovered, and there are other rocks in its vicinity.

CORME and LAGE BAYS.—Roncudo point forms the north-east extreme, and Lage point, distant 2½ miles, the south-west extreme of a deep bight, open to north-west gales, when it is generally covered with broken water; but there is no danger except the reefs off the points of entrance, and a patch of 4½ fathoms lying S.S.W. about one mile from Roncudo point. There are two summer anchorages in this bight, one,

Corme bay, in its north-east corner, and the other, Lage bay, in its south-west corner, the former better than the latter; in the winter it will be prudent not to enter either, unless in a case of necessity, when Corme bay should be preferred, where with good ground tackle a vessel may ride safely.

An abundance of fresh water will be found in both bays. At the head of Corme bay there are three different spots of low shore; in each of which is a stream where a squadron may conveniently water. Vessels anchor off the low shore in 7 or 8 fathoms water, sand, with a cable fast to the shore on the north, and an anchor to the south, lying safe from all winds except the south, which sometimes blows hard, but with good cables there is little danger to be apprehended, as the bottom is good holding ground.

At the east end of the beach is an islet, difficult to distinguish from the land, with a hermitage on it; thence a high and steep coast runs southward to Canteros point. From Canteros point begins a tract of low beach, extending to the head of the bight where rises monte Blanco, which from the middle of its height to its small peak, is sandy, and a good mark from seaward. The river Canduas here falls into the sea.

Lage bay has at its head a clean beach, and there is an abundance of fresh water. An anchorage should be chosen in the middle of the bay in $8\frac{1}{2}$ fathoms water, with Cabalo point, the east extreme of the bay, in line with monte Blanco; but small vessels may take up a berth nearer the town in 4 or 5 fathoms. Lage point, the south-west extreme of the bight, is high, and surrounded by reefs to a distance of 2 cables.

CAPE VILLANO.—Catasol point, at $1\frac{1}{2}$ miles south-west of Lage point, is high and of a sandy colour, with large rocks and shoals extending some distance from its foot; on its north-east side is a low sandy shore, and on its south-west side another called Arenal de traba de Lage. The small bay of Camello, at $3\frac{3}{4}$ miles westward of Lage point, has shoals at its entrance, and is used only by fishing boats. Cape Trece, at about $4\frac{1}{4}$ miles farther on, is low and foul, and at the distance of two-thirds of a mile to the north-west are the rocks named Baleas de Tosta; a little way back from the point, the land is high and rugged, terminating in peaks, and extending from Camello bay to cape Villano.

Cape Villano is of steep rock of moderate height, with a lighthouse on it. A peak of a red colour with a sharp point rises at its back, which at a distance resembles a tower, and it may also be known by a large patch of a sandy colour $1\frac{1}{2}$ miles eastward of it. About half a mile N.N.W. from the cape lies the Bufardo rock, being the pinnacle of some sunken rocks of small extent, on which the sea breaks, but all round it the water is deep.

LIGHT,—The lighthouse on cape Villano exhibits, at an elevation of 243 feet above the level of high water, a *fixed* white light, visible in clear weather at a distance of 10 miles.

CAMARIÑAS BAY, southward of cape Villano, is somewhat obstructed by rocks and shoals, and frequented only by coasters. Merejo bay, on its southern shore, has excellent clean holding ground, in 4 to 7 fathoms water, sheltered from all winds but north-west, which send in a heavy sea ; it is therefore seldom used, and on the appearance of the wind coming from this quarter a vessel should be prepared to gain the anchorage off Camariñas on the northern shore.*

Cuerno point, at half a mile south-west of the cape Villano, is low, with rocks extending 2 cables from it, the greater part of which are visible, and steep-to. At about 1¼ miles south of the cape is a round hill named Monte del Virgen; the coast between should not be approached too close, as off it there are one or two outlying rocks. At three-quarters of a mile south-eastward of Monte del Virgen, is a fort on a point, and 4 cables farther eastward is another fort on a point, which should be given a berth, as there are only 2½ fathoms water at 2 cables southward.

Close to the north-east of this latter point, stands the town of Camariñas on the shore of a small sandy bay, with a small pier used by coasters at high water, but it dries when the tide is out. To the north-east of the bay is the entrance of a shallow inlet which runs northerly for a mile ; a short distance southward of the entrance is a small river, the Puente del Puerto, with a bar at its mouth.

Merejo point, on the south shore of Camariñas bay, is high and steep, with a small town of the same name on the summit. Between this point and Chorente point, two-thirds of a mile farther westward, is Merejo bay, with two rivulets running into it. Chorente point is high and precipitous, and a quarter of a mile off it is the Higuera shoal, about the size of a boat, with only 6 feet on it. About three-quarters of a mile north-west of Chorente point is the town of Mugia, on the beach at the head of a clean sandy bay, and on the south side of a hill with a rugged summit. The north side of this hill terminates in Cruces point, which is bordered with breakers, and at 2 cables north of the point is the Peneiron rock.

Water may be had in abundance at the town of Camariñas.

The QUEBRANTAS, off the entrance of Camariñas bay, is a dangerous rocky shoal about half a mile long, N.N.W. and S.S.E., with depths of 1½ to 7½ fathoms on it, except at the north end, which at low water shows a head of rock resembling a buoy. From this end of the

---

* *See* Admiralty plan :—Camariñas bay ; scale, *m* = 2·5 inches, on Chart, No. 2,728.

shoal, which is called the Great Quebranta, cape Villano bears N.E. by
E. ¼ E. distant 1¼ miles, and the chapel on Cruces point S. ½ W. 1¾ miles.
The south-east end of the shoal is named the Small Quebranta, and the
above chapel bears from it S. ¾ W. distant 1¼ miles; it has 1½ fathoms
water on it, and the sea breaks during a swell; and in bad weather the
water breaks all over the shoal.

At about 1½ miles W.S.W. from the Great Quebranta lies another rocky
shoal with 5½ fathoms over it, and the sea breaks on it during a heavy
swell from the westward.

Tides. — It is high water, full and change, in Camariñas bay, at
2h. 33m.; springs rise 13 feet, neaps 9 feet.

Directions.—Entering Camariñas bay with the wind from the
eastward, keep cape Villano aboard, taking care to avoid the Bufardo
rock, which will be known by its breakers, and may be passed on
either side. The rocks off Cuerno point may be approached to a quarter
of a mile, as they are steep-to. From then steer to pass half a mile
from Virgen point, and when midway between the two points of entrance,
haul to the eastward by the lead, giving the inner points a berth of a
third of a mile, when with a couple of short boards, a vessel will gain the
anchorage abreast, and a short half mile from the beach of Camariñas,
in 4½ fathoms water, saud. The most dangerous wind is from the
southward. Several vessels that have parted their cables in southerly
gales, have been saved by running ashore in the inlet at the head of
the bay.

If the wind is too strong to allow a vessel to turn in, temporary
anchorage may be found where convenient in the bay; or she may run
into Merejo bay, which is safe with all winds but those from the north-
west. Entering with westerly winds, give a wide berth to the Quebrantas
shoal, and run in mid-channel between it and Cruces point.

CAPE TORIÑANA.—Nearly 2 miles westward of Cruces point
is the high and steep point of Buitra, and between, the coast forms a bight
open to the northward, Near Cruces point, a flat beach of the same
name is almost entirely covered when there is much swell and a high tide,
all the way to the town of Mugia. Cape Toriñana, 3 miles from the
latter point, is low and rugged, and at a distance is not easily recognized,
being blended with the high land at its back. A short distance off its
western face is a small rocky islet, high and round, with two small peaks
and shoals around it. A reef of sunken rocks runs from the cape nearly a
mile to the north-eastward.

CAUTION.—Mariners are warned not to make too free with this
dangerous coast, off which it is more than probable that there are other

dangers than those marked on the chart. In May 1833, H.M. steam vessel *African* struck on a sunken rock, from which cape Finisterre was said to bear S. by W., and cape Toriñana E.S.E. distant one mile. This rock had been seen previously from H.M.S. *Confiance*, when the sea was breaking over it. The Spanish steam vessel *Santander*, in May 1863, is reported to have struck upon a rock in this vicinity, in all probability the same.

Tofiño states that W.N.W., 2 cables distant from cape Toriñana, there is a sunken rock on which the sea breaks when there is any swell; this may be identical with the *African* rock, as the Spanish chart of 1847 shows only one rock, lying about W. ½ N. two-thirds of a mile from the north extreme of the cape, and half a mile from the nearest shore.

CAPE FINISTERRE.—At 9 miles S. by W. ½ W. from cape Toriñana is the Navé of Finisterre; the coast between forming an indentation, and at 4½ miles from the same cape is Lemiña point, with the bay and beach of the same name on its south side. Vessels may safely anchor off the beach during north-east and easterly winds, in 6 to 8 fathoms, sand (but not in deeper water, for there the bottom is rocky), abreast a rivulet, where water may be obtained; the north shore of the bay is foul. From thence to the Navé the coast is bold, with some small bays and patches of beach, but none of them deserving notice.*

The Navé is high land with a flat summit, having its foot, named cape Navé, washed by the sea; about a third of its height above the sea is a short projection with hummocks on it. A small but high island lies at the foot of the Navé, and at 1¾ miles N.W. by W. from it is a small ledge, named the Munis, with 3 fathoms water, upon which the sea breaks in bad weather; it is steep-to, having 20 to 30 fathoms around.

Cape Finisterre, 2¾ miles farther on, is neither so high nor so flat as the Navé, but more uneven on the summit. Without being precipitous over the sea, it is of steep ascent, and landing under it, even in the most favourable weather, extremely inconvenient. It will be easily recognized at sea by the lighthouse on its south point, and also between it and the Navé there is a bight with some low beach, and the land behind is less elevated. It may be further distinguished by the coast trending from it to the east and north, and by monte Lozaro or Lezara to the E.S.E. of it, which may be known, not merely from its height, but from its singular formation, as its summit consists of numerous small pinnacles resembling the teeth of a saw.

---

* *See* Admiralty chart:—Cape Finisterre to cape St. Mary, with Plans, No. 87; scale, *d* = 6 inches.

About 3 cables from point de los Oidos or Enquieira the north-west point of the cape is the little rocky islet of Centolo ; and N. ¼ W., half a mile from this islet, is a small ledge named Carraca, awash at low water. Nearly one mile from the shore between point los Oidos and the cape lies a pinnacle rock named Peton de Mañoto, with 9 fathoms water and 32 fathoms close around ; the sea nearly always breaks on this rock. At 3 cables S.W. ¼ W. from the extremity of the cape is the Turdeiro rock, about the size of a boat, with 2 fathoms water on it ;* and nearly a mile about S.W. by W. from the cape there is a small shoal with 5¼ fathoms on it, named Peton de Socabo, which breaks in bad weather.

LIGHT.—The lighthouse on the south point of cape Finisterre exhibits, at 466 feet above the level of high water, a *revolving* white light, which is described as giving *alternate flashes and eclipses every thirty econds* (November 1880),† and should be seen in clear weather from a distance of 20 miles.

The COAST from cape Finisterre to the frontier of Portugal, on the river Miño, 64 miles to the southward, is much broken by a series of deep inlets and bays. The headlands are rugged and uneven, and as many dangers lie some distance off shore, the approach is dangerous at night or in thick weather. In the daytime, if the weather is clear, the coast may be seen 25 to 30 miles distant, the land near the shore being generally high, and some of the mountains not far inland attaining altitudes of 1,400 to 2,000 feet.‡

CORCUBION BAY.—The deep bight immediately eastward of cape Finisterre, between the cape and Remedios point, is about 7 miles wide. From the cape the coast, which is high and precipitous, trends to the north-east for about 1½ miles to the village of Finisterre, inhabited only by fishermen on the shore of a small bay. The shore in front of the village and half a mile north of it is skirted with rocks, at the distance of 3 cables ; then begins a low beach about a mile in length, named Costeira, and at a long half mile beyond it is Sardiñeiro point, which is high and steep.

To the eastward of the village, off Costeira beach, there is good anchorage on sandy bottom, and shelter during northerly winds. It is much frequented by vessels in the summer, when north-easters are often of

---

* The Spanish Chart of 1835 places this rock nearer the point.

† Published in Notice to Mariners, No. 246 of 1880. Also in Spanish Notice to Mariners, No. 119 of 1880.

‡ *See* Admiralty chart:—Cape Finisterre to Vigo bay, No. 1,756 ; scale, *m* = 0·5 of an inch ; and plan of Corcubion bay ; scale, *m* = 1 inch on chart No. 1,755.

long continuance, but as soon as there are signs of the wind coming round to the S.E. or S.W. quarters, it is necessary to get under way, for all on-shore winds are dangerous. The inlet running in, a mile to the north-east, between Sardiñeiro point and cape Nasa, has a rocky patch lying in the middle of it, and is only used by fishing vessels. At its head there are two villages, one named Esteiro, where there is a small rivulet, and the other, which is the westernmost, Sardiñeiro.

From cape Nasa, which is high and steep, a high level shore trends eastward 1¼ miles to cape Cé, the west entrance point to the bay of Corcubion, formed between the cape and Galera point, 1¼ miles to the southeast.   Cape Cé is a high bluff, with an octagonal granite light-tower standing 36 yards within its extremity. It should be given a berth of 3 or 4 cables, as it is bordered with rocks, and shoal water extends some distance off.   Galera point is low, with a number of large rocks near it; but the bottom close to them is clean, and the water deep.

The shore trends easterly from Galera point, and then south and westerly to Piñeiro point at the foot of monte Lozaro or Lezara, forming the bay of this latter name.   In this little bay there is a good depth of water, and at its head a flat shore with a small river, where water may be procured, which comes down through a gully, in the middle of high land.   Piñeiro point is high, and on its south side is a small cove, and the fishing village of Pindo, at the termination of a valley.   At 3 miles to the southward of Piñeiro point is Caldebarcos point, the coast between being the base of monte Lezara, is high and skirted by rocks, and beyond it is the bay and beach of Carnota, and then follows Remedios point.

Caldebarcos point, bearing S.E. ¼ E. 6 miles from cape Finisterre, is low and fronted by large rocks. A little north of the point is the village of Quilmas.   Remedios point is salient, surrounded by rocks, which extend a mile to the north-east. Near the point is a small conical hill, and a quarter of a mile farther eastward, there is another of the same shape but larger.

Corcubion bay, formed in the north-east part of the great bight thus described, runs in northerly 2 miles from cape Cé, affords good anchorage for all classes of vessels, and is well sheltered from all winds but those from the southward, which send in a heavy sea. Its shores are high, with several small coves and patches of beach, two of which are near the head of the inlet. About half way in, are two forts, that on the west shore is named Cardenal, and that on the east Principe; the distance across abreast the forts is about 6 cables, but the inlet narrows towards its head, where, on the west side, stands the town of Corcubion, with a population of about 1,200, and on the east side, called Fernelo, is a small river, and farther in on the same side is the town of Cé. The inhabitants of these places are principally employed in fishing, and rearing cattle.

Anchorage.—The usual anchorage is between the forts in about 11 fathoms water, sand, the depth gradually decreasing to within a short distance of both shores. Vessels sometimes anchor farther in abreast the low beach of Fernelo in 7 fathoms; but in winter the former anchorage should be preferred, for should the wind come in from the southward, and blow hard, the vessel would tail near the shallows at the head of the inlet, and have no room to veer or let go an anchor, in case she should drive or part.

DANGERS.—At two-thirds of a mile S. ¾ W. from cape Cé is a small rock, covered at high water, named the Carromeiro chico. It has a rocky ledge extending southerly 2 cables, beyond which the water is deep across the channel separating it from the Lobeira grande islet, nearly 1½ miles to the south-west. At 2 cables from its north side there are 4 fathoms water, increasing to 6, and then shoaling to 3 fathoms on the edge of the bank of rock and gravel extending from cape Cé.

About a mile S.S.E. ½ E. nearly from the above rock is an islet or rock, named Carromeiro viejo. It has large rocks on its east and south sides, with shallow water all round, but only to a short distance, for at one cable off, there are 11 fathoms, and soon after 17 and 22 fathoms.

Between this islet and Lobeira grande the channel is 1¼ miles wide, clean and deep, as it is also between the islet and Quilmas point on the south, between which there is summer anchorage. It is necessary to give a berth to both sides of this latter channel, but in case of doubt the safest plan is to pass nearer the islet than the shore, on account of the Asno shoal, which lies N.E. by E. ¾ E. half a mile from the islet, with the north-west part of the islet on with the south-east part of the Lobeira grande, and Galera point on with the low shore of Fornelo. Large vessels, if requisite, may pass between this shoal and the land.

The Bueyes (the oxen), at about 3½ cables southward of Galera point, are three large rocks forming a triangle, and resembling three fishing boats lying together. They are clean, and have deep water on all sides except the west, from which a rocky ledge projects more than a cable, and at its extreme the depth is 5 fathoms. Vessels may pass between those rocks and the east shore, between them and Galera point, and between them and the Asno shoal; the latter passage carries 9 to 13 fathoms, but is narrow.

Lobeira Grande is an islet composed of reddish coloured boulders, and rocks lying N.N.W. and S.S.E. From its centre cape Finisterre bears

W.N.W. 3¾ miles, and cape Cé N.N.E. ½ E. 2¼ miles.   At a cable distant, all round, the bottom is clean, and the water deep.

Lobeira Chico, about three-quarters of a mile S. ¾ E. from the Lobeira grande, with a clear passage between of 18 to 24 fathoms water, is another similar cluster, but smaller, and intersected by numerous channels, through which fishing boats pass at high water.   It is low, and in a swell the sea washes over it ; shoals surround it in all directions, particularly on the south-east side.

Duyo Rock is a dangerous patch with 2¾ fathoms water on it, 4 miles S.S.E. from cape Finisterre, in a direct line between that cape and Remedios point.   It is of small extent, with deep water close to on all sides.

At nearly a mile westward of Remedios point are some large rocks, always above water, surrounded with shoals, named Miñarzos.   The passage between these rocks and the ledge bordering the point is used only by coasters.   At the distance of about 1¾ miles, and between the bearings of N. ¼ W. and N.N.E. from the point, are other dangerous shoals called Arrosas and Arrosiñas.

LIGHT.—The octagonal granite light-tower on cape Cé, the west point of entrance to Corcubion bay, exhibits, at 82 feet above high water, a *fixed red* light, visible at a distance of 8 miles.

Pilots for Corcubion bay reside at the village of Finisterre, and come off to vessels requiring their services, the usual signal being hoisted.

Tides.—It is high water, full and change, at Corcubion at 3h. ; springs rise 12 and neaps 7 feet.

Directions.—Bound into Corcubion bay, with a leading wind from south-east or south-west, steer towards the Lobeira grande, passing it on either side, and then between the Corromeiro chico and Corromeiro viejo for the entrance.   The best leading mark in is a conspicuous waterfall pouring down a mountain gorge, which will be seen bearing E. ½ N. on getting abreast cape Finisterre.   It falls over the spur lying between mount Lezaro and mount Pindo, and when in line with the northernmost of two white houses on the beach in Lezaro bay, will lead between the Corromeiro chico and the Lobeira grande.   When cape Cé bears North steer for the anchorage, which will now be visible.   Give the Corromeiro chico a berth of two cables, and proceed up the harbour, anchoring as convenient.

With a north-west wind it will be advisable to run between cape Cé and the Corromeiro chico, keeping nearer the latter than the cape.   Haul to the wind directly the shoal ground off the cape is passed, anchoring where the vessel can fetch, or, if the tide be flowing, work to the anchorage off the forts.

If unable to work into the bay with a north-east wind (as generally happens during the north-easters of summer), anchor either at the entrance or off Costeira beach, or on the east shore with Corromeiro viejo bearing about N.N.W., and Lobeira grande W. ¼ S.; this latter is a good berth, and much used by coasters.

The COAST from Remodios point trends, in a southerly direction, 5 miles to monte Louro, which forms the north-west point of entrance to Muros bay. The land between is high in the interior, but the shore low, and bordered, as far as Lens point, by rocks which extend some distance off. This latter point is also low, and fronted by a ledge, and there are sunken rocks off it, on which the sea breaks at low water. The bay on its north with a sandy beach is named Lariño.

The bay between Lens point and monte Louro has a flat clean shore, named Arena Mayor, which extends across to Muros bay, separating monte Louro from the other hills on the north, so that at a distance it appears like an island. Monte Louro is a round hill 787 feet high, with two peaks on its summit, the higher of which, the southern, is crowned by a watch-tower. On its south extreme, named Queijal point, stands an hexagonal light coloured granite light-tower, 24 feet high, with the keeper's dwelling adjoining it.

About 5 miles N.W. ¾ W. from the above lighthouse is a circular shoal about a cable in diameter, named the Meixido, consisting of several dangerous sunken rocks, on one of which there are only 3 feet water, but their position is nearly always pointed out by breakers. A patch of 3¾ fathoms, called the Yusua rock, lies half a mile distant from the west side of the shoal, and there is another of the same depth about the same distance from the north side. The channel between the Meixido and the land is deep and clear of danger, but it will be more prudent to pass outside, which may be done by keeping the Navé of Finisterre open of the north-west extreme of cape Finisterre, N. ¼ E., until the lighthouse on Queijal point bears S.E. by E., when a vessel will be south of these dangers.

Nearly 3 miles W. by N. ¼ N. from the tower on monte Louro, are some large rocks named the Bruyos, which are low, and in a heavy sea the water washes over them. A sunken ledge extends some distance from their west side, and about three-quarters of a mile northward of them, lies another rocky patch named the Mean.

The Leixon rocks, off Queijal point at the foot of monte Louro, are large, and clear on all sides except the north; the channel between them and the land, is deep but narrow.

LIGHT.—The light-tower on Queijal point, on the north side of entrance of Muros, exhibits, at 37 feet above high water, a *fixed* white light, visible in clear weather at a distance of 10 miles.

MUROS BAY.—This bight, running in E.N.E. between monte Louro and Castro point, 3½ miles distant to the S. by E. ½ E., has on its north shore the port of Muros, and at its head on the south the inlet of Noya, which may be navigated by small vessels as far as the town of this latter name, but a pilot is requisite as there are several shallows. The whole bay is almost surrounded with high land, and has general depths of 12 to 24 fathoms over clean ground, but it is open to the south-west, and there are many sunken dangers off its rocky shores.

Francisco Bay, the first bight on the north shore between monte Louro and Bouja point, has a beach, but there are many rocks both above and below water close to it. The depths are convenient at a short distance offshore, but no vessel should anchor here as the bottom is foul. Bouja point is high and precipitous, with a reef running some distance from it to the southward, having on its extremity, which is steep-to, only 6 feet water.

About a mile north-east of Bouja point is the Atalaya de Muros, a high hill, perpendicular over the sea, with deep water close to ; from thence the shore bends round to the north-west and north, forming port Muros, the head of which is shallow. At half a mile within the Ataleya is a beach and the little town of Muros, which possesses a few coasting vessels and fishing boats.

Bornalle Bay, 2 miles north-east of the Atalaya, has a beach and rivulet at its head; from thence a rocky coast runs southward three-quarters of a mile to an islet surrounded with rocks, which must be given a good berth. From this islet to a point, 1½ miles eastward, the coast is of moderate height, with a number of large rocks and shoals stretching off in places about a third of a mile. Then follows a bight with sandy beaches, and at its head is the Esteiro rivulet. Huia point is low and foul, but the land rises behind it ; Quiebra island, lying off it, is high, with rocks extending from its north-west and south-east ends; the passage between it and the point being only fit for boats.

Noya Inlet has 9 fathoms water at the entrance, between Quiebra island and Plancha point on the opposite shore, but it should not be entered by a stranger without a pilot, as there are rocks and shallow water within. The town of Noya stands on the southern shore of an inlet, and the rivers Sierra and Tambre run into the sea on the north. Plancha point is high and projects but little, with four fathoms water near it. Cabeiro point, 2¼ miles westward, is also high, broad, and on its west side is the beach of Polveira, which terminates in a low point at nearly half a mile westward, from which a reef extends half a mile to the north-west, and at low water a large rock Filgueira, appears in the middle of it.

Between the low point and the Atalaya de Son, the next point westward the shore is a beach with several rocks off it, some of which are visible at low water. The Atalaya de Son is a hill of moderate height, dark coloured and precipitous, with a chapel on its summit. Close to its east side is the town of Son with a small mole. The shore hence to Castro point, 2¼ miles to the south-west, is skirted by rocks. Castro point is of moderate height, perpendicular, dark coloured, and foul; and N.W. by W. ½ W. 1¼ miles from the point, and S. ¼ W. 2⅝ miles from the light-tower on Queijal point, is the middle of a reef called the Baya, nearly awash at low water. Nearly midway between it and the point is a rock called the Con, between which and the ledge off the point is a narrow channel with 13 fathoms water, used only by coasters.

Las Basoñas.—This extensive rocky bank may be mentioned here as it is in the track of vessels approaching Muros bay from the southward. The largest rock on the bank is like a sloop's hull, having other smaller rocks around it; the lighthouse on Queijal point bears from it N.N.E. ¼ E., 5¾ miles, and Castro point N.E. by E. ¾ E. about 4 miles. The bank extends westward from the rock about 2 cables to a rock which dries at low water; here the bank turns to the northward. There are 7 fathoms water close to on its east side, and 14 fathoms on its west side.

Pilots for Muros bay are to be obtained by day, the usual signal flag being hoisted.

Directions.—The position of Muros bay may be easily recognized when coming in from sea by monte Louro, which being isolated from the hills at its back will appear like an island; or if this hill is not seen it will be known by cape Finisterre and monte Lozaro or Lezara to the northward of the bay, and the peak of Curota to the southward. The latter is the highest land on this part of the coast. It is broad, and from the summit down, a fourth of its height appears to be cut perpendicularly on the side facing the west, but afterwards sloping gradually.

Entering the bay with a northerly wind, keep the northern shore aboard, giving a berth to the Leixon rocks off the foot of monte Louro, and to the reef extending from Bouja point. From thence a board or two will reach the anchorage abreast the town of Muros, in 8 or 10 fathoms water, mud. The easterly winds, although off the land, raise a heavy sea, and have occasioned the loss of many vessels.

If the wind be from the South or S.E. keep the southern shore aboard, avoiding the Basoñas, and pass outside the Baya reef, by keeping the lighthouse on Queijal point eastward of N. by E. until Cabeiro point bears

E. ¾ N.   Castro point will not at first be easily made out, as it lies at the foot of high land.

The COAST from Castro point, on the south side of entrance to Muros bay, trends S.W. 7½ miles to cape Corrobedo, and is backed, at a short distance inland, by the lofty range of the Sierra de Barbanzo, with the remarkable Fanegueira and Curota peaks at its extremities; Fanegueira peak, at the northern extreme, is elevated 1,910 feet, and Curota peak, near the southern, 2,041 feet above the level of the sea.   Between Castro point and Roncadora point, the next projection to the southward, the shore is low with rocks and shoals off it, as well as about the latter point, which is high and steep like the former.

Southward of Roncadora point the shore is low as far as Careisiñas point, which is bordered with rocks.   Espiñeiria point, 1½ miles farther south-west, is also low and rocky, with a reef extending from it to the northward about a third of a mile; there is also a rock, called Teilan, about half a mile from the point in a W. by N. direction, being separated by a depth of 9 fathoms.   Between Careisiñas and Espiñeiria points and a little island, there is a hill of moderate height, called monte Taume, which slopes towards the south-west, and terminates in another hill, neither so high nor so sharp pointed as the former, called monte Facho.

Cape Corrobedo, nearly 1½ miles south-west of the latter point, is low, salient, and surrounded by rocks, but it will be easily recognized by its lighthouse.   Between the Cape and Falcoeiro point, 4 miles southward, is a large bay, with a flat beach, skirted here and there with large rocks. As far as the beach the shore is high and rocky, and beyond the beach to Falcoeiro point it is again of moderate height and steep, but of a sandy colour.

This bay has anchorage in 11 fathoms water, sand, occasionally used by coasters in off-shore winds, but off its entrance are dangerous ledges, steep-to, on which the sea breaks when there is any swell; the outermost ledge, named Pragriña, lies S.W. ½ W. 2½ miles from cape Corrobedo, and between are four others named Cobos, Tomasa, Rinchador, and Marosa. About 2¼ miles S. by E. ¾ E. from the Pragriña is the Canteiro, the outer of three other ledges lying nearly 2 miles westward of Falcoeiro point. This point has off it some islets and rocks, which, with the large rocks off the north-east part of Salvora island, resemble from a distance a number of vessels under sail.

Salvora Island, 2¼ miles southward of Falcoeiro point, is about a mile in length, N.N.E. and S.S.W., of a reddish colour, high in the middle, but low at each end, particularly the north.   A chain of rocks extends from its north end, and off its north-east part are several large rocks, the highest of which is named the Noro.   A lighthouse stands on the south end of the island, off which, at 1¼ cables, there is a rock which seldom uncovers, but with breakers around it.

LIGHTS.—The lighthouse on cape Corrobodo exhibits, at 103 feet above high water, a *fixed* white light, visible in clear weather at a distance of 15 miles.

Salvora Island.—The lighthouse, on the south end of Salvora island, exhibits a *fixed* light varied every *two minutes* by a *red flash.* It is elevated 82 feet above high water, and visible in clear weather 12 miles.

AROSA BAY extends 13 miles in an E.N.E. direction, with a varying breadth of 2 to 7 miles, having its entrance between Salvora island on the north, and Grobe peninsula on the south. The island of Arosa and numerous small islets and rocks are scattered about within it, and there are many reefs off the points and islands, but the navigable channels leading to the principal anchorages are sufficiently clear to enable the prudent mariner with a good chart, and a leading wind and daylight, to take his vessel safely in. This bay may, therefore, be resorted to in case of emergency, as there are many good and well sheltered anchorages within it.

The entrance is two miles wide, with 32 to 34 fathoms water, mud bottom, which depths continue about 6 miles to the north-east. Brisan point, the east extreme of Salvora, has some rocks above water off it. The north-west extreme of the Grobe peninsula is low and rocky, with large rocks fronting it ; the southern part of the peninsula is connected to the main by a narrow neck of sand.

The towns of Villa Garcia and Carril being connected with the capital of the province, the historic town of Santiago de Compostella, by a railway, the bay of Arosa is becoming of some importance, and is visited twice a month by the large English steam vessels of the Pacific and River Plate lines.

Con de Baixeu Rock, having a depth of 7 feet water on it and 7 fathoms close around, lies about 1½ cables south of Sinal del Maño shoal, on the west side of Arosa bay ; from this rock Arosa island lighthouse bears E. by S. ¼ S., and Rua island lighthouse S.W.

Mascatino Rock, with 4 feet water and 5¼ fathoms close around, is surrounded by seaweed nearly awash at low water, it lies about midway between Sinal del Maño shoal and Cabio point ; from the rock Arosa island lighthouse bears S.E. ¾ E., and Rua island lighthouse S.W. by S.

Bajo Ter, a sunken rock with 12 feet water, lies about a third of a mile from Barbafeita point ; the north-west point of Arosa island, Vig

Ancados, bearing N.E. by E. ¼ E., leads half a mile north-westward of this rock.

La Barsa, a conical rock which uncovers about 3 feet at low water, and has deep water close to, lies about half a mile south of Chazo point.

Las Novias, Bajo Seijo, and Las Hermanas, form a rocky patch, at one mile W.N.W. from Sines point; Las Novias shows about 4 feet at high water, but the other two rocks are covered at high water and show about 4 feet at low water. There is 7 to 8 fathoms, 1½ cables to the north-east and east of them.

Mount Xiabre kept E. ¼ S., and steered for on that bearing, will lead between Bajo Seijo and La Barsa, or should mount Xiabre be obscured by clouds, the island of Benencia, kept well to the northward of the first rise in the mountain range to the N.W. (behind Puebla), will also lead clear of them.

Anchorage.—There is a fine weather anchorage in 10 to 15 fathoms water, on the north-east side of Salvora, with Brisan point bearing about S. by W. ½ W., distant two thirds of a mile. Vessels may anchor in summer with easterly winds in 8 to 12 fathoms in the bay on the south side of the peninsula, taking care to avoid the Corzan and Aguiera rocks on which the sea generally breaks. The principal anchorages on the north-western side of the inlet are in the bays of Santa Eugenia and Puebla; the former cannot be recommended, as it is open to the southward. Small vessels will find good shelter in the northern corner of the inlet, about a mile off the mouth of the river Meluzo, in 2 fathoms mud bottom. In the eastern corner of the inlet are the town and bay of Carril, the town of Villagarcia, and, several villages scattered along the south-east coast; Carril bay affords a roomy and well sheltered anchorage in 7 to 9 fathoms. H.M.S. *Agincourt* (with Channel fleet), 1874, anchored in 7 fathoms, with Sines point bearing S.W. by W. ¼ W., and Ferrazo point S.E. by E. ¾ E. There is anchorage off the north end of Arosa island, abreast the village of Arosa, in 8 to 11 fathoms, this is considered a good winter anchorage, and with a southerly wind is preferable to Puebla bay. Anchorage will also be found off the west side of the island in 14 fathoms, with Pedregosa isle W. by S., distant about a mile.

LIGHT.—On Caballo point, the north extreme of Arosa island is a lighthouse, which exhibits, at 36 feet above high water, a *fixed* white light, visible in clear weather at a distance of 10 miles.

Rua Island.—On Rua island is a round gray coloured granite tower, which exhibits, at an elevation of 78 feet above high water, a *fixed* white light; visible in clear weather at a distance of 11 miles. The tower is attached to the keeper's dwelling.

Pilots for Arosa bay are generally found at Salvora island. Vessels requiring their services must fire a gun, in addition to hoisting the usual signal flag.

Tides.—It is high water, full and change, at Arosa island, at 3h. 45m. The flood runs 5 hours, and the ebb 7 hours.

Directions.—If bound to any of the anchorages in Arosa bay from the westward or north-westward in fine weather, Salvora island, which is of moderate height and rocky, will be soon recognized. The lighthouse is not easily discernible from seaward, being very low and of the same colour as the rock on which it is built.

During the fishing season—April until December—care must be taken to avoid the nets of the innumerable fishing boats belonging to the district. The regulations of the port which compel them to leave a clear space in the fairway leading up to Rua island are generally disregarded.

After passing Salvora island, at a convenient distance, steer into the bay with the hill next west of Cabio point in line with Rua island bearing N.E. ¼ N., pass Rua island at a distance of 1½ or 2 cables, and continue to the northward until the Vigia de Ancados is seen open of Benencia island, N.E. by E. ¼ E., which will lead nearly midway between Con de Baxieu rock and Bajo Ter; if bound for the anchorage in Carril bay, bring mount Xiabre to bear E. ¼ S., and steer for it, which will lead between La Barsa and Bajo Seijo, anchoring as convenient in 7 to 9 fathoms water.

ONS ISLAND, lying 5 miles southward of the entrance of Arosa bay, is nearly 3 miles long, N.E. by N. and S.W. by S., with a general breadth of about half a mile, and affords some shelter from north-west gales to Pontevedra bay, the next inlet to the southward. The island is of moderate height, and level on the top, but its western side is rugged and bordered with rocks. Its eastern side is cleaner, and has two spots of beach where boats may land; there is anchorage at about a third of a mile off this side in 16 fathoms water, sand, shells, and mud; within this distance the bottom is of rock. The north end of Ons is separated from the coast by a passage 2 miles wide, but there are several rocky patches in it, and the Fagilda bank, a rocky ledge, extends two-thirds of a mile from the coast, a little southward of Corbeiro point. There are 6 to 9 fathoms water, rocky bottom, in the channels between these dangers, and vessels locally acquainted run through in fine weather; but when there is much swell the sea breaks all over them.

Onza is a small round island separated from the south point of Ons by a passage not half a mile wide, which is only used by fishing vessels, as there are several rocks in it, and a shoal with but little water on it r----

in mid-channel. The island is about the same height as Ons, and has a beach on its eastern side; but all the other sides are bordered with rocks. Galera point, its south extreme, is foul to some distance off, and S.W. ¼ W. three-quarters of a mile from the point there is a rocky patch on which the sea breaks, and W.S.W. 1¼ miles from the point there is said to be another patch, on which the sea sometimes breaks in bad weather.

The Coast.—The point from which Fagilda bank extends is of moderate height, perpendicular, with some large rocks fronting it, thence a level coast trends S.S.E. nearly 3 miles to Cabicastro point; midway is monte Montalvo, which is higher than the rest of the coast, and has on either side of its point a small beach. Cabicastro point is steep, and forms with cape Udra, 2¾ miles to the S.S.W., the points of entrance to the inlet of Pontevedra, which runs 8 miles to the eastward.

LIGHT.—On the most elevated part of Ons island, and 1¼ miles from its north point, is a tower which exhibits, at 421 feet above the level of the sea, a *fixed* white light, varied by a *flash* every *two minutes*, and visible in clear weather at a distance of 12 miles.

PONTEVEDRA BAY is easy of access, but large vessels should not enter it in the winter season on account of the little shelter it affords; in summer, however, it furnishes good anchorage. The soundings in it are 23 to 5 fathoms, mud and sand, except in the neighbourhood of cape Udra, the south point of entrance, where the bottom is of rock and gravel, and on the northern shore of the bay, about Fertiñanzo point, where it is of rock.

The land on both shores of the bay is high, but broken into many pleasant and well cultivated valleys. Porto-novo point, on the northern shore, three-quarters of a mile eastward of Cabicastro point, is high, with a large rock and some sunken ones off it. Vessels bound northward with northerly winds, generally anchor abreast the flat shore, between these points, in 8 to 10 fathoms water. On the east side of Porto-novo point is the bay and fishing village of the same name. From thence the shore continues eastward three-quarters of a mile to another village named San Genjo; in the interval are some spots of beach separated by rocky points, with shallow water off them.

To the south-east of San Genjo is a rocky point, and nearly a mile farther on is Fertiñanzo point. This point is rocky, low, and shoal water extends from it to the south-west; at two-thirds of a mile beyond it are a cluster of large rocks, named the Bueyes (or Bulls) de Rajo, which are covered at high water. From thence to Marinulos point, 2¼ miles farther eastward, are several small points with spots of beach. A rocky patch lies off Caero point, and a large rock off the south-west side of Marinulos point; the rest of the coast is clear, but give the points a berth of 2 cables, as the ground off them is generally shallow.

Tamba Island, 270 feet high, lying half a mile south of Marinulos point, is round, with rugged shores, excepting on the east side, where there is a small beach, its shores are clear of danger; but between its northern extreme and Marinulos point the depth is only 1¾ fathoms.

To the north-eastward, between Marinulos point and the entrance of the river Leres, is a shallow bay, parts of which dry at low water springs, named Combarro from a town of that name at its head.

The entrance of the Leres between the points is three-quarters of a mile wide, but the whole space, as well as the river itself, dries at low water, so that even coasters must wait for a flowing tide to take them to Pontevedra. The low sandy point of Placeres, the south point of entrance, has a chapel on it, and between it and Pesquera point, 1¼ miles westward, is a bight with a flat shore, in the midst of which stands the town of Estrivela, and farther on, near Pesquera point, the town of Marin, and a small river used by fishing craft, which ground in it at low water.

Town of Pontevedra is situated on the south bank of the river Leres, about 2 miles within the entrance; it is well built and surrounded by walls; a long bridge of 12 arches here spans the river, up to which small craft can come at flood tide. The population may be about 5,100, and there is little or no trade.

Pesquera Point is high and rocky, with a battery about one-third of the way up to its summit, on which is a look-out. Shoal water extends nearly half a mile from the point, the northern extremity of which is marked by a red and white striped buoy.

From thence the coast, which trends S.W. 2¼ miles to Condeloiro point, has several spots of beach separated by points, off some of which are large rocks, but the water is deep and the ground clean at half a cable outside them. Condeloiro point is easily recognized, being the foot of a hill with a flat summit.

Between Condeloiro Point and Cape Udra is a deep bay, 4¼ miles wide, with general depths of 7 to 16 fathoms in it. San Clemente point, the first projection southward of Condeloiro point, is rocky and uneven, with several rocks fronting it, and appears at a distance like an island, from the flat shore on either side, and the low ground behind it. Monte-gordo point, three-quarters of a mile farther on, is less projecting but higher than that of San Clemente; and here begins a low shore, which terminates 1½ miles westward at Suspiros point, which is high; the coast then becomes steep, and there is another point running out from it, named Cabalo de Bacu, and a rock called Piedra Blanca, with several sunken rocks near it.

Thence the ¨coast continues steep, with the exception of two small patches of beach, called the Maurisca sands, as far as Sentoiera point, which is low, with a ledge extending from it N.E. one-third of a mile. This point and cape Udra form a broad rocky front, having many large rocks off it, some of which are covered at high water when the sea breaks over them. The cape is low at its extreme, but rises into a rocky hill, beyond which the interior of the country is high land.

Pilots.—The fishermen of Pontevedra are competent to act as pilots for the various anchorages.

Directions.—Pontevedra bay may be easily known when approaching it from the westward during the day, by monte Curato and the islands Salvora, Ons, and Onza, to the northward of the entrance, and the Bayona islands to the southward ; and at night by the respective lights. In entering give a berth to the breakers off the south end of Onza, and to the ledge surrounding Cape Udra. Having arrived between this cape and Cabicastro point, the course in is E.S.E. until Tamba island bears E. by N. ½ N. when steer for it.

Anchorage.—As before stated no large vessel should seek for anchorage in this bay in winter. Small vessels moor in 3 to 4 fathoms water, gravel, abreast the town of Marin, and are sheltered from all winds, but a sea sets in with westerly gales. There is better shelter from these gales in 3 fathoms on the east side of Tamba, with a cable made fast to the island. Large vessels should not go farther than 7 to 8 fathoms, mud, between Tamba and the town of Marin, but here they will be exposed to the west.

ALDAN BAY, formed between cape Udra and Couso point, 1¾ miles to the south-west, will accommodate vessels of the largest draught, but it is exposed to north-west winds, which bring in some swell, although the islands of Ons and Onza in some measure cover its entrance. The bay runs in south nearly three miles, gradually narrowing to its head, where there is a small bend to the eastward, but so shallow as only to admit coasters and fishing craft, which lie safe in all weathers. At the head of this bend is the town of Aldan, with a stream of excellent water.*

The coasts of the bay are steep, with patches of beach, and fronted with rocks and shoals, which should be avoided. From cape Udra the eastern coast trends S. ¾ W. 3 miles to Piedra Rubia point, thence to

---

* *See* Admiralty plan:—Vigo, No. 2,548 ; scale m = 1·1 inches.

Con point, a third of a mile farther south, the coast is lower but steep and clean. About 3 cables W.S.W. of Con point is another point, with a large rock off it, and here ends the low shore at the head of the bay, between which and the Bouteye shoal with 6 feet water on it, on the north, is the best anchorage for small vessels.

Dangers. — Area Brava point, about half way in on the western shore, is of moderate height, and surrounded with rocks at the distance of a cable. About 3 cables N.E. by E. from the point is a patch with 4 feet water on it, and there is another with 9 feet, named the Dado-Con, lying nearly half a mile S.E. by E. ¼ E. from Couso point. This latter point is also of moderate height and steep, with a shoal lying N.N.E. 3 cables from it; the least water on the shoal is 3¾ fathoms; there are 13 fathoms without it, and 11 fathoms between it and the point, and its extremity is marked by a red and white chequered buoy. Another shoal of larger extent fronts the coast between this point and that of Osas, a third of a mile to the W.S.W.; it extends about half a mile from the lands, and on it are several large rocks, named the Osas islets, always above water.

Directions.—Aldan bay should be navigated with a leading wind, on account of the rocks and shoals fronting its shores. In entering give a good berth to the shoals off cape Udra and Couso point, then keep in mid-channel, steering south for Con point, and passing eastward of the shoals on the western shore.

Anchorage.—There is good anchorage for large vessels above Area Brava point in 10 to 11 fathoms, mud bottom. The best berth for small vessels is southward of the Bouteye shoal, over sandy bottom, about 2 cables off the Playa de Arneles.

CIES or BAYONA ISLANDS.—The coast from Couso point trends S.W. by S. 3½ miles to cape Hombre, the west extreme of a promontory forming the north point of entrance of Vigo bay, and is all the way high and steep. This cape and Subrido point, half a mile to the south-east, are both moderately high, and bordered with reefs. At 2 miles W.N.W. of the cape is Caballo point, the north extreme of the Cies or Bayona islands, two in number, which from thence trend in a southerly direction, and cover an extent of nearly 4 miles in front of the entrance of Vigo bay, to which they form a natural breakwater. They are high and uneven on the summit, steep on the west side, but less so on the east, where there are some sandy beaches. A lighthouse stands on the summit of monte Faro, being the highest land, and at the south-west end of the northern island.

The northern island is 2¼ miles long, but at two-thirds of its length from Caballo point, its north extreme, it seems from a distance to be divided into two parts; this is not, however, the case, for these two parts are connected by a low narrow neck of sand, over which the sea sometimes washes in a heavy swell. At a quarter of a mile N.N.W. from Caballo point is a rocky shoal of some extent, named the Roncosa, which dries at low tide, leaving between it and the point a channel with 7 fathoms water; and N. ¾ W. nearly 1¼ miles from the same point is another shoal with 2¼ fathoms water on it, named the Biduido. The latter is about the size of a launch, with depths of 5 to 12 fathoms and sunken rocks between it and the Roncosa, and steep-to on the north side.

The two islands are separated by a pass, a quarter of a mile wide, named Freu de la Porta, with 4½ fathoms least water in it. Both shores of the pass are lofty and steep, with a rocky ledge extending a cable from the north end of the south island, and 3 cables from the south-west end of the north island, and which continue along the west sides of both islands.

St. Martin Island, the southern island, is about 1¼ miles in extent, and at 4 cables W. by S. ½ S. from its south-west point is a small rock which dries 4 feet at low water, named Forcado. The islets or rocks named Boeiro, 70 feet high, lie W. by S. ½ S. one mile from cape Vicos, the south point of the island. There is also at three-quarters of a mile S.W. of the Boeiro a dangerous shoal with 3 fathoms water on it, named los Castros de Agoeiro, with 6 to 12 fathoms close around it, and on which the sea breaks during heavy gales; and at 2½ cables S.S.W. from cape Vicos lies a rock which is awash at half ebb. There are passages between the dangers which, with a pilot, and in case of necessity, may be attempted. Another patch of 2½ fathoms, the Carrameiro, lies off the east side of the island, and 2 cables E.N.E. from its southern end.

VIGO BAY runs in about 15 miles in an easterly direction, from its entrance between cape Hombre on the north, and cape Silleiro on the south, and is entirely enclosed with mountainous land, broken by cultivated valleys, which form a pleasing landscape. From the entrance, the bay gradually diminishes in breadth to the castle of Bestias on its north shore, 12 miles within, where it is only a third of a mile wide; within this it forms a basin to the north-east 3 miles long, and in places 1½ miles wide, but the water in it is shallow.

A series of small bays are formed on both shores of Vigo bay, between high projecting points. The bay on the north shore of entrance, between Subrido and Castros points, has a flat shore, of which vessels sometimes anchor with northerly winds in 9 to 11 fathoms, sand. Castros point and the shore half a mile westward, is of moderate height, and fronted by a reef extending upwards of half a mile in a southerly direction.

Borneiro point, 1¼ miles farther eastward, is low and salient, with a reef running 4 cables S.S.W. from it, and near its outer end lies a rock of the same name, which uncovers at low water. At the distance of three-quarters of a mile S.E. ½ E. from the same point, is a small patch with 2½ fathoms water, named the Zalgueiron rock, with 4 and 5 fathoms close around it, and which has a red buoy with a white top, on its southern side. On the east side of the point is the bay of Cangas, with a beach at its head, and the town of the same name; the bay terminates to the eastward at Rodeira point, between which and Con point, 1¼ miles farther eastward, the shore is fronted by an extensive ledge of rocks, covered at high water, the southern extreme of which is marked by a buoy coloured black and white in horizontal stripes with staff and cage, and the south-western, named Piedra de Pego, at half a mile from the land, is marked by a beacon.

From Con point begins another bay and beach, and at its head is Bartolomé chapel on a steep black rock; from thence the eastern shore is high and rocky on to Ruas point, off which, at 1¼ cables eastward, is a large rock above water, named Ruas islet. The shore then extends 2¼ miles eastward to Bestias point, between which and Ronde point, bearing S.S.W. a third of a mile, is the narrowest part of the bay. Both points are clean and steep, and between them in mid-channel the depth is 16 fathoms, mud. Within these points the bay opens out, and forms to the north-east a shallow basin with one to 3 fathoms water, the head of which dries at low tide; the river Payo disembogues in its north-east corner, and the river Redondela in its south-east; both are navigable for boats at high water. On the east shore is San Simon islet, of moderate height, with large rocks at each end.

The southern shore of the bay takes a W.S.W. direction from Ronde point, and at the distance of 2 miles is the village and bay of Teis, at the foot of the hill of la Guia. This hill is of moderate height, round, steep, and of a reddish colour, with a chapel on its summit, and a castle with a light-tower well down towards the point; a sand-bank with shoal water extends 2 cables from its north and north-east sides, and a cable from its west side, and off its north-west face, is a large rock named Cabron islet. Between the hill and the battery of San Andres, 1¼ miles westward, is a bight with a beach, and the town of Vigo, the latter stands partly on the beach, and partly on the ground rising gradually behind it.

Bouzas point, 1¼ miles westward of San Andres battery, is low and rocky, with a reef projecting 3 cables from it. Cape Mar, 1½ miles farther westward, is low and of a sandy colour; a reef, part of which is visible at low water, extends 3 cables from it to the north-west. From thence to cape Estaya bearing W.S.W. 2¾ miles, the coast forms a bight with a low shore, off which is a small island named Toralla, which is of equal height with a shore abreast, and at a distance appears to be part of it; the island is surrounded with shoals, and only separated from the land by a passage scarcely fit for coasters. Near the extremity of the reef at the west end, is a red buoy, with staff and cage.

Cape Estaya is of black colour, and fronted by a reef which continues along the shore of the bight between it and monte Ferro. The hill is round, of a reddish colour and has a look-out on its summit; its north-west extreme is named cape Sentaulo, and its south slope forms the northern shore of Puerto de Bayona, which, having many shoals and sunken rocks in it, should not be entered without a pilot. The best shelter is abreast the town of Bayona to the south-east of Tenaza point, which is the north extreme of a peninsular hill of moderate height, but steep over the sea, with the walls of an extensive castle on its summit.

At 3 cables off the western face of monte Ferro is a small island, the Estela de Tierra, of moderate height, between which and the land is a narrow passage, with 3 fathoms water between the shoals, and may be used by small craft in case of necessity with a smooth sea, by keeping close to the island. At 2 cables westward of this island is another of equal size and height, the Estela de Mar, the passage between them being only 1¾ fathoms deep. At about three-quarters of a mile in a N.W. and W. by S. direction from this latter island, is a reef named the Restinga de Laxe, some of the rocks on which dry at low water.

The town of Vigo, which stands in a small bend of the south shore, about 9 miles within the entrance of the bay, has good anchorage off it, and was of great importance as a port, previous to the formation of the naval establishment at Ferrol. The town is enclosed by walls, with a ditch, and is defended by the castle of Castro, which crowns the heights behind. There is a good export trade in wine, maize, and bacon, and an active pilchard fishery. In 1871, 1,876 vessels of 168,430 tons entered inwards, and about the same number cleared outwards; the imports of the same year were valued at 270,352l., and the exports at 121,759l. Population about 6,000. There is steam communication with London, Liverpool, and Southampton, and a British vice-consul resides here.

Telegraph.—There is a submarine telegraph between Vigo and England, and between Vigo and Lisbon.

Water may be obtained in ship's boats from San Bartolomè on the northern shore, or it can be purchased and brought off in sailing tanks, for three shillings a ton.

Supplies are plentiful and cheap; coal is easily procurable, and brought alongside in lighters.

Anchorage.—With the exception of the neighbourhood of the points, the whole of the bay affords good anchorage in 14 to 23 fathoms, mud and sand. The usual anchorage is off the town of Vigo in 11 to 6 fathoms, mud, sheltered by the Bayona islands from westerly winds, which throw in the heaviest sea. The bay of Teis, the next bend of the shore eastward of Vigo, affords safe anchorage sheltered from all winds; vessels may lie here in 6 fathoms, with a cable fast to the shore, and an anchor to the northward. There is also space sufficient at a quarter of a mile eastward of Bestias and Ronde points, at the entrance of the shallow basin, for a number of vessels to lie in 15 to 6 fathoms safe from all winds. There is also an outside anchorage in 11 fathoms, sand, off the east side of the low sandy neck, uniting the two parts of the northern of the Bayona islands. The other parts of this basin may also be serviceable to vessels taking the bay without anchors or cables, as they may run aground anywhere on the mud, until necessaries be procured, and then by lightening they may be got off without the least damage.

Buoys.—In July 1879 the following were the buoys in Vigo bay :—

North Shore.—A nun buoy, painted red with staff and cage, is moored in 9 fathoms, near the south extreme of Castros da Barra. A nun buoy, painted red and white in vertical stripes, lies in 6 fathoms, near south part of Bajo Borneira. Zalgueiron rock, a red buoy with staff and cage marked Zalgueiron ; at the south-west extreme of the reef extending from Rodeira point, a black and white horizontal striped buoy ; in the middle of the anchorage, about 4 cables west of Santa Tecla point, a black buoy in 9 fathoms water.

South Shore.—A black nun buoy with staff and cage, marking south-west extreme of shoal off Toralla island. A can buoy, red and white in vertical stripes, lies in 5 fathoms near the north entrance of El Caberon. The buoys are often out of position, and cannot be depended upon.

CAPE SILLEIRO, the south part of entrance of Vigo bay, is high and rugged, and may be known by the light coloured granite light-tower, 33 feet high, standing on it about 30 yards from the water's edge. The first story is square, the two upper octagonal, and the tower is joined to the keeper's dwelling. The extremity of the cape is a low point, which terminates in a ledge of rocks extending three-quarters of a mile to the N. by W., a part of which dries at low water, and the sea breaks when there is the least swell.

Caution.—The Restinga de Laxe reef, and los Castros de Agoeiro, bearing from it about N.W. by N., distant 1¾ miles, were formerly buoyed ;

these are the dangers on either side of the southern entrance to Vigo bay, and it may be in contemplation to replace the buoys which of late years have disappeared.

LIGHTS.—Cies Island.—The lighthouse on monte Faro, the highest and most prominent part (at the south end) of the northern of the Bayona islands, exhibits, at an elevation of 604 feet above the level of the sea, a white light which *revolves* once *every minute*, and should be seen, in clear weather, at a distance of 30 miles.

Caution.—Too much dependence should not, however, be placed on the regularity of the revolution, or the duration of the eclipses of Cies light.

Cape Silleiro.—The light coloured granite lighthouse on cape Silleiro, shows, at 72 feet above the sea, a *fixed* white light visible 17 miles.

La Guia.—On the castle of La Guia, near the point of that name, about 1¼ miles eastward of Vigo, is a *fixed* white light, varied every *three minutes* by a *flash*. It is elevated 102 feet above the sea, and visible at a distance of 7 miles, the flash is seen 12 miles.

Pilots for Vigo are in general on the look out for vessels in the neighbourhood of the Bayona islands, in the daytime only.

Tides.—It is high water, full and change, in Vigo bay at 3h. ; springs rise 12 to 13 feet, and run about half a mile an hour; the rise is much influenced by the wind.

Directions.—Vigo bay is readily known when approaching from north or south by the islands of Ons and Bayona. At a distance in the offing, however, these islands appear to be part of the main land, and it will then only be known, if the weather is clear, by monte Curota, 28 miles northward of the south entrance, and by monte Señora del Alba, which is a sharp pointed hill with a chapel on its summit about 3 miles inland on the south shore of bay. The land is high and level to the southward of the entrance ; and no opening will be seen until at the mouth of the river Miño. The bay may be entered by the north passage between cape Hombre and Caballo point, the north extreme of the Bayona islands ; or by the south passage between the dangers south-west of the southern island, and those extending westward from monte Ferro. In a case of necessity, vessels may, if their draught will permit, run through the passage between the Bayona islands.

To enter by the north passage, which is the best with a northerly wind, steer with mount Señora del Alba just over cape Hombre on a S.S.E. ¾ E. bearing, until monte Ferro, the black round hill on the south side of the entrance to the bay, is seen in the middle of the passage, bearing South a little westerly.   Keep the mount on this bearing until southward of Caballo point, when steer in mid-channel, and haul gradually into the bay giving a berth to the dangers.   Monte Ferro open of the east side of the north Bayona island, also clears the Biduido shoal.

The chapel on the summit of the hill of la Guia bearing East, leads up to the anchorage off Vigo.   This chapel is not readily recognized by a stranger ; it is a very small whitewashed building upon a hill, apparently half the height of those beyond it, and is the next projecting land beyond Vigo.

To enter by the south passage, the rocks off cape Mar in line with point la Guia E. by N. ¼ N. will lead in mid-channel between the Castros and Restinga de Laxe shoals, in depths of 32 to 27 fathoms. When the high summit of mount Faro de Domayo bears N.E. by E. ¼ E. steer for it, until the chapel on the hill of la Guia bears East, when proceed as before.

At Night, with cape Silleiro light bearing S.E., bring the *revolving* light on Faro island N.E., and then steer E. by N.; should the *flashes* of La Guia light be seen, keep it on this latter bearing until cape Silleiro light bears S.S.W. distant 3¼ miles, then steer about N.E. by E. ¼ E. until La Guia light bears East, and proceed as before.

Should the wind prevent the vessel from following these courses, give a good berth to the ledges extending from the different points and to the Zalgueiron rock, and do not approach the shore to a less depth than 8 fathoms.   To clear the Borneira reef, keep Caballo point (the north extreme of the Bayona islands) open of Subrido point until Cangos church is well open.

The COAST from cape Silliero trends about S.S.W. 15 miles to the entrance of the river Miño, and is nearly all the way bordered with rocks. Orulluda point, at 4½ miles southward of the cape, is a little salient with some large rocks off it.   About 2 miles beyond the point and close to the shore is the town of Oya, with a small rivulet.   At 5½ miles farther on is the little town and port of la Guardia, the latter, a small creek used by fishing craft.   The coast is backed by a lofty rugged range, rather level along the summit, which begins at cape Silleiro.   At about a mile south-ward of la Guardia is a hill named monte Santa Tecla, having two peaks, on the highest of which is a chapel.   This hill greatly resembles monte Louro, the north point of entrance of Muros bay, and serves to indicate the position of the Miño, of which it forms the north side of entrance.

The RIVER MIÑO rises in the north-east part of the province of Galicia, about 40 miles north-east of Santiago, and from thence flows southward until it reaches the borders of Portugal. It then takes a westerly direction, and forms the boundary between Spain and Portugal to the sea, which it enters after a course of about 180 miles. The entrance between Picos point on the north, and Castillo point on the south, is 1¼ miles wide, but nearly midway is a small low islet named Insua, with a fort on it. Formerly there was a channel on both sides this islet, and that on the south side (called the Portuguese entrance) was the best; but the sands in this channel now dry at low water springs, while the channel on the north side (called the Spanish entrance) has 5½ feet in it at that time of tide.

The Miño being barred, and having many banks within, which change their shape and position according to the strength of the current can only be navigated by vessels of light draught, with an experienced pilot. A short distance within the bar there is a small space with about 3 fathoms water, but off Camiña there is only one fathom. This small town stands on the left bank, about 3½ miles within, and is strongly fortified. The inhabitants are chiefly employed in fishing and the manufacture of salt. Population about 1,800. The river is navigable for small craft to Moncao, on the left bank, about 11 miles further up.

Tides.—It is high water, full and change, on the bar of the Miño, at about 2h. 30m., and ordinary springs rise 7 feet.

CHAPTER V.

COAST OF PORTUGAL. RIVER MIÑO TO RIVER GUADIANA.

VARIATION IN 1881.

River Miño   - 21° 0′ W. | Cape St. Vincent   - 19° 0′ W.

COAST.—There is no available harbour of refuge along the whole coast between Vigo and Lisbon. From the entrance of the river Miño the shore runs in a southerly direction for about 44 miles to the entrance of the river Douro. From monte Santa Tecla to the mouth of the Lima, the coast is of moderate height, but backed by the Sierra de Santa Lucia which rises a little inland, higher than the land to the northward, and visible from sea at a distance of more than fifty miles, forms a good mark for distinguishing this part of the coast. At about 8 miles southward of monte Tecla is the mouth of the little river Ancora, with anchorage off it for small craft in fine weather, and 5 miles farther on, is a point with a round hill called mount Dôr; the shore here should not be approached nearer than 7 or 8 fathoms water. The town of Areoza, forming an amphitheatre, may be seen on the slope of mount Santa Lucia.

LIMA RIVER.—This river rises in the sierra de San Mamed, and enters the sea at Vianna, after a course of about 60 miles. Its mouth is 11 miles southward of monte Santa Tecla, between two low points, and fronted by rocks and shoals, which partly protect it from the sea. There are 7 or 8 feet water over the bar at low water, and vessels of 13 or 14 feet draught cross it at high water; the river is navigable for small craft up to the bridge of Lima, 9 miles from the entrance. The bar offers no impediment to navigation as the channel is always open, the course of the river being diverted by means of artificial works.

The river swells out near its mouth into a broad estuary, more than two-thirds of the area of which is exposed at low water. On the northern bank there is a wet dock and quays, and on the same side of the entrance, a cluster of rocks and a break-water, all of which serve to direct the stream of the river to the southward, which prevents the accumulation of sand. A pilot is necessary to enter, and the principal anchorage is within the southern point.

Vianna do Lima is a fortified town, standing on the north bank of the river Lima; having a white appearance, it is visible at some distance and may contain about 7,500 inhabitants. It carries on a fair trade in salt fish with Newfoundland. A fort on the point commands the entrance.

LIGHT.—From the northern bastion of fort Vianna, is exhibited a fixed *red* light, elevated 48 feet above high water, visible in clear weather from a distance of 7 miles.

Semaphore.—On the south-west corner of the fort there is a semaphore station with which vessels can communicate by the international code.

Anchorage.—In fine weather vessels may anchor off the mouth of the Lima, in 8 or 9 fathoms water, with the town bearing E.N.E.

Directions.—A vessel should have a pilot to enter the Lima, but if unable to obtain one, and in case of actual necessity, the following directions may enable the mariner to save his vessel. It is necessary to double the rocky ledge which extends nearly a mile southward of the entrance; to do which, bring a small round hill, covered with pines, on the south shore opposite the town to bear East, and steer for it till at the distance of half a mile from the shore; then haul to the northward, passing nearer the rocks—or about two-thirds over—then the west extremity of the south point, until the river is well open, then steer in, thus entering from the south.

The south shore is of low sand terminating in a sharp point at the entrance, from which a wooden pier or breakwater projects seaward, and off it the sand banks dry at low water. The channel for some distance is between the sandy shore and the rocks; a rock said to be covered at high water lies southward of the main ledge, which is left on the port hand. There is a northern passage, which is the deeper but narrower, and runs nearly east and west; the southern lying nearly north-east and south-west is preferred, as being the wider and easier to take.

ST. BARTHLOMEW ROCKS.—For 3 miles southward of Vianna, or as far as the bar of Nieva, the shore is a low beach, when it becomes higher and level, backed by high land as far as Villa do Conde, at the entrance to the Ave 17 miles farther on. The St. Bartholomew or Pedra do Pontel rocks, to the southward of the river Neiva, and the raven rock to the south-west of them, are 2¼ miles and 2½ miles off-shore respectively. These dangers are formed of several patches, some of which show themselves at low water, and others are always covered. This part of the coast should not be approached nearer than 3 miles, nor into less than 11 fathoms water. To the southward of these rocks, the coast is clean, as far as Espozende, 10 miles from Vianna.*

---

* The *Corinthian* steamer was wrecked in July 1864 on a rock from which the fort at Vianna was said to bear N.N.E. distant 3¼ miles, and Castello de Neiva E.S.E. 2¼ miles.

CAVADO RIVER rises in the sierre de Gerez, on the frontiers of Galicia, and after a course of 65 miles to the south-west runs into the sea between the towns of Espozende and Faõ, each having a high steeple. Espozende, with a population of about 2,000, is the principal place, and stands on the north bank, nearly opposite Faõ, at a short distance from the coast. It gives its name to the bar, over which none but small vessels can pass, there being only 7 feet over it at high water, and even then a pilot is necessary, as the bar shifts with fresh winds and strong tides. The river is navigable for about 6 miles.

DANGERS.—There is a sunken rock lying nearly 2 miles from the shore abreast Cavado river entrance, with Espozende light bearing E. ¼ S. Abreast of Faõ, at 1¼ miles from the coast, there are two rocky ledges, even with the water's edge, and parallel to each other ; they are named Cavallos de Faõ. At 2 miles south of Cavallos de Faõ, and about one mile from the shore, there are two dangerous sunken rocks. This part of the coast should not be approached nearer than 3 miles ; but to the south-ward of these rocks, a vessel may stand into 10 or 12 fathoms until near the reefs northward Villa do Conde.

A little to the north-west of the lighthouse at Povoa de Varzim there is a ridge of rocks.

LIGHT.—A *fixed red* light is exhibited at the old fort of Espozende, at an elevation of 45 feet above the level of the sea, visible in clear weather at a distance of 7 miles.

AVE RIVER.—The mouth of this river is about 11 miles south-ward of the bar of Espozende ; for the first 8 miles, the shore is low and sandy, with the mountains of Franqueira lying nearly parallel with it, a few miles inland ; at Ablemar, the coast becomes higher, and trends more easterly to the mouth of the Ave.

Villa do Conde is a small seaport town, on the north bank near the mouth of the Ave. On an elevation near it is the convent of Santa Clara, surrounded by houses which have the appearance of a small town ; this and its high long aqueduct parallel to the coast, are generally the first objects seen from a distance at sea ; they are visible 17 or 18 miles. Opposite Villa do Conde, and on the left bank of the Ave, is the small town or suburb of Azurara, with a remarkable steeple ; and by these objects, the entrance of the river may be easily recognized.

Dangers.—There are numerous rocks above water before the bar of the Ave, and others to the northward near the coast, amongst which there are passages, but they are intricate and dangerous ; it is therefore more prudent to pass to the southward of them all if intending to enter the river, in order to cross the bar.

Bar.—Vessels drawing more than 8 feet water cannot enter the river, and as the bar shifts at times, a pilot is necessary.

LIGHT.—At Povoa do Varzim, 2 miles north of Villa do Conde, a white light is shown occasionally in dark and foggy nights, and when the fishing boats are at sea. The light appears *revolving* to the south and north, but its revolving character is less distinctly seen from the westward.

ORESTES ROCK.—This danger, on which H.M.S. *Orestes* struck in 1833, was considered to be distant 3½ miles from the shore ; with the north part of the village of Vilha do Conde bearing E. ¼ N. and the south part E. ½ S. This rock was found to be steep-to; at a distance of one cable no bottom could be obtained with the hand line.

To avoid this dangerous ground, vessels in the neighbourhood of Vilha do Conde should be careful not to approach the shore nearer than 4 or 5 miles.*

LEÇA RIVER.—From the bar of the Ave, the coast trends about S. ¼ W. 10 miles to the mouth of the Leça. It is mostly a sandy beach with low land, but there are hills of moderate height in the interior ; and near the shore are some rocks above water. The Leça, a small sluggish stream, runs into the sea at nearly three miles northward of the mouth of the Douro; at the entrance (one opposite the other), are the two small towns of Leça and Matozinhos.

The Leichoes rocks, between half and two-thirds of a mile from the land, and lying somewhat in the direction of the coast, form a crescent about half a mile in extent, are always uncovered, and within them there is shelter in about 6 fathoms water, from northerly and north-west winds. At half a mile to the E.S.E. of the southern rock, is a small shoal with about 11 feet water on it, upon which the sea breaks heavily. This shoal is a quarter of a mile from the land, and lies nearly W.N.W. from the chapel of Arèa near the shore. At nearly half a mile westward of this chapel is the chapel of Matozinhos in the middle of a grove of poplar trees, but it cannot be seen at any distance.

Anchorage.—The 10-fathom line of soundings passes but a short distance from the Leichões; and in the north channel, between these rocks and the land, the depth is said to be 6 fathoms. This anchorage is convenient for pilot and fishing vessels, as they can nearly always get to sea, and it appears to be the only place on this coast where a vessel in distress could run on the beach with a chance of saving the crew.†

---

* Nautical Magazine, 1834, page 520.

† It has been in contemplation to make a secure harbour, by forming a breakwater trending towards the shore, from each extremity of the Leichões ; and to build quays and docks along the banks of the Leça, with a railway to convey the goods landed here to Oporto.

DOURO RIVER.—From the mouth of the Leça, a sandy beach trends in a southerly direction 1¼ miles to fort Queijo (Black fort), from whence the land begins to be rocky and more elevated, but continues in nearly the same direction 1¼ miles farther to fort San Joaõ da Foz, on the north point of the mouth of the Douro. This river takès its rise in the sierra de Urbion, in Castile, and traverses the most mountainous portions of Leon and Salamanca before it reaches the Portuguese frontier. In Portugal it passes through the soft crumbling granites of Tras-os-Montes and then enters the long strip of country in which the port wine is produced. From thence to Oporto the land is laid out in vineyards, wherever the soil along the banks admits of the vine being cultivated.

The course of the Douro lies mainly through a soil, which, during heavy rains, is easily carried down by the stream, and in Portugal its channel is everywhere narrow, with a rocky bed. The waters being thus confined the strength of the current is considerable, and at some points its rate is said to exceed 9 miles an hour, and the average rate is probably not less than 3 miles an hour. It is navigable for several vessels for 70 miles from the entrance, and boats of light draught may proceed 30 miles higher. Grain and other produce is floated down from Spain on flats, but its navigation is frequently interrupted, from the swelling of the river by rain and melted snow.*

OPORTO, the second city of Portugal, and having a population of upwards of 90,000, stands on the side of a steep eminence of about 200 feet elevation, which rises from the north bank of the Douro about 2 miles from the sea, and is bounded by hills 500 feet high, of which that of Congregados is the most elevated; these heights are fortified, and the city is otherwise defended by lines of defence, bastions, &c. The houses extend on the north side to the Lapa convent, and are continued along the shore for a considerable distance down the river. The climate is considered healthy, but the heat during July and August is oppressive.

The city is profusely supplied with excellent water, and the necessaries of life are abundant and cheap. Wine is the chief article of trade, and no less than 41,558 pipes of port have been shipped in one year; oil, shumac, fruit, wool, cream of tarter, salt, leather, and cork, are also exported. The chief imports are corn, beef, sugar, coffee, deals, woollen and cotton goods hardware, rice, hemp, flax, and dried fish. There is steam communication with Liverpool, Lisbon, &c., and many English families reside in the city and suburbs.

Villa Nova da Gaya, formerly called Calle, was the original town. It extends along the south shore of the river, opposite Oporto,

---

* See Admiralty plan, Douro river and views, No. 87, scale m = 3·9 inches.

between the Serra convent and the heights of Furada ; in it are the principal wine lodges and depôts : it formerly gave the name of "portus calle" to the port, from which, it is said, the present name of the kingdom is derived. A handsome suspension bridge connects Oporto with this town.

LIGHT.—Near the chapel of Nossa Senhora da Luz, is a square white tower with a red band 6 feet wide, from which, at an elevation of 170 feet above the level of the sea, is exhibited a *fixed* white light varied by a *flash* every *minute*, and visible in clear weather at a distance of 15 miles.

Semaphore.—At the lighthouse, there is a semaphore station, with which vessels can communicate by the international code.

Aspect.—The land in the vicinity of Oporto may be easily recognized, as the heights of monte da Rabida and of Furada, which form the river gap, being 200 feet high, and only 1½ miles from the coast, will point out the entrance of the river by the peculiar haze behind them. It may also be known at a considerable distance, if the weather be moderately clear, by the hills of Congregados and Lapa, on the northern limits of the city. The latter hill, which is the nearer of the two, and 500 feet high, may be distinguished by a round tower near a gloomy-looking convent on the heights over Matozinhos. To the northward is the conspicuous chapel of San Joaõ da Apollonia ; it is easily known by its three large umbrella-shaped trees. On the southern range, and at nearly the same distance from the Lapa, is San Ovidio, about the same apparent magnitude as the chapel of Santa Apollonia ; and, at the entrance close to the water, the church of San Joaõ da Foz, if the weather be fine, is also very conspicuous.*

To a vessel coming from the southward, into 12 fathoms water, the probable outline of the land to the northward will be the Queijo fort, black, with four white-capped turrets at its angles ; Crasto hill, flat-crowned, and rising close north of the lighthouse ; and in the distance the chapel of San Joaõ da Apollonia, capped by the umbrella trees. The coast to the southward of the Cabedello or sandspit, is sandy, but may be distinguished from it by the fisherman's huts, which commence a few miles to the southward, and continue a great distance. Should the weather be too lazy to distinguish the outline above described, it will be necessary to pay attention to the soundings, which cannot far mislead, if to the southward of the Leichões.

Off the bar, in 9 fathoms, the bottom is hard and sandy ; to the northward or southward of it the sand is mixed with mud. In this depth, if near

---

* The directions for the Douro are by Commander Edward Belcher, of H.M.S. Ætna-1833.

the bar, the vessel will be a little more than a mile off the land; and here the rollers on the bar, if they top, will be perceived. If to the northward of the bar, the convent of Santa Clara, nearer Villa do Conde, will be seen in clear weather.

If, on making the land in hazy weather, its higher outline cannot be defined, it will be well to look narrowly to the beach, bearing in mind that, although a considerable range of sandy beach lies to the southward of the Douro, yet it is there studded with huts, whereas none are to be seen near the Douro. Should the beach appear to be sand, with a few boulders of large rounded rocks, the eye should be carried northerly, to ascertain whether the slope of the dark land terminates in sand, with a clump of these boulders there, as well as on the land. If this be the case the vessel will be to the southward of the bar, and off its shoalest part. By tracing the sand (which is a long spit) northerly, the fort of San Joaõ da Foz will be discerned, and the South Filgueira. This rock is connected by sunken rocks with the mainland at the fort.

If on the other hand, the shore should exhibit rough rocky ledges, with sandy bays between them, the vessel will be to the northward of the bar, and the Black fort (Queijo) will be seen where the long sandy beach commences to the northward. Here the water should not be shoaled to less than 10 fathoms, and it would be advisable to keep to the south-west to avoid the Leichões.

Approaching the Bar.—The city of Oporto may be seen in clear weather at the distance of 12 or 14 miles. The steeple of Los Clerigos is a very prominent object, and when brought E.S.E. the land may be approached on this bearing until this water shoals to 9 fathoms. By night a vessel should not go into less than 15 fathoms, unless the weather be very fine, in which case she may run into 12, where it would be advisable to anchor until daylight, as in the event of calms, currents, morning fogs, or easterly winds, much delay and loss of tide might be occasioned.

If the fog be not very thick, the church of Santa Catharina and the white dome of Anjo will probably be seen; keeping these objects in line vessels of 12 feet draught should not shoal to less than 5 fathoms; but as long as the Black fort is kept open westward of the North Filgueira, four times the length of the latter, there is no risk in this depth, provided the vessel's head be off shore, with steerage way. If there be much swell this will probably be the line of the rollers, when a vessel should not stand so far in.

If the chapel of St. Joaõ de Apollonia be made out, bring it and the lighthouse in line, N.E. by E. ¼ E., and stand on in that direction, until Santa Catharina church and Lapa convent are in a line; these cr~

bearings will place a vessel in 6 fathoms, and in the best position for taking a pilot on board. If compelled to wait, give West to S.W. the preference in laying the ship's head to seaward. A considerable offset will secure her from danger of indraught in this position; the offset especially during the winter, prevailing until the freshets have been overcome by the ordinary flood tides, which are pretty regular from June until November.

The bar of Oporto is an unsafe lee shore, especially with the wind from West to S.W.; but, with the wind from N.W. vessels may with safety approach to examine the state of the bar, provided always that the latitude be known (or land made out), and the usual precautions of the lead and a good look out be attended to. If the weather should be so hazy that San Joaõ da Foz fort and the lighthouse cannot be distinguished, it will be unsafe to approach the bar; at the same time it should be borne in mind, that, if the haziness commenced before 10 a.m., and not the result of bad weather, it may be expected to clear off about noon.

It is unsafe to trust boats outside the bar on the ebb, unless they have a vessel to resort to, as the overfalls on freshes or springs would prevent their evading any roller which might follow them in.

Bar Signals used at the telegraph adjoining the lighthouse :—A drum at mast head, and one at each yard arm, signifies close the bar. A drum at each yard arm, you may be piloted if you approach. A drum at masthead and one at right yard arm, you cannot be piloted. A drum at mast-head, the coast is dangerous, keep at a distance.

The Anchorage outside the bar is good in any depth between 10 and 14 fathoms : but if bad weather be anticipated, the Leichões should bear at least North from the anchorage. Slip ropes and buoys should always be on, as the swell at times renders weighing dangerous, as well as impossible.

The Bar.—To give sufficient directions to a stranger for entering the Douro is impossible, for the channel is so intricate that even with a considerable acquaintance with the place much care and promptitude is requisite and most particularly with regard to the helm. The bar—the great obstruction to its navigation—is a broad and constantly shifting belt of sand having generally about 20 feet water over it, at ordinary high tides. From November until May the bar is seldom free from rollers. Those which endanger vessels, rarely top heavily at the distance of a mile from the shore, unless in gales; but should the ebb have made, the attempt to enter against it would be attended with extreme danger.

Although the bar may be impassable, it does not follow that there can be no communication with the shore, as even at half-ebb, the worst time of tide for the bar, boats can go off from the beach between Foz and the lighthouse, and nearly at all times from the huts of monte Crasto. The boats used for this purpose (Catraias) go through very heavy seas safely, when no ship's boats could live. The dangers at, and within the bar, are much exaggerated by the pilots, whose noise and confusion in bringing a vessel in, is intended to produce undue impressions of intricacy and danger, whereas vessels drawing from 9 to 12 feet may safely enter at high water, and even at half-flood without a pilot, many cases having occurred in which masters who would not be imposed upon, have brought the vessels over the bar, in defiance of the pilot's assertion, that such a step would be impracticable.

Tides.—It is high water, full and change, at the bar of Oporto, at 2h. 30m.; springs rise on an average about 10 feet, and neaps 8 feet, which may be further increased by nine inches or a foot in easterly winds. The pilots affirm that in the heaviest freshets the tide is not increased on the bar more than one foot. The western swell being checked by the freshets from the Douro, the rollers on the bar become terrific, and not unfrequently detain vessels entering or departing for five or six weeks.

The Freshets are occasioned more by extensive thaws in the mountainous country which feeds this river, than by heavy rains, and may be expected in their greatest force during the months of March and April,— even as late as May,—but the increased rise and rapidity of the tides which is occasioned by rain alone, may occur between November and May. The latter do not produce any dangerous consequences; but the effects of thaws and rain combined, occasions such an increase in the rapidity of the stream, that vessels cannot then trust to their anchors, which are sometimes undermined by the current, and not unfrequently trees and other large bodies are brought down by the stream.

The rise of the river under these circumstances is very great. It is said by actual measurement to be 10 feet above springs, and the velocity from the sudden fall at the bend has been estimated by the pilots at almost 14 miles.

Precautions.—During the freshets the vessels are secured in tiers, the innermost being secured to stone bollards or rings let into the piers for the purpose, and are kept about 40 feet from the shore by brows both forward and aft, and well lashed to admit of rising. During the months of March and April additional precautionary measures will probably be necessary. It is said that the eddy, during the freshets, has been strong enough to bring a boat from Lazaretto point up to the Cavaco gate.

Pilots.—The constant shifting of the sand forming the bar renders it necessary to sound the channel every three or four days, and to maintain a numerous body of experienced pilots, who are always ready to go off when a vessel is in sight, unless the weather prevents their getting out, or if the marks cannot be seen. They will also go off at night if fine. The pilotage dues are heavy.

Life Boats.—A society at Oporto for the rescue and preservation of wrecked seamen, and an establishment with life boats and apparatus for reaching vessels in distress, exists on the banks of the Douro, just within the bar.

Anchorage in the River.—The best anchorage is in the bight of San Antonio, where the freshes cause a kind of eddy, and as near the convent as possible; not allowing the dome of the Serra Convent to be seen outside the quay. There will be no danger of grounding at low water springs. A good berth for a vessel of war will be to bring the wine company's store (a white house, on the starboard bow,) and the eastern red gate of the garden wall of the Cavaco abreast the starboard gangway. It is customary to make the starboard bower cable fast to the shore. The holding-ground in the stream is very loose; however, a bower is usually laid out there at a long scope, for the off strain, and as the stream swells gradually heave in shore, until the starboard cable is nearly ahead. In this position but little strain is experienced and the port chain will bury itself in the mud, which is very deep.

Directions.—The long leading mark is Santa Catharina church on with the south belfry of Lapa convent, bearing E. ⅜ S., and on this course vessels should stand in for the bar, particularly if the bar or pilot-boat is on the look out. Should the haze prevent the Lapa from being seen, Anjo dome and Santa Catharina will answer the same purpose; and when on the bar, it is rather safer, although the space between those marks is apparently trifling.

Two cross bearings will now come on nearly at the same instant, and even in the thickest navigating weather, can be discovered, viz., Queijo fort and North Filgueira, and the Northern or Pilot's Staff of San João da 'Foz over South Filgueira. This is the shallowest part of the bar. Now edge northerly to bring a building named the Bar mark and Santa Catharina in line, and stand on, keeping a little northerly withal, but bearing in mind that the cross bearings of Bar Mark and the cross of Anjo chapel, as well as the two staffs of San João da Foz, in line, meet on a very small rock named the Staff rock, which is awash at low-water springs, with deep water around it. The moment the line of the two staffs is passed, get into the line of Anjo chapel cross and the Bar Mark, and stand on until abreast the semicircular stone wall, against which a vessel may almost rub her side.

From thence pass on the south side of the Cruz, but very close, as a rock named the Agulha or Needle, having 1½ feet on it at low water,

lies S. ¼ W. from it, distant half a cable. After passing the Cruz
(looking astern) keep the centre of South Filgueira in line with the
south side of the Cruz, until the dome of the Foz is seen over the south
extremity of the Anjo Battery ruins. The course should then be shaped
for the willow-tree at the fountain under the Monte de Rabida, until
Santa Catharina is well open of swamp island, when steer direct for
Clerigos, recollecting that all the danger, after passing the fountain steps
are on the south side. Merchant vessels anchor above and below these
steps; ships of war abreast the steps in the fine season, and higher up, as
noticed in the freshes.

Dangers within the Bar.—The channel between the Lages (flat
topped rocks) carries from 3 to 4 fathoms water. This channel is comprised between those rocks, or rather between the line Bar Mark and Anjo
chapel, and the Lapa turret and Anjo dome. The south Lage has 9 feet
on it at low water, the cross mark for it being the North Filgueira, seen
through the gap of the southern.

A little more than a cable inside the North Lage, lies Staff rock,
small in size and awash at low water springs, with deep water close
round; it lies in the most dangerous part of the channel, because on the
ebb, particularly in the freshets, the tide sets directly on it, and consequently, by the slightest sheer a vessel would risk being laid broadside on.
Even a steam vessel may be detained some minutes at this spot. The
marks for it, however, are good, viz., the Bar Mark over the Cross of Anjo
chapel, and the two staffs of San João da Foz in line. To clear it, the
south edge of the Bar Mark should be kept in line with the Cross, as the
instant it is fairly passed, it is necessary to edge northerly.

The next danger is a patch about 40 fathoms N.N.W. of the Cruz, and
dry at low water springs. The marks for it are the south staff of the Foz
over the south pillar of the hospital, and Clerigos steeple, just clear of
the south edge of the large detached rock between Cruz and Anjo. This
patch, however, is generally avoided by hauling over to the Cabedello
side, except on a strong ebb, when the course from the circular wall is
direct for the Cruz rock, which allows the tide to sheer the vessel clear
of it. In summer weather, with slack water, there is no danger within
Cabedello bay, and rings are secured in the rocks to admit of vessels
mooring in the 6-fathom hole. At 10 yards from the beach there are
3 fathoms water.

The Agulha,—a small pinnacle, with only 1½ feet water, bears S. ¾ W.
distant half a cable from the Cruz. The channel is quite clear on either
side of it, but that generally preferred is on the north side close to the
Cruz. The marks for it are well defined, and always visible except in
dense fog. The first is the dome of the Foz over the second pillar of the

hospital: the second, the Cross of Anjo church on with the left edge of Anjo dome.

Within the Cruz will be found three patches to be avoided by vessels drawing above 12 feet. The first is on the line of Anjo and Foz Domes in one, and may be avoided by bringing in line the South Filgueira and the large rock N.E. of the Cruz, just before bringing the former mark on, so as to pass close to the edge of the Northern flat. The next patch has Anjo chapel cross and Foz dome in line, and may be avoided by hauling northerly the moment the whole church of Santa Catharina is seen over the west end of the high-water mark of Swamp island. The last patch is a continuation of an irregular flat extending from the lazaretto; but that side of the channel vessels ought not to approach.

COAST.—From the bar of Oporto the coast trends with scarcely any deviation S.W. ¾ S. 96 miles to the north point of Pederneira bay, on which is the church of Nazareth; the whole distance nearly is a sandy shore, but some 13 or 14 miles inland a range of hills called the heights of Feira, continues rising from the banks of the Douro, and at about 18 miles to the southward they become more elevated, and form the peak of Ornellas or Carregoza, which may be seen 28 miles from the coast. The hills become less elevated as they continue thence to the southward, where they unite with the mountains of Saude and Talhadas, and these join the high peak of Caramulo.

These mountains lie nearly parallel with the coast, and the Caramulo slopes gradually to the southward and may be seen 45 miles off, or 20 miles westward of the land near Aveiro for which and Oporto it is a good mark, and the only distinct object to be seen above the sandy plain of the coast. The configuration of Caramulo is so like that of Ornellas that it is necessary to consider the latitude to prevent mistake.

Immediately to the southward of the bar of Oporto, a beach, for the most part rocky, extends to the south for about 3 miles, and thence to the S.S.W. From the first fishermen's huts named Espinhos, the shore is a sandy beach with huts dispersed along it, and one remarkable building named Casa Branca (White House), about 6 miles south of Espinhos. Here, at 4 miles inland on rising ground is seen the town and castle of Feira, which is easily distinguished from sea in clear weather.

At 17 miles beyond Casa Branca is the new bar of Aveiro; the whole of this coast is clean, and may be navigated as near as 2 miles, in 10 or 12 fathoms water; but in hazy weather, if the peaks of Caramulo and Ornellas are not visible, it is difficult to distinguish the particular parts of the coast, the peaks and the tower of Aveiro being the only remarkable points on this low sandy shore; also, the vapour and sand raised by the heat and wind, render it frequently very difficult to see the mountains, so that it is necessary for the mariner to be certain of his latitude when running for the bar of Aveiro.

LIGHT.—Aveiro.—*Light proposed.*

The ˙RIVER VOUGA rises in the north-east of the province of Beira, and after a course of about 48 miles flows into the sea at the new bar of Aveiro, rendering the province one of the richest and most fertile in Portugal, and facilitating its commerce, and the exportation of its productions, by its commodious navigation. The entrance is about 27 miles northward of cape Mondego, in lat. 40° 38½′ N., and maintained by a dyke thrown up about a mile to the southward of the hermitage of San Jacinto· A circular white tower 73 high has been erected in the fort, nearly a mile east of the bank at the bar, to point out its position, and from which signals are made to vessels approaching the bar.

The harbour has sufficient depth and space for a great number of vessels, there being good anchorage in 3 and 4 fathoms water, from the dyke to the town of Aveiro, and thence nearly all the way to Ovar, a distance of 9 miles.

The town of Aveiro stands in a flat marshy country upon both banks of one of the arms of the Vouga, about 4 miles from its mouth, and on such low land that it can only be seen at a short distance. Its manufactories are earthenware; and salt from the marshes is produced in large quantities· There is an active fishery, and its oysters are celebrated.

Bar.—The depth on the bar at high-water springs is from 12 to 13 feet, at high-water neaps 10 feet, and immediately seaward of it there are 6¼ fathoms. In the channel, made through the beach between the dyke and the north shore, there are from 3½ to 8 fathoms. The hermitage of San Jacinto near the shore, half a mile northward of the bar, serves as a sea mark, but is difficult to be discerned 4 miles off, and the tower has been erected for the purpose. The plan of Aveiro shows the position of the bar and the dyke, and the formation of the estuary; but it is, however, proper to obtain a pilot before entering, as the tides are rapid, and no directions can be given on account of the unsteady nature of the sands.

When the sea is smooth the entrance is easy, and accessible with all winds except when blowing strong from the eastward, and with south-east winds there is much sea. In case of a heavy sea preventing boats going off, vessels of about 9 feet draught may run for the bar at three-quarters flood, providing the wind is fair and sufficient to keep the vessel under command. In fine weather vessels may anchor outside near the bar.

Tides.—It is high water, full and change, at the bar of Aveiro, at 3h., and the rise is 7 to 8 feet, but at the town of Aveiro the rise is scarcely 4½ feet.

Pilots are always ready to go off, but it sometimes happens that the sea is too heavy for boats to cross the bar, when vessels can. In this case the pilot boats remain inside the bar, and a pilot stationed at the tower, who will signalize in conformity with the boats.

Bar Signals.—On approaching the bar great attention should be paid to the signals from the tower and pilot boat, which are made by a staff with a flag attached to it. When the staff is inclined to the north or south, the vessel should steer in the direction to which it inclines, and if it is held upright she should steer direct on. When a red flag is hoisted at the tower it is a signal that vessels can enter, but they ought not to approach near the shore unless the flag remains hoisted.

If the red flag is hoisted and immediately lowered, and at the same time a gun is fired, it is a signal for vessels to make the best of their way to sea, to avoid being embayed, and that they may return at a more convenient opportunity. When the sea is smooth and the wind fair, the red flag is hoisted at low water as a call for vessels to approach and keep near the bar, the flag is then lowered, and when the tide is high enough to allow vessels to enter it is hoisted again. If a gun be fired and the flag remain hoisted, it is a signal for vessels to make more sail in order to save the tide.

MIRA.—The lagoon and town of Mira are 10 miles to the south-west of the bar of Aveiro; there are a few huts built on the beach abreast the town, which may be seen 6 miles off. A large portion of the population of this place is composed of fishermen. The old entrance to the Vouga was over the bar of this lagoon.

The COAST from the bar of Aveiro to cape Mondego continues low, forming an extensive waste of sand in places 4 miles wide, only interrupted by the houses of Mira, and those of Tocha, which are 9½ miles northward of the cape. Beyond this belt of sand the land is high, particularly the peak of Bussaco, which is about S.W. by W. 12 miles from that of Caramulo, and connected with it. Nearly E.S.E. from the peak of Bussaco are the Cantaros, or lofty peaks of the great chain of the Estrélla mountains, which are the highest in Portugal. The most elevated part, being 6,400 feet above the level of the sea, is 56 miles inland, and visible from seaward in clear weather at a distance of 36 miles from the coast.

CAUTION.—This coast, between Aveiro bar and cape Mondego, is more dangerous than it is generally understood to be. At some distance from the sandy beach, banks of sand are said to form at intervals at some distance from the shore, caused by the influence of the winds or currents; these banks are not stationary, but disperse and re-form at other points, and vessels coasting have been known to ground on them. Mariners are therefore recommended to keep at a distance of 3 or 4 miles from the coast, until they are to the southward of cape Mondego, when bound to Figueria.

CAPE MONDEGO is the western termination of mount Buarcos, which has a signal house standing on its level summit, 700 feet high, and can be seen about 30 miles off; the mount at a distance has the appearance of an island, and must not be mistaken for the Burling island. The cape itself is a sandy point, with a reef running more than a cable to the south-west, and the sandy beach extends several miles both north and south, by which it may be known. On the south side, at 1½ miles from the cape, is the small fishing village of Buarcos, whence boats go off to vessels with pilots for Figueira harbour, but they are frequently prevented from getting off by the heavy surf on the beach.

There is good anchorage for vessels off the village with north and off-shore winds. At about 3 miles S.S.E. from cape Mondego is fort Santa Catherina, on the northern point of the entrance of Mondego river. The soundings abreast of and near to the cape are 7 fathoms, a little farther off 20, and at about 7 miles distance 30 fathoms, brown sand and shells. Vessels standing off and on, on account of weather, should not come into less than 30 fathoms off the cape, or into 40 fathoms when to the northward of it.

LIGHT.—On cape Mondego is an octagonal lighthouse, which exhibits at an elevation of 302 feet above the sea, a *fixed* white light, visible at a distance of 20 miles.

The MONDEGO RIVER has its source in the mountains of Estrélla, and after a course of about 90 miles forms the harbour of Figueira, and falls into the sea at the town of this name, which is on the north bank a third of a mile from its mouth, where a trade is caried on in salt, oil, wine, dried and other fruits. Population about 5,000.

The Harbour formed within the mouth of the river would be spacious, but it is nearly filled with flats of shifting sand; its entrance is less than a cable wide, and the greatest depth of water in it is 12 feet. The bar frequently shifts, and has sometimes as much as 11 feet over it at low water, but at other times is so shallow that the smallest vessels cannot pass over it ; generally, however, there are 5 or 6 feet upon it at low water springs.*

Tides.—It is high water, full and change, at Figueira Bar, at 2h. 30m., and the rise is about 7 feet.

Pilots.—From the strength of the tides, and the uncertain state of the bar, pilots are necessary, and when they cannot get out, a red flag is hoisted at fort Santo Catherina north of the bar.

Bar Signals.—If the flag just mentioned is afterwards lowered or struck, it shows that the tide is not sufficiently made, and that vessels are

---

* See Admiralty plan, of Figueira bar, on chart No. 87.

to keep at a prudent distance till the flag is again hoisted. When a gun is fired without the flag being hoisted, it is a signal for vessels to make the best of their way to sea, in order not to be embayed, and to return at a more convenient opportunity. If a gun be fired with the flag hoisted, the vessel to make more sail to save the tide. On approaching the bar, great attention should be paid to the signals from the fort and pilot boat, which are made by a staff with a small flag attached to it. When the staff is pointed to the north or south, the vessel should steer in the direction indicated; but if held upright keep on the same course.

Anchorage will be found with off-shore winds, at about 5 miles southward of the cape, in from 10 to 7 fathoms water, sandy bottom ; but should the wind veer to southward, vessels should weigh immediately and stand out to sea, for westerly gales generally commence from the southward, send in a heavy sea, and are frequently of long duration.

COAST.—From Figueira the coast trends to the south-west for 17 miles to the river Vieira, and 19 miles farther on is the church of Nazareth at the north point of the small bay of Pederneira. The shore is a long flat, composed almost entirely of sand, but rises in the interior to hills of a moderate height. This level coast is covered here and there with woods of fir and larch trees, the most extensive of which are the Leiria and Concelho, together occupying an extent of 13 by about 27 miles. In fine weather with off-shore winds small vessels anchor off Vieira river, or near the chapel of San Pedro de Muel, in from 8 to 10 fathoms water, sandy bottom, at about a quarter of a mile from the beach.

On the shore between Figueira and the river Vieira there is no remarkable object, except three small sand hills. The forests are not visible more than 4 or 5 miles from the coast, from which they are separated by extensive sandy plains. The north point of Pederneira bay, formed by a rocky headland, which is considerably elevated above the flat sandy coast, is abrupt, and projects a mile in a south-west direction. There is a fort on its outer point, and on its summit, the church of Nazareth, the high and pointed spire of which, is an excellent mark for the place. No other edifice on the coast can be mistaken for this church, which is surrounded by a number of houses appearing like a village, but they cannot be seen from a great distance; there is a grove of pines to the north-west of the headland, planted to protect the church and houses from the shifting sands.

The small vessels which anchor in Pederneira bay, are sheltered from easterly winds, but exposed to all other winds. The town of this name is partly on a hill connected with the height of Nazareth, about a mile to the south-east of the church, and the same distance from the beach. The population may be about 2,000, and are principally employed in fishing.

From Pederneira the coast is of steep cliffs as far as lake Obidos, about 12 miles to the W.S.W. These cliffs are backed by the hills of Boiro, which terminate in a headland named Foz, near the mouth of the lake. At about 6 miles south-west of Nazareth church, is the small bay of San Martinho (St. Martin), where small vessels load with wood. The town with about 1,000 inhabitants, is on the north shore of the bay. Lake Obidos is about 8 miles in circumference, and communicates with the sea by a small outlet not more than 40 or 50 yards wide, which is choked up in summer. It abounds with excellent fish, which give constant employment to a large number of boats from the different establishments on its banks.

The **PENINSULAR of PENICHE** is a rocky surface of about 5 miles in circumference; it is steep, projects seaward, and is connected with the main by a sandy isthmus a mile in length, which is completely overflowed by high tides, in strong winds, either from the northward or southward. A line of fortifications extends along the south-east face of the peninsula; at the north end of it is the upper town of Peniche, and at the south end the lower town, near which is the citadel : a sandy shore with downs extends westward to cape Carvoeiro, the outer point of the peninsula of Peniche. A lighthouse stands on cape Carvoeiro, and near it is a battery and chapel. Close off the cape is a detached rock named Nau.*

LIGHT.—A *fixed* white light is exhibited from a square lighthouse on the highest part of cape Carvoeiro, at an elevation of 182 feet above high water, and visible in clear weather at a distance of 15 miles.†

Semaphore.—At cape Carvoeiro, there is a semaphore station, with which vessels can communicate by the International code.

The Anchorage in the bay on the north of the isthmus, between point Baleal and upper Peniche, is not good, the bottom being very rocky and all winds, having northing in them, send in a heavy sea. But the bay on the south side of the isthmus between the lower town and the rocky point at Consolation fort, affords shelter, with winds from East to North, and even as far round as N.W., in 6 and 7 fathoms water; the bottom, however, is for the most part rocky. If using this anchorage be careful to anchor as soon as the arch of the bridge between the fortifications, and an isolated rock to the east, begins to open. Small vessels can enter the ditch of the fortifications from the southward at high water, and haul up on the shore.

---

* *See* Admiralty plan:—Peninsula of Peniche, Burling and Farilhões islands, and anchorage on the east side of Burling island, on chart No. 87.

† A telegraphic cable station—Falmouth and Lisbon—is established at Peniche for reporting the passage of vessels.

CAUTION.—In thick weather the peninsula of Peniche appears like an island, and has been mistaken for the Burling, whereby vessels have been wrecked on the isthmus; such a mistake may, however, be avoided by remembering that when the Burling island is seen, so also will be the Farilhões, which are 4 miles to the north of it, and also that the breadth of the passage between the Burling and the peninsula is much greater than the apparent opening to the eastward of the peninsula can appear under any circumstances. Besides which, the position and height of the light-houses should be considered, that of Carvoeiro is on the extremity of the cape, and its base about 90 feet above the sea, whilst the base of the Burling is higher, being about 288 feet above the sea.

BURLING or BERLENGA ISLAND, of an irregular oblong form, and about three-quarters of a mile in length, in an E.N.E. and W.S.W. direction, is level on the summit, and bounded for the most part by perpendicular cliffs. An isthmus, about 140 yards across, divides it into two unequal parts, between which, two small narrow inlets are formed; the northern one, named Carreixo dos Caçöes (Frying-pan road), is bounded by high and almost perpendicular cliffs. This inlet has a depth of 5 fathoms at its entrance, and 3 fathoms close to the isthmus, against which the sea breaks with great violence during westerly winds.

The south-east inlet, named Carreiro do Mosteiro (Monastery road), has 8 fathoms at its entrance, diminishing to 2 fathoms close to the beach, where landing is easy. On an islet to the south-west of the inlet is a small fort connected to the island by a bridge, from which a road leads to its summit; boats land at the north part of this islet in fine weather. There are two small springs of fresh water on the island. Vessels may anchor abreast of the fort in from 12 to 15 fathoms sand, but only with winds between N.W. and S.W.

A small detached high rock lies close to the north-east end of the island, and near it a rocky shoal occasionally shows. Also, a rock which uncovers at low tide, lies about a cable off the south end of the island. The lighthouse, standing on the highest part of the island, bears N.W. by N., 5¾ miles from the lighthouse on cape Carvoeiro.

LIGHT.—The lighthouse on Burling island is square, and exhibits at 365 feet above the level of high water, a *revolving* white light, attaining its greatest brilliancy every *three minutes*, and may be seen in clear weather at a distance of 25 miles.

The ESTELLAS, a group of islets, lying from half a mile to a mile to the north-west of Burling island, extend three-quarters of a mile W. by S. and E. by N.; a rocky shoal near the western islet shows at low water. The channel separating these islets from Burling island, is deep but dangerous, from the rapid currents, and its foul rocky bottom affords no anchorage.

The **FARILHÕES,** a cluster of rocky islets covering a circular space about three-quarters of a mile in diameter, are steep, and that called the great Farilhão rising to the height of 315 feet, bears North 4 miles from Burling island. Some sunken rocks, which break at low water, lie nearly three-quarters of a mile on their north and eastern sides. A small bay formed by the large islet affords shelter to fishing boats in winds from N.N.E. round westward to W.S.W.

The **Strait** between the Farilhões and the Estéllas is from 20 to 50 fathoms deep, and its navigable breadth 2¼ miles, but the current before spoken of sets strongly from the former to the latter, and renders great caution necessary; also there should be wind enough to keep the vessel well under command when passing through it.

The **channel** between Burling island and the main is clear and deep; at half a mile from the shore on either side there is a depth of 14 fathoms, increasing to 24 fathoms; the bottom is rocky with sand and gravel. Both the Farilhões and the Burling may be seen from the deck of a vessel at a distance of 24 miles, and the peninsula of Peniche at nearly the same distance; all are easily distinguished, and too remarkable to be mistaken with common attention. This channel may be taken, therefore, without fear at any time when the above points are visible.

Caution is necessary in sailing along this part of the coast in thick weather, to avoid running on these isles, as they lie so far from the land and the depth around, and almost close to them, on every side, is so great that the lead would hardly give warning in time to clear them.

The **Coast** from cape Carvoeiro trends S.S.W. ¼ W. for about 35 miles to cape Roca. At Consolation fort, 3 miles from the former cape, the ⌐sandy beach terminates, and steep rocky cliffs, with some breaks in them, follow nearly to the town of Lourinha, where there is an extensive beach; at the end of it the coast again becomes steep, and continues so as far as Porto-novo or the small river Maceira. From this the Praia formosa (beautiful beach), so called on account of its length, regularity, and cleanness, extends to the south-westward for 5 miles. The town of Vimeiro stands in a valley 1½ miles inland of Porto-novo, at the foot of the hill of Valongo.

The Monte Junto, rising 15 miles inland, 2,180 feet high, may be seen 53 miles off, or 38 miles from the coast. It summit is in the latitude of Vimeiro, and in the middle of the range of conspicuous mountains which have a direction somewhat parallel to the coast. From the Praia Formosa the coast is steep for 13 miles to Nabas point, on a height to the southward of which is the fishing town of Ericeira, with about 3,000 inhabitants; near the town is a small creek used by boats. From Ericeira to cape Roca the coast is steep and rocky, except a small place named Macaas, 3 miles from the cape, off which small coasting vessels occasionally anchor.

Mafra Palace, built of a species of white marble, on the summit of a hill 4 miles East of Ericeira, contains a palace, convent, and superb church; its front is 825 feet in length, the church being in the centre of the structure, having the palace on one side and the convent on the other. This magnificent building, having no other like it on the coast, is remarkable and conspicuous.

The CINTRA MOUNTAINS, rising a little south of cape Roca, extend in an easterly direction 5 miles, the summit presenting an irregular and rugged outline. At each extreme is a convent, that at the eastern end is named Pena, and that at the western Peninha.

They are visible from a great distance, the former being 1,735 feet, and the latter 1,617 feet, above the sea. The town of Cintra, on the northern acclivity of the mountain, may also be seen from a long distance.

CAPE ROCA (or Rock of Lisbon) is the westernmost point of Portugal, and of the continent of Europe. It is about 550 feet high, its cliffs are bluff and steep, and a lighthouse stands upon its summit. Near the cape is a high rock, and farther out a reef, on which the sea continually breaks ; close off this reef are 25 fathoms water.

At about 4 miles S. by W. from cape Roca is cape Razo, upon which is fort Sinchette. This is a low rocky point, with a small shoal close off it, which it is necessary to avoid. Between these capes, the coast forms a bay bounded by steep cliffs, till within a mile of the latter, where there is a small beach.

Semaphore.—Upon an elevation about half a mile south-east of cape Razo, is a semaphore station with which vessels can communicate by the International code.

From cape Razo the coast of steep cliffs trends to the south-eastward rather more than 2½ miles to fort Santa Martha, at the western extreme of Cascaes bay. Between these points are the chapel and light tower of Guia ; the latter is a mile from the west point of Cascaes bay.*

LIGHTS.—Roca light.—The circular light tower on cape Roca, situate nearly a quarter of a mile N.E. of the cape, exhibits a white light which *revolves* every *one* and *three-quarter minutes.* It is elevated 596 feet above high water, and visible in clear weather at a distance of 21 miles.

Guia light.—The hexagonal light-tower of Guia, situated one mile to the south-east of the west point of Cascaes bay, near the chapel of Guia,

---

* *See* Admiralty plan:—Entrance of the river Tagus, with views, No. 89, scale m = 1·75 inches.

exhibits a *fixed* white light, at an elevation of 167 feet above high water, and should be seen in clear weather through an arc of 288°, or between the bearings of S. by E. ¾ E. and S.W. ¾ W., from a distance of 15 miles.

CASCAES BAY is formed by the shore from fort Santa Martha sweeping to the north-east, east, and south-east to Rana point, at one mile beyond which is fort San Julian, at the entrance to the Tagus. A sandy shore extends around the bay between fort Santa Martha and that of Velho for about 1¼ miles; thence it is rocky to Rana point, off which for 2 cables the ground is foul. The shore again becomes sandy to fort San Julian, midway between which and Rana point is a bank with 3¼ fathoms water over it, the outer edge of which is 3¼ cables from the shore, and very near the fair way of the North channel into the Tagus. The town of Cascaes stands on the shore, half a mile from fort Santa Martha and between them is fort Cascaes, which is conspicuous on a high, steep point.

Anchorage.—There is good anchorage in Cascaes bay during the summer months, the wind being almost invariably from the northward; southerly winds throw in a heavy sea, when vessels should either put to sea or endeavour to stand through the North channel into the Tagus. Large vessels anchor in 7 to 10 fathoms, mud and sand, with Guia light-tower in line with the light-tower on Santa Martha fort. Small vessels lie farther in, and coasters close off the town.

LIGHT.—On fort Santa Martha near the village of Cascaes (north side of entrance to river Tagus) is a square tower, with a blue horizontal stripe half-way up from the base; which exhibits at an elevation of 52 feet above high water, a *fixed red* light, visible in clear weather at a distance of 5 miles.

Semaphore.—At Cascaes there is a semaphore station with which vessels can communicate by the International code.

LISBON, the capital of Portugal, on the northern bank of the Tagus, is about 7 miles from its mouth. The broad estuary of the Tagus forms an extensive and safe harbour, in which the largest vessels can anchor close to the city, and is admirably adapted for commerce, both the north and south shores presenting a very pleasing prospect, from the numerous villages, buildings, gardens, and cultivated land.

The City rises from the bank of the river in the form of an amphi-theatre, being built on a succession of hills, the highest of which is the Estrélla to the west, and the castle hill on the east. Most of the streets are steep, irregular, badly paved, and dirty: one part of the town, however, is regular and handsome. This space contains 8 or 9 well built, paralle' and wide streets, and contains the best shops of the city : these are crossed at right angles by others, that terminate in a handsome square, the Prada de Commercio, one side of which is formed by the Tagus, and the others by the Arsenal, Custom House, Exchange, Royal Library, and other public buildings ; the whole presenting a magnificent aspect from the river.

The Arsenal formerly was one of the finest establishments of the kind in Europe, but it is now, with the dockyard, on a reduced scale. A handsome aqueduct brings water into the city from the springs near Bellas, a distance of 9 miles ; this, as a work of art, is not surpassed in boldness of design and grandeur of effect by any in Europe. The British Minister, in addition to a Consul and a Vice-consul resides in Lisbon. ·

The climate is hot and dry in the summer months, when the thermometer often shows 96° Fahrenheit. Heavy rains fall in November and December. It is cold in January, but snow is of rare occurrence and in February the spring begins.

Supplies.—Shipping can be abundantly supplied with fruits and necessaries of all kinds ; coal is easily procured, and brought off to the ships in lighters.

Trade.—Lisbon has a moderate amount of trade. There are manufactories of silks, paper, soap, leather, sugar refineries, and potteries ; among the exports are wines, fruits, salt, and oil. In 1871, 1,521 vessels, of 748,065 tons entered inwards ; of which 745 vessels, of 210,468 tons, were British : and 1,443 vessels, of 471,630 tons clear outwards. The coasting trade in the same year was carried in vessels amounting to 102,000 tons. There is steam communication to all the countries of Europe and Brazil, and monthly to the West coast of Africa.

Docks.—There is a floating dock at Lisbon, but it is adapted only for small vessels ; there is also a dock at Cacilhas on the south side of the Tagus, abreast Lisbon, capable of docking a vessel of 10 feet draught.

Time Signal.—On the north bank of the river, between the Caes do Sodre and the Arsenal, is the Observatory, from the flagstaff of which, a time ball drops at 1 h. p.m. Lisbon *mean* time.

The RIVER TAGUS, or Tejo of the Portuguese, the largest in the Iberian peninsula, which it traverses from east to west, and divided into two nearly equal parts, has its source in the Sierra Albarracin, on the borders of Aragon and New Castile, in about lat. 40° 25′ N., long. 1° 35′ W. It enters Portugal near Alcantra, above which the river is not navigable, and below this town it begins to turn to the south-west, and after a course of about 540 miles, enters the sea about 7 miles below Lisbon. Above Lisbon, the Tagus opens out into a wide expanse of water from 2 to 7 miles in breadth, and here any number of ships may be accommodated in a convenient depth of water, and although hitherto beyond the city the river has not been of much commercial importance, it is navigable for vessels of 150 tons, as high as the mouth of the Zezere.

Opposite Lisbon, on the south shore, is Cassilhas point, being the eastern point of what may be termed the port of Lisbon, and from whence the wide expanse already alluded to opens out; here the river is a long mile wide, but it narrows to about three-quarters of a mile at Belem, when it becomes considerably wider, and at its entrance it is 1¾ miles across.

Belem castle, on the north side of the Tagus, 5 miles above fort San Julian, and about 2 miles below Lisbon, is a prominent feature in entering the river, as it stands on a projecting point, and is nearly insulated at high water; near it is the quarantine station.   Here the health and customs offices are established, and off it, all vessels are boarded on entering.   The church, houses, and straggling quintas of Belem almost connect it with the capital.

CACHOPO or CACHOP SHOALS.—Off both points of the entrance to the Tagus there are dangerous sandy shoals extending in a westerly direction, and having between them a deep channel, which is nowhere less (between the 5-fathom lines of soundings) than nine-tenths of a mile in breadth.   These shoals are named the North and South Cachopo.

From the depth of 4½ fathoms, at the west end of the North Cachopo, fort San Julian bears about E. by N. ¼ N. distant 3½ miles.   Thence the shoal, with 2½ to one fathom water on it, extends in the direction of the fort, leaving at its east end a narrow passage into the Tagus, named the North channel.

From the south-east point of entrance to the Tagus, the South Cachopo extends to the West and W.S.W. for 2½ miles.   From the depth of 4½ fathoms, at the west end of the shoal, Bugio fort bears N.E. by E. ½ E. distant nearly 1¾ miles.   The larger portion of this shoal has little more than one fathom water on it, and around Bugio fort the sand is dry at low water.

The BAR, between the western extremes of the Cachopos, has 6 and 7 fathoms over it at low-water springs; the channel within it soon deepens to 9 fathoms, increasing to 19 fathoms, abreast Bugio fort.   Notwithstanding the depth upon the bar, and the distance between the extremes of the Cachopos, the sea in south-west gales rolls over it with great force frequently forming one tremendous roller that breaks with irresistible violence the whole distance across; at such times the bar is impracticable, and in winter, or when the freshets are strong and accompanied with westerly gales, continues so for several days together.

LIGHTS.—St. Julian light.—From a tower in fort San Julian, at the north point of entrance to the Tagus, a *fixed* white light is exhibited at an elevation of 128 feet above high water, and visible in clear weather at a distance of 13 miles.

Bugio light.—A round tower in Bugio fort exhibits at 110 feet above high water, a *revolving* white light, attaining its greatest brilliancy every *minute* and *three-quarters,* and visible in clear weather 16 miles.

Leading lights.—At 2½ miles west of Belem Castle two *fixed red* lights 470 yards apart N.E. by E. ¾ E. and S.W. by W. ¾ W. from each other, are exhibited for leading over the bar of river Tagus. The high light which is shown from an octagonal stone tower, with cupola of lantern painted red, situated on Alto de Caixas, is elevated 310 feet above high water, and should be visible in clear weather from a distance of 18 miles.

The low light, elevated 60 feet above high water, is shown from a tower painted red with a white roof, at Porto Côvo, and should be visible in clear weather from a distance of 10 miles.

Belem light.—From the eastern side of Boã Successo fort, 200 yards N.W. ¼ W. from the tower of Belem castle, a *fixed red* light is shown at an elevation of 30 feet, and visible in clear weather 5 miles.

Semaphore.—There is a semaphore station at Fort San Julian, with which vessels can communicate by the International code.

Tides.—It is high water, full and change, at Belem, at 2 h. 30 m.; springs rise 12 feet, and neaps 9 feet. The great danger in entering the Tagus is occasioned by the tides. Off the city of Lisbon the ebb sometimes runs at the rate of 6 or 7 miles an hour, particularly when the freshes come down after rain, so that anchors frequently come home. The flood is commonly much weaker than the ebb. When a strong ebb is opposed by a gale from seaward, the sea breaks completely across the bar, so that the breakers cannot be distinguished from those on the Cachopos. In the South channel the current sets directly through, and over the bar on the flood 3 miles an hour, and on the ebb 4 miles an hour. Therefore, to enter during the ebb requires a strong breeze and the vessel well under command.

Within the river, the wind, unless it is west or south-westerly, comes irregularly through the valleys on either side. It is, however, pretty steady when it blows in the direction of the river. It is also to be remarked that the tide draws strongly towards the Bugio bank, and divides the water in that vicinity into several counter currents, so that a vessel approaching too near that bank is liable not to obey the helm.

Pilots are usually to be found some distance from the entrance of the Tagus, their boats are to be distinguished from others by a blue flag hoisted at the yard-arm of their lateen sails. There are also some pilot schooners with letter **P** on the mainsail; pilots may always be obtained at Cascaes.

LEADING MARKS.—Santa Martha fort, to the southward of Cascaes, is white and of a triangular form to the eastward, with a low battery extending to the northward, and on its south-east angle is a square light-tower, with a blue horizontal stripe, half-way up from the base; Guia lighthouse in line with the bastion of this light-tower, N.W. ¾ W., leads through the north channel.

Cascaes fort is large and conspicuous, and stands to the north-east between Santa Martha and the town of Cascaes, the outer northern wall extending to the town.

Fort San Julian is an extensive fortification erected on a high steep point on the north-west side of the entrance to the Tagus. A ledge of rocks with 3½ fathoms extends a short distance to the south-eastward of the fort.

Bugio fort stands upon the highest part of the South Cachopo, about two-thirds of a mile from Medão point, the south-east point of the mouth of the Tagus; the fort is of a circular form, and the sand around it is dry at low water.

The Paps are very difficult to be distinguished, particularly on the bearing used for the South channel, from whence they appear over some flat ground which scarcely shows above the land to the south-west of it; they lie to the eastward of a ridge of hills with several windmills. "When seen to the northward of San Julian, or to the southward of the Bugio, they show like two small hummocks, but when in a line with either of the turning marks, or with the leading mark, they appear as a single hummock with a flat top."[*]

The Mirante or Turret of Caxias is a small white dilapidated building, formed of two octagonal turrets, with red cupolas, on a hill nearly 3 miles E. by N. of San Julian fort, and is used as the northern turning mark for the South channel when in line with the Paps bearing about E. by N. ¾ N.

Jacobs Ladder is a range of white masonry or stone wall that supports the cliff, and is not easily distinguished; it is between two conspicuous white buildings, and there is a stone wall resembling an aqueduct to the eastward of it, and another to the westward. Jacobs ladder is used as the centre leading mark for the South channel when brought in line with the Paps, bearing E.N.E. A large conspicuous cypress tree stands one third of a mile to the eastward of Jacobs ladder, and when in line with the Paps, bearing E.N.E. northerly, is used as the southern turning mark for the

---

[*] R. Stokes, Master of H.M.S. *Prince Regent*, May 1852.

South channel. This tree is above, and a little westward of the Boaviagem convent, a long regular white building with numerous windows.

The tower of Belem is an ancient building 92 feet high, and formed of three distinct parts, with a battery just above water; it is about 5¼ miles above San Julian, and at high water is nearly insulated. It stands on the extremity of the point, from which the coast bank extends along shore to the westward, and appears to be increasing. To guard vessels from this danger, the *fixed red* light is shown on the eastern side of Boä Successo fort, N.W. ½ W. 200 yards from the tower of Belem.

The dome of Estrélla is an excellent mark and readily distinguished by its great size, being the largest dome in Lisbon, and towering above all other buildings in the city; when in line with Bugio fort it bears E. ¼ N.

Beacons.—There are three beacons, painted in red and white bands which in line indicate the fairway of the South channel, Tagus river entrance. The southernmost beacon is on Jacobs ladder; the middle beacon on a hill nearly midway between Jacobs ladder and the Paps; and the inner beacon on the Paps.

Caution.—To afford protection to a submarine telegraph cable crossing the river Tagus, vessels are prohibited from anchoring within the space enclosed by lines drawn between Ponte d'Argés and Trafaria on the west, and between the Lazaretto and the telegraph station at Bom Successo on the east.

Also, that should a vessel, from any cause, anchor within this prohibited space, the anchor is not to be lifted without an express order, to be obtained from the office of the Captain of the port.

DIRECTIONS.—In steering for cape Roca, commonly named the rock of Lisbon, it should be borne in mind that with northerly winds, the current has a general southerly trend, varying between S.W. and S.E. at the rate of a half, or a mile an hour. The soundings from Burling island to the southward are regular; a depth of forty fathoms will ensure an offing of about 10 miles until near cape Roca, when a greater depth will be found at that distance. At night, in clear weather, the light on the cape will be seen, having passed which, the Guia light will soon be observed, vessels should then keep off the coast sufficiently to open out Cascaes *red* light; thus avoiding the rocks of Pombeira, Nau, and Ponta da Insua.

The North Channel into the Tagus requires a knowledge of the tides, and in a sailing vessel a commanding breeze. Having passed Guia and Cascaes, bring Cassilhas point (the eastern termination of the south shore) in line with the southern face of fort San Julian bearing E. by S. ¼ S. —or, if wishing to borrow on the North Cachopo, Belem tower in line with the south-east extreme of San Julian point ;—steer in with either of the above marks until Guia lighthouse is in line with the light-tower on Santa Martha fort, N.W. ¾ W.; then keep this latter mark on, and it will lead in mid-channel, and in not less than 5½ fathoms at low water.

When the centre of mount Cordova (on the south shore) is in line with Bugio tower, bearing about S.E. ¼ S., steer for Bugio until San Thomas fort (which is white and a long half-mile north-east of San Julian) is seen open eastward of the yellow fort of Catalazete; then steer into the river carefully allowing for the tides, as the flood sets strong towards the shoal extending to the south-east from San Julian, while the ebb sets directly on the North Cachopo.*

Mount Cordova is 12 miles from San Julian fort, and may not be visible ; in this case, having entered the North channel, as soon as the rocks at Catalazete point are open of the south-east angle of fort San Julian, steer for Bugio fort till the battery at Catalazete point, San Thomas fort (the next to it), and the outer windmill, are in line bearing N.E. by E., and then haul more to the eastward into the river. Rana church in line with Quinta Nova is a good mark to check a vessel's position when proceeding through the North channel, with Cassilhas point in line with the southern face of fort San Julian, for she will then be in the centre of the fairway, and have Guia lighthouse just open south of the light-tower on Santa Martha fort.

The South Channel is the principal passage into the river. On entering it with a fair wind, and rounding the southern extremity of the North Cachopo, keep the Peninha (or western part of the mountains of Cintra) bearing N. ¼ E,, and open westward of Cascaes fort, until Bugio fort comes in line with the Estrélla dome, E. ¼ N. Then steer towards Bugio, keeping it in line with Estrélla dome, which leads over the bar connecting the north and south Cachopos, in the deepest water, (not less than 6½ fathoms) ; and when the Paps are in line with Jacobs Ladder, or the three beacons (page 280), E.N.E., a vessel will be inside the bar, and the depth of water will have increased 12 and 13 fathoms. Steer with the Paps in line with Jacobs Ladder, or if the wind be from the northward, borrow as far as the northern turning mark (the Paps in one with Caxias, E. by N. ¾ N). On the contrary, if the wind be from the south-east, borrow towards the southern turning mark, with the Paps in line with the

---

* The rocky ledge of San Julian fort extends 90 yards from its south point where a depth of 3 fathoms will be found at low water, but in approaching it great caution is necessary, as the flood sweeps over it with great velocity.—*J. Richards, Master of H.M.S. Hecate*, 1851. In June 1872 the steamer *Gibraltar* was wrecked close to San Julian fort.

Cypress tree, bearing E.N.E. northerly, but avoid going too near Bugio, as the tides there are strong and irregular, and the south Cachopo steep-to.

Having passed between Bugio and San Julian, keep to the northward, so as to clear the sandy flat inside Bugio, till Belem castle is in line with the south part of the city of Lisbon, bearing E. ¾ S. Pass Belem castle at the distance of 2 or 3 cables, and then proceed to the anchorage, keeping the whole of fort San Julian and all its outworks open to the southward of the parapet of Belem castle, which will clear the shoals of Alcantara, until the vessel arrives off the Packet Stairs, where there is anchorage in from 10 to 14 fathoms water, or farther up in 12 to 16 fathoms, mud.

At Night, vessels should cross Tagus river bar with the leading lights in line bearing N.E. by E. ¾ E., and when Bugio light, *revolving*, bears South, alter course to E. by S., which leads in mid-channel to a position 4 cables south of Belem castle.

Turning through the South channel.—A vessel from the north-west standing towards the west tail of the North Cachopo, should keep Peninha peak bearing N. ¼ E., open westward of Cascaes fort, and in not less than 12 fathoms water, until the south part of the city of Lisbon is in line with Bugio fort, East; then haul to the wind. The turning mark for the north side of the channel is the Paps in line with the Mirante or Turret of Caxias E. by N. ¾ N.; and the Paps in line with the Cypress tree (which stands a little above the convent of Boaviagem and a third of a mile eastwards of Jacobs Ladder); E.N.E. northerly leads just clear of the breakers fringing the edge of the shoal.

Vessels working in or out should in approaching South Cachopo shoal tack directly the Paps come in line with Jacob's Ladder E.N.E.

The flood and ebb tides set strongly towards the north point of South Cachopo shoal, and must therefore be guarded against.

Rana church open westward of Quinta bearing N. by E., clears the tail of the South Cachopo, and in working in, a vessel need not go to the east-ward of this line until well in the channel. A mill on a height 1¼ miles north-eastward of fort San Julian, open eastward of fort San Thomas, N.E. by E., clears the eastern edge of the North Cachopo, and this is a good fairway mark in running out through the South channel. The shallow ground around San Julian extends a short distance from the fort, but deepens immediately to 5 and 6 fathoms; San Thomas fort well open east of the small battery of Catalazete, on the intermediate point, clears the south extremity of this shoal.

Having passed forts San Julian and Bugio, stand to either shore into 12 fathoms; a good mark for clearing the shoulder of the sands, inside of Bugio, is Belem castle in line with the citadel of Lisbon, which stands on the first rise of the land from the south point of the city. Between Medão point and the village of Trafaria, the south shore is bordered by a bank of the latter name, which extends off full a third of a mile, with deep water close to it. The houses at Torre Velha north of Trafaria cliffs, clears the bank. Above Trafaria the south shore of the river is clear, with deep water as far as Cassilhas point.

Between fort San Julian and Belem castle the north shore is bordered at a short distance by a narrow bank, but westward of the castle it extends off a quarter of a mile. The shore on the south side of the castle is steep; thence it is again bordered by a bank which in places extends nearly 2 cables off, with 5 fathoms on its edge, and deep water close-to.

When nearing the Alcantara bank the mark for clearing it in 7 fathoms is San Julian castle and outworks open of the parapet of Belem castle, until Alcantara, which appears like the angle of a fort with a watch-tower, bears N. ¼ W. The bank will then be passed, and the shore may be approached until the tower of San Julian is in line with the parapet of Belem Castle; and this is a good mark for anchoring in 7 or 8 fathoms water, off the Packet stairs. A vessel of heavy draught will be far enough out in 12 or 14 fathoms, good holding ground of stiff mud, and out of the strength of the tides.

At Night.—If coming from the northward, bring Guia *fixed* white light to bear North, and steer on that bearing until Bugio *revolving* light bears East: then steer for Bugio on this latter bearing until San Julian *fixed* white light bears N.E.; when an E.N.E. course will lead between the two lights. When Belem *red* light is seen, bring it to bear E. by S., as the vessel will be nearly in mid-channel, and steer up the river. These night marks will also assist a vessel by day.

In entering from the southward, bring San Julian light to bear N.E., and steer on that bearing until Bugio light bears East; then proceed as directed before. San Julian light N.N.E. just clears the South Cachopo in 4 fathoms, at a cable from the depth of 2¼ fathoms.

When cape Roca light is shut in with Guia a vessel will be nearing the shoals, and within the influence of the river tides, and therefore a cautious and constant reference to the bearings will be necessary. Should the ebb tide be running, be careful not to be set too near Bugio, and if in any doubt, steer more to the northward.

CAPE ESPICHEL.—From Bugio fort the land trends in a southerly direction with a sandy beach to within 2 miles of cape Espichel, when it becomes rocky, steep, and high to the cape, which is about 13 miles from Bugio. About 6 miles northward of the cape is the lake of Albufeira, the mouth of which is closed at times. Cape Espichel is a steep bold headland, above 500 feet high, presenting a bluff to the W.S.W.

about a mile in extent; its summit is level, of a whitish colour on the north side, and reddish on the south; and on it is a convent and a lighthouse. From the cape the coast trends suddenly to the eastward for 14 miles to the entrance of the port of Setubal or St. Ubes, then southward for 27 miles to the small river André, and then W.S.W. 8 miles to cape Sines, forming a deep bight between the latter and cape Espichel.

The land on the north side of this bight is remarkable not only for the sudden turn in the coast to the eastward at cape Espichel, but also for the mountains in its neighbourhood, the highest of which, the peak of Formozinyo, is 1,637 feet above the level of the sea, and visible 46 miles off. This peak is about 11 miles eastward of cape Espichel, and 1½ miles from the peak of Arrabida. The mountain is 4½ miles long in an east and west direction, so that when seen from the northward or southward, it seems of considerable extent, but from the westward it appears isolated.

At 3½ miles to the north-east of the latter mountain is the Serra de San Luiz or mount Cordova, the leading mark for the North channel into the Tagus. It is 1,190 feet high, round, and resembling a haystack; and 2¾ miles N.E. by E. ½ E. from it is the castle and town of Palmella, which being isolated and built on an elevation of 875 feet may be seen a considerable distance. The mountains of Arrabida, San Luiz, and Palmella form a triple range of land clearly distinguishable, and when seen at a great distance from the south-west are good marks for cape Espichel.

In case of necessity, and with northerly winds, there are two anchorages under the land between cape Espichel and the shallow ground fronting the entrance to Setubal. The first is in Balieira bay, 3 miles from the cape, in 15 to 30 fathoms, sandy bottom: the next, Cezimbra bay,* with the fishing town of the same name, to the west of çape Ares, which is high, salient, with a small detached rock close to it, and 4 miles from Balieira. The best anchorage here is off the town in 7 or 8 fathoms, near the shore, for in 10 and 12 fathoms there is a bed of rocky ground from 100 to 150 yards wide, which extends a considerable distance along shore.

To avoid this rocky ground close the shore until the detached rock near cape Ares is shut in. When at the anchorage inside, in 7 or 8 fathoms, this rock will be shut in with the cape, but it is advisable to anchor outside this foul ground in order to have room to weigh and work off, should the wind change to the southward. From cape Ares, the land continues high and steep with rocky cliffs for about 8 miles to the town of Setubal, and about mid-way is fort Arrabida with a convent and chapel, on the high land over it.

LIGHT.—On cape Espichel is a hexagonal tower standing southward

---

* See Admiralty plan :—Cezimbra bay, scale m = 2·0 inches, on chart 87.

of the convent, which exhibits at 625 feet above the level of high water, a *fixed* white light, visible in clear weather at a distance of 12 miles.

Semaphore.—There is a Semaphore station at Espichel lighthouse, with which vessels can communicate by the International code.

SETUBAL (St. Ubes) is the third port of Portugal. The town stands on the north side of the estuary of the river Sado, which rises in the south of the province of Alemtejo, and after a course of about 110 miles, 35 of which are navigable, it forms a wide estuary, and falls into the sea.

The harbour, formed at the estuary of the Sado, is enclosed from the sea by a tongue of sandy land which leaves the southern shore and extends in a northerly direction ; between the end of the tongue and the opposite shore is the entrance, about three-quarters of a mile broad, with 9 to 20 fathoms water. Within this, and along by the north shore, there are 15 to 10 fathoms.

Anchorage.—In front of the town there is good anchorage in 6 to 8 fathoms. Between the tongue of sand and the eastern shore is an extensive sand bank, which uncovers at about half ebb, with channels on either side of it, in which there is also good anchorage in 12 and 13 fathoms, sandy bottom.*

The trade of this port is considerable : its principal exports are corn, wine, fruit, and salt, for which last article it is celebrated, and the facilities for shipping it are such that vessels of 1,000 tons can be loaded in 24 hours. In the year 1869, 346 vessels amounting to 64,221 tons entered inwards ; and the same cleared outwards, wholly laden with salt. Population, about 20,000. A British Vice-consul resides here.

The Bar.—At about three-quarters of a mile west of fort Arrabida a shallow sandy flat leaves the shore, and sweeping to the south and east for a distance of 6 miles, covers the entrance to the harbour, and joins the tongue of land about 4 miles southward of its north end. A channel into the harbour, carrying from 3 to 20 fathoms water, is formed through the sand, having at its entrance a bar with about 12 feet over it at low water, which lies about 1½ miles south of Arrabida fort, and which is marked by two buoys. The northern buoy is white, has the letter N. painted on it, and lies S.W. by W. ¼ W. nearly 2½ miles from the lighthouse at Outão point ; the southern buoy, about 3 cables S.E. by S. of the first is red, and marked with the letter S. At high water springs there are 25 feet over the bar, and at high water neaps about 21 feet.

LIGHT.—On Outão point, near the fort of the same name, on the north-west side of entrance to the harbour, is a circular tower, which

---

* *See* Admiralty plan :—Setubal, No. 2,714, scale m = 2·7 inches, and plan on chart, No. 87.

... at an elevation of 40 feet above high water a fixed white light ... in ...

Tides.—It is high water, full and change, at Setubal at 3h. 10m.; springs rise 9 to 11 feet, and neaps 3 to 4 feet. Westerly winds increase the rise of the tide.

Pilots.—The pilot station is in the entrance, off ... point, and when the pilot cannot get onboard, they guide ships entering the river by signals from the pilot boat, which is anchored at such times in a fairway just within the bar.

Directions.—To enter from Setubal should bring the lighthouse to bear about N.E. ¾ E., and steer for it; when Fort Arrabida bears ... by E., ... 1¼ miles along then steer for the bar, steer for the fairway channel between the white and red buoys, with the south-east part of Fort ... open to the southward of Outão; with these marks on, pass close to Outão fort, keeping along by the north shore, and having passed Albarquel fort, an anchorage may be selected off the town in from 5 to 9 fathoms at low water. The best time for passing the bar is, of course, with a rising tide.

CAPE SINES.—From Setubal to the southward, the shore is generally low, with a sandy beach and some towns. Pesquiera point projects, and to the southward of it are two small hills with houses on them, which serve to mark this part of the coast; the southern hill is named San Thiago de Cacem, on which is a castle and town, and can be seen from a considerable distance. Two small rivers, the Melides and André, here fall into the sea, but are fit only for small craft. Cape Sines, about 31 miles southward of Outão lighthouse, is steep-to, with two small ... called Perceheiras, close off it. The castle and town of Sines are built on the shore just to the south of the cape; its exports are cork wood and fruit, and in 1872, 55 British vessels loaded with those articles. The population amounts to about 2,000, and are chiefly engaged in fishing. A sweep of the beach here forms a bay, which affords shelter from northerly winds, but is open to the south-west. Vessels generally anchor off the town in 9 to 15 fathoms, sand.

Approaching cape Sines from the northward, at a distance of 3 or 4 miles, it appears low, but will be known by the windmills upon it. A short distance from the innermost mill is a dwelling house or farm, and at a cable or so outside the cape the rugged islets of Perceheiras will be seen. The next object of notice is a square built and cement-fronted building, and soon after the town will be visible. From the haze which frequently overhangs the land, the objects on shore are extremely difficult to distinguish.

LIGHT.—On cape Sines, stands a lighthouse 75 feet high, from which, at an elevation of 130 feet above high water, is exhibited a *fixed* white light, visible through an area of 270° (from the bearing of S.W. ¼ S. southerly, round to N.W. ¼ W. westerly) and should be seen in clear weather from a distance of 19 miles.

The COAST from cape Sines is generally low and sandy as far as Aljezur, about 35 miles; from thence to cape St. Vincent, it becomes higher, with steep rocky cliffs. The Serra de Monchique, the highest part of which, named Foia, 2,963 feet high, is a remarkable feature of the coast, rising about 25 miles E.N.E. of cape St. Vincent, and about 12 miles eastward of Aljezur. At 9 miles southward of cape Sines is the islet of Pacegueiro, separated from the main by a narrow channel, where small craft may anchor in fine weather, in 2 to 3 fathoms, stony bottom; a little to the northward of the fort there is an inlet visited by coasting vessels.

At about 5 miles southward of Pacegueiro islet are some small steep cliffs of a reddish colour, and about 4 miles beyond it is the bar of the river Odemira. The mouth of this river is from 170 to 200 yards in breadth; a sandy shoal projects from the southern side, leaving the passage along the northern shore, upon which is a fort, and a mile above it the town of Villa-novo, containing about 2,500 inhabitants. The bar has 9 or 10 feet water over it, and within it the river is 12 feet deep, and navigable by coasting vessels as far as the town of Odemira, which has a population of about 2,300, 12 miles from its mouth. The coast continues sandy for nearly 3 miles to the southward of the bar of Odemira, where there is another patch of red cliffs like those to the northward, and which are excellent marks for this part of the coast.

Cape Sardaõ, a projecting high cliff, is about six miles southward of the red cliffs, and the same distance farther on is the mouth of the river Odeseixe, which divides the province of Alemtejo from that of Algarve. At 6 miles southward of the Odeseixe is the entrance of a small river leading to the town of Aljezur, on a sand-hill, crowned by the remains of an old castle; and 3½ miles farther on are the ruins of Arrifana battery, on the point of the same name with a sandy beach, and about a cable off it there is a remarkable rock named the Agulha. At 4 miles beyond this rock is the point and ruins of Carrapateira fort; thence follows, at 11 miles more to the southward, cape St. Vincent. From the red cliffs to the cape the coast is composed of high, steep, rocky cliffs, except the beach at Arrifana point, and another small one a mile northward of the cape.

GORRINGE or GETTYSBURG BANK, the area of which comprised within the depth of 100 fathoms, is nearly circular in shape, has an average diameter of 5 miles, and is included, between the parallels of 36° 29½' and 36° 34' N., and long. 11° 32' and 11° 38' W.

The shoalest part, within the depths of 35 to 30 fathoms, appears to be a narrow ridge 2 miles in extent, running nearly east and west; the least depth of 30 fathoms being confined to a small patch in lat. 36° 31½' N. and long. 11° 35½' W.

The nature of the bottom at depths under 50 fathoms was found to consist of rock and coralline matter; in depths exceeding 50 fathoms, pebbles, corralline substances, shells and sand.

Beyond the depth of 100 fathoms the soundings increase rapidly. The depth of 1,000 fathoms from the shoal ground being about 5 miles in a northerly direction; 6 miles in a southerly; 13 miles to the westward; and 11 miles to the eastward. At 20 miles distant in a north-westerly direction, 2,750 fathoms were found, and in a north-easterly direction 1,640 fathoms.

The tide was observed in H.M.S. *Salamis*, when at anchor on the shoal ground, on the 4th March 1877 (spring tides), to set regularly north-east and south-west, with a maximum velocity of about 1½ knots.

Fish in abundance were caught on the bank.[*]

CAPE ST. VINCENT or San Vincente, is about 200 feet high, bluff, and level, having a convent on which is a lighthouse, and other buildings on its summit. At about 50 yards from the pitch of the cape there is a high isolated rock, with 15 fathoms water, sand and shells between them; at a cable from the rock there are 20 fathoms. From the cape the coast, composed of high steep cliffs, trends to the S.S.E. for 4 miles to Sagres point, which is about 200 feet high, with a small village and signal tower on it; at a long mile from the convent is fort Belixe.[†]

The position of the cape will be known by the Serra de Monchique, which terminates in two distinct peaks; the western named Foia, is, next to mount Estrella, the highest land in Portugal, and may be seen at a great distance; the eastern peak is named Picota, and both being of rocks that reflect the light, appear whitish when seen from a distance, particularly from the northward.

LIGHT.—The circular lighthouse on the convent on cape St. Vincent exhibits at 220 feet above high water, a *revolving* white light, attaining its greatest brilliancy every *two minutes*, and seen in clear weather at a distance of 20 miles. This light is reported to revolve irregularly.

Semaphore.—At Sagres there is a Semaphore station, with which vessels can communicate by the International code.

---

* *See* Admiralty plan of Gorringe or Gettysburg bank, No. 434, scale m = 1·0 inch.
† *See* Admiralty chart :—Cape St. Vincent to the strait of Gibraltar, No. 92, scale m = 0·2 inches.

Currents.—In light winds, sailing vessels should preserve a good offing when in the vicinity of cape St. Vincent, as the currents generally set strong along shore, and have a tendency towards the cape. Ripples are occasionally seen off the cape.

SOUTH COAST OF PORTUGAL.—On the east side of Sagres point is the bay of the same name, where vessels will find shelter from northerly winds by anchoring in 11 fathoms water, about half a mile from the shore. Balieira point is the east extreme of Sagres bay, and on its north side is Morlinhal bay, with three rocky islets, where anchorage for small vessels may be found in 5 or 6 fathoms. Vessels should leave these bays directly the wind changes. At 13 miles eastward of Balieira point is Piedade point, at the entrance to Lagos bay, and the termination of some whitish high land named the Alto de Barril, which extends two miles in an east and west direction; the coast all along being generally of steep cliffs, with patches of beach.

Piedade point is steep and rocky, with a battery on it; several large rocks lie along its eastern face, and a reef extends from it about a cable to the southward.

The principal features of this coast, from a distance, are the Serra de Monchique, already described, monte Figo, and monte Gordo. Monte Figo is a low double peak, about 800 feet high, and is just seen over the low land of the coast rising about 11 miles to the north-east of cape St. Mary; it is more distinctly visible from the eastward or westward, as it then appears separated from the mountains to the northward of it, but from the southward it is blended with them. In approaching from the westward this mountain is not visible until 10 miles eastward of cape St. Vincent, and it should not be mistaken for a smaller mountain to the north-west of it. Monte Gordo in Spain, is 5 miles to the eastward of the Guadiana river, and about the same height as mount Figo. The town and ruined castle of Ayamonte, on a hill on the eastern bank of the Guadiana, is seen from seaward 10 or 12 miles, and is a good mark for entrance to that river.[*]

LAGOS, the chief town on the south-west coast of Algarve, stands about 1½ miles to the northward of Piedade point, on the west side of the entrance to the river Lagos. It has a cathedral, is surrounded with ancient walls, and contains about 9,000 inhabitants, who carry on an extensive fishery. The river Lagos is a small stream, and vessels of 7 or 8 feet draught may enter at high water, with the aid of a pilot. The north shore of Lagos bay is a sandy beach, the land rising and presenting a pleasing appearance, with numerous towns, villages, and houses; the town of Mexilhoeira is sufficiently elevated to be seen 12 or 15 miles at sea.[†]

---

[*] Navigating Lieutenant F. W. Jarrad, April 1871.
[†] See Admiralty plan :—Lagos bay, on chart, No. 87.

Water and Supplies.—Water may be obtained from the river at a suitable time of tide, and other supplies are plentiful.

Alvor.—The town of this name, with about 1,500 inhabitants, is 3 miles from the mouth of the river Verde, which is navigable also at high water for small vessels up to the town, but the bottom at its entrance, which is 3¼ miles eastward of Piedade point, is rocky and foul.

Tres Irmaõs Point, (three Brothers), nearly 3 miles farther on, is the east extreme of Lagos bay, and of moderate height, with three small rocks off it, and hence its name; to the eastward of it is the bar of the river Silves; the coast being generally rocky, with a few patches of open beach.

Anchorage.—Lagos bay affords good anchorage with northerly winds. Large vessels anchor a mile or more east of Piedade point in 12 or 15 fathoms water, sand; and smaller vessels nearer the town, in 8 or 10 fathoms. Coasters lie close in, and find shelter even from south-west winds.

Tides.—It is high water, full and change, at Lagos, at 2h. 7m.; springs rise 13 feet, and neaps 7 feet. The bar of the river is just covered at low water.

The RIVER SILVES is much frequented by coasters, but can only be entered at two-thirds flood, with the aid of a pilot. The bar has only about 7 feet on it at low, and 16 feet at high water springs, but within, the water is deeper, and for nearly 3 miles up there are from 11 to 3 fathoms; thence the river is navigable as far as the town of Silves, about 7 miles from the entrance. On each side of the entrance there is a fort, and in winter the bar is rarely passable for vessels, as the breakers are dangerous, and there is a swell a long way outside them.

Villa Nova de Portimão.—This town, containing about 4,000 inhabitants, stands on the west shore, about 1¼ miles within the mouth of the river Silves. The exports consist chiefly of cork wood, of which several British vessels loaded in 1872.

Tides.—The time of high water and rise of tide, may be considered the same as Lagos.

Water is scarce and has to be brought from a distance of 4 miles.

COAST.—At nearly 4 miles S.E. by E. of the bar of the Silves is Carvoeiro point, rocky, of moderate height, with a fort on it; thence the coast trends eastward for 3 miles to Santa Rocha, a bluff point with a battery on it: then a low beach follows to the mouth of the river Algoz, which flows into a bay about 5 miles from Carvoeiro point, and the same distance westward of Balieira point. The town of Pera, with about 1,500 inhabitants, is picturesquely situated on the east bank of the Algoz, 1¼ miles from its entrance.

Between Balieira point and Albufeira point, about half a mile east of it, is a small bay, fit for small vessels, and at the head of it is the town of the latter name, with a population of about 3,000, chiefly employed in fishing. From point Albufeira the coast trends eastward with a bend northward for 5 miles to Vallonga fort, and about a mile beyond it is the mouth of the river Quarteira. At about a mile S.S.E. ¼ E. from the entrance of the Quarteira river is a tower of the same name ; thence follows a sandy beach and plain—called the beach of Ançaŏ—in the above direction for 10 miles to the south-east end of Barreta island, at 3 miles beyond which is cape St. Mary. Loulé fort stands on the coast, about 2¼ miles from the tower of Quarteira.

FARO, one of the chief towns on the coast, stands at the entrance of the little river Valfermoso, nearly 4½ miles north of the lighthouse at cape St. Mary. It is visible from every direction, and easily recognized by its two white steeples, as well as by the chapel of San Antonio on a hill east of the town, which is white, and can be seen at some distance abreast. The population of Faro may amount to 10,000. The exports are dry figs, raisins, and cork wood. In 1862, 29 British vessels cleared with cargoes.

Directions.—The approach to Faro is by either of three channels, one west of cape St. Mary, and two east of it ;. there is a bar at each entrance having from 9 to 12 feet at high water, but as the depths frequently alter, the aid of a pilot is necessary. The channel by which vessels generally enter is abreast the town of Olhão, eastward of the lighthouse.

CAPE ST. MARY is the south extreme of several low sandy islands, which border the coast for a long distance to the north-west, and to the eastward of it. Vessels in the vicinity of the cape should not approach the coast at night or in thick weather, as at 1¼ miles southward of the lighthouse there are only 3¼ fathoms water, and 2 miles 8 fathoms, when the depth rapidly increases, so that at 5 miles from the cape there are about 90 fathoms, and a little farther out no soundings with 150 fathoms ; the bottom is generally sandy, with small shells.

LIGHT.—On cape San Mary is a circular tower, which exhibits at 109 feet above high water, a *fixed* white light, seen in clear weather at a distance of 15 miles.

TAVIRA.—At about 29 miles eastward of cape St. Mary light-tower is the mouth of the river Guadiana. The coast between, for the greater part of the distance, is bordered by a series of long low sandy islands, with salt ponds, separated by narrow navigable channels for boats, and backed by high land. On the longest of these islands are several sand-hills, to

T 2

the north-east of which at 17 miles from the light-tower is the tower of Tavira, built on both sides of the river Gilão, with about 9,000 inhabitants, who carry on a brisk coasting and fishing trade. Tavira bar is of loose sand, and continually shifting; pilots are therefore necessary. There is anchorage with off-shore winds outside the bar in 4 or 5 fathoms water. The coast thence for 12 miles to the Guadiana is low and sandy, and between are the churches of Conceicão and Cacela.

The **GUADIANA RIVER** rises in New Castile, and after a tortuous course through Spain, forms its boundary for some distance, and then enters Portugal, through which it flows for nearly 100 miles more; then again, forming the boundary of those kingdoms, to the sea. Of its whole length of more than 400 miles, about 40 miles only are navigable up to the town of Mertola, and it discharges itself into the sea a little south-ward of the towns of Villa Real and Ayamonte. Villa Real, containing about 2,000 inhabitants, and Castro Marin with 3,500 (Portuguese towns) are on the west bank, the former about a mile, and the latter about 3 miles from San Antonio point. In 1872, 212 British vessels, amounting to 29,814 tons, entered inwards at Villa Real. About midway between the towns the Castro Marin creek takes a N.N.W. direction, and has 8 to 10 feet in it at low water springs. The town of Ayamonte, with a population of 6,000, is on the Spanish side, about 2 miles from Canela island, at the entrance of the river.

Pomarão is a Portuguese village on the right bank of the Guadiana, and said to be about 40 miles from its mouth. Vessels of 500 tons ascend to this place, and a steam tug plies between it and the bar of the Guadiana for the assistance of sailing craft in contrary winds. The navigation for steamers is easy, by keeping the side of the highest bank. The anchorage off the village is good, but the tides are strong, and if any stay is intended, it is requisite to moor. There are piers for the accommodation of vessels shipping ore, large quantities of which is brought down by rail from the mines of San Domingo, situated some 10 miles off. These mines employ about 3,000 people, and the ore is exported at the rate of from 8,000 to 10,000 tons a month. Two vessels of 500 tons can be loaded in 24 hours.* About a third of a mile below Pomarão, where a small river runs into the Guadiana, a vessel can be grounded on a sandy beach, and at low water have her bottom cleaned.

Supplies.—Fresh meat is cheap but of inferior quality, other supplies are scarce.

The Bar.—The entrance to the Guadiana is encumbered with shoals, which extend to seaward for a considerable distance from both points, and

---

* Lieutenant Smail, H.M.S. *Wizard*, October 1869.

as the sands are constantly shifting, the bar cannot be crossed without a pilot. At low springs there are said to be only about 6 feet water on the bar, but within, vessels of 12 feet draught may navigate as far as Pomarão at any time of tide without touching the numerous sand-banks; vessels drawing 16 feet have reached Pomarão, but they go up and drop down with the tide; one shoal has only 15 feet on it at high water neaps. In most parts of the Guadiana, as far as Pomarão, the depth is said to vary from 3 to 6 fathoms, ánd the river is safe and convenient to lie in.

Off Villa Real, where the breadth of the river is about 840 yards, the depth is 27 feet. At Ayamonte the breadth is about 420 yards, and depth 20 feet, whence it opens out wider with 20 and 22 feet water.

Pilots for the Guadiana river will generally be found cruising near the bar, their boats are distinguished by having the letter P inscribed upon the Portuguese national flag. In strong southerly winds, when unable to come out, they remain just inside the bar, and by waving a red flag, indicate the direction in which the vessel should steer.

LIGHTS.—Ayamonte light.—On Canela island, near Canela point, at the east side of entrance to the Guadiana, two *fixed red* lights are exhibited to aid in crossing the bar of Ayamonte. The northern of the two is at an elevation of 22 feet, and the southern one 21 feet above the mean level of the sea, and should be visible in clear weather from a distance of 5 miles. These lights are 3 miles from the bar, and their position is changed as the bar alters.

Higuerita Bar lights.—Two *fixed green* lights are exhibited for crossing Higuerita bar; one is 24 feet, the other 17 feet above the sea, and are seen in clear weather from a distance of 10 miles. The channel alters, and the position of the lights is changed accordingly.

Tides.—It is high water, full and change, at the bar of the Guadiana, at 3h. 0m.; springs rise 12 feet.

CHAPTER VI.

SOUTH COAST OF SPAIN.—RIVER GUADIANA TO GIBRALTAR. —NORTH-WEST COAST OF AFRICA.—CEUTA BAY TO MOGADOR.

VARIATION IN 1881.

Cape St. Mary -   - 18° 40′ W. | Gibraltar -   -   - 17° 40′ W.
Mogador 17° 40′ W.

COAST.—From the river Guadiana the low sandy coast trends eastward and southward,—forming a bay about 10 miles deep,—for nearly 58 miles to Chipiona point on the south side of the entrance to the river Guadalquiver. The most prominent features in the land are monte Gordo, page 289, the town and ruined castle of Ayamonte, and a hill a little eastward of Chipiona point. The coast consists of low sand hills, and there are several small towers at intervals along the shore. Several rivers discharge their waters into the sea, having low islands formed at their entrances, but they are navigable only by coasters, on account of the shifting and shallow bars. The soundings are regular, and there are from 9 to 12 fathoms water at about 5 miles from the shore.*

AYAMONTE, on a declivity of a hill, upon the summit of which is a ruined castle, on the east shore of the Guadiana, about 2 miles from Canela point, is a Spanish town, with a population of nearly 6,000. Between Canela point and Ayamonte are the mouths of two creeks, which run eastward parallel with the coast ; they are almost dry at low water, but navigable for the boats of the coast with a flood tide. The southern creek leads to Higuerita, a distance of 4 miles, where there is a shallow entrance from the sea, and two *fixed green* lights are exhibited to guide vessels through the channel, their position being changed as the channel alters. There are 3 fathoms at low water off the town of Higuerita, at which time there is only 3 feet water upon the bar. The northern creek passes by Higuerita, and continues past Tuta, near which place it flows into the sea, forming the low island called Cristina.

---

* *See* Admiralty chart:—Cape St. Vincent to strait of Gibraltar, No. 92, scale, m = 0·2 of an inch.

The bar of Tuta is 5 miles to the eastward of that of Higuerita; it is formed between two low sandy points, that on the west being the east end of Cristina island, and its eastern the main land. It is dry at low water, and at high water only fit for small coasting and fishing vessels.

PIEDRAS RIVER.—The tower of Catalan stands upon an eminence of rugged reddish ground upon the west bank of the river Piedras, which has a narrow mouth and two entrances 3 miles apart, called the bar of Terron, and Marijato bar.

The bar of Terron, eastward of which a sandy island called Levante lies parallel with the main, extending 3 miles, has a depth of $3\frac{3}{4}$ feet at low water. Two white perches, upon each of which a *fixed* white light is shown at night, when in line lead across the bar; their position is changed as the bar alters.

Marijato bar lies between the east end of Levante island and a sandy point running out from the main. To cross this bar it is necessary to keep nearer to Levante island than the main; the broken water points out the narrow channel, and having entered it, proceed between Levante island and the main to the westward, and anchor as convenient in 4 or 5 fathoms. It has only 3 feet water upon it at low water, and both this and the preceding entrance, merging into the river Piedras, lead up to the towns of Lepe and Cartaya, both of which have a considerable trade; the former has a population of about 3,500, and the latter of 4,500.

LIGHT.—At Rompido de Cartaya, on the left bank near the eastern entrance of the river Piedras, is a white circular tower, which exhibits at 81 feet above the mean level of the sea, a *fixed* white light, varied by a *flash* every *four* minutes, and visible in clear weather at a distance of 14 miles.

As a guide over the bar of Terron (the western entrance to the river Piedras) two white perches on the north shore show at elevations of 66 and 56 feet above high water, each a *fixed* white light, visible in clear weather at a distance of 4 miles. When in line they lead across the bar: the positions are changed as the bar alters.

ODIEL and TINTO RIVERS.—Umbria point and tower at the entrance to the rivers Odiel and Tinto, is 6 short miles to the S.E. of the bar of Marijato. On the east side of the point—within the entrance—is the low and sandy island Saltés, about $2\frac{1}{4}$ miles in length, the south-east extreme of which is the west point of the main entrance to the rivers. Sandbanks extend to the south-eastward from Umbria point, and from the island for a distance of nearly 6 miles, running parallel to the coast; the latter bank is separated from the former and broken in places, forming narrow channels into the main entrance, with from the 2 to 5 feet in them at low water.

The canal del Padre Santo, formed between the termination of these banks and a bank extending 1¼ miles from the coast, is nearly 2 cables wide, carries from 8 to 16 feet at low water, and is the principal passage into the rivers; but as the bar constantly shifts, strangers should not enter the river without a pilot. From the 'position of the Padre Santo lights, the shore trends north-westward 6 miles to the point and tower of Arenilla where there are 14 fathoms water at the confluence of the rivers, and here, the river Tinto trends to the E.N.E. to the town of Palos and Moguer.*

Huelva.—The town of this name situated on the eastern bank of the Odiel river about 3 miles above Arenilla point, has a population of about 7,500. Among the manufactures are rope, sails, blocks, and other articles for shipping. There are several mines in the vicinity which produce manganese and copper pyrites, the largest is the Tharsis, which exports from 8,000 to 10,000 tons a month. The trade is carried on in sailing vessels of about 130 tons, to steamers of 1,100 and is increasing; there is also a small trade in fruit, and a tunny fishery. In 1870 the number of ships that cleared from this port was 445, amounting to 149,860 tons.

Anchorage off Huelva is good, the depth being from 17 to 22 feet at low water, but it is requisite to moor, as the tides run as much as 3¼ knots an hour.

Moguer is 5 miles from Arenilla point, or the left bank of the Tinto; agriculture, flour mills, brandy distilleries, a few hand looms for coarse linens, and hempen stuffs, are the chief means of employment. Oil, wheat, &c., are imported, and wine the principal production of the district, exported; population 5,500.

Palos, a small town about 2½ miles from Arenilla point, with a population of about 1,100, is celebrated and interesting as the place from which Columbus sailed on his first voyage to America, August 3rd, 1492. The depth here abreast the town is from 8 to 14 feet.

Tides.—It is high water full and change, at Huelva, at 2h. 16m., and at the bar 1h. 54m.; and the rise is about 14 feet. The stream at the anchorage of Huelva runs at the rate of 3¼ miles an hour.

LIGHTS.—Near Padre Santo point, on the eastern shore of the mouth of the river Odiel, two *fixed* white lights are exhibited; the northern one at an elevation of about 27 feet, and the southern one 16 feet above the mean level of the sea, visible in clear weather from a distance of 7 miles.

---

* *See* Admiralty plan :—Entrance to rivers Odiel and Tinto, port of Huelva, No. 72, scale, m = 2.8 inches.

These lights are nearly 1¼ miles from the outer part of the bar, and when in line lead in the deepest water, the sand-bank on the western side of entrance is marked by a buoy, which is seen at some distance.

The positions of the lights and buoys are altered when the bar changes.

GUADALQUIVER RIVER.—At about 27 miles S.S.E. from Picacho point is the mouth of the river Guadalquiver. The shore between is of sandy downs, and on it are the towers of Oro, Asperilla, Higuera, and Carbonera. The Guadalquiver rises on the borders of Murcia, and intersects Andalusia, draining all its northern portion; it rapidly increases in size by the accession of numerous streams on both sides, and after passing the town of Andujar its course is to.the west-south-west to Cordova and Seville. At some distance below the latter, the islands Minor and Major divide it into three branches; it unites again below the latter, and forms a harbour near its mouth above San Lúcar de Barrameda. The whole course of the river is 250 miles, but it is only navigable up to Seville, where it is crossed by a bridge about 70 miles from the sea, to which, and sometimes beyond it, the influence of the tide is felt.

Occasionally the river becomes swollen by the melting snow, and when retarded in its course by high tides, the inundations that ensue cause great ravages, and serious loss to the inhabitants on its banks. The river is navigable for vessels of about 100 tons, at certain seasons of the year, as far as Seville, the capital of the province, but generally speaking vessels of more than 10 feet draught are obliged to load and unload about 8 miles below the city.*

Malandar point, on the north side of entrance, is covered with trees, and a lighthouse (which is merely a dwelling house) stands on the low sandy spit ; and 1½ miles northward of it is the tower of San Jacinto, seen among the sand-hills on the coast, and a prominent object on approaching the river from the northward. The coast bank extends in a W. by S. direction 2¼ miles from the tower, and at this distance from it the depth is about 3 fathoms, the bank with various shallow patches on it, here trends southward and joins the coast bank south of the mouth of the river.

Baxo Picacho, the outermost shoal, is of rock, has only 4¼ feet water on it, and lies W. by S. about 2¼ miles from the tower of San Jacinto, and N.N.E. ¼ E. from the church tower of Chipiona; at 2 cables southwest of this shallow part there are 1¼ fathoms. The Regla convent, standing a long half-mile south of the town of Chipiona, well open of the town leads westward of the shoal.

---

* *See* Admiralty plan:—Entrance of Guadalquiver river, No. 2,341, scale м = 3 inches.

Chipiona point, at 4 miles from Espiritu castle on the south side of entrance, is low and rocky, and has the town or village of the same name on it. An extensive rocky bank surrounds the point, and at 1¼ miles from it the Salmedina rocks uncover at low water; from the north-west extreme of the bank the church tower of Chipiona bears about E. by S. ¾ S. distant 2 miles. To clear these dangers keep San Lucar church tower, which is conspicuous, open of Montijo point, until the steeples of Rota are open of the termination of the sand hills at Almadrava. There are 6 to 8 fathoms water near the edge of the band, and it should be rounded with caution.

From Chipiona point eastward the shore is bordered at some distance by rocky ledges and shallow water, and at Espiritu point the Riza reef, which partly dries at low water, projects nearly a mile to the north, leaving between it and the shore west of Malandar point a channel into the Guadalquiver 1½ cables wide and 4 to 7 fathoms deep. Within this reef the channel widens, but opposite Malandar point, the sands of the south shore extend more than half way across the river to the Riceta shoal, with 1¾ fathoms water over it; above which it again widens, and in the navigable part of the river there are from 3¼ to 8 fathoms.

SAN LUCAR de BARRAMEDA.—This city and seaport stands on the south bank, at the mouth of the Guadalquiver; the country about it is sandy and undulating, and cultivated with vineyards and gardens. Agriculture is the chief occupation, and fishing employs a considerable portion of its inhabitants, who form a population of about 17,500; it is also a mart for inferior wines. At Bonanza, a mile above the city, is the custom-house and quay. From San Lúcar de Barrameda, Columbus sailed on his third voyage to America, May 30th, 1498, and Magellan on the first voyage of the circumnavigation of the world, August 10th, 1519.

LIGHTS.—Chipiona Light.—On the Perro rocks, and about 45 yards from the sea, between the town of Chipiona and the Regla convent, is a light yellow coloured tower, which exhibits at 225 feet above the sea, a white light eclipsed every *minute*, and visible in clear weather at a distance of 23 miles. The tower stands about 1½ miles within the Salmedina rocks.

Espiritu point light.—On Espiritu point, at the south side of entrance, and a cable from the castle, there is a *fixed red* light to indicate, when bearing S.S.W., that a vessel is within the Riza spit, and the moment when the course should be altered; it is not seen from the offing.

Malandar point light.—On the beach of Malandar point, north of San Lúcar de Barrameda, a *fixed* white light is shown 36 feet above the level of the sea, visible 6 miles.

Bonanza light.—Near the quay at Bonanza, 52 feet above the sea, a *fixed* white light is exhibited, visible 7 miles.

Anchorage. — There are two anchorages off the mouth of the Guadalquiver where vessels may safely bring up in fine weather; that of Pozo, in 7 fathoms water, with the Perro light-house bearing about south distant 3 miles, Chipiona church S. ¾ E., and the castle of Espiritu S.E. by E. ¼ E.

Grajuela anchorage is nearer the shore, in 5 fathoms, clay, with the convent of Regla open of Chipiona, Chipiona church S. by W., and Espiritu castle E. ¾ S.

Pilots.—The many dangers at the entrance, and within the Guadalquiver, render it necessary for strangers to have a pilot, and weather permitting one may always be obtained, but they only put to sea when a vessel is off the port. The pilot station is at Chipiona point.

Tides.—It is high water, full and change, at Salmedina rocks, at 1h. 27m., and at Bonanza at 2h.; springs rise from 11 to 13 feet, and neaps 8 feet.

Directions.—With a fair wind, bring the Bonanza and Malandar lighthouses in line, bearing about East, and steer for them until Espiritu lighthouse bears S. by E., when the vessel will be about half a mile from the end of the Riza reef; then keep a little to the northward, and bring Malandar lighthouse in line with the south end of Bonanza custom house, which will pass the spit in 4 fathoms water. When off the end of the reef, Espiritu lighthouse will bear about S. by W. ¼ W., and when that line is crossed and the reef rounded, steer for Salvador castle till Malandar light bears N.W. ¼ N., then steer about N.E. ¼ E. for Bonanza road, and anchor with the light bearing S.E. ¼ E. in about 4 fathoms, sand.

The passages between the shoals at the entrance of the river are adapted only for small vessels.

COAST.—From Chipiona point the low coast with sandy downs trends nearly South for 6½ miles to Candor point, at about 2 miles to the south-east of which is the town of Rota, at the entrance to Cadiz bay. The shore all along is rocky, and at 2 miles southward of Chipiona point, the rocks extend off nearly half a mile; and at about three-quarters of a mile farther on is a rocky patch with 1½ fathoms water on it, lying two-thirds of a mile from the shore, with the tower on the high land of Beva, bearing E. ¼ N. Between Candor point and the town of Rota the reefs extend from a half, to a long mile from the shore. Rota pier gives shelter to small vessels, which can only go in at high water.

In approaching Cadiz from the westward in clear weather, the first land which will probably be identified are the mountains of Ronda, Ubrique, and Medina. The mountain of Ronda, named also Cabeza del Moro, is the highest part of an extensive chain, appears rounded, rises about 45 miles inland, and when brought to bear E. ¾ S. leads direct to Cadiz. The mountain of Ubrique is about 40 miles inland, and nearly on the same parallel as Cadiz, but less conspicuous; it forms a peak from which the land descends in gentle slopes. The Medina assumes a pyramidal shape, is of less elevation, and about 20 miles nearer the coast than Ubrique. There is a remarkable tower a little below the summit, and easily distinguished everywhere at the entrance of Cadiz bay. The white houses of the town of Medina, on the west slope of the mountain, appear as a white patch.

The tower of Beva, standing on a high ridge of hills, about 11 miles northward of Cadiz, is a good mark for recognizing the coast, as it can be seen from a long distance. It is square, with a round cupola at the top, and between 2 square houses. From the northward, the light tower of San Sebastian should not be brought to bear southward of S.S.E. until southward of Rota.

CADIZ, the capital of the province of the same name, and one of the most important seaports of Spain, occupies the rocky and comparatively elevated extremity of a long, narrow, low tongue of land, which projects northward for about 5 miles from the isle of Leon, comprising between it and the main land a spacious bay with excellent anchorage. This tongue of land has a causeway along it, and connects the city with the main land; it is in places not more than from 200 to 300 yards across, and is strongly fortified. The access to Cadiz from the sea is almost impracticable, from the rocks, ledges, and sandbanks by which it is surrounded; and being everywhere defended by ramparts, bastions, and detached forts, is all but impregnable.*

The streets of the city though narrow, are straight, well paved, and lighted. The houses in general are lofty, and well built of white freestone, with a court in the centre, and are generally crowned by a mirador or turret. There are but few public buildings of importance, the cathedral being the most conspicuous. Along the ramparts is a fine promenade, known as the Alaméda, with an extensive view eastward of the different towns and the mountains in the distance, and westward, of the wide Atlantic. Seen from a distance, Cadiz presents a magnificent display of snow-white buildings. From its almost insular position it enjoys a mild climate, the mean annual temperature being about 64° Fahrenheit, while the mean

---

* See Admiralty plan:—Cadiz harbour and approaches, No. 86; scale m = 1·4 inches.

summer and winter temperatures, do not vary more than 10° above and below this point.

From the same cause it labours under a deficiency of water, which is either collected in cisterns, or brought at a great expense from Santa Maria, on the opposite side of the bay. The population may be about 60,000. Wine is the principal export, and in 1865 the total value exported amounted to 2,134,280*l.* sterling. The principal articles of import are sugar, coffee, cocoa, fish, tobacco, and foreign manufactures.

In 1865 there were only 882 arrivals of foreign vessels, of which 426 were English.

Water and Supplies.—Ships can obtain water from tank vessels brought from Santa Maria. Provisions and supplies are plentiful.

Santa Maria, on the north-east shore at the mouth of the Guadalete (across which there is a bridge of boats) is a town with a population of about 18,000, and a considerable trade, particularly in wine; it supplies Cadiz with fresh water, conveyed across the harbour in vessels constructed for that purpose; steamboats also ply between it and Cadiz, and it is connected by a railway with Xeres. Two small *red* lights mark the entrance to the Guadalete river.

Puerto Real, on the mainland at the head of the harbour, has a mole, a slip, &c.; its manufactures are coarse linens, leather, pottery, vermicilli, and starch; population about 4,000.

Trocadero stands on the projecting point of land near forts Matagorda and Luis; the Caño (channel) runs past it to the mole of Puerto Real.

Carraca, on the main, at the north-east entrance of the Sancti Petri, is the site of the Royal dockyard and arsenal, containing docks, slips, basins, &c., formerly of the highest order.

San Fernando stands on the eastern shore of the isle of Leon, which is connected to the main land by the drawbridge of Suazo, which crosses the river Sancti Petri; the Camiño Real, or high road from the bridge, leads through it to the Torre Gorda, and thence to Cadiz. The Royal Observatory is near this town, and considered to be in latitude 36° 27' 41" N., and longitude 6° 12' 16" West of Greenwich. There are here numerous flour mills and extensive salt works, and manufactories of starch, leather, and vermicilli; many of the inhabitants are employed in fishing. Population about 10,000.

At San Carlos, to the north of San Fernando, is the residence of the Captain-general, that of the Intendent of the Marine, the Government Boards, &c.

Timeball.—San Fernando mean time is shown daily by the dropping of a black ball from a staff on the roof of the Observatory at San Fernando.

The ball is hoisted slowly 10 minutes before 1 p.m., and is dropped at the instant of 1 p.m. San Fernando mean time.

If, owing to any circumstance, the ball should not drop at the precise moment, it will be re-hoisted, and dropped a second time at 1h. 10 m. mean time. Should the ball be obscured by a squall or fog at 1 p.m. the signal will be repeated at 2 p.m. mean time. In heavy gales the ball will not be dropped.

Docks.--Near fort Matagorda there is a dry dock 500 feet long, and 64 feet wide, with a depth of 26 feet at its entrance. Contiguous to this dock are wharves where vessels may lie afloat in 19 feet water at low tide, bottom soft mud.

There is a patent slip in the creek at El Trocadero, suitable for vessels, 136 feet long, with a draft of 10 feet 6 inches aft and 7 feet 5 inches forward.

Repairs can be effected to wood or iron vessels ; also to engines and boilers.

CADIZ BAY.—From the town of Rota the coast defended by several batteries, trends eastward and southward to the rocky point and castle of Santa Catalina and together with the Galera and Diamante shoals, and the Puercas rocks, may be considered the boundaries of Cadiz bay ; the lighthouse of San Sebastian and the town of Rota being the two extremes, the former is 5¼ miles southward of Rota. Banco de Rota, about a mile in extent, lies in the north-west part of the bay; it has 4 fathoms water on it, and its southern edge is situated about 1¾ miles S. by E. from Rota.

LIGHTS.—Cadiz light.—On a bed of rocks at the western extremity of Cadiz, stands the white circular light tower of San Sebastian surrounded by a fort. A *fixed* white light varied by a *red flash* every *two minutes* is shown from it, at a height of 146 feet above high water, and should be seen in clear weather at a distance of 20 miles.

Santa Maria light.—On the east side of entrance to the Guadalete river are two iron columns 47 yards apart, from each of which, at elevations of 25 and 15 feet above high-water level, is exhibited a *fixed* red light ; visible in clear weather a at distance of 3 miles.

Rota light.— On the molo of Rota, a *fixed* white light is proposed.

Torpedo caution.—A red flag with a white T, hoisted on the flag-staff at fort St. Sebastian (on the south side of the town), indicates that a torpedo is anchored near, close to which there will be a buoy, painted red and white vertical stripes, with a staff terminating in two rings, also with red and white vertical stripes. The flag-staff on the fort, the torpedo, and buoy will be in line. During night a *red* light will be substituted for the flag, and will throw a ray to within 100 yards of the buoy. No boat or vessel should approach within 100 yards of the buoy or line between the buoy and fort. Should there be more than one torpedo, each will be marked with a buoy.

The above-named flag hoisted on any boat or vessel signifies that there are torpedoes on board, or that they are operating with some, and it is strictly forbidden to go alongside any such boat or vessel.

Outside Anchorage.—Should it be desirable vessels may anchor in 10 or 11 fathoms water, with San Sebastian lighthouse bearing about S.S.E. distant 2¼ miles nearly, and fort Santa Catalina in line with Xeres hill about East. In this position, should the wind veer to the south-west, as it does generally in winter, a vessel will be to windward of the entrance to the harbour. In summer a vessel may anchor more to the north-east, there being no danger then of sudden gales, and as the wind generally draws off the land in the mornings at that season the vessel will be more to windward, and in a better position for entering the bay. The strongest winds are those from East and S.E.

Winds.—The sea breezes vary from West to N.N.W., and are generally strongest at the full and change of the moon, when they not unfrequently blow during the whole night. They set in most commonly with the flood, and are of less strength when the tide makes near noon, indeed at that period calms are not uncommon throughout the day. The land wind seldom reaches the anchorage, although above Puntales castle there is scarcely a night without it.

The S.E. and East winds are most dreaded by the inhabitants, but they are by no means so destructive in their effects as the S.W. and Westerly gales, which send a heavy sea into the bay ; whereas the East being an off-shore wind seldom creates any swell of consequence. These winds most commonly set in at the full and change of the moon, particularly the former, and blow with great violence ; they are seldom known in the winter months, and generally commence in May or June, with intervals of a fortnight or three weeks, and their average duration is three days, but at times five.

The sensation occasioned by these winds is oppressive in the extreme the stronger it blows the warmer the wind, and the atmosphere is always impregnated with particles of sand. The thermometer rises 10 or 12 degrees in a few minutes after it has set in, averaging from 84° to 92° Fahrenheit, and there is a singular circumstance connected with it, viz., that the temperature between decks is but little affected.

The inhabitants consider that when the hills of Ronda appear near and distinct, it is a sign of an easterly wind, but there are exceptions to this rule. It may however be considered almost to a certainty, that when the hills have the above appearance, an easterly wind exists in the strait of Gibraltar. Whenever there is any southing in the wind, the atmosphere is always hazy; and if to the westward of South a dampness ensues, but if to the eastward of South it becomes hot and dry.[*]

Tides.—It is high water, full and change, at Cadiz, at 1h. 56m. springs rise 12 feet, and neaps 9 feet. The tides are generally regular except in winter after a series of westerly gales, which not only forces a large quantity of water into the port, but causes the time of high water to be 2h. later than ordinary springs, and the flood to run eight hours, and the ebb only four. At the entrance of the channel the first of the flood sets to the S.S.E.; at half tide directly through towards Puntales: and the last quarter, from the lighthouse towards Santa Maria. The ebb sets nearly from the opposite directions. In the anchorage off the city, the first hour of 'flood, and the last hour of ebb, generally sets from St. Felipe point towards Santa Maria, and the remainder of the tide in a S.S.E. and N.N.W. direction.

When in the vicinity of El Frayle, Puercas, and Cochinos, especially with a beating wind, it should be borne in mind, that the tidal stream sets strongly over these dangers. The velocity of the stream at springs is from 1½ to 2¼ miles an hour, and at neaps from 1 to 1¼ miles.

Pilots are generally found off the port of Cadiz, but vessels cannot depend on finding them at night.

Dangers.—From the light tower on San Sebastion, the reefs extend nearly 4 cables westward, and at 1¼ miles to the south-west of it there are only 3¼ fathoms water, At nearly 4 cables N. W. ¾ N. from the light tower is the Olla shoal, having one fathom water on it, with Santa Catalina castle in line with the centre of Puercas rocks; and the high house at San Fernando, half open of the sea bastion at the lighthouse.

The Cochinos are two small black rocks which uncover at half tide, at 1½ miles N.N.E. ¼ E. from the light tower, and with the two small steeples of the Carmelite convent in line, at the west end of the Alaméda. Shallow water, extends a third of a mile south-west of them, and the north-western edge is marked by a black bell buoy, No. 1, in 5½ fathoms water.[†]

---

[*] J. F. Boxer, Master H.M.S. *Trinculo*, 1839.

[†] The positions of the buoys at the entrance to Cadiz cannot always be relied upon; in June 1873, the Cochinos bell buoy, and the buoys that mark the Galera and Rota reefs, were missing.

The Puercas are a cluster of rocks lying E. by S. and W. by N. three-quarters of a mile nearly off the north extreme of Cadiz, and half a mile eastward of the Cochinos. These rocks are covered at high water springs, when they are distinguished by the breakers, but they are uncovered at neap! tides. A black and white beacon, the top of which is 10 feet above high water, stands on the west extreme of the Puercas.

El Frayle is a rocky shoal with 6 feet water, extending half a mile S. E. by E. ½ E. of the Puercas, and 6 cables N. ¼ E. from the end of St. Felipe mole. After passing the Puercas rocks, caution should be observed in rounding this rocky shoal, which has on its north-east edge a black buoy, No. 5, in 3¾ fathoms water.

There are other rocky patches within the above dangers, rising from the shallow bank which surrounds all the northern shore of Cadiz.

The Diamante and Galera are two rocky shoals lying at the entrance of the harbour, and covering a space of more than three-quarters of a mile in a N.E. and S.W. direction. The shoalest part of the Diamante with 2¼ fathoms water on it lies with the flag staff of Santa Catalina castle, in line with the easternmost part of Xeres hill; the northern part of Puerto Real in line with the southern hill of Medina; and the Puercas rocks, in one with fort Santa Catalina, at the north-west angle of Cadiz. From the depth of 4 fathoms at the southern end of this shoal to the same depth near the Puercas, the distance is about two-thirds of a mile across, with 6 fathoms water in mid-channel, and forms the south-west entrance into the harbour. The southern edge of El Diamante is marked by a red buoy, No. 3, surmounted by a ball, in 4¾ fathoms water.

The Galera to the north-east of the former has 1¼ fathoms water on it and is separated from it by a narrow channel. Between this shoal and Santa Catalina point, about three-quarters of a mile apart, there are 5¼ fathoms water in mid-channel, which forms the north entrance into the harbour. A black buoy, No. 4, lies in 6 fathoms water on the north-west edge of La Galera.

CABEZO de los ASNOS.—A red buoy, No. 2, lies in 4¾ fathoms on the outer part of Cabezo de los Asnos, about a mile south-west from Rota.

Dangers within the Harbour.—From the Puercas rocks, the edge of the shallow bank trends eastward round the Frayle shoal, and thence along the whole shore of Cadiz, forming to the southward of Puntales castle, a wide expanse of black mud with shallow water over it. That part of the bank on the north side of Puntales castle is named St. Domingo bank (Palma shoal). On the eastern shore from Santa Catalina castle, the whole space southward to fort Matagorda is one extensive flat. The southern part of this flat is called Cabazuela shoal, and its edge northward of Matagorda fort is marked with a red buoy, No. 6, in 5½ fathoms. The high tower San Fernando on with the north end of Matagorda S. by

E. ¾ E. easterly leads along the western edge in 3 fathoms water, and with the tower open westward of the fort there is not less than 5 fathoms.

The Corrales is an extensive rocky shoal, which extends from the shore at the ditch of the land port of Cadiz, about a third of a mile, and then trends southward, uniting itself to the shore at nearly a mile from its commencement.

St. Domingo Bank (Palma shoal).—The shallow ground between the Corrales shoal and Puntales castle is named the St. Domingo bank. It extends off nearly three-quarters of a mile, and on its edge there are 2½ fathoms water, sand, marked by a red buoy, No. 7, which lies in 4¾ fathoms with Gorda tower just open of Puntales castle, and the Cathedral in line with the Landport Battery.

CAUTION.—Entering Cadiz harbour, the beacon, and the buoys painted black must be left on the starboard hand, and the buoys painted red on the port hand.

Directions.—Vessels entering Cadiz harbour between the Puercas rocks and Diamante shoal, should keep Medina and Puerto Real steeples in line bearing S.E. ¾ E., until the gates of St. Domingo open of the low point of Phillip, which has a flagstaff and saluting battery on its extremity or the small mole—named the mole of Seville gate—is seen open of the point ; when the lead will be a sufficient guide, and a convenient anchorage may be taken.*

Working in, the Diamente should not be approached nearer than to bring the south end of Medina in line with the north end of Puerto Real. In standing to the southward the north end of Medina should not be opened southward of the south end of Puerto Real.

North Channel.—Vessels entering Cadiz harbour by the North channel, or between the Galera shoal and Santa Catalina castle, should steer with Puerto Real church steeple in line with the southern hummock of Marrucco hill, S.E. ⅞ S., until St. Domingo steeple in Cadiz is well open eastward of St. Felipe point, when a vessel will be within the shoals. If turning in, do not open any part of Marrucco hill north or south of Puerto Real.

Anchorage off the City.—The best for vessels of moderate size, is with the Barracks (in ruins) on the isle of Leon, touching or on with Matagorda fort, and the dome of the Cathedral twice or thrice its apparent breadth open east or west of St. Domingo gates, in 5 to 6 fathoms mud. Small vessels and coasters lie nearer the city. Large vessels should anchor farther out, with the high house—the first large building north of the

---

* Staff Commander McFarlane remarks :—"That the leading marks are difficult to distinguish, and that the pilots appear to have marks of their own."

tower—at San Fernando, a little open west of Matagorda fort; and the Cathedral open eastward of St. Domingo gates.

Vessels proceeding up the harbour after having opened St. Domingo gates of St. Felipe point, should steer for Puntales castle, keeping the high tower of San Fernando open westward of Matagorda fort, and when abreast St. José church, a remarkable solitary palm tree will be seen on the summit of Martyrs hill—the first rising land eastward of Gorda tower, with two magazines on it a short distance apart—which, just touching the south gable end of a large white building at the water's edge near Santibañez mills lead clear of all the shoal water until abreast of fort Luis.   The anchorage between Puntales and the entrance to the Carraca channel is excellent, and requires no other guide than the chart and lead.

The COAST from Cadiz trends in a southerly direction for 25 miles to cape Trafalgar, and as between there are several dangerous rocky shoals having from $1\frac{1}{2}$ to $3\frac{1}{4}$ fathoms water on them, and lying from 2 to 3 miles from the shore, vessels of heavy draught should not stand nearer than about 4 miles, or into less than 15 fathoms water, during fine weather, and 6 or 7 miles when there is any sea or unsettled weather.   In rounding the dangers surrounding the north-west end of Cadiz, a vessel should not steer to the southward until the town of Rota bears eastward of N. by E., so as to avoid the $3\frac{1}{4}$ fathom patch on the tail of the bank S.W. $1\frac{1}{4}$ miles from the lighthouse.

Channels inside the several dangers between Cadiz and cape Trafalgar are used by coasters and even larger Spanish vessels, but none than those locally acquainted should go inside the shoals.   Should however, the mariner from any particular motive do so, the vessel's position should be constantly checked, the lead kept going, and the tide considered.   The flood runs strong to the northward, and the ebb to the southward.

Leon bank is about $2\frac{1}{2}$ miles southward of San Sebastian lighthouse, and its western edge $2\frac{1}{4}$ miles from fort San Fernando.   The shallow part of the bank, over a space of about three-quarters of a mile, has from $2\frac{3}{4}$ to $3\frac{1}{4}$ fathoms water on it, and there are 11 fathoms at about half a mile outside it.   The marks for it are Xeres bluff a little open northward of St. José church having three towers, and Torre Vista at Chiclana in line with Gorda tower.

Gorda tower, named also the Tower of Hercules, is round, with a battery at its base, and stands on a small sand-hill about $5\frac{1}{2}$ miles southward of the lighthouse.   Care must be taken not to mistake it in thick weather for the lighthouse, as the coast here is everywhere low.

Martyrs bank lies southward of the Leon bank, fronting the shore and parallel to it, between the Torre Gorda and the south end of the isle of Leon, and about 2¼ miles distant from the coast. It is 3½ miles in length, and has from 3¼ to 4¾ fathoms water on it.

Sancti Petri river, which separates the isle of Leon from the mainland will only admit vessels of light draught, as at its mouth the depth is only about 3 feet at low water. At the entrance is the islet of Sancti Petri, having a fort and square tower on it, surrounded by rocks and sand-banks, over which the sea breaks heavily when there is any swell; the islet is 5½ miles southward of Gorda tower.

Bermeja tower is a round tower 1½ miles eastward of Sancti Petri islet; it stands near the beach, at the east end of a portion of coast of reddish colour, level on the top and steep towards the sea, a little higher than the land westward of it, and covered with fir trees, being part of the wood of Barrosa. A little north of this tower, in the middle of the trees, will be seen a white house named Coto, and near it a remarkable tree higher than those in the neighbourhood. At 1½ miles southward of the tower of Bermeja, is a large white building named Barrosa.

HASTE AFUERA SHOAL.—In a W.S.W. direction from fort Sancti Petri is the north end of a narrow rocky bank, which runs to the southward for 3 miles, parallel to the coast and at the distance of about 3¼ miles from it. The general depths on the bank are from 3¾ to 5 fathoms but near its north end is a shallow patch with only 1½ fathoms water over it, called the Haste Afuera shoal, which lies S.W. by W. nearly, distant $1\frac{8}{10}$ miles from fort Sancti Petri, and N.W. by N. 6 miles from cape Roche.

At nine-tenths of a mile southward of the Haste Afuera is another shoal with 3½ fathoms on it, named Mogote. There are 12 fathoms water at about half a mile outside the bank, and as the swell rolls heavily over it, and the sea occasionally breaks, vessels should give it a wide berth.

CAPE ROCHE, at about 5½ miles southward of Bermeja tower, is somewhat low, steep, of a red colour, and has a square tower on it. From the tower of Bermeja the land gradually rises to the height of the cape, but the shore all along is a flat beach to 1¼ miles north of it, whence commence the cliffs Castillejos. At nearly 2¼ miles north of the cape is the tower of Puerco, and at half a mile to the N.E. of it is a little hill. On the east side of the cape, the little river of the same name runs into the sea.

MARRAJOS SHOAL.—This is a rocky shoal, 1¾ miles in length in a N.N.W. and S.S.E. direction, over the greater part of which there are only 2¼ fathoms water. From its north end Puerca tower bears E. ½ N., distant 2 miles, and cape Roche S.E. $3\frac{2}{10}$ miles; and from the depth of $2\frac{1}{4}$ fathoms at its south end, cape Roche bears S.E. by E. $\frac{1}{4}$ E., 2 miles nearly. The sea generally breaks over it. In passing between this shoal and the land, the town of Conil should be shut in with cape Roche. There are a few scattered patches with $3\frac{3}{4}$ to $4\frac{3}{4}$ fathoms on them, northward of the Marrajos and between the bank south of the Mogote shoal and the land.

CAPE ROCHE SHOAL is $1\frac{1}{2}$ miles in length N.W. by N. and S.E. by S. immediately off the pitch of the cape, which bears E. $\frac{3}{4}$ N. distant one mile from the shoalest part. The shoal has from $2\frac{3}{4}$ to $4\frac{3}{4}$ fathoms water on it, and 6 fathoms between it and the cape.

CONIL.—This town, with about 7,000 inhabitants, stands on rising ground $2\frac{3}{4}$ miles south-east of cape Roche; its church steeple is conspicuous, and east of it on the summit of a hill are several windmills, and on its south is the little river of the same name, which admits small craft at high water, but they lie dry when the tide is out. Thence the coast trends southward for $6\frac{1}{4}$ miles for cape Trafalgar; between are the towers of Castilobo and Blanca, the former square and in ruins, the latter round and white. The shore all along is a flat beach backed a little inland by hills, varying from about 300 to 650 feet high.

CONIL SHOALS.—Between Conil and cape Trafalgar, at about $1\frac{3}{4}$ miles from the shore, are two rocky shoals, called the Little and Great Conil, on which the water breaks when there is any sea. They lie parallel to the coast, with irregular depths on them of from $1\frac{1}{2}$ to $4\frac{3}{4}$ fathoms, and the two together extend over $2\frac{1}{4}$ miles. The Little Conil on the north is separated from the Great Conil by a passage a quarter of a mile wide, with 9 fathoms water. From the north extreme of these shoals the tower of Atalaya de Conil bears N.E. distant 2 miles, and Castilobo tower E. $\frac{1}{2}$ S. $1\frac{8}{10}$ miles; from the south extreme Blanca tower E. by N. $\frac{3}{4}$ N. $1\frac{3}{4}$ miles, and cape Trafalgar lighthouse S.E. $\frac{3}{4}$ S. $3\frac{3}{4}$ miles.

CAPE TRAFALGAR is a low steep sandy point having a tower and lighthouse on it, and being separated from the high land to the north-east by a low sandy plain, appears at a short distance from the north-west or south-east like an island. High table-land, divided in two, rises abruptly to the eastward of the cape at a short distance from it, and extends to the hills of Patria, which reach an altitude of about 625 feet at $3\frac{1}{2}$ miles eastward of Conil. This table-land extending north-east and south-west bears the name of the Altos de Meca, which in connexion with a white round tower on the western part, called the Torre de Meca, forms the most remarkable land on the Spanish coast westward of Gibraltar.

The site on which the tower stands, in whatever direction it may be seen from seaward, presents almost always the same appearance; its colour is dark, and on its northern part there are some sandy patches, which contrast well with the green hue of the surrounding land. From the tower of Meca, the table-land trends in the direction of the tower of Tajo declining gently on approaching the sea, where it terminates abruptly to a steep cliff, the whiteness of which is remarkable. The table-land formed by Altos de Meca extends also to the north for some distance, and preserves its height as far as the town of Vejer, which contains about 8,000 inhabitants, and stands 725 feet above the sea, 5½ miles N.E. by E. ¼ E. from cape Trafalgar lighthouse. This town can only be seen from Barbate bay, but the windmills are visible being on a hill a short distance south-west of the town.*

LIGHT.—The lighthouse on cape Trafalgar is conical, built of white stone with a red and yellow dome, and exhibits at 168 feet above the mean level of the sea, a *revolving* white light attaining its greatest brilliancy every *half minute*, and visible in clear weather at a distance of 19 miles. It bears N. ½ E. 24 miles from cape Spartel; N.W. ¼ W. 13 miles from cape Plata; and S. by E. ¾ E. 8¼ miles from cape Roche.

Tides.—It is high water, full and change, near Conil, 6 miles northward of cape Trafalgar, at 1h. 18m.; springs rise 12 feet, and neaps 7 feet.

The ACEYTERA is a dangerous rocky shoal, on the west side of cape Trafalgar, a mile in length, N. by W. and S. by E., having from about 3 to 20 feet water on it, and on which many vessels have been wrecked. From the depth of 4 fathoms, at its north extreme, the lighthouse on cape Trafalgar bears E. by S., distant 1¾ miles; and from the depth of 5 fathoms on its south extreme, the lighthouse bears about N.E. by E. ¼ E., 2 miles.

The south end of the Aceytera is connected with cape Trafalgar by a rocky ridge about a quarter of a mile wide, over which the general depths are from 2½ to 5 fathoms, but there are two shallow patches, one called the Requin, with 1½ fathoms water on it, at about 1¼ miles from the lighthouse; and the other the Animas, with one fathom on it, at half a mile from the lighthouse. None but small vessels, under favourable circumstances, should therefore pass between the Aceytera and the cape, as over the rocky ridge there is a race about half a mile in extent, caused by the unevenness of the ground and the effect of counter streams.

The MECA is a rocky shoal covered with a slight layer of sand, with from 2¾ to 5 fathoms water on it, which extends in a N.W. and S.E. direction nearly 1½ miles. From the north-west end in 5 fathoms, cape

* *See* Admiralty chart :—Strait of Gibraltar, No. 142, scale m = 0·78 inches.

Trafalgar lighthouse is in line with Tajo tower S.E. by E. ¾ E., distant 3¾ miles; and from the south-east end, the lighthouse is in line with a white sandy patch named Boqueron between the lighthouse and Tajo tower.

The Phare, to the south-west of the Meca is a rocky bank, on which there are 7 to 10 fathoms water. From its centre the lighthouse is in line with Meca tower, and bears E. by N., distant 4¾ miles.

In about the same direction, 14½ miles from the cape, is another shoal, called the Little Phare, of 9 fathoms, with 13 to 26 fathoms round it.

Anchorages.—From cape Trafalgar the coast trends in an easterly direction with a slight bend to the northward, forming a bay with a sandy beach, terminating in cliffs, on which, at 3 miles from the cape, is the tower of Tajo, 150 feet above the sea. On the shore, and nearly midway, there is a small white guard-house seen at some distance, and off it, at 2 to 3 cables, is a reef named the Cañaveral, which uncovers at low water, protecting the little cove of Baradero de Meca, which affords convenient landing. In this bay vessels may anchor with northerly winds, in any convenient depth, sheltered from the north-west swell.

A good berth will be found off the Baradero de Meca, in 8 or 9 fathoms, with a break or cut in the heights of Meca bearing N.E. ½ E., and the south extreme of the cliffs, on which is the tower of Tajo, about E. by S. ½ S.

Coasting vessels find shelter from easterly winds between cape Trafalgar and Castilobo tower, close to the shore, in about 6 fathoms sand, but when the wind draws northward of N.E., the former anchorage is the safer.

BARBATE BAY.—At 3 miles eastward of Tajo tower is the mouth of the river Barbate, and 1¼ miles farther on is a coast-guard house ; the shore between forms a bay about a mile deep, named Barbate. From the tower the land becomes lower, and changes to sandy ground, as the mouth of the river is neared; the shore under the cliffs of the tower is clear of danger and steep-to, but from a little beyond it to the mouth of the river, reefs extend off about a third of a mile; and at three-quarters of a mile off the coast-guard house, in the eastern part of the bay, is the Sara shoal with 3¾ fathoms water on it.

The river Barbate runs into the sea between low sandy banks, after winding through a deep valley ; there are 3½ feet over the bar at low water but at high tide the banks at the entrance are overflowed, when its mouth appears wide. The village of the same name with about 250 inhabitants stands on the right bank, about three-quarters of a mile from the entrance. A large extent of white sandy ground, between the cultivated land east of the Tajo tower and the river known as the Picacho de Barbate, is conspicuous, and serves as a mark for the Cabezos shoals.

Anchorage.—Coasting vessels which frequent Barbate, anchor in the river on its western shore, off the houses, in $3\frac{1}{2}$ to $4\frac{1}{2}$ fathoms water; but those unable to cross the bar, anchor in any convenient depth, southward of it, where they ride safely with northerly winds, but this anchorage must be left should the wind blow from seaward.

Between the cape and Tajo tower the soundings are very irregular, there being rocky patches of 9 and 10 fathoms, with 12 and 20 fathoms, sand, between, at $1\frac{1}{2}$ and 3 miles off shore.

The COAST.—From the mouth of the river Barbate, the shore is low and sandy, and trends to the south-east for 6 miles to cape Plata. At $2\frac{1}{4}$ miles beyond the coast-guard house before mentioned, is the tower and village of Sara or Zahara, with about 370 inhabitants. Between is mount Retin, a hill of an irregular form with several peaks, which is seen at some distance, and then appears like a bold headland, having on its slope two large ancient towers. On the east side of the hill the land is level, and a small stream runs into the sea between its foot and the village of Sara; this stream flows from the laguna de la Janda, an extensive sheet of water lying nearly parallel with the coast at about 3 miles from it.

Cape Plata, is of a moderate height, but appears low from the near vicinity of the sierra de Plata from which it descends. A reef extends off about 2 cables from the point, some of the rocks of which are high and remarkable.

Point Camarinal, at $4\frac{3}{4}$ miles southward of Sara, is low, salient, and surrounded by rocks, for some distance off; it is backed as is also the point north of it, by the sierre de Plata, the north-western hills of which rise from the level land of Sara. On one of the heights over Camarinal point, at some elevation above the sea, there is a circular tower; on the point north of it there is a square tower (Gracia tower) not so high as the former and at the foot of it a small white coast-guard house; whilst at a little distance from the sea and to the north of the latter tower there are several white buildings. Between the two towers is a sandy beach.

The steep ridge of the sierra rises to a height of 1,567 feet at a distance of 3 miles E.N.E. from the point, and is named the Pope's chair, or Silla del Papa.

From Camarinal point on the west, an extensive white sandy patch extends across the foot of the mountain to Bolonia bay, and is seen at some distance from seaward. From this mountain, the land eastward is of considerable elevation all along the north shore of the strait.

Anchorage.—The coast between Sara and cape Plata is named the bay of Sara; the bottom is sandy, but not clear of rocks, and here vessels will find shelter from strong easterly winds. The best anchorage is westward of Camarinal point, at a short distance from the shore; but the mariner must be prepared for the heavy squalls which come over the land. In front of the sandy beach off the point north of Camarinal there are rocky patches close to the shore, outside of which the holding ground is indifferent. Coasters also find shelter off a small beach between Camarinal point and cape Plata. Although this is a convenient stopping place when easterly winds prevent vessels getting through the strait of Gibraltar, it must not be forgotten that it is exposed from the south-west, and partly from the north-west, and is therefore a dangerous anchorage in any but easterly winds.

BOLONIA BAY, on the east side of Camarinal, is about three-quarters of a mile deep; it has a sandy beach, and at its head is a coastguard station, and the ruins of the ancient town of Bolonia, from which it derives its name. The bay is backed at from one to 2 miles on the north by the sierra de Plata.

MOUNT SAN BARTOLOMEO.—From the head of Bolonia bay the coast trends to the south-east for 3½ miles to Paloma point, and is of moderate elevation, and bordered by a rocky bank which extends off about a third of a. mile. The point is the termination of mount San Bartolomeo, which at about 1½ miles inland rises to the height of 1,542 feet above the sea, and is conspicuous from its peculiar jagged summit, and by a long patch of yellow sand with no vegetation on it, which commences near Paloma point, rises to about half way up the mountain, and terminates near the middle of Val de Vaqueros bay. It is known by the name of the Picacho de San Bartolomeo, and is the most remarkable feature anywhere seen on the north shore of the strait. A small white guard house will assist in distinguishing the look-out tower from the houses north of it.

VAL de VAQUEROS BAY.—Between Paloma point and Peña point east of it, the shore recedes northward and forms Val de Vaqueros bay, which is about half a mile deep. Coasters seek shelter here from north-east winds, anchoring near the beach at the head of the bay, where the holding ground is good. Two small rivulets, on the banks of which are some houses, fall into the bay, that nearest Paloma point being the larger, and named Puerco.

SIERRA de ENMEDIO.—To the eastward of mount San Bartolomeo is another similar mountain, 2,191 feet high, not so broken, but more isolated, which bears the name of Sierra de Enmedio. It is not so remarkable as San Bartolomeo, and from the westward some small peaks appear a little above the main body of the mountain, not very conspicuous, but known to the local navigators.   The Sierra de Enmedio, named also Peña, slopes in declivities to the south, and forms Peña point, which terminates abruptly in a remarkable conical, and apparently isolated rock on which is a tower reached by an ascent of 84 steps.   Seen from the westward, the tower and rock appear to be detached, and stand out in bold relief from the high land.

SIERRA de NUESTRA SEÑORA de la LUZ.—To the north-east of the Sierra de Enmedio, is the lofty chain of mountains named Nuestra Señora de la Luz, which decline gradually to the coast and terminate at Tarifa.   The summit of this range is moderately even, and presents nothing remarkable, with the exception of two peaks near each other, which are 7 miles inland, 2,431 feet above the sea level, and named by the local mariners las Tetas (the Teats).

LANCES de TARIFA.—From Peña point to Tarifa, the distance is 4 miles, and the shore all along a sandy beach named Lances de Tarifa. The little rivers Salado and Vega here run into the sea; and several buildings are scattered along the base of the Enmedio; and in the plains of Salado, a coast-guard house stands on the shore about half a mile south-east of Peña tower, and a bridge crosses the Salado at a short distance from its mouth.

DANGERS.—The **CABEZOS** is the general name of a cluster of dangerous rocky patches lying westward of Tarifa, and nearly midway between it and point Camarinal.   There is as little as one foot of water on these dangers, over which the sea breaks with great violence during strong westerly winds; but in calms or easterly winds, a ripple with dangerous eddies is all that is seen.   These shoals are separated from each other by deep water; they are steep-to, and consequently the lead gives no warning, hence a wide berth should be given them.

Placer Nuevo or **Luyando bank,** the southernmost of these dangers, is a bed of conical rocks about three-quarters of a mile in length in an east and west direction, with 9 fathoms on it.   From its west end Poloma towers bears N.N.E., distant about 3 miles; and Tarifa lighthouse E.S.E. 5¾ miles.   There are from 10 to 18 fathoms water near it.   A heavy swell rolls over the bank during strong westerly winds, and a berth should be given to it.

Piedra Verde or eastern shoal, the principal danger, having only one foot on it at low water, is separated from Placer Nuevo by a narrow channel having 20 fathoms water. It lies 2¾ miles from Paloma point with Tarifa lighthouse bearing S.E. by E. ¼ E., distant 5 miles; Peña tower N.E. by E. ¾ E. 3½ miles ; and point Camarinal N.W. by N. ¼ N.

Placer del Oeste or **del Puerco** is another rocky bank, and the most western of these dangers ; it lies about 1¼ miles in a N. by W. ¼ W. from Placer Nuevo, with 9 fathoms water on it. Close to on its west side there are 18 to 24 fathoms.

Bajeta is a dangerous rocky patch with only 5 feet water on it in the channel between the Cabezos and Peña point. It lies 1¼ miles from the land, with Peña tower bearing N.E. by E., and Tarifa lighthouse S.E. ¾ S. 4 miles. In south-west gales the sea breaks heavily on this shoal, and at times there are strong eddies and ripples over it. There are irregular soundings from 6 to 3¼ fathoms between it and the shore ; and 10 to 20 fathoms between it and the Cabezos.

The Anchorage westward of Tarifa, off the Lances de Tarifa, is good and sheltered from easterly winds. It is, however, exposed to heavy squalls from the north-east, but as the holding ground is good, and the sea smooth, vessels ride easily. Landing on the beach is easy. Vessels should leave the anchorage when the easterly wind subsides.

Directions.—Coasters and small steam vessels in order to avoid the sea and the strength of the easterly winds, when bound westward, and also in working to the eastward, usually pass between the Bajeta and Peña point. Nevertheless the channel between the Bajeta and Cabezos is preferable, being 1½ miles wide with deep water, regular soundings, and current direct. The leading mark through in mid-channel is Tarifa lighthouse in line with the el Hacho of Cueta ; when Peña tower is in line with the two peaks of Nuestra Señora de la Luz, a vessel will be between the Cabezos and Bajeta. To avoid the Bajeta, the sierra Bullones or Apes hill, on the African coast, should not be shut in with the south extreme of Tarifa peninsula.

To pass southward of the Cabezos, keep the Picacho de Barbate (the white sandy ground east of Tajo cliffs, page 310) well open of cape Plata, until the peaks of Nuestra Señora de la Luz, are open eastward of Peña tower ; or do not bring cape Plata to bear westward of North, until Tarifa lighthouse bears E. by S. ¼ S., when the lighthouse may be steered for.

TARIFA, formerly an islet, is now a small peninsula, being connected to the main by an artificial causeway. It is level and moderately high, and surrounded by steep cliffs with deep water close to, except on the southern side, where a reef extends off to the distance of a cable, with 12 feet water on it ; half a cable from the shore, W. ¼ N. from the light-tower one of the rocks uncovers at low tide; and at a cable from the shore in the same direction the depth is only two fathoms. The lighthouse, some small batteries, barracks, magazines, and other buildings are erected on the peninsula, and on its north-west side there is a small artificial harbour for fishing craft.

The town and arsenal of Tarifa, ancient *Julia Joza*, with about 6,000 inhabitants, stands on the shore a short half mile N.W. of the peninsula; it was built by the Moors, and is surrounded by a wall flanked by several towers, the principal of which is named the castle of Guzman, at its south-west angle. Santa Catalina, a fort on rising ground on the causeway or neck of the peninsula, is surrounded by sand, and appears isolated.*

Camorro point, about three-quarters of a mile north-east of the peninsula, is high, steep, and of a whitish colour; seen from the westward it is readily distinguished. There are several rocks on the shore between the point and the town, with 6 to 9 feet water between them, where small craft load and unload.

LIGHT.—The white circular light-tower, standing at the south end of the peninsula of Tarifa, exhibits at 130 feet above high water, a *fixed red* light, visible in clear weather at a distance of 17 miles. This light is shaded eastward to about half a mile southward of the Pearl rock.

CAUTION.—Vessels passing within gunshot of any fortress on this part of the coast should show their colours, and by night a light, which if neglected, expose them to be fired at.

Tides.—It is high water, full and change, at Tarifa, at 1h. 46m. springs rise 6½ feet, and neaps 3½ feet. The flood runs westward, and the ebb eastward.

The Anchorage, on the east side of Tarifa, between the peninsula and Camorro point, is near the beach, for the bottom is shelving, and there are 5 fathoms water at 2 cables from the shore. Coasters, and particularly lateen vessels that can readily make sail, are the only kind of vessels that can frequent the anchorage with confidence, as Camorro point is difficult to clear should the wind change to the southward. Large vessels will find temporary anchorage in 8 to 10 fathoms, sand and gravel; but should the wind haul to the south-west, it generally blows hard, and the anchorage becoming exposed, a vessel should leave.

The COAST from Camorro point trends eastward for 9¼ miles to Carnero point at the entrance to Gibraltar bay. It is generally composed of cliffs separated by sandy beaches, with ledges of rocks which do not extend

---

* A semaphore has been erected, by the Spanish Government, on the western turret of the Castle of Guzman.

far off, and backed by gentle undulating hills, upon which are numerous farms and cultivated ground.   Behind those hills the land becomes mountainous, reaching 1,774 feet above the sea, and forming part of the range of Nuestra Señora de la Luz.   Gualdamesi point, at 4½ miles from Tarifa light-tower, is a dark bold cliff with a tower on it, and on its north-east side is a valley through which a small stream runs into the sea.

Tolmo bay, with a white sandy beach scattered with rocks, is 2 miles eastward of Gualdamesi point; Acebuche point, the east extreme of the bay is low, and although projecting but little can be distinctly made out.   A short distance outside are several rocks, some of which are nearly awash at low water.   A castle stands upon a hillock near the head of the bay about which are some country houses, and two guard houses near the beach towards Gualdamesi point.   The bay affords good anchorage for small craft with off shore winds.

Frayle point, a mile beyond Acebuche is bold, and the termination of high land which rapidly declines from an elevation of nearly 1,000 feet; a white house stands above the cliff, and a square tower upon the summit a little west of it.   Off the point are several rocks, one of which from its size and shape gives the name of Frayle or Friar to the point.   Thence to Carnero point is a succession of rock and sand for above 1½ miles.   A small bight with a beach named Cala Arena lies to the eastward of Frayle; off its western point which separates it from a similar bay, are some rocky heads which project out for some distance.   Cala Arena offers shelter to coasters from north-west winds, and will be recognised by a house near a stream upon the east side; there is also another surrounded by wood upon the slope of the hill, half a mile to the northward.

CARNERO POINT.—This is a broad projection (sloping from the mountains within) towards the south-east, and forms the western entrance to the bay of Gibraltar; the shore is bordered by rocks, but a bight between it and point Secreta, half a mile to the westward, is resorted to by fishing boats.   Off the southern extremity of the point is Cabrita rock always above water, and conspicuous above the several others which appear when the tide is out.   Upon the summit north-west of Carnero point is a square tower, and a lighthouse upon the point below it.

LIGHT.—The lighthouse on Carnero point is painted yellow, and exhibits at an elevation of 135 feet above high water a fixed *green* light, visible in clear weather from a distance of 11 miles, between the bearings of S. ¾ W. round by West and North to N.E. by E. ½. E.

Palomas island.—Nearly mid-way between Frayle and Carnero points, and about 2 cables from the shore, is Palomas or Pigeon island.   It is small and low, and nearly connected with the shore by a rocky ledge over which is a passage for boats, there are also several rocks extending about 1¼ cables off the west end of the island.

PEARL ROCK, lying a long half mile south of Palomas island, is a dangerous rocky shoal in the way of vessels bound to and from Gibraltar bay. It lies with the middle of San Roque in line with the inner part of Cabrita rock bearing N.E. by N.; Gualdamesi tower in line with the outer rock off point Acebuche W. ¼ N.; and Tarifa lighthouse W. ¼ S. This danger is formed of pinnacle rocks, having 8 feet only on the shoalest part; the passage between it and Palomas island is over uneven ground, the depths varying from 5 to 10 fathoms.* To pass between the Pearl rock and the shore, keep Tarifa lighthouse in line with the outer rocks off Frayle point, and with the Gualdamesi tower shut in, but unless it is absolutely necessary, none but small vessels should use this passage.

CAUTION.—In the neighbourhood of the Pearl rock and Carnero point, the tides and eddies run nearly always either north-west or north-east, and consequently will carry a vessel towards them, rendering this part of the coast the most dangerous in the strait, and resulting in many serious accidents to shipping. There are 6 fathoms 1½ cables south-east of the rock, and above 100 fathoms three-quarters of a mile outside side of it; the stream at times runs past it at the rate of 3 knots.

Clearing marks.—To pass to the southward of the Pearl rock, keep Black hill (a conspicuous peak rising over the west side of Tolmo bay, with a white house nearly under it) in line with point Acebuche bearing W.N.W.; and to pass to the eastward, bring San Garcia tower (upon the point between Carnero point and Algeciras) in line with Carnero point bearing N. ½ E.

Directions at Night.—To mark the position of the Pearl rock at night, a ray of *red* light is shown from the lighthouse on Europa point, which is seen between the bearings of N.E. by E. ¾ E. and E. ¼ N., and extends half a mile southward of the rock. Therefore, in approaching the Pearl at night from the westward, a vessel should open Europa *white* light, until Verde islet light, Algeciras, is seen, when she may steer to the northward into Gibraltar bay. A vessel from Gibraltar bay, or the eastward, should open the *white* light of Europa before shutting in Verde island light.

The BAY of GIBRALTAR is formed between Carnero point on the west, and Europa point on the east, distant from each other 4 miles.

---

* *See* Admiralty plan : — Gibraltar bay, No. 1,448 ; scale m = 2·9 inches. Two electric cables are laid inside the Pearl rock; vessels should avoid anchoring there if possible.

Between the points the coast recedes about 5 miles, forming a large bay open to the south, in which, midway between the points, the depth is about 235 fathoms, and nearer Europa point 278 fathoms, with a lane of deep water running in for three miles, when the bank on either side and at the head of the bay rises although the water continues deep to the anchorages around the bay.   The land on the west side of the bay is high, being the lofty range of mountains which follow the direction of the coast from Tarifa, rising over Carnero point about 1,000 feet above the sea, continuing northward and gradually decreasing in elevation towards the head of the bay.

The town of San Roque with a conspicuous church stands on a hill 442 feet high, about 2 miles inland ; and to the south-east of it is mount Carbonera with a tower on it, 971 feet high ; thence the land declines to the Neutral ground, at the termination of which rises the Rock of Gibraltar.

LIGHTS.—Europa point light.—At the south-east extreme of Europa point on a cliff 98 feet high, is the gray coloured tower of Victoria, which exhibits at 156 feet above high water, a *fixed* white light, visible in clear weather at a distance of 15 miles.

From the same tower a ray of *red* light is shown in the direction of the Pearl rock over an arc of 23°, and seen from the westward between the bearing of N.E. by E. ¾ E. and E. ¼ N.

New Mole light.—On a stone column near the extremity of Gibraltar New mole is a *fixed red* light, elevated 28 feet above the level of the sea, and visible in clear weather at a distance of 8 miles.

Ragged Staff light.—On a lamp-post at the Ragged Staff landing place is a *fixed green* light.

Verde Islet light.—At Verde islet near Algeciras a *fixed white* light is exhibited at an elevation of 62 feet above the sea, visible in clear weather, between Europa and Carnero points, at a distance of 9 miles.

Getares Bay.—Carnero point is skirted by rocks, and it should not be approached too close on account of the currents.   At 1½ miles northward of Carnero point is San Garcia point, with a tower over it, and skirted by rocks; the shore between recedes westward and forms Getares bay, which is sandy, nearly three-quarters of a mile deep, and affords shelter from north-west and south-west winds, in 9 or 10 fathoms water sand.   The bay is exposed to north-east and south-east winds, which send in a heavy sea, and vessels should therefore leave directly there is any sign of an easterly wind.   Two small streams here run into the sea ; there is a guardhouse and ruined fort at the foot of the slopes.

At a short half mile northward of San Garcia point is Rodeo point, surrounded by rocks which extend off about a cable; and between is a small bay with a sandy beach, the entrance to which is nearly choked by a reef of rocks from point Rodeo.

Verde Islet.—At a short half mile northward of Rodeo point, and about 4 cables from the shore, is Verde islet. It is about 30 feet high, barren and rocky, partly occupied by fortifications for the defence of Algeciras road, and surrounded at some distance by rocks. These rocks extending a third of a mile from it N.N.E. and S.S.W., are partly un-covered, and afford some shelter to small craft, which anchor north-west of the islet. The passage inside the islet carries from a half to 1¼ fathoms water, over rocky bottom, and can only be used by those acquainted with it. Between Carnero point and Verde islet, the shore may be approached to the distance of a short half mile, in from 10 to 16 fathoms water.

ALGECIRAS.—At half a mile north-westward of Verde islet is the mole of Algeciras projecting from the south-east angle of the town, and from the north point of the entrance to the river Miel, which coasters enter at high water. The town of Algeciras, the Al-Djezirah of the Arabs, stands on a hill which rises gradually from the shore to a height of 220 feet, and contains a population of about 12,000. The river Miel on its south, separates it from a small suburb named Villavieja, with which it communicates by means of two bridges. It is an open town, and on its north side, on a steep incline of the sea shore, is the fort of Santiago, which with the fortifications of Verde islet protects the roadstead. There is a steam ferry between Algeciras and Gibraltar.*

Galera Rock, lying one cable E. ¼ N. from the extremity of the mole is level with the surface of the water, nearly circular, and about 20 yards in diameter. At less than a cable N.N.E. of the Galera there is another rock, with 1¾ fathoms water on it, and in the channel between there are 2¼ to 3¼ fathoms. A rock with about 2¼ fathoms on it, lies 4 cables northward of Verde islet, with Galera rock bearing West nearly, and the flagstaff of Verde islet S. by W. ⅓ W., and in line with the highest peak of the sierra Bullones. There are 5½ and 6 fathoms round it. Besides the above dangers, rocks extend along the shore of the town and fort.

At about three-quarters of a mile N.N.E. ¼ E. from fort Santiago, and on a hill, is the tower of Almirante, round, white, and conspicuous; from the cliffs at the foot of the tower a reef extends off, and at 4 cables from

---

* *See* Admiralty plan of Algeciras roads on sheet No. 1448.

the tower the depth is 3¼ fathoms. Inland, W. by N. ¼ N., three-quarters of a mile from the tower, and on the slope of another hill, is a square tower, called Pólvora, 356 feet above the sea, in ruins, and surrounded by a wall. With these towers in line and near the shore, the bottom is rock and gravel, so that vessels should avoid anchoring with those marks on, or in the vicinity.

The Anchorage off Algeciras is sheltered from westerly winds, and has good holding ground. Vessels of moderate size will find a good anchorage at 6 cables from the shore in 9 fathoms water, mud bottom, with Verde islet in line with San Garcia tower; fort Santiago bearing West; and the highest belfry of the town W.S.W. It is desirable to anchor northward rather than southward of this position, as the depths are there regular and not greater than 12 fathoms, mud; but vessels should not go north of the parallel of the cemetery (a large white wall extending north and south, on level ground, not far from the shore), which is the most remarkable building next north of the fort. Large vessels anchor in 16 or 17 fathoms, muddy bottom, at a mile from the shore, with fort Santiago West, and the light tower on Verde islet S.W. Attention should be paid to keep a clear anchor. Small craft anchor between the islet and the river Miel.

The roadstead of Algeciras is exposed to south-easterly winds, which send in much sea, and vessels should leave when there is any sign of these winds blowing, and proceed either to Mayorga or Gibraltar.

TIDES.—It is high water, full and change, at Algeciras, at 1 h. 49 m. ; springs rise about 4 feet, and neaps 2¼ feet ; the floods sets to the northward, the ebb to the south.

Palmones River.—Between Almirante tower and Rinconcillo point, at half a mile northward of it, the shore is skirted by reefs. From the point the shore is low and sandy, and continues so round the circuit of the bay to Gibraltar, excepting the two points of Mirador and Mala. The river Palmones, the largest of those which fall into Gibraltar Bay, has its mouth 1¾ miles N.E. by E. from Rinconcillo point, and is so obstructed by sandbanks, that large boats only can enter. The Guadarranque, a small stream, runs into the bay about three-quarters of a mile eastward of the mouth of the Palmones. The tower of Entre Rios is square, and stands on a hill between the mouths of the two rivers.

Anchorage.—Between Rinconcillo point and Mirador point there is good anchorage, with winds from N.E. round north to S.W., at about half a mile from the shore, in from 10 to 18 fathoms water, mud   Near the latter point the water is deep. A south-east wind, however, sends in a sea, hence a vessel should leave for the anchorage at Gibraltar directly the wind sets in from that quarter.

Mayorga.—At about three-quarters of a mile eastward of the mouth of the Guadarranque is Mirador point; the coast between the point and a square tower a little west of it is closely skirted by rocks, with 10 fathoms water, at two cables from the shore. Between Mirador point and Mala point 1¼ miles farther on, the coast forms a small bay, and near the shore northward of the latter point are the villages of Campamento and Mayorga, the former with 450 and the latter with 550 inhabitants. Mala point is low and surrounded by rocks, a large part of which are dry at low water, they extend off about 2 cables, and are steep-to.

The Anchorage off Mayorga is considered the best in Gibraltar bay with easterly and south-east winds, being free from the squalls over Gibraltar. It is much frequented by Spanish vessels seeking shelter from levanters, whilst strangers anchor at Gibraltar. The water is, however, deep, there being 16 to 18 fathoms at 3 cables off shore, rapidly deepening outside; sand and muddy bottom.

Water and Supplies.—Both at Mayorga and Campamento, water and vegetables can be procured.

Neutral Ground.—At Mala point commences the level plain of ground, which surrounds the base of the Carbonera hills, elevated 971 feet, it continues southward, and forms the isthmus which connects the rock of Gibraltar with Spain. The plain is about 1¾ miles north and south, but that part named the Neutral ground, from the remains of the Spanish lines to the foot of the rock, is nearly three-quarters of a mile in length, and half a mile across. It is low, being in places not more than 2 feet above the level of high water, whilst in other places there are small downs 5 or 6 feet high, the sand accumulated by the sea reaches a higher level on the eastern than on the western side. To appearance it is a mere strip of sand, but it has been ascertained that the sand is only a superficial covering of a prolongation of the solid rock itself. It is green near the rock; but as it approaches Spain it becomes sandy.

All that is to be seen on it are the remains of the Spanish lines of fortifications of 1732, the ruins of the two castles of San Felipe and Santa Barbara forming the terminations. Near the rock are some gardens, the cemetery and racecourse, and on the western shore some temporary houses, and a wooden pier for watering.

GIBRALTAR.—This singular rocky mass, known generally by English seamen as the rock of Gibraltar, is the *Mons Calpe* of the Phœnicians and Romans, the Gibel Tarik of the Arabs, and the Monte de

Gibraltar of the Spaniards. It is oblong in shape, rising abruptly like a wall at the termination of the Neutral ground, to the height of 1,337 feet above the sea, extends 2¼ miles south, and is scarcely three-quarters of a mile in breadth. It is formed of compact rock covered with a vegetable soil, and on its north and east sides it is quite precipitous, being accessible only to the monkeys which inhabit its rocky recesses; whilst on the west it falls in rugged slopes, on which there is some cultivation. It presents to the south, several successive short terraces, which descend one under the other, until terminating in Europa point (ancient Leon), which forms the southern extreme of the rock, and the east extreme of Gibraltar bay.*

For many years it was the object of various contests between the Moors and Spaniards, until 1462, when it was ceded to the latter. In 1704 it was taken by the British, and with one memorable exception has since continued an undisputed possession. The town stands on the western side of the rock and shelves down to the bay; it contains the governor's house, cathedral, and other churches, exchange, library, and in 1878 contained 18,014 inhabitants, exclusive of military. The naval and victualling departments are established south of the town, and the New mole, which extends from the shore more than two cables in a N.N.W. direction, forms an admirable breakwater to an area sufficiently large to afford shelter from south-westerly winds to ships of any draught. The Old mole originally constructed by the Spaniards in 1618, extends from the north end of the town in a north-western direction, for 1,200 feet; it shelters the mole used by the small trading vessels, the depths admitting those only drawing from 8 to 10 feet of water. There is also a small mole in Rosia bay, near the victualling stores.

The formidable batteries, the vast galleries in the rock (one above the other nearly to its summit), and the strength of the military works, altogether renders Gibraltar one of the strongest fortresses in the world. The signal station is on the hill, 1,294 feet high, and nearly midway between O'Hara tower on the south, and Rock Gun fort; the highest part of the ridge, 1,396 feet, is over the harbour within the New mole.

Gibraltar is a free port and the trade is considerable, exporting wool, lead, copper, &c., and importing cottons, woollens, hardware, coals, iron, silk, tea, &c. In 1871 the total tonnage of vessels which frequented the port was 2,795,173 British, and 822,124 foreign, exclusive of the coasting trade; and the value of British imports was 830,120*l.*, and of exports 59,672*l.*

* See Admiralty plans :—Gibraltar, No. 144, scale, ＝ 5·9 inches; and Gibraltar New Mole, No. 524, scale, ＝ 52·0 inches.

Supplies.—Gibraltar is well supplied with meat and vegetables from Spain and Morocco, and there are water-tanks or reservoirs near the victualling establishment in Rosia bay. Shipping are supplied by means of a hose if within the harbour, and from a floating tank if at the anchorage outside.

Telegraph.—A submarine cable is laid from Gibraltar to Malta, a distance of about 1,050 miles; also to the river Guadiana and Lisbon, and thence to Falmouth.

Anchorages.—Off the Old mole are moored several coal depôts in from $3\frac{1}{2}$ to 11 fathoms of water; the P. and O. Company's depôt carries a red light, which bears N.W. nearly a mile from the Old mole; and N. $\frac{1}{4}$ W. $1\frac{3}{4}$ miles from the New mole; it is necessary to be cautious in approaching these depôts at night. Vessels may anchor off the Neutral ground in any convenient place, but it is necessary to have the Devil's tower (which stands at the foot of the rock, and at the north-east end) open of the rock, to avoid the heavy squalls and eddies from the rock.

As south-west winds blow directly into the bay, and send in much sea, vessels during winter on an approaching gale from that quarter should either leave the anchorage for Palmones, or immediately let go a spare anchor, and otherwise make the vessel snug, as in consequence of neglecting this timely precaution, the shore of the Neutral ground has often been strewed with wrecks.

The bottom between the Old mole and the Ragged staff is uneven and rocky, and as anchors are liable to drag or break, vessels should not anchor there. Moreover, during strong easterly winds, heavy squalls and eddies blow down over the rock, causing a vessel to continually swing in every direction.

There is, however, very fair temporary summer anchorage off Jumpers bastion, in 9 to 13 fathoms water, sandy bottom.

New mole.—Vessels intending to go alongside the New mole are generally boarded by an officer from the Naval Department, who gives the requisite directions for berthing. If it be necessary to proceed at once to the mole without such assistance, the red, and the white beacons at the landing place in the naval yard in line lead in. When the red beacon on the breakwater in front of North Jumpers bastion is in line with a white stripe on the wall a little north of the bastion, the off shore anchor should be let go for the outer berth; and when the white cage beacons on the mole (denoting the inner berth) come in line, the starboard anchor should be let go and the helm put hard to port, bringing the vessel's bows close to the mole, when she may be finally secured with her head out.

These marks for anchoring will not afford sufficient scope of cable for very long vessels, the anchors of which should therefore be let go before either of the marks come in line, but the line of the leading beacons in should in all cases be preserved.

Tides.—It is high water, full and change, at Gibraltar New Mole, at about 2 h. ; springs rise 3½ feet, and neaps 2½ feet.*

The stream of the flood sets in round Europa point towards Carnero point, off which it divides, one branch continuing westward, whilst the other trends northward along the western side of the bay ; and as the tide sweeps by Europa point, its inner edge branches northward along the eastern side of the bay. The water which thus runs into the bay on either side, re-unites at its head at about half flood, and causes a stream to the southward down the middle of the bay, which re-unites with the general current.

The stream of the ebb sets by Carnero point to the north-east, nearly in the direction of Mala point, and divides into two counter streams near the head of the bay ; one stream curves round the bay to the westward, the other to the eastward, and at about half ebb runs out on either side. These streams are occasionally checked by strong winds.

Directions.—A sailing vessel from the westward, with the wind from that quarter, and bound into Gibraltar bay, should give a fair berth to the Pearl rock (page 319) and Carnero point ; bearing in mind that the current has a tendency towards the latter, and squalls come down from the high land over it. But with an easterly wind and any sea Carnero point should be carefully avoided, and the southern board continued until the vessel can reach the middle of the bay on the starboard tack ; then keep in the steady wind westward of the strong squalls and eddies, which blow down over the rock, and work up to a convenient anchorage.

If from the eastward with westerly winds, a vessel should work round Europa point with the flood tide, standing but little off, and towards the point to a prudent distance, and it will be passed in two or three boards. But with an easterly wind, after having rounded the point, keep up the middle of the bay in the steady breeze beyond the reach of the squalls the demarcation of which will be seen. The edge of the bank at the Neutral ground is steep-to ; at night, the red light at the New mole will assist a vessel in anchoring.

Should the wind be fresh and from the southward of East, the squalls on the west side of the rock will be from the southward, when a vessel

---

* Strong easterly gales sometimes cause the water to rise several feet around Gibraltar. During one of these, on November 3rd, 1868, the sea rose as far as the houses in Catalan Bay, on the east side of Gibraltar.

bound for the New mole may steer for it before the squalls. If, however, the wind be northward of East, the squalls will be from the northward, a vessel should then work up in the steady breeze until near the anchorage at the Neutral ground, and then run down for the mole before the squalls, under easy sail.

Eddy winds from the rock on its east side, caused by westerly winds, are as dangerous as those on its west side produced by easterly winds, and vessels should never go within the line of a steady breeze when approaching it to round Europa point. The winds render sailing in boats and small craft to, and from the shore, particularly dangerous.

COAST OF AFRICA.—CAPE SPARTEL TO CEUTA BAY.

The COAST of AFRICA, forming the southern boundary of the strait of Gibraltar, is part of the state of Marocco (Moghrib-el-Aksa, ancient *Mauritania*), one of the largest of the Barbary states. The general surface of the country is mountainous with many rich plains and fertile valleys; at from 3 to 10 miles inland, the ranges of the former attain an elevation of from 3,000 to 6,000 feet. The country possesses many natural advantages, has a good geographical position, and a healthy and temperate climate. In 1870, the number of British vessels entered at the several ports of Marocco amounted to 617 of 108,702 tons.

The coast of Marocco from cape Spartel has a general direction of E. ¼ S. to Lanchones point, whence it turns E. by S., thence trending S.E. by E. ¼ E. to the termination of the strait at point Almina.

CAPE SPARTEL (Raz-el-Skukkar), the north-west extremity of Africa, and the south-western limit of the strait of Gibraltar, terminates in a mass of black conical-shaped rock, which, seen from the north and south, appears detached like an islet. It is commanded by high land which reaches 1,068 feet above the sea, being part of a chain extending east and west; south of the cape the land falls rapidly, forming an extensive plain, in the middle of which is mount Nipple, remarkable by its isolation and conical form. The cape is skirted by a reef which extends off about 2 cables; and foul ground extends to the south-westward. With the lighthouse between the bearings of East and E.S.E., the shore should not be approached within three-quarters of a mile. The high land over cape Spartel is conspicuous when bearing S.E., as there are two remarkable gray patches about a third of its height from the summit.*

---

* See Admiralty charts:—Strait of Gibraltar, No. 142, scale, m = 0·73 inches; Africa, sheet I., No. 1,226, scale, d = 1·5 inches; and Africa, west coast, sheet I., No. 1,227, scale, m = 0·13 inch.

Spartel Bay.—Half a mile south of the cape is a sandy bay, where small vessels find shelter from easterly wind, in 6 or 7 fathoms water, a half to three-quarters of a mile from the beach ; but heavy squalls blow off the land, and a continual swell make it difficult to land, even when not opposed by the Moors.

LIGHT.—Half a mile eastward of cape Spartel is a stone tower, which exhibits, at 312 feet about the sea, a *fixed* white light, which should be seen in clear weather at a distance of 20 miles ; from it the lighthouse on cape Trafalgar bears N. ¼ E., distant 24 miles.

JEREMIAS ANCHORAGE, about 2¼ miles southward of cape Spartel, is much resorted to by vessels prevented from entering the strait of Gibraltar by strong easterly winds. At a mile from the shore there are about 20 fathoms water, over clean sandy bottom, and good holding ground. With these winds it is preferable to keep over on the African coast rather than the Spanish, as it is free from danger, and vessels are in a better position to profit by any change in the direction or force of the wind, and for this purpose it is prudent for a sailing vessel to keep under sail.

Directions.—Approaching the strait of Gibraltar, if a levanter comes on, stand well to the southward, and work up to bring mount Nipple to bear E. ¼ N. before anchoring, that being generally the southern limit of heavy squalls. A good berth may be obtained in 24 fathoms, and at half a mile from the shore there are 7 fathoms.

H.M.S. *Vulture* in 1872 anchored at Jeremias anchorage in 14 fathoms water, with a white marabut tower (the only building in the vicinity) bearing S.E.

COAST.—North of the cape, the coast is high and of uninterrupted steep cliffs, at the base of which a little beyond the cape, are some black pinnacle rocks above water named the Needles.   About 1¼ miles N.E. of the cape is Fraylecito point, at the termination of which is a small black islet surrounded by rocks. The coast thence trends eastward for 3 miles and is less cliffy, but still high and irregular, to Judios point ; the most projecting part between being Pigeon point, remarkable and well defined when seen from east or west. Judios point is more salient and remarkable than either of the other points, and is known from seaward, rather by the white cliffs that form it than the point itself, which is only well defined from east or west. The coast between cape Spartel and Judios point is steep-to.

JUDIOS BAY.—At nearly three-quarters of a mile eastward of Judios point is a bay with a small sandy beach, named Judios bay, the only one on this part of the coast. A small stream of the same name disembogues in it, and runs down a narrow valley which separates the mountain of cape Spartel from the Mesa de Marchan—table-land of Marchan—which is contiguous to Tangier. These two heights form good points for recognizing the coast from sea, to vessels bound to Tangier, even at night, should the weather be clear. The valley through which the Judios rivulet flows presents a remarkable break, which completely separates the mountain of cape Spartel, that is uneven and irregular, from the Mesa de Marchan, which is level and not so high, being only 342 feet above the sea.

On the eastern point of the bay are the ruins of a fort, and a marabut tower stands on the slope of the western part of the mountain. To the northward of Tangier, and especially at the time of springs, and however little sea there may be, the stream of the tide is strong and causes eddies resembling breakers.

TANGIER BAY.—A white and reddish cliff commences at Judios bay, and terminates at Tangier point, distant one mile, and which seen from a distance appears like a patch in the middle of the coast. The shore is here skirted by reefs, and Tangier point terminates in a bed of rocks. The town of Tangier stands by the sea, and on the eastern slope of the table-land of Marchan; its most remarkable objects (from their height) being the castle (la Casbah), and a mosque in the north-west angle of the town; the north-east angle being at Tangier point. The houses standing above each other and being entirely white are seen at some distance, but to a vessel from the westward, the table-land of Marchan prevents the town from being seen until abreast of it.*

The bay is three miles wide and one deep, Tangier point forming its western extremity, and Malabata point its eastern, which bears from the former point about E. by N. ¼ N. The bay from the offing appears much deeper than it is, from being surrounded by high land; nearly all its western shore is a clean sandy beach, with 5 to 6½ fathoms water at 3 cables distant, but eastward of fort Arabi-el-Said (2¼ miles east of the town) rocks and foul ground extend 1½ cables from the foot of the cliffs at the coast line.

Tangier point is foul on its northern sides for a distance of 2 cables; and eastward and southward of it for a distance of three-quarters of a mile the 3-fathoms line is found at a distance of 3 to 4 cables from the shore. There is an isolated conical hill about two-thirds of a mile inland named mount Direction, which serves as a mark for the anchorage; and a little east of it is another hill not so high, on which is a whitish tower. Between these two hills winds a small stream which falls into the sea near the

---

* *See* Admiralty plan, Tangier bay, No. 1,912, scale, *m* = 3·5 inches.

scattered ruins of old Tangier, crossed by two bridges, one of which is white, and that nearest the sea in ruins.

Another rivulet joins the above, east of old Tangier; the shore of the bay here trends northerly to Malabata point, skirted here and there by reefs which extend about a cable from the shore. There are two batteries on the eastern side of the bay; one (Arabi-el-Said) at the termination of the sandy shore, close to which there is a tower in ruins, and another half a mile farther to the north-east.

From the foot of the battery at Tangier point, the extensive bed of rocks which covers at high water, and upon which are the remains of an old mole, extends 2 cables eastward, and affords shelter for small craft from northerly and north-west winds. About 1½ cables farther southward, is another reef consisting of a group of rocks, one of which is 12 feet high.

Between the two reefs is a curved beach, off which the water is shallow, but where small vessels load and discharge; the custom-house being on the beach, and this being the only place where landing is permitted. The easterly and south-east winds, however, send in a sea, when the beach cannot be approached without considerable risk. The town of Tangier (Tanjah of the Arabs and Tingis of the Romans) at the west side of the bay is enclosed by walls, indifferently fortified, and may contain a population of about 10,000. It is the residence of the Consuls-general and Consuls of the principal nations, and a few European merchants reside here. Small supplies may be obtained. The gates of the town are locked at sunset. There is communication by steam vessel with Marseilles, Oran, &c.

Trade.—In 1875 the value of the imports at Tangier amounted to 331,331*l.*, and that of the exports to 222,457*l.*

Light.—From the extremity of a wooden landing stage near the custom-house at Tangier is exhibited at an elevation of 20 feet above high water, a fixed *red* light, visible in clear weather from a distance of 3 miles.

Bourée Rock.—A sunken rock lies about half a mile from the south-eastern shore of the bay, named Bourée. It is about a cable in extent, and the least water on it is 3 feet, but the sea seldom breaks on it. From its shoalest part, mount Direction bears S.W. ¼ S., White tower (east of mount Direction) S. by W. ¾ W., and fort Arabi-el-Said S.E. by E. ¼ E. There is a depth of 12 feet for a distance of about three-quarters of a cable west and south-west of the rock, and from 4¼ to 6½ fathoms water between it and the shore, and about the same depths at half a cable northward.

Anchorage.—Tangier bay is the only anchorage of any consideration on the south coast of the strait of Gibraltar, where a vessel of any size may anchor. Although exposed to winds from N.W. round by north to N.E., it affords security with winds from the other points of the compass. Nevertheless N.W. winds only are to be apprehended, which coming over an extensive range of ocean send in much sea, that is felt even with the wind as far round as S.W.; those between North and N.E. do not last long nor send in much sea. A vessel may anchor anywhere in the middle of the bay in about 7½ fathoms water, sand and good holding ground, with mount Direction bearing about S.S.W. A large vessel should keep Judios point open of the fort in ruins on the east point of Judios bay, and also Europa point open of Malabata point. Small vessels go nearer the shore. During the winter months vessels should be prepared to leave.

A vessel entering Tangier bay during an easterly gale, will find convenient anchorage off a small beach about a mile southward of Malabata point, in 8 or 10 fathoms water, where she will be better sheltered, and in a fair position for continuing her voyage when the wind slackens or changes. When working out of the bay and standing towards old Tangier, keep Europa point open of Malabata point to avoid the Bourée rock.

Tides.—It is high water, full and change, at Tangier point at 1 h. 42 m.; springs rise 8¼ feet; neaps 5 feet. The flood off the coast runs from east to west, and the ebb in the reverse direction, turning in mid-channel at high and low water by the shore. Three hours after it is slack water in the offing or at about half ebb by the shore at Tangier, the ebb stream within the bay runs from east to west or in a direction contrary to the offing stream. Northward of Tangier, the stream of tide is strong, causing eddies, resembling breakers, however little sea there may be; this occurs more especially during springs.

Malabata Point, at the eastern extremity of Tangier bay, is a bold prominent headland, terminating in cliffs, and bordered by rocks, having on it a battery and a circular white tower, the land rising from the point 792 feet high.

Almirante rock.—At 7 cables from Malabata point and N. ¼ W. from the tower, there is a rocky shoal with 3½ to 4¾ fathoms water on it, named the Almirante rock. There is generally a sea over it, and with strong winds from the westward the water breaks. Between this rock and the shore there are from 8 to 12 fathoms; no larger vessel should, however, use the channel except in cases of necessity, but give the point a berth of a mile in from 12 to 15 fathoms water.

The COAST from Malabata point trends nearly East for 3¼ miles to Al Boassa point, and between is point Altares, recognized by the cliff of a triangular form which terminates it; it is all along high, steep, rocky and commanded by high land.   At about a mile from the former point lie the Peril rocks, a dark group, most of which are above water, and about a cable north of them there is a sunken rock on which the sea occasionally breaks.   Between Altares and Al Boassa points there is a slight bay with several small white sandy beaches separated by rocky points; of these latter the most remarkable is Kankush point, which separates the two largest beaches, one known as Cala-Baja, and the other Hermosa.

The shore is here bordered by a bank with several rocky heads, and the Caña Coja reef in the middle of the bay dries at low water, and is separated from Kankush point by a channel nearly a cable wide with 6 and 7 feet water.   The fishermen of the strait, and at times coasting vessels, seek shelter off these beaches from strong easterly winds, by anchoring near the shore.   A rivulet falls into the sea, a little east of Kankush point.

JASEUR BANK.—At a third of a mile to the N.N.E. of the Caña Coja reef, and about N.W. ¼ N. distant three-quarters of a mile, nearly, from Al Boassa point, lies the Jaseur rock with 13 feet water on it. There are other rocky heads inside it with deep water between, and the bank northward of it between Al Boassa and Altares points, extends 1¼ miles from the shore, with from 6 to 9 fathoms on it.

Phœnix Bank lies 1½ miles N. by E. from Altares point, with 8 fathoms on it, and half a mile south-west of it is another bank with 9 fathoms; 2 miles north of these the depths are above 100 fathoms.

In the vicinity of the Jaseur and Phœnix banks, the tide is nearly always running strong either east or west.   To clear the Jaseur rock keep mount San Simonito open eastward of Al Boassa point, until the town of Tangier is its apparent length open of Malabata point.

AL BOASSA POINT is the termination of high land, which at about 2 miles southward of it attains the height of 905 feet, descending rapidly to the sea.   It only appears salient when seen from east or west, presenting then a bold headland.   It is rocky, and at 2 cables N.N.E. of it is a rock with three feet water on it.   At about 1¾ miles south-eastward of Al Boassa point is Cala Grande, a bay with a sandy beach more than half a mile in length.   Small vessels passing the strait from east to west may anchor here to wait the turn of tide, in 9 or 10 fathoms water, sandy bottom, at half a mile from the shore.   The bay affords no shelter, except with the wind off shore.

The river Ostras runs into the sea at the east end of the beach after descending through an extensive valley; small but excellent oysters are found in the river, from which it takes its name.   In the interior, mount

San Simonite, 803 feet high, terminates in two peaks, the western being the most pointed.

ALCAZAR POINT.—From Cala Grande the coast backed by high mountainous land trends eastward for 4 miles to Alcazar point; it is composed of sandy beaches interrupted by rocky points, and at the distance of half mile there are from 10 to 15 fathoms water, generally rocky bottom with patches of sand. Alcazar point projects northward and is fringed with rocks. A river falls into the sea on the east side of the point, and at its mouth are the ruins of a town ; eastward of it is a small beach.

The beach before mentioned forms a bay on the east side of the point, where there are 5 or 6 fathoms water, and were it not for the hostility of the Moors, it would be a most convenient place for small vessels to seek shelter from westerly winds.

CIRES POINT.—From the above bay the coast, which is chiefly of cliffs with sandy beaches interrupted by rocks, trends to the N.E. for 3¼ miles to Sainar point, which is low and projects but little. At a third of a mile from the shore there are from 9 to 12 fathoms water. At 1¾ miles farther on is Cires point, with two rocks or islets off it, the rocky channel between being nearly 2 cables wide; the coast between the two points forms R'Mel bay, in the southern part of which is a fine sandy beach. From Cires point the land suddenly rises 740 feet high, and forms a remarkable hill extending north and south, known as mount Cires, which, in some positions, has a resemblance to Gibraltar.

At the foot of the mount, on the south-west, is the sandy beach before alluded to, and at its south end the river R'Mel falls into the sea after winding through a deep valley. At about 3½ miles south nearly from Cires point is a rounded summit of a mountain 1,561 feet above the sea, visible from nearly every part of the strait.

LANCHONES POINT at a mile eastward of Cires point is high and bluff, with a rocky base, the land at a mile within it rises 1,161 feet. Cires bay between the two points is about half a mile deep, with a sandy beach and deep water off it. The coast between Lanchones point and Cruces point east of it, forms a bold front for three-quarters of a mile ; it is shallow close in, but at a distance of half a mile there are 100 fathoms ; the current here is very strong.

ALMANZA BAY, between Cruces and Almanza points, is about half a mile wide, 4 cables deep, with a small sandy beach. In the middle of the bay there are 3 and 4½ fathoms water, sandy bottom, offering convenient anchorage for small craft, and one of the best on this part of the coast of Africa. A small stream runs into the bay, and in the interior there is a long narrow valley, in the middle of which is a remarkable conical height with its rocky summit crowned with verdure. Almanza point is clear of danger, bold and remarkable, has a level summit, and rises from the sea like a wall.

PEREGIL ISLAND.—From Alamanza point a high rugged coast continues to the east as far as Peregil or Coral island, and then turns north-east to Leona point. The centre of this island is exactly midway between each point, or a short mile from both. It lies at the base of the sierra Bullones or Apes hill, with the land of which it appears blended. The island is nearly triangular, a mile in circuit, and its northern part 241 feet high. It is entirely rock, but covered with shrubs, presenting to the northward cliffs of the same colour as the rugged height of Bullones, from which it is separated by a channel full of rocks, a cable and a half across.

The island on its western side is bold, there being from 11 to 22 fathoms close to it. On its eastern side there are two coves; the northernmost called Rey or Levante, and the southernmost Reina; they are fit only for small craft. There are other coves on the north and west, where landing may be effected to climb the cliffs, should it be necessary to reach its summit for any purpose, or to obtain fuel. It contains a cave called Palomas, in which 200 men could find shelter. There are the remains of a tower at the entrance to Reina cove, and a cistern commenced, a work probably of the Portuguese, and of the time of the conquest of Ceuta.

This island belongs to Spain, and is a dependant of the Government of Ceuta. In 1746 a plan was made of it, with the view of fortifying it and converting it into a presidency.

Peregil Rock.—A reef extends a short distance from the north-east extremity of the island; and a rock which scarcely uncovers at low water springs, lies rather more than a cable about N.E. by E. of it, with 5 fathoms between it and the island. Another rock with 3¼ fathoms water on it lies E. by N. nearly of the former, 2 cables from the north-east point of the island, there being between the two a depth of 22 fathoms.

Anchorage.—Between Peregil island, and the coast, there is good shelter for small vessels both from easterly and westerly winds, and the island would be resorted to but for the unfriendliness of the Moors Smuggling craft and fishing vessels are all that frequent it, when overtaken by bad weather on the African coast. In case of necessity a vessel may obtain water on the shore of the mainland opposite the island; but the greatest precaution must be used against any sudden attack. Fuel may also be had from the shrubs which abound on the island.

LEONA POINT.—The north extreme of the south coast of the strait projects northward from the high range of the Bullones; it is high and level, terminates in cliffs, and can be seen from a great distance. The point is very bold, there being 200 fathoms but a short distance off.

SIERRA BULLONES (APES HILL).—This celebrated mountain, named by the Moors Jibel Mousa,* and by the ancient Romans *Abila*, rising near the eastern entrance of the strait, is very remarkable, and with the Rock of Gibraltar is a good mark for the eastern entrance to the strait. The Bullones, rugged in outline, is very precipitous, ascending in a series of sharp inaccessible cliffs and peaks, which are nearly of the same elevation, to its summit—the highest, 2,808 feet above the sea, commanding the whole chain of mountains on this part of the coast.

This mountain, and Gibraltar under the name of Mons Calpe, were called by the ancients the Pillars of Hercules; and in very early ages were considered by the people dwelling east of them as the western boundary of the world.

BENZUS BAY.—At 1¾ miles eastward of Leona point is Blanca point, high, steep, and of a dark reddish colour, with the ruins of a tower on it. The coast between the points forms a bay more than half a mile deep, bounded on the west by high accessible cliffs which terminate in Leona point, and on the east by high land. The land at the head of the bay rises rapidly in terraces one above the other, on some of which are the remains of towers and buildings. In case of necessity, with winds southward of east or west, small vessels will find anchorage here close to the shore.

Benzus rock.—To the north-west of Blanca tower, and 4 cables from the shore, there is a rocky shoal with 2¼ fathoms water on it, and 7 to 10 fathoms around it. Between it and the shore the space is encumbered with rocks, which extend from the east point of Benzus bay.

Susan rock, situated E. by S. ¾ S. 3 cables from Benzus rock, is about 30 yards long north and south, and 10 yards broad, with 16 feet water and 6 to 9 fathoms close around. From Susan rock, Leona point bears W. by N. ¾ N. 1½ miles, and the north angle of old Ceuta wall seen just open of Bermeja point.

MARABUT MOUNTAIN.—About a mile south-east of Blanca point is Bermeja point, on which are the ruins of a tower; it derives its uame from the reddish colour of the land. The coast between is the base of the Marabut mountain, which has several breaks or fissures, more or less deep covered with vegetation to the shore. A white marabut tower

---

* Jibel or Gibel, by the Moors, signifies mountain.

stands on its summit 1,079 feet above the sea; upon the hill to the south-ward are several Spanish redoubts, and on the eastern slope, towards the boundary, are other batteries, a mosque, &c.

CEUTA BAY* is formed between Bermeja point and Santa Catalina point about 2¾ miles eastward. It is a mile deep, but affords no shelter for large vessels except from south-west winds, as fresh south-east winds cause much sea, and those from the westward send down heavy squalls over the mountains. Hence no vessel should seek shelter in this bay, and much less with easterly or westerly winds with any northing in them. At a long mile from Bermeja tower, is the low point of Benitez with reefs extending from it; between the two points the coast forms a bend with sandy beaches, interspersed with rocks at a short distance from the shore.

Campo rocks extend about 2 cables north-east of Benitez point having 1½ and 2 fathoms water between them and the shore; they are surrounded by sunken reefs, some of which uncover at low water to the distance of nearly three-quarters of a cable, on which the sea nearly always breaks, and shallow water extends off nearly a third of a mile from the shore.

The eastern slope of the Marabut mountain descends in proportion as it advances eastward, and continues narrowing until it becomes a mere tongue of low land a little more than a cable across, which forms the isthmus of Ceuta, and at the commencement of which are the fortifi-cations that protect the port from the land side. The ruins of the old town of Ceuta are at the foot of the hill, about half a mile west of the fortifications, which are separated from the modern town by a channel or canal running from Ceuta bay to Madraga bay on the south. The modern town, or rather that of the barrio Almina, occupies the northern and western slope of the peninsula of Ceuta, in the form of an amphitheatre, the peninsula being a series of seven small hills, which ascend gradually eastward to the largest and highest called Monte el Hacho, on the summit of which is the castle of the same name, 665 feet above the sea.

The land east of the town of Ceuta is named the Almina, and embraces an extent of nearly 2 miles east and west, and is nearly 5 miles in circuit, with a rocky coast. It includes the seven small hills above mentioned, the new town or barrio of Almina, the castle el Hacho on the mount of that name, a modern building erected on the ruins of the old one attributed to the Romans, and various forts. This mount is remarkable from its isolated

---

* See Admiralty plan of Ceuta, No. 2742; scale, m = 4·7 inches.

position and the strong castle which crowns it, the walls and buildings of which are seen from a great distance. The town of Ceuta proper (the Sebtah of the Arabs, and the *Septa* of the Romans) stands on the lowest and narrowest part of the isthmus, constituting, with the batteries and out-works, the third part of this military post.

To the westward of the fortifications the land gradually ascends, and on a small hill is the watch tower of the Spanish sentinel. A little farther on is a walled district in ruins, the remains of the ancient town, known by the name of Ceuta la Vieja, and beyond it is the line of separation between the Moors and Spanish territories. The modern city or barrio ed la Almina is the most handsome part, the houses being seen among the shrubs and trees of the gardens which surround them, at a distance pre-senting an agreeable and pleasing prospect.

As a fortress Ceuta is strong and well supplied with the munitions of war. It is the principal presidency of the Spanish possessions on the African coast, and destined to figure in the commercial world if it should, as intended, be ever declared a free port, but at present there are no supplies of any kind. This important fortress, one of the keys of the strait, was gained by Don Juan I. of Portugal, who took it from the Mahometan power on the 14th of August 1415, but since the revolution of 1640, when the Portuguese detached themselves from Castile, it has remained in the hands of the Spaniards, who have been increasing their fortifications and converting it into another Gibraltar. The population, including the military, in 1860 was 10,395.

Anchorage.—The best anchorage in Ceuta bay is N.W. of the middle of the new town in 8 to 13 fathoms sand and rock. It should be observed that the Obispo street should be kept open; this is the principal thoroughfare, and begins on the side north of the Governor's house, which is the most conspicuous at the commencement of the Almina; the belfry of the church of San Francisco at the higher end of the street may assist in recognizing it. A vessel at this anchorage should be prepared to leave should it come on to blow hard from east or west. The mail vessels which run between this and Algeciras make fast to buoys.

At the western end of the town near the Government house is a mole, to which small craft such as feluccas may be secured, and about 2 cables off the mole small vessels anchor in 6 and 7 fathoms water.

Tides.—It is high water, full and change, at Ceuta, at 2h. 6m. ; springs rise 3¾ feet, and neaps 2¼ feet. The flood sets west, and the ebb east.

Santa Catalina point, the eastern extreme of the bay of Ceuta, is low, projects northward, is surrounded by rocks and reefs, and a fort of the same name commands it.　The rocks off the point are high, and extend about 1½ cables to the northward; and a rocky bank with 3¼ fathoms water on it, known as Queen Isabel bank, extends about a quarter of a mile northward of the rocks, and in heavy seas the current sets very strong over it.　At the distance of 4 cables from Santa Catalina point, the depth varies from 11 to 23 fathoms, rocky bottom, and there are above 100 fathoms at three-quarters of a mile eastward of the peninsula.　This point bears S. ½ W. distant about 12½ miles from Europa point.

Almina point, the eastern extreme of the Almida de Ceuta, is low, being the termination of mount el Hacho.　It is commanded by a battery, and a little to the south of it, and on the summit of the hill called the Mosqueros, stands the light tower.　From Almina point the coast trends southward, south-west and west, forming the peninsula of Ceuta, and with the coast of Africa the great southern bay of Ceuta, in which vessels find good shelter against winds from south-west to north.

LIGHT.—The lighthouse on Mosqueros hill exhibits at 476 feet above the sea a *revolving* white light attaining its greatest brilliancy every *minute,* and visible in clear weather at a distance of 23 miles.　The light in conjunction with that on Europa point, shows by night the eastern entrance of the strait of Gibraltar.

Soundings, Westward of the strait of Gibraltar.—

Between Cadiz and cape Trafalgar, at 20 miles from the shore, a depth of 100 fathoms is obtained; the bottom is mud and sand on the parallel of Cadiz; sand and shell between that place and Trafalgar; and coarse sand and gravel mixed with rocky substances as Trafalgar is approached. Northward of Trafalgar, from the line of 100 fathoms to within 7 miles of the land, the soundings decrease gradually to 25 fathoms: to the south-west of the cape towards the Phayre and Aceytera banks the depths shoal more rapidly.　Between cape Trafalgar and the Cabezos shoals the water is deeper, there being 30 fathoms within 2½ miles of the shore; the bottom here is similar to that obtained anywhere along the northern shore of the strait, viz., coarse gravel mixed with broken shell and pieces of rock.

On the African coast south of cape Spartel, at 20 miles from the shore the water shoals gradually from 100 fathoms (mud), but this bank of soundings narrows as Spartel is approached and rounds the cape at 2½ miles, the bottom changing to coarse sand and shell.　Eastward of cape Spartel the bank of soundings extends to an average distance of 3 miles from the shore, as far as Cires point, from which to point Almina it does not extend further than one mile from the shore (excepting in the bay of Ceuta).

The deep water channel (between the lines of 100 fathoms) on a line with capes Trafalgar and Spartel is 9¼ miles in breadth; the bottom being very irregular and having a general slope on both sides of a ridge, the deepest water on which, apparently, does not exceed 150 fathoms.

On the above-mentioned ridge which separates the waters of the Atlantic from the Mediterranean, and at about two-thirds the distance across from cape Trafalgar, is a bank of coral, sand, and weed, on which is a depth of 45 fathoms, with 100 fathoms round it at 1¼ miles.

From the meridian of Spartel the width of the deep water channel gradually decreases to 5½ miles on that of Tangier, continuing that breadth until near the meridian of Carnero point, where it gradually widens. The bottom in the deep-water channel is rock, gravel, and broken shell.

DIRECTIONS.

STRAIT of GIBRALTAR (West to East).—Vessels bound to the Mediterranean from the westward usually make cape St. Vincent; steam vessels then steer direct for the centre of the strait; a sailing vessel, however, with winds from West round by south to East had better make cape Spartel; with winds from N.W. round by north to East she may make cape Trafalgar. If making the latter cape in thick weather the safety of the vessel may be assured by the use of the lead and chart, as the soundings extend some distance from the land; the shoals off the cape and the Cabezos should be carefully avoided. In clear weather, and with ordinary care, there is no difficulty, none of these dangers extending beyond 4 miles from the land; in thick weather, however, caution is necessary, the currents and eddies between cape St. Vincent and Tarifa being very variable. Cape Spartel is safe of approach, being clear of danger and having 100 fathoms water at 3 miles from the shore; the land above the cape being about 1,000 feet in height, can be seen from a considerable distance. The lighthouse on cape Trafalgar exhibits a *revolving* white light, whilst that on cape Spartel shows a *fixed* white light, and as they are 24 miles apart N. ½ E. and S. ½ W., and either light in clear weather is seen at the distance of about 20 miles in all directions seaward; the extreme range of these lights embraces more than 60 miles of latitude, and thus, on approaching the strait of Gibraltar, unless in very thick weather, one or other of these lights are seen.

With a fair wind through the strait, keep in mid-channel, so that the vessel will have the advantage of the easterly current; for the same reason a sailing vessel with an easterly wind should work in mid-channel whilst the flood tide is making, but on the ebb (which sets to the eastward) she may approach either shore, with a chance of meeting with favourable slants of wind; if it be blowing fresh, a vessel will (especially if she be able to gain the meridian of cape Plata or Malabata point) get through the strait, provided she keep in mid-channel and can carry at least her topsails (even close reefed). When Tarifa is passed, the force of the wind will have lessened and an attempt should then be made to reach Gibraltar or to enter the Mediterranean. If the easterly wind be so strong as to prevent a vessel carrying sail, shelter should be taken under cape Spartel, keeping under easy sail to await more favourable circumstances. Coasting vessels which keep the Spanish shore on board reach Tarifa easily, availing themselves of the set of the tide, and anchoring off Los Lances (*see* page 315), if the wind be too strong to admit of their keeping under sail. When the easterly wind inclines to the northward, it is advisable to keep on the Spanish coast, remembering the Pearl rock (*see* page 318), but when to the southward the African coast is preferable.

WORKING through the STRAIT from EAST to WEST.—The passage through the strait of Gibraltar from east to west against the general easterly current from the Atlantic is, even with a fair wind, (especially during neap tides) somewhat difficult for sailing vessels, but with westerly winds which increase the strength of the current, it is, for a large ship, almost impossible. Some instances are known of vessels of war having achieved it, but these cases, favoured by circumstances, are rare. From Europa point, vessels should continue to work along the coast of Spain during the flood tide until reaching Tarifa where, if necessary, they should anchor to await the next flood tide. If from Algeciras, they should get under weigh at half ebb in order to reach point Acebuche, by the commencement of the flood. If a vessel cannot reach Tangier by following these directions she should cross to the African coast (not before half flood) and work up with the favouring tide, anchoring when necessary until Tangier bay is reached. Unless strong S.W. winds render it necessary, however, the Spanish coast should not be abandoned for the African, the flood stream being felt at a greater distance from the former than from the latter; in any case Tarifa should be fetched before standing across, otherwise there will be no certainty of weathering point Cires, and should a vessel fall to leeward of it, difficulty will be experienced even to regain Gibraltar bay.

Having weathered point Cires, work within the counter current and near the shore to take advantage of any slant of wind that may occur, and then doubling Malabata point, gain Tangier bay whence, with a single flood, it will be easy to regain the Spanish coast. When once the meridian of Tangier is passed, there is less current and a more manageable wind than in the narrows.

If a vessel succeeds in doubling Tarifa by keeping the Spanish coast, she should continue working up the bay of Lances, while the tide remains favourable, when, gaining Peña tower she should ; if it be preferred not to work inshore of the Cabezos) cross to the African coast and work up under that as above directed. If the wind be S.W. with moderate weather the Spanish coast should be kept, as by crossing to the African shore, where the wind will probably be found lighter, a vessel will be set to leeward. Should the wind haul to W.N.W. or N.W. the Spanish coast should still be kept. (To avoid the Cabezos shoal *see* page 314.)

The greatest difficulty is in gaining the meridian of Tangier (more especially during neap tides) after passing which the strength of the easterly current and the force of the wind diminishes, and a more rapid progress can be made.

Vessels beating through the strait to the westward, should get under weigh or sail from shelter at *low* water, keeping inshore; at *half flood* long tacks may be made from shore to shore regaining shelter, or anchoring *before high water*.

From the eastward with a fair wind (whether in sailing vessel or steamer) careful attention should be given to the set of the tides (*see* page 21), making either one coast or the other (that of Spain being preferable), and following it with the object of keeping as much as possible out of the influence of the easterly current. Unless the wind is sufficiently strong to keep good way on the ship, do not approach too near the projecting points, such as Carnero, Acebuche, Tarifa, Cires, &c. If the wind be light it would be prudent to anchor.

WINDS.

CADIZ to CAPE TRAFALGAR.—On the coast between Cadiz and cape Trafalgar the easterly winds are squally, with a clear sky overhead. These winds are dry, and small scanty white clouds (*cirrus*) are seen occasionally high, which soon disperse; a white mist hangs over the land, increasing in density as it nears the horizon, and continues while the easterly winds last, and even indicates their approach. In the fine weather season, when the easterly wind prevails, it is generally more constant and stronger than the westerly wind. It may last over a fortnight, and blow hard all the time. The native seamen say that it always blows for periods of three, six, or nine days.

In general, easterly winds attain considerable strength in a short time, and may freshen to a gale in a few hours. Near the land these winds are often squally, and although scarcely felt on deck, are severe aloft, the squalls are at times hot, sudden, and give no warning. At a distance from the land the breeze is steady, and gradually goes down.

The Solano.—At Cadiz the easterly winds, there called the Solano, often blow strong ; but in April, instead of as usual being warm and dry, they are accompanied by heavy black clouds, and often with rain and hail. They are squally at times, and sometimes attended with thunderstorms. They slacken in the evening, freshen in the morning, become strong during the day, with occasional sudden gusts at night.

At Cadiz, and in its neighbourhood, when the morning dew ceases and the atmosphere assumes a remarkable stillness, when the sun at rising and setting has no defined edge and has a greasy appearance, so that it may be viewed by the naked eye while the sky is clear in the zenith, and when the gossamer web is observed about the rigging of ships, the Solano may be expected.

Westerly Winds.—On this coast, between Cadiz and cape Trafalgar, south-west winds are the most dangerous. They are generally preceded by a fall in the barometer, and commence from the southward, and unlike easterly winds they take a certain time to veer to S.W., from which direction they blow hardest. Like the south-west winds of the Bay of Biscay, they shift suddenly to west, and even to N.W. ; if they continue at N.W. the weather becomes fine, but with heavy squalls at intervals, and sometimes thunderstorms ; and generally go down at North. The above account of the westerly wind specially applies to winter. In the fine season of April and May these winds are usually moderate, with fine weather, although the sky may be overcast.

STRAIT OF GIBRALTAR.[*]—It may be said that two winds prevail in the strait of Gibraltar ; they are those from east and west, and known to the local seamen as the Levante and Poniente. These winds are, generally speaking, the results of those from north-east and south-east, as also from north-west and south-west that are blowing at the outside ends of the strait, and which reaching the narrows, become east and west. Nevertheless strong south-easters are occasionally experienced in the strait, producing serious damage in the bay of Gibraltar, particularly in winter, and are quite as severe as south-westers commonly called Vendavalves. There have been years which navigators called years of easterly winds, when these have greatly prevailed in the strait, vessels then being rarely detained in their passage westward.

There have also been periods called years of westerly winds, when it has been especially difficult for sailing vessels to get from east to west, the bays and anchorages along the Spanish coast near the strait affording temporary refuge to hundreds of vessels waiting a spell of easterly wind to

---

[*] Abridged, with some alterations and additions, from the "Manuel de la Navigation," by M. Dumolin.

get away: instances have been known of vessels having been detained from one or two months waiting to clear this short distance.

The following table is the result of observations made at Gibraltar and Cadiz during the years from 1850 to 1855, showing the average number of days of easterly and westerly winds for each month during the period. From the table it is evident that easterly winds at Gibraltar predominated during the months of March, July, August, September, December; while at Cadiz the winds most prevalent were from the westward. It also appears that the direction of the wind at Gibraltar, is frequently contrary to that experienced at the same time at Cadiz.

DAYS OF EASTERLY AND WESTERLY WINDS.

Months.	Gibraltar. Days of		Cadiz. Days of		Gibraltar. Days of Variable Wind.	Cadiz. Days of Variable Wind.
	Easterly Wind.	Westerly Wind.	Easterly Wind.	Westerly Wind.		
January - -	8·2	20·6	6·7	12·3	2·2	12·0
February - -	11·2	16·1	8·8	10·6	0·7	8·6
March - -	16·0	13·6	7·7	16·1	1·4	7·2
April - -	12·2	17·3	10·2	13·8	0·5	6·0
May - -	7·3	23·3	4·4	20·2	0·4	6·4
June - -	11·8	16·6	7·7	18·5	1·6	3·8
July - -	18·5	12·2	6·9	19·9	0·3	4·2
August - -	19·5	11·0	11·8	15·5	1·5	3·7
September -	17·3	12·6	11·0	15·7	0·1	3·3
October - -	12·7	17·3	9·8	14·2	1·0	7·0
November -	10·5	17·8	8·5	11·4	1·7	10·1
December -	15·0	13·5	13·4	7·0	2·5	10·6
	160·2	191·9	106·9	175·2	13·9	82·9

From observations made at Tangier in 1825, as compared with those at Gibraltar, there appeared a considerable difference, although these places are only 30 miles apart. At Tangier there were 195 days of westerly winds, 134 days of easterly, and 36 days of variable; at Gibraltar there were 180 days only of westerly winds, and 185 days of easterly. In confirmation of preceding remarks with reference to seasons of prevailing winds in the above table, Gibraltar shows a result of only 160 days easterly and 192 of westerly winds, and 14 variable; calms were very rare, and it often blew very hard. Again the mean of the daily record for the years 1868-70 gave the following results, by which it will be observed that easterly winds again prevailed:—66 days north, 145 east, 36 south, and 107 west, without a single calm day.*

* Observations by the Army Medical Department at Gibraltar.

January, February, and March are the months that are generally bad for the navigation of the strait. About the end of October and November there is occasionally bad weather in the strait, it being the time of the short rainy season, which lasts from 15 to 20 days. In January, February, and March, S.W. (shifting to W. and N.W.) and S.E. gales are frequent. These gales are at times very heavy, accompanied by rain, and follow each other at short intervals.

Easterly winds.—In the strait of Gibraltar the easterly winds (known by the name of the Levanters) have peculiarities different from those on the coast between cape Trafalgar and Cadiz. They are squally near the land, but in the strait are uniformly strong. In shore, and principally in the bays, a dead calm prevails both morning and evening ; or the wind is light near the land, whilst outside it is blowing hard, especially in the middle of the strait. Easterly winds, instead of being dry as they are on the coast between Cadiz and Trafalgar, are often very moist. They are generally accompanied by a mist, and the thicker the mist the stronger the wind.

During the fine season, easterly winds are seldom attended with rain in the strait ; but as they cause more moisture in the eastern entrance of the strait than in the western, it often happens that the mist which is formed on the heights of Gibraltar and Apes Hill, occasions rain at the foot of these mountains, while there is fine weather in the strait. Again, in the fine season, and particularly in June, if, after a strong easterly wind, large white clouds are seen collected about the land in round masses, with light south-west or westerly wind, and a thick fog bank is formed in the western part of the strait, it gradually gains on the land, and soon envelopes the whole strait. These fogs are sometimes as thick and wet as those which are met with on the coast of Newfoundland in the month of August; but they are only of a few hours duration and disappear as rapidly as they form.

In the bad season, usually during February, March, and April, north-east winds frequently bring rain, and when they veer to east or south-east, they generally freshen to a gale. These winds are squally and shift suddenly to N.E. and sometimes North. In these changes they blow hard at times, however, in changing to N.E. they moderate, but if they again veer quickly to East or S.E. the bad weather will continue. In this season also, easterly gales veer to S.E. and are accompanied by torrents of rain; the weather then is nearly always murky, and the sky overcast ; the south-east is the rainy wind of the strait.

Signs of the Levanter.—The Levanter gives timely warning of its approach ; on shore, and especially at Algeciras, Gibraltar, and Ceuta its approach is known 24 hours beforehand. An abundance of dew, a mist over the land especially over Gibraltar and Apes hill, over the heights of which it hangs in dense masses, are almost certain indications of an approaching easterly wind ; and these continue while the wind lasts ; sometimes a swell from the eastward anticipates the wind.

It often happens, and particularly in the summer time, that the Levanter does not reach cape Trafalgar and Cadiz until two or three days after it has been blowing at Algeciras, where it will often be found blowing fresh when in other parts of the strait it is calm or a westerly wind is blowing. But at Cadiz and thereabouts it is very well known when the Levanter is prevailing in the strait, by the whitish clouds in the form of strips of cotton which hang about the summits of the neighbouring mountains.

Westerly winds in the fine season are generally moderate ; the sky is clear, and the land remarkably distinct ; but if they freshen, it soon becomes overcast, and squally with rain ; with a considerable sea in the strait. Generally westerly winds in the fine season bring favourable weather, and it is principally in October, November, or December that a strong breeze may occasionally occur from the westward. These winds are attended with much moisture at the western entrance of the strait, but are mostly dry at Gibraltar.

In the fine season easterly winds in the strait are always fresh, while the westerly winds are mostly moderate. But easterly or westerly winds in the strait have this peculiarity, that in the vicinity of the coast they follow its direction. Thus, when the wind is due West in the strait, it becomes N.W. near the coast of Spain, while near the African coast it is S.W. In like manner, easterly winds in the strait draw to the N.E. near the coast of Spain, and to S.E. near the coast of Africa. As the wind penetrates into the strait, it becomes stronger as it reaches its narrowest part. Thus, although the easterly wind may be light between Gibraltar and Ceuta, it blows hard between Tarifa and Cires point as well as in all the western part of the strait. And in the same manner westerly winds, which are moderate between cape Trafalgar and cape Spartel, attain their greatest strength south of Tarifa, and preserve it in all the eastern part of the strait.

In the bad season, that is, in February, March, and April, westerly winds are squally, and attended with heavy rain. The worst winds of the strait are the south-west, and in the squalls by which they are attended, it changes suddenly to West, or N.W., and even to North, and sometimes N.N.E. When they remain between North and West, they generally diminish in strength. Between the squalls there are intervals of fine weather, with moderate wind ; and if the wind settles between N.W. and N.E., it goes down, and fine weather ensues. But if, on the contrary, after suddenly changing to N.W., the wind backs round again to S.W., it mostly redoubles its force, and brings rain in abundance.

Winds from N.W. round by north to N.E. are rare in the strait; and when moderate they are attended with fine weather. In the bad season they blow with considerable force; but the local mariners say that although north-west winds may blow hard outside, they are not much felt in the vicinity of Tangier bay.

Signs of Westerly winds.—When the summit of Gibraltar, and that of Apes hill, after being covered with mist by a continuance of the easterly wind, become more clear and conspicuous, it is a tolerably certain sign of the approach of the westerly wind, and it will be more certain still if the mist or clouds entirely disappear. At Algeciras, Gibraltar, and Ceuta, the atmosphere becoming dry, or when the lassitude occasioned by the easterly wind is sensibly less, are also signs of the approach of the westerly wind, and when once set in, the hills and sky become clear and especially so if the wind be N.W. A swell from the north-west or south-west also indicates the approach of a westerly wind.

Rain.—By observations made at Gibraltar and Cadiz there appears to be considerable difference between the rainfall of the two places. For while at Gibraltar an average of 68 days rain is looked for every year, at Cadiz they have only 18 days. The following table shows the number of days rain for each month of the year at the two places from six years' observations. Another column is added of the observations made afloat for a different year; from which will be evident not only the great difference between the two places at simultaneous periods, but also the difference between one year and another in places so closely approximate.

DAYS OF RAIN.

Months.	Gibraltar.	Cadiz.	Afloat.	Observations.
January - -	9·1	2·5	15·5	
February - -	7·1	1·6	18·0	
March -. -	6·2	2·0	12·0	
April - -	10·1	1·7	4·3	Afloat at the anchorage of
May - -	6·1	1·6	3·5	Caraca, or Cadiz, from
June - -	1·8	0·2	0·7	17th February to 20th
July - - -	0·4	0·0	0·7	April. On other days in
August - -	0·9	0·2	0·2	the strait or its vicinity.
September - -	2·9	0·7	2·5	
October - -	5·7	2·0	3·0	
November - -	9·5	3·8	9·0	
December - -	8·8	2·0	0·7	

It will be seen by the table, that the most rainy month at Gibraltar was not the same as at Cadiz. At times with south-west winds rain falls at Tangier while it is dry at Gibraltar; and often while easterly winds bring rain in the eastern part of the strait, it does not reach the western part. It is generally considered that there are two rainy seasons in the strait; one of them, which commences in November and at times in December, or even in the early days of January, seldom last more than 15 days. The weather afterwards becomes fine before the heavy winter rains, which sometimes last till May. In the years 1854 and 1855 the little rainy season occurred in November; December was dry; the rains recommenced in January and lasted through the first fortnight of April.

Thunder storms.—Thunder storms are most frequent in the months of September and October; they are not so common in April, May, and November, and rarely happen in other months. They most frequently occur in the afternoon or at night, when the weather is uncertain, and the wind variable. Heavy gusts of wind, but of short duration, blow from opposite points, as from East and West, and clouds are seen, of different elevations, pursuing opposite directions, which is nearly a certain sign that the evening will not pass without a storm. The local mariners affirm that in the months of September and October about 15 or 20 miles outside the strait squally weather is experienced and most frequently accompanied by thunder.

The squalls are attended with a considerable quantity of rain, with intervals of fine weather and calms or light winds. When these squalls are strong they assume something of the character of whirlwinds, and shift rapidly through four, six, or even eights points, blowing harder as the changes are more rapid and considerable.

Barometer.—During summer in the strait the changes of the barometer are of little importance and cannot be depended on, but in winter they seldom deceive. When it falls, wind or rain may be expected. With winds from N.N.W round by North to East it is generally high, and keeps so even when it rains. But as soon as the wind has any tendency to the southward, it falls; thus a rising barometer indicates a northerly or easterly wind, and a falling barometer the contrary. South-west and south-east winds, being those which generally bring bad weather in the strait are indicated by a considerable fall in the barometer. But frequently this fall is only on account of rain, for generally speaking, these changes of the barometer are more frequently followed by rain than force of wind.

The following table, the mean result of six years' observation at Cadiz, will convey an idea of the movements of the barometer and thermometer near the strait of Gibraltar.

Months.	Barometer.			Thermometer.		
	Max.	Min.	Mean.	Max.	Min.	Mean.
January - - -	30·40	29·49	30·08	68	30	49
February - -	30·40	29·96	30·20	72	41	55
March - - -	30·32	29·60	29·88	67	45	57
April - - -	30·20	29·49	29·88	82	50	64
May - - -	30·08	29·57	29·88	78	50	64
June - - -	30·08	29·77	29·88	82	60	68
July - - -	30·08	29·80	29·88	90	62	74
August - - -	30·08	29·80	29·88	87	58	75
September - -	30·16	29·69	29·88	82	59	72
October - -	30·08	29·60	29·88	82	47	64
November - -	30·20	29·69	30· 0	72	41	59
December - -	30·40	29·88	30·08	65	37	53

TIDES AND CURRENTS.—Within the bend of the coast comprehended between cape St. Vincent in Portugal and cape Rabat in Africa, the general direction of the surface current is to the eastward towards the strait of Gibraltar, increasing in strength as the strait is approached, and acquiring its greatest velocity between Tarifa and Cires points. On the coast of Spain the stream runs to the S.E., on the coast of Africa it has a tendency to the N.E. Near Tarifa the current runs S.E. towards the African shore, and off Cires point to the E.N.E., the mass of water thus combined setting East through the strait, causes a stronger current along the coast of Africa than the coast of Spain. Continuing in this direction between Tarifa and Europa points, the easterly stream enters the Mediterranean, inclining to the N.E. on the Spanish coast, and to the S.E. towards that of Africa.*

The movement of the whole body of water in the strait of Gibraltar, however, is tidal, affected by the above-mentioned surface current running into the Mediterranean from the Atlantic.

Within a cable of Tarifa the flood at springs runs westward at the rate of 2 or 3 miles an hour; but at neaps it is reduced to little more than one mile an hour. At springs the stream of the tide near the coast and the bays runs at the rate of 1½ to 2 miles an hour, but at neaps there are places where it nearly ceases. These in-shore streams always run much faster on the ebb than on the flood, thus showing the effect of the general current.

Thus it will be seen that independently of the general current that runs to the eastward through the middle of the strait, there is a regular ebb

---

* South-west gales, however, cause a northerly current of at times 2 knots an hour; it runs to the N.E. on the African coast, North and N.N.W. on the coast near Cadiz, and N.W. and West towards cape St. Vincent, where it joins the northerly set along the coast of Portugal.

and flood stream running, the former of which, setting to the eastward
unites with the general current, therefore when the water is falling, the
whole stream in the strait is running to the eastward, attaining at a
cable's distance from Tarifa a velocity of from 4 to 5 knots an hour, and
from 5 to 6 knots an hour at 4 miles north of Alcazar point. When,
however, the water is rising, the tidal set to the westward meeting the
incoming current from the Atlantic is, under ordinary circumstances,
overpowered by it in the middle of the strait (where the easterly current
is connected into a narrow and rapid stream) though along the shores (at
a greater or less distance according to the time of tide) the flood stream
to the westward is experienced, but always at a greater distance from
the Spanish than the African coast. The velocity of the easterly current
during this tide is considerably checked, its rate being only from 2 to 3 miles
an hour in the middle of the strait on the meridian of Tarifa; 2 miles
on the coast of Africa, and rather more than one mile in the vicinity of
Tarifa. It is only during easterly winds and calms that a decided set
to the westward (flood stream) is experienced in the middle of the strait.

This, however, is only the case with the surface water, the bottom
stratum is unaffected by the in-running current of the Atlantic and sets
east or west for equal periods according to the tide.

On the shallow ridge at the western entrance to the strait, the surface
streams are tidal, the in-running current from the Atlantic being insuffi-
ciently strong to over-run the westerly (flood) stream.

The change in the tidal stream in the bottom water corresponds with the
time of high and low water at Gibraltar, with the easterly winds, the surface
current ceases running to the East, at from one to two hours after low
water; it turns to the East again at high water.

From the foregoing it will be understood that, from the Narrows to the
western entrance to the strait, there is either no easterly current, or else a
decided set to the westward, from about one to two hours after low water
until high water; and that the velocity of the latter at about half-tide is
from one-half to one knot an hour; and that even off the African coast,
where the current from the Atlantic runs the strongest, there is no
easterly surface current from $1\frac{1}{2}$ hours before, until high water.

Off the salient points in the strait, as Europa, Tarifa, and Trafalgar on
the coast of Spain; and Spartel, Cires, and Leona, on the coast of Africa,
the stream of the tide turns at the moment of slack water.

" As a general rule the tide sets westward along shore in the strait from
the time of the moon's rising till it is on the meridian, then eastward until
it sets, then westward until the lower culmination takes place, then eastward
until it rises."[*]

---

* Commander James Penn, R.N.

The tidal wave arrives simultaneously at Mogador in Africa, and Conil in Spain, continuing on into the strait, and causing high water at the same time on all the coast between cape Plata and Europa point.

It is not however until about twenty minutes after it has attained its highest level on the coast of Spain, that the water reaches its highest level on the African shore opposite. In the narrows, the last of the ebb and first of the flood set across from Tarifa towards point Cires, joining the inshore stream running to the westward along the African coast.

It is high water, full and change, with the rise of tide at the several places as mentioned in the following table.

Places.	High Water, full and Change.		Springs Rise.	Neaps Rise.	Neaps Range.
	H.	M.	Ft.	Ft.	Ft.
Chipiona - -	1	30	12·5	8·0	3·6
Rota - - -	1	24	12·6	8·0	3·6
Cadiz - -	1	23	12·9	8·2	—
Conil - - -	1	18	12·0	7·5	3·3
Cape Plata - -	1	45	8·0	5·3	2·6
Tarifa - -	1	46	6·0	3·6	1·3
Algeciras - -	1	49	3·9	2·6	1·3
Gibraltar - -	1	47	4·1	2·7	1·3
Ceuta - - -	2	6	3·7	2·5	1·3
Tetuan - -	2	23	2·6	1·6	0·6
Tangier - -	1	42	8·3	5·1	2·0
Rabat - -	1	46	11·0	7·1	3·3
Mogador - -	1	18	12·4	8·0	3·6

Eddies or Counter Currents, which are so numerous in the strait of Gibraltar, generally occur in the vicinity of the most salient points of both coasts, and near their off-lying banks. In Tangier bay the ebb stream strikes against Malabata point, a portion of it turns to the south, and runs along the whole shore of the bay in a direction opposite to that of the current outside of it. Observations show that this effect, which take place in all moderately deep bays, results in streams as periodically regular as those produced by the tide : only this reversal of the stream does not take place at slack water, like that of the outer current, but at three hours after, and thus it will be not until half ebb at Tangier, that the counter stream will run westward, and the tide will have three hours to rise when the counter stream to the east commences.

In the bay between the points Al Boassa and Cires, the ebb stream, which is strong off the latter point, produces a counter current, while the flood, by no means so strong, and meeting a less salient point, Al Boassa, is attended with no counter current. In this case, as at Cala Grande, the stream on coming in contact with the land between point Alcazar and Cires, produces on the ebb a counter current to the west along the coast between them.   With the flood stream all the water runs to the west, along shore, and the consequence is that the bay of Cala Grande, has this great advantage, that near the shore the stream runs continually to the westward. This fact is of great importance to sailing vessels passing the strait from east to west with foul winds.

In Ceuta bay the counter currents are much the same as in Tangier bay, but weak.

In Gibraltar bay there are special counter currents.   On the flood tide the stream enters the strait by Europa point, and sets towards Carnero point; off which it is divided into two branches, one of which continues on its westerly course; another takes the western shore of the bay, making a northerly course from Carnero along by Algeciras; and as the flood passes Europa point a portion of the stream branches northward, and continues along by Gibraltar to the head of the bay.   It there meets with the stream from the western side of the bay, and then, by their combined action, a current to the southward is established down the middle of the bay, until it joins the flood stream which is running in the strait.

Thus, during the flood, there are actually three streams in the bay, two of which run north along either shore, and, uniting at the head of the bay, form together a current running south out of the bay.   The stream on the western side is much stronger than that on the eastern side of the bay, and it commences at point Carnero as soon as the flood makes there.   In about an hour it reaches Getares, and does not penetrate to Algeciras until two hours after the turn of the tide.   The stream on the eastern side of the bay does not reach the anchorage off Gibraltar until three hours after the flood makes; the consequence of which is, that on the flood it never lasts so long as on the ebb, nor does it run so strong.

As soon as the ebb commences in the strait, the tidal stream enters Gibraltar bay round Carnero point, and runs north-east across the bay. Having gained the edge of the bay, it divides, one part running along the shore towards Gibraltar, the other, which is the larger branch, sets round the head of the bay and along the western shore by Algeciras to the south ; and thus on the ebb, as on the flood, there are three currents in the bay. These streams are quite periodical, changing regularly with every tide, and about two or three hours after high and low water.   It has also been observed, that these particular currents produced by the general stream of the tide, are subject to considerable variation.

Not only has the wind a considerable influence over them, but their velocity and their extent depend much on its force.   Off Carnero point the tide runs almost always either N.W. or N.E., and consequently in general towards the shore.   Carnero point, or perhaps Acebuche point west of it, is one of the most difficult points for vessels to get round from the eastward; besides which, Carnero point is the most dangerous in the whole strait, and many accidents occur on this point, in consequence of the currents above mentioned.

On the east side of Tarifa the flood tide is never sufficiently strong to cause any counter current; but with the ebb, the stream which runs S.E. occasions a counter current along the coast to the westward, and which at times is felt some distance eastward of Tarifa.

Tide races.—There are probably few places in which the tide races are more numerous than the strait of Gibraltar. They are generally found off all the salient points of the strait where the direction of the coast changes, and near the banks in their neighbourhood. They form on a sudden, without warning of any kind, the sea gets up like water boiling over a fire, short, irregular, and deep. These races are dangerous, not only for boats, but even for small craft; the wind, of course, contributes to form them, and always augments their violent character. The most turbulent races in the strait are generally where the angle of the point is most acute, and off which the water is not so deep, and they are generally formed at half tide, when the current is strongest.

In some parts the stream of flood, as well as that of ebb, produces these races; in others, the race is only produced on the ebb. The points on the coast of Spain where races are found are,—cape Trafalgar, the Cabezos shoals, the south point of Tarifa, Frayle point, the Pearl rock, and Europa point. On the coast of Africa, cape Spartel, points Malabata, Altares, Al Boassa, Cires, Leona, and the north-east point of Ceuta have also races off them.

The most violent race is off cape Trafalgar, and it forms there both on half flood and half ebb. It extends to a considerable distance off the cape in a W.S.W. direction, crossing the bank of Aceytera, and over all the small banks of the Pharc. This race, which is more formidable both in extent and violence than any in the strait, most probably arises from two causes, the sudden change of direction in the coast, and the number of banks off it.

At every half tide, a race is also formed on the Cabezos shoals, or near them, varying both in its extent and direction; and sometimes by following the small shoals it becomes considerably extended, although not so violent as the races generally are off the points; it gets up a troubled sea even in calm weather, and in bad weather, with much sea on, extends over the whole breadth of the strait, from the Cabezos to the flats between Malabata and Al Boassa points, on the African coast.

The race off Tarifa point is comparatively of limited extent; on the ebb it extends to the south-east, but with the flood south-west. It appears at every half tide, and that on the ebb is generally more considerable than that on the flood. The races off Frayle and Europa points are much the same as those just mentioned, the first resembling that of the Cabezos, and the last that of Tarifa; their only difference is in being less extensive and less violent.

On the African coast, off cape Spartel, Judios point, and Tangier point, the races are generally of small extent and of little importance, although they are found both with the ebb and the flood. The worst races are between Malabata and Al Boassa points, over the Almirante, Phœnix, and Jaseur banks, and, as above mentioned, reach across the strait to the Cabezos. The races off Cires, Leona points, &c. as far as Ceuta, are of small extent : they are sometimes rather violent, like the tide which produces them : but this is only on the ebb. In fact, in the strait, and pirncipally to the northward of Tangier, there are occasional eddies as well as counter streams at springs, but they are of small extent and short duration.

CAPE SPARTEL SOUTHWARD TO MOGADOR.

ARZILLA.*—The coast from cape Spartel is nearly straight S.W. by S. 19 miles to Arzilla, and, with the exception of a few rocky projections, presents a clean sandy beach with a line of low hills, which from the distance of half a mile inland slope gradually to the beach. At 13 miles farther inland there is a range of very conspicuous mountains, the loftiest of which, named Jibel Habib, is about 3,000 feet above the level of the sea. Another peak, mount Raven, lies 6 miles farther to the northward, 10 miles inland, and is about 2,200 feet high. Just north of the town of Arzilla there is a castle built by the Portuguese, but now in ruins. Date trees, which overtop the walls, are growing in the court. The wall fronting the sea is strengthened by three towers apparently of more recent date. Under the southern angle of the wall, the well-whitewashed tomb of a Mahommedan saint, contrasts singularly with the mouldering ruins adjoining. The country in the neighbourhood of the town is well wooded, and much land is laid out in gardens.

General Anchorage.—There is good anchorage on this part of the coast ; a good berth is in 15 fathoms, on a bottom of sand and small shells at 1¼ miles from shore, with cape Spartel bearing N.E. ½ N., and the town of Arzilla S. by W. ¾ W. 5 miles; but further to the southward, in 13 fathoms, coral rock will be found mixed with gravel, when the centre of Arzilla town bears S. ¼ E. 2½ miles. There is said to be a mackerel fishery

---

* *See* Admiralty chart :—Africa, west coast, sheet I., cape Spartel to Azamor, No. 1,227 ; scale *m* = 0·18 of an inch.

about this part of the coast, on which 20 or 30 Spanish and Portuguese feluccas are employed during the fishing season.

Caution.—It is against the law of this country for any one to land on any part of the coast where there is not a port for their reception.

The Coast from Arzilla continues in the direction of S.W. ¾ S., and presents nearly the same appearances, the depth at a distance of 3 miles from the shore being 25 to 30 fathoms, gravel. At 4 miles south of Arzilla the outer hills rise to about 700 feet. Haffat-el-Beïda, or the White cliff, situated 8 miles south of Arzilla, stands about 300 feet above the sea, and presenting in all directions the form of a wedge, serves to identify this part of the coast. The face or section of this cliff shows the strata lying at an angle of 70° with the horizon.

El Aráish or Larache.—About 8 miles south-west of White cliff is El Aráish, on the steep southern point of the Wad el Khos (the bow), which here meanders through a fertile valley; the sudden bends in the river having probably suggested its Arabic name. A large castle on the summit of the hill, a lofty mosque and several towers, give this town from the sea an imposing appearance, which, however, soon vanishes on approaching it. The environs are laid out in gardens, from whence the town derives its name (El Aráish, signifying a pleasure garden), but they are in a very wild uncultivated state; in 1875 there was a population of about 5,000 persons at El Aráish.*

Trade.—In 1875 the value of the exports from El Aráish amounted to 143,352l., and that of imports to 28,925l.

Tides.—It is high water, full and change, at El Aráish at 1 h. 30 m.; springs rise from 9 to 12 feet.

On the bar at the entrance of Wad el Khos at low water there is a depth of 5 or 6 feet, deepening inside to 24 feet. The river takes an abrupt turn to the northward, and in the bend vessels moor.

Anchorage.—The best anchorage in the outer road of El Aráish for vessels intending to enter the river is about a mile off, in 12 fathoms, on a sandy bottom, with a distant conical mountain named Jïbel Sarsar, appearing in the centre of the entrance bearing S.S.E. or in 10 fathoms with the north entrance point S.E. by E. ½ E., distant about 1¼ miles. The Pap, or rising ground, on the north side of the river is 200 feet above the sea.

Old Mámorah.—About 21 miles southward of El Aráish is situated the outlet of a stream said to flow from a small inland lake; on the north point of the entrance there are several tombs kept well whitewashed, the

---

* See Admiralty plan of El Aráish, on sheet, No. 1,227.

[17801.   z

chief of which is named after Mulai-Abou-Sallūm. Though the coast is straight there is tolerable anchorage off this river during the summer; at 2 cables from the bar of the river there is a depth of 5 fathoms, gradually increasing to 34 fathoms, at 2 miles off shore. The coast between El Aráish and this spot is generally about 300 feet in height, with reddish cliffs for the first 10 miles, and then sandhills partly covered with brushwood.

Rocky Shoal situated 15 miles southward of Old Mámorah, and one mile off shore, has 8 fathoms on it, with 13 fathoms inside. From this shoal Black rock bears E.S.E.

Mehediyah or New Mamorah lies 60 miles S.W. from El Aráish. The town stands on the lower slope of a hill which rises to the height of 456 feet, on the southern bank of the Wad Sebou. It is noted for its ruins ; the population is said not to exceed 400, who subsist by the sale of a fish resembling salmon (shebbel), and are not friendly.

Anchorage.—There is good anchorage off the river Wad Sebou during the summer, there being 16 fathoms muddy bottom at 2 miles from the shore, but in winter the S.W. and S.S.W. winds render it unsafe. Vessels approaching the land from the latitude of Mehediyah will strike soundings in 100 fathoms, coarse sand, when distant 18 miles from the shore, and will shoal to 50 fathoms at a distance of 8 miles.

The Coast from Mehediyah trends in a S.W. direction, generally resembling that before described, but rather more level, and wooded.

Sali.—At the distance of 17 miles the town of Slá, or Sali stands on the northern bank and near the mouth of the river Abū Rakrak. It is encompassed by a wall 35 feet high, strengthened and flanked by towers at regular distances.

Rabāt.—The town of Rabāt extends along the opposite or southern bank of the river, and is larger than Sali. The population of both together is estimated at 30,000. Rabāt is defended by fortifications which extend round the river faces of the town.*

Trade.—The value of the imports during the year 1875 amounted to 84,403*l*., and of the exports 59,450*l*.

Hassan Tower.—The well-known tower of Hassan, to the south-eastward of the town, is 180 feet in height, and, standing on a cliff which rises 70 feet above the river, may be seen from a distance of 15 or 20 miles.

Tides.—It is high water, full and change, at Rabāt at 1 h. 46 m. (approximate) ; springs rise 9 to 12 feet.

---

* *See* Admiralty plan of Rabāt and Sali, on sheet, No. 1,227.

Anchorage.—The best anchorage in the road, is with Hassan tower seen just open of the south entrance point of the river, and 2 miles from the shore, in 21 fathoms mud, or a steam vessel in fine weather might anchor in 10 fathoms, at 1¼ miles off shore, with Hassan tower in line with the angle of the fort.

Bar.—A sand bank, which dries at low water, is situated at the mouth of Abū Rakrak river: of the two channels into which this bank divides the entrance, the northernmost is the deeper. The southern channel has a depth of 2 feet at low water; Hassan tower in line with the east angle of the fort on the south entrance point, leads through this channel.

Landing.—There is always a very heavy rolling swell hurrying onwards to break on the bar, but with the aid of local pilots it may be crossed in two places with 5 feet at low water; it is, however, very dangerous, as the banks constantly shift, and cause the loss of many coasters. Landing is effected in lighters kept by the Government, ships' boats being unfit.

CAPE FEDÁLAH.—The first conspicuous object, situated 7 miles W.S.W. from Rabāt, and built on the slope of a hill, is Massa tower, 190 feet high; and 22 miles further the little town of Mansoriyeh will be seen, the principal mosque of which rises to 180 feet above high water. At 5 miles further is the village of Fedálah, with its projecting cape, which at a short distance has the appearance of an island, and affords some shelter to the small bay in front of the village. Vessels may anchor there in 5 or 6 fathoms, but very near the shore.

From Rabāt to cape Fedálah there is no danger at 3 cables off the shore, and the bank of soundings is upwards of 20 miles in breadth and tolerably regular. At 22 miles N.W. of Rabāt, there are 162 fathoms, whence towards the shore it suddenly shoals to 90 and 80 fathoms, between which depth and 60 fathoms it continues for many miles to be fine sand and mud. The coast between these places is slightly embayed, but the inland features scarcely vary in appearance; two lines of barren and gently undulating hills lying nearly parallel to the coast. The distant hills are from 200 to 400 feet high, and lie 5 or 6 miles from the sea, while the near hills are not more than 200 feet in height, nor more than a mile from the beach, on which many patches of rocks are intermixed with the sand, and down to which they gradually slope.

Banks.—At 6 miles N.E. by E. from cape Fedálah, there is a bank of 17 fathoms from which others extend about 9 miles in an E.N.E. direction parallel with the shore, and at a distance of 3 or 4 miles from the coast. The least water on these banks is 15 fathoms, and there is deep water between them.

z 2

Cape Dar el Beïda bears W. ¾ S. 13 miles from cape Fedālah. Reefs extend from it to the distance of nearly half a mile, and further off here is a rocky bank of 6 fathoms; a safe distance at which to pass the cape is 3 miles.

Anchorage.—Northward cape Dar el Beïda, and between it and cape Fedālah the bottom is rocky in many parts of the bay, which must be a very unsafe anchorage during the winter, not only from its foul bottom, but from the current, which sets obliquely on the cape, rendering it difficult for a vessel when weighing to clear it with an on-shore wind. A good berth for a steam vessel is three quarters of a mile off shore in 10 fathoms sand, with the centre of the wall of the town of Dar el Beïda bearing S.S.W., and the fort, on which is a white tower, S.W. by W.; or in 6½ fathoms hard sand, with British Consulate Flagstaff bearing S.W., and the extreme of the north-west fort West.

Dar el Beïda is also generally known by the name of Casa Blanca.

Landing.—A reef of rocks, which projects from the town, affords some shelter to a landing place.

Trade.—In the year 1875 the value of the exports was 304,054*l.*, and of the imports 386,819*l.*

The Coast from Dar el Beïda is nearly straight, and trends W. ½ S., 35 miles to Azamor point, the first two miles being rocky, but the rest becoming a broad sandy beach, inside of which two parallel ranges of hills, of 300 and 400 feet in height, rise at the distance of 2 and 6 miles from the sea, and are partially covered with brushwood.*

AZAMOR.—At Azamor point the coast suddenly bends to the southward in to the mouth of the river Om-er-biych (mother of herbage), on the south bank of which, at 120 feet above the sea, stands the town of Azamor. The river has a bar of sand across its mouth, which dries nearly across at low water; though on the inside it is said to be deep and rapid.

Effect of Refraction.—"As we approached the town," says Lieut. Arlett, R.N., "towards sunset it was refracted through the haze into a magnificent looking place, and a tomb in the centre of the town had the appearance of a stately cathedral; but the morning light showed all to be mere heaps of ruins."

CAPE MAZIGHAN.—The small town of Mazighan stands on a low rocky point, 8 miles to the westward of Azamor, the coast between them forming an extensive bay. From cape Mazighan a reef extends more than a mile to the north-eastward, with shoal water beyond it. This reef somewhat shelters the anchorage for small craft in westerly winds, notwithstanding which a heavy swell rolls in.

---

* *S* ‹‹Admiralty chart: West coast of Africa,[sheet ii., No. 1,228; scale, m = 0·13.

A shoal with 4 fathoms on it gravel bottom lies East from the north extreme of cape Mazighan distant 1½ miles from the shore; vessels should not attempt to pass between this shoal and the coast.

Directions.—Cape Mazighan should not be approached nearer than 2 miles. A small mosque, situated about 1½ miles eastward of the town, should be brought to bear S.W., until the ruined tower at Mazighan bears West, this latter mark then kept on leads to a good anchorage in 7 fathoms, mud and sand, about 1 mile from the town.* Further eastward, in the larger bay, the general depth is from 7 to 10 fathoms (fine dark sand), but this would be a wild and dangerous anchorage during winter.

The town or rather fortress of Mazighan is well situated for defence, being nearly at the extremity of the cape.

Landing may be easily effected after half flood in a camber on the east side of the town.

Trade.—The value of the exports during the year 1875 amounted to 260,410l., and the imports to 154,228l.

The Coast between Mazighan and north cape Blanco, 11 miles in a W.S.W. direction, should not be approached nearer than 1½ miles, as scattered rocks lie off the shore, and the soundings are very uneven. The beach also, though in many places a broad sand, is generally lined with craggy rocks. A barren line of hills, 200 feet above the sea, slope to the beach throughout the above interval, and terminate just to the northward of the cape in a low, dark, and rocky cliff.

NORTH CAPE BLANCO no doubt derives its name from a white cliff 170 feet high, a little to the southward of the headland that forms the cape; it is named north cape Blanco, to distinguish it from the other cape of the same name which is in latitude 20° 47′ N.

Anchorage.—The bight on the S.W. side of the cape is said to afford a stopping place, but it is only recommended for summer use.

Soundings.—At 19 miles N.W. b. N. of north cape Blanco, 111 fathoms, gravel, will be found, and at 22 miles N.W. b. W. 100 fathoms, broken shells, from whence it shoals gradually to the shore.

CAPE CANTIN.—From 3 miles off north cape Blanco, to 3 miles off cape Cantin which rises precipitously 200 feet above the sea, the course is S.W. by W. ¼ W., distance 50 miles. At 4 miles to the southward of cape Blanco there is a dark cliff which projects from the shore, and in some directions has an insular appearance.

---

* Navigating Lieutenant W. P. Haynes, H.M.S. *Aurora*, 1878.

About 6 miles to the southward of north cape Blanco, the hills rise gradually from the beach to the height of 450 feet, and seem to be the highest land on the coast.   About 10 miles from the cape, near the coast, there is a black tower with some ruins near it ; and 21 miles further to the south-westward the ruins of the El Waladiyeh may be seen on the shore, with a smaller patch of ruins 2½ miles further.   There is said to be here an extensive lake, communicating with the sea ; but the boats of H.M.S. *Raven* did not discover the entrance; it was probably concealed by the high surf which rolls along this forbidding shore.   At 4 miles north-eastward of cape Cantin, the profile of the land, which is here about 450 feet above the sea begins to lower gently, but just inside the cape it again rises into a hummock, on the outer edge of which there is a white patch, seen both from the northward and southward, and apparently the site of the former town. A singular-looking gap in the ridge of the cape is also seen on both sides.

Current.—Northward of cape Blanco there is a slight southerly set ; south of cape Blanco a stronger set in the same direction.   Off cape Cantin in November there is a set of 1½ miles per hour to the south eastward.*

Westerly Swell.—Between cape Spartel and cape Cantin, allowance should be made for a heavy swell that generally sets directly on the coast.

Soundings.—At 16 miles to the westward of cape Cantin, soundings may be obtained in 100 fathoms, fine sand ; and at 11 miles, 40 fathoms, sand and shells, decreasing irregularly to the cape, from which a reef or sandy spit extends to seaward more than a mile, with 5 fathoms on its extremity, and 3 miles from the shore the depth is only 17 fathoms.

Cape Safi, the northern point of Safi bay, bears S.S.W. 12 miles from cape Cantin ; the intermediate coast is a continued line of white cliff with a broad sandy beach at its foot ; the cliff gradually rising to upwards of 500 feet at cape Safi, which may be known by a square tower, said to be the tomb of some celebrated Moorish saint.

SAFI BAY.—At the cape the land suddenly recedes to the south-eastward into Safi bay, and the cliff drops into a ravine, the bed of a winter torrent.   On the slope of the hill which rises from the south side of this ravine, stands the town of Safi, or more properly Asàfi, a place of considerable antiquity and importance, but which, in 1855, was reduced to a population of about 6,000.   Water is scarce, and during the summer it has to be procured from wells a short distance to the southward of the town. The country in the neighbourhood appears from seaward to be sandy and barren, but travellers assert that it is remarkably fertile.

---

* Remark Book of Navigating Sub-Lieut. E. S. Greaves, H.M.S. *Lee*, 1871.

Trade.—During the year 1875 the value of the imports amounted to 36,761*l.*, and of the exports to 93,086*l.*

Anchorage.—Safi bay, during the summer months, affords as good anchorage and smoother water than any other on the coast, but is entirely exposed to westerly winds; the bottom is sand und mud, and there is generally about 15 fathoms water a mile from the shore, shoaling gradually to 5 fathoms a few yards from the rocks. Small steam vessels may anchor off the town with the castellated rock bearing E. by½N., distant one quarter of a mile, if prepared to quit at short notice.

The landing at Safi is at all times bad.*

WAD TENSIFT.—At 7 miles to the southward of Safi, a red cliff called Sharf-el-Judi or Jews cliff, rises to 280 feet above the sea; 10 miles further is the mouth of the Wad Tensift, the principal river of Marocco; the general character of the coast continuing throughout that space is high sandhills, terminating occasionally in low cliffs, and sloping points, backed by brushwood hills above 600 feet in height; the Wad Tensift, though a very considerable river in the interior, had, in the month of August, its bar entirely dry at low water. On the northern bank of the river there is a castellated building in ruins.

From that river the coast trends in a S.W. b. W. ¼ W. direction 9 miles to the tomb of Sidi Abd Allah; and further on, other tombs with the ruins of a town will be seen at the base of the Iron mountains. The coast which from the Tensift is barren and uncultivated, and from 200 to 300 feet in height here shows renewed signs of cultivation. Jibel Hadid, or the Iron mountains, a large mass of high land extending more than 20 miles in length, rises to the height of 2,300 feet; and on one of its summits the tomb of Sidi Wasman forms a very conspicuous object, useful in recognizing the land, and verifying a ship's position.

Hadid Point.—At 45 miles S.W. ¼ W. from cape Safi is a sandy spit called Hadid point, which projects a mile beyond the general trend of the coast, terminating in a reef half a mile in length, and at 2 miles from the shore the depth is under 10 fathoms.

The Coast.—From Hadid point the sandy beach continues in a south-west direction 12 miles to Mogador; the view inland being bounded by the Botof high sandhills, which run parallel to the beach at about a mile distant.

Soundings.—At 6 and 7 miles from the coast, between Safi and Mogador, the depth is 25 and 20 fathoms, whence it gradually decreases to the shore, except off Hadid point.

---

* Captain S. Douglas, H.M.S. *Aurora,* 1873.

MOGADOR.—Approaching the land in the parallel of Mogador, the first remarkable features are the distant craggy summits of mount Atlas, capped with snow, and contrasting with the dark ridges of intermediate hills ; while to the northward, the Jibel Hadid, or Iron mountains, appear like a large island. On a nearer approach to the shore, a narrow white streak of sandhills, fringed at the top with verdure, seems to rise out of the sea ; and at a distance of 8 or 10 miles, the mosque towers and castles of Mogador begin to be distinctly seen, as well as its low black island.*

Soundings in 100 fathoms may be obtained at 22 miles from the shore, in the parallel of Mogador, when the water almost immediately becomes discoloured ; and from the depth of 78 fathoms the soundings decrease gradually, the 50-fathom line being 8 miles from the shore.

The town of Mogador, or Suïra, dates only as far back as 1760, when the Sultan Mohammed Ben Abdallah, having been attracted there by the wreck of a European vessel, laid its foundations. Unlike those of any other town in his dominions, they were planned by a Genoese architect, with some little attention to convenience and regularity ; and the effect was so pleasing to his Majesty, that he gave it the name of Suïra, or the Beauteous Picture. It is, however, better known to Europeans by its more ancient, though less flattering name of Mogador. It stands on a low sandy spot, which is surrounded by the sea at high-water springs, and the adjacent ground is therefore a swamp. The town is encompassed by a wall with flanking batteries at each angle.

Fresh Water.—Formerly there was a great want of water, as the river is a mile and a half distant, but an aqueduct now conveys the stream to several large tanks, built in different parts of the town. One of these has been placed very conveniently for the vessels in the harbour, as it lies close to a jetty inside the fortified bridge ; and boats may fill there towards high water, perfectly sheltered from all winds.

Supplies.—The market is excellent ; provisions of all sorts, including fish, poultry, and game, are abundant and cheap, as are also fruit and vegetables. The price of beef is regulated every dry by a superintending officer. The port charges for merchant vessels are high, as well as for ballast. Boat-hire is also expensive, but the number of boats that are every year destroyed by the surf, satisfactorily accounts for a little exorbitance in that respect.

Trade.—In 1875 the value of the imports amounted to 109,240l., and that of the exports to 253,986l.

---

* See Admiralty plan of Suïrah or Mogador harbour, No. 1,594 ; scale, m = 4 inches.

Coals can be obtained in small quantities.

Population in 1871 consisted of 12,000 Moors, 8,000 Jews, and a few Europeans.

Mogador Island, about half a mile long and a quarter of a mile broad, lies about half a mile from the opposite beach, and three-quarters of a mile from the town; it rises about 94 feet above the level of the sea, and except upon the harbour side, it is surrounded by large detached rocks and reefs, which extend 3½ cables from its south-west extreme; the shores are cliffy, and defended by several batteries. A high islet, nearly joined to Mogador island, lies off its north-east extreme, and immediately north-east of this islet there is a rock above water.

Mogador Harbour, or, as it is generally termed, the bay, is formed by a double bight in the coast line; the northern part of which is somewhat sheltered from the long Atlantic swell by Mogador island.

To enter.—The north entrance affords a clear channel, about 3 cables wide, with from 4 to 6 fathoms water, into the bay; but there the depth decreases to 3, 4, and at most 5 fathoms, on a rocky bottom with only a superficial covering of sand; and the clear space for anchoring is contracted to a little more than half a mile by the reefs of the town point and by the 2 fathoms flat which extends from the shore to the island.

Leading Mark.—The sanctuary of Sidi Mogodol kept on a S.E. by S. bearing leads safely in through the north entrance.

Anchorage.—The actual extent of the anchoring berths is of very small dimensions; vessels generally haul close in to the eastward of the middle of the island, at little more than half a cable's length distance, and therefore in only 14 or 15 feet at low water, loose sandy bottom. A more central position in the bay, and in deeper water, would be directly open to the swell of the Atlantic, which occasionally sets in with great violence even in moderate weather. But greater facilities for discharging cargo, induce merchant vessels to anchor in the eastern part of the harbour, well under the shelter of the rocks that extend off the town. With the prevalent north-east wind, this northern entrance is so distinct, as to require no further directions than to keep mid-channel, and to haul round the rock off the north end of the island as closely as may be practicable.

South Entrance.—The bight to the southward of the island is never used as an anchorage, but vessels of not more than 12 feet draught find it more convenient to cross the above-mentioned flat, or bar, and to run *out* in that direction with the benefit of the current, than to work out through the northern entrance. The lead will be a sufficient guide not to deviate much from mid-way between the island and the opposite shore in passing through this south channel; or the great mosque of Mogador, standing near the beach, in one with a house with an angular roof (the only one in the town) will cross the flat, or bar, in the deepest water.

This channel is said to be filling up.

Caution.—Vessels should moor in the above-mentioned anchorage, with a very short scope of cable, and with an open hawse either to the northward or southward, according to the prevalent winds or season of the year. But from November to April this bay can scarcely be considered tenable, although it has often been asserted that vessels with good ground tackling need be under no apprehension. To which the prudent seaman will reply, that the equivocal nature of the bottom shows that no reliance can be placed on the hold of the anchors; and that the necessity of veering more cable to a westerly gale, will infallibly increase the exposure of the vessel to the effects of the swell which rolls round both ends of the island, and which again reacts from the opposite shore.

Anchorage for Steam Vessels.—A good berth for small steam vessels is in 4 fathoms, 400 yards from the reef off the water-gate, with the N.E. extreme of Mogador island bearing West, and the ruined battery S.S.W. ¼ W.

Mogador Road.—Vessels of more than 14 or 15 feet draught, would find it imprudent, unless in fine summer weather to anchor in the harbour; and if intending to remain but a short time, fair anchorage can be obtained outside the island, open indeed to the south-west round to N.E. by E., and at all times exposed to a long swell, but comparatively safe during the summer. This roadstead is three-quarters of a mile from the castles, and the pilots consider it to be the best outer anchorage, but the ground is loose.

Caution.—During the winter months, south-west winds come on without the slightest warning, rendering anchorage in the road dangerous; and with the first sign of a falling barometer an offing should be sought.

Tides.—It is high water, full and change, at Mogador at 1h. 18m. Springs rise 10 to 12 feet. The tides are generally regular in their ebb and flow, but their direction varies with the wind, and their strength is at all times weak.

Current.—The current in-shore is said sometimes to set to the northward; but in the offing always to the south-westward; average strength about half a mile per hour. In the offing between Mazaghan and Mogador, a set of 2 knots per hour to the S.S.E. has been experienced in November.

Winds and Weather.—North-east winds with fine weather prevail from March to December; during the remaining months the winds are variable and the weather stormy.

East and south-east winds are rare; they are locally known as the simoon and are dry and hot. Southerly winds are usually gentle, and accompanied by fog, these winds generally run to N.W. before dying away.

Gales usually blow from W.S.W., and are preceded by a falling barometer.

The climate of Mogador is agreeable, the range of the thermometer being from 64° to 70° F.

APPENDIX.

The following information has been received, subsequently to the publication of the 3rd edition of this work, and is given herein, in the order of the paging of the 4th edition; the pages referred to are given in the margin.

INFORMATION RELATING TO CHAPTER I.

Variation in 1885.

The Iroise -   - 19° 0′ W.

CURRENTS—Caution.—The Committee of Lloyd's having p. 4. drawn attention, through the Board of Trade, to the large number of vessels that during the last few years have been wrecked or otherwise lost in the neighbourhood of cape Finisterre, it is deemed desirable in the interests of seamen to draw attention to the following information bearing on the navigation of that part of the coast of Spain.*

At page 4 (as was also stated in the editions of 1867, 1873, and 1881):—

"The easterly current from the North Atlantic strikes the land near cape Ortegal in Spain, and then appears to divide into two branches; the northern (Rennell current) flowing eastward along the coast of Spain, then north along the west coast of France. * * * The southern branch turns gradually to the south-east and southward along the coast of Portugal until having passed cape St. Vincent, when it runs eastward to the Strait of Gibraltar. It must not however be presumed that the current along the west coasts of Spain and Portugal always sets to the southward, for during

---

* According to a statement furnished by Lloyd's, the following are the losses in the neighbourhood of cape Finisterre, from the year 1877 (inclusive) to July 1882, namely :— Wrecks, 15 ; losses by collision, 7 ; foundered, 8 ; abandoned, 6.

westerly winds it sets strongly towards the land, and immediately after a continuance of southerly gales or strong breezes the current will probably be found setting to the northward."

" The mariner will perceive that caution is necessary in crossing the bay [of Biscay], and that due allowance should be made both for the outset and indraft, but especially the latter, when standing to the southward during thick weather for a position westward of cape Finisterre."

It is also stated at page 224—" The coast between capes Ortegal and " Finisterre is dangerous to approach at night, especially in the winter " season, or in thick and foggy weather, which is frequent here, for not " only does a powerful current at times set towards the land from the north- " west, but the streams of flood and ebb often draw vessels out of their " computed position."

As some of the recorded wrecks in the neighbourhood of cape Finisterre may have arisen from the effects of the indraft or set towards the land, as above described ; the attention of mariners is again drawn to the necessity of caution and of a vigilant look-out when approaching the parallel of the cape.

Also, between capes Roca and Espichel, caution must be exercised by guarding against the indraught to the Tagus, on the flood.

Mariners are also cautioned when approaching cape Finisterre, especially in vessels from ports of the United Kingdom, to lose no favourable opportunity of ascertaining the errors of the navigating compass :—one of the unsuspected causes of vessels being found, in thick weather, in dangerous proximity to the land, being doubtless due to the disregard of these necessary observations.

p. 18.   **PASSAGE du FROMVEUR.—Ile de Molène.**—The semaphore or Molène island midway between Ushant island and the mainland, has been replaced by an ordinary signal-staff which is in telegraphic communication with Corsen point.*

Leading mark.—A square tower 10 feet high, has been erected on the south end of Trois-Pierres rock, which when kept in line with Molène church leads westward of the plateau de Helle.

p. 19.   **CHENAL DU FOUR.—Plateau des Fourches.**—A rock, awash at low water spring tides, has been found on the north-west edge of the Plateau des Fourches, with the central Grande Fourche bearing S. 10° E. distant 7 cables.

p. 22.   **Loquejou shoal.**—A small black spire buoy has been placed about 70 yards westward of Loquejou shoal, northward of pointe de St. Mathieu.

---

* See Admiralty charts :—France west coast, channels between Ile d'Ouessant and the mainland, No. 2,694.

CHAUSSÉE DE SEIN (SAINTS).—Armen rock light-house.—A steam fog signal has been established at Armen rock lighthouse.   The signal is a steam horn, which, during thick and foggy weather, will give a sound of about *five seconds* duration every minute.*   p. 24, 31.

THE IROISE.—La Vandrée shoal.—Buoys.—A large red automatic whistle buoy has been again laid out, 220 yards northward of the one-fathom patch of La Vandrée ; this buoy is liable to be washed away.   A red spire buoy marks the north-eastern side of this shoal.†   p. 24.

Guepratte shoal.—This shoal of small extent, upon which a least depth of 5 fathoms was found, and 20 to 27 fathoms around, lies West, distant 1¾ miles from Basse de l'Iroise, or in lat. 48° 11′ 55″ N., long. 4° 50′ 23″ W:

RADE de BREST.—Anse du Fret.—Beacon.—A wooden beacon, surmounted by a barrel, painted in red and white horizontal stripes, and elevated 5 feet above high water, has been erected on the extremity of Roche Noire mole, south shore of Rade de Brest.   p. 27.

DOUARNENEZ BAY.—Beacon.—A stone beacon surmounted by a ball 6 feet above high water and painted red, has been constructed on the Pierre de Laber.   p. 30.

ILE DE SEIN.—Beacon.—A stone tower has been erected on Cornac-au-Vasnevez rock, about one cable northward of Plass-ou-Normand, on the western side of Raz de Sein.   p. 32.

GLENAN ISLANDS.—Pourceaux Bank.—A stone beacon surmounted by a staff and ball, 15 feet above high water and painted red, has been constructed on the principal rock of the Pourceaux bank, S.S.E. of Moutons island, in lat. 47° 45′ 40″ N., long. 4° 0′ 30″ W.‡   p. 36.

Landmark.—On Ile du Loch there is a conspicuous factory, useful as a landmark.

Beacons.—Beacon towers surmounted by iron perches, have been erected on Basse Rouge rock, south-west of Moutons isle; and on Men Diou rock, north-west of Moutons isle, entrance to Benodet bay.   p. 37.

BENODET BAY.—Beacon.—A tower painted black, surmounted by a spherical vane 12 feet above high water, has been erected at   p. 38.

---

* *See* Admiralty charts :—English channel, Nos. 1,598 and 2,675b ; Raz de Sein to Ile d'Ouessant, 2,643 ; I. de Groix to Raz de Sein, 2,645.

† *See* Admiralty charts : —Raz de Sein to Ile d'Ouessant, No. 2,643 ; Brest roadstead, No. 2,690.

‡ *See* Admiralty chart :—I. de Groix to Raz de Sein, No. 2,645 ; also No. 2,646.

the extreme of the spit extending nearly half a mile S.E. of Kareck-hir point, about three-quarters of a mile N.N.E. from Men Diou beacon.

p. 48. **ILE DE GROIX.—Semaphore.**—A semaphore has been erected on Bec Melen point in place of that on Grognon point, situated about 780 yards to the eastward, on the northern side of Isle de Groix.*

INFORMATION RELATING TO CHAPTER II.

Variation in 1885.

Lorient - - 18° 20′ W.

p. 45. **PORT LOUIS and LORIENT. — Approaches. —
Buoys.**—The following additional buoys have been placed in the South pass, viz., La Paix rock is marked by a conical red buoy placed on its western side; on the north-west side of Bastresses rocks, is placed a conical red buoy, with staff and vane, and marked Bastresses Nord; the other buoy is marked Bastresses Sud. A pear-shaped buoy, painted black, lies south of the end of the 9 feet bank extending eastward from Les Errants rocks, (marked by a statue).†

In the western pass, a conical black buoy, surmounted by a vane, has been placed to mark the shoal lying North from Les Trois Pierres.

Beacons.—An iron beacon surmounted by a can painted red, about 9 feet high, has been placed on Pesqueresse rock, westward of Bangatres point, at the entrance to, and on the south side of the channel leading to Locmalo bay. Le Roliou rock, entrance to Stole bay, westward of Lorient, has been marked by two beacons painted black, and surmounted by vanes. The north beacon is about 13 feet high, and the south beacon 10 feet high.

p. 49. **BELLE-ILE.—Palais Harbour.**—Two buoys are placed to mark the extremity of the breakwaters under construction at Palais harbour, the buoy at the northern mole is red; that at the southern mole is black, and the passage to the harbour is between them.

p. 52. **QUIBERON BAY.—Beniguet Causeway.—Beacon.**—
The beacon on Sœur rock consists of a red stone tower.

p. 53. **Houat island.—Rock.**—A rock with 7 feet over it, upon which the French corvette *l'Euménide* struck, lies half a mile N.E. of Houat island, in lat. 47° 24′ 10″ N., long. 2° 58′ 0″ W.

---

* *See* Admiralty chart :—Ile de Groix to Raz de Sein, No. 2,645; Bourgneuf to I. de Groix, No. 2,646.

† *See* Admiralty plan :—Port Louis and Lorient, No. 304.

Haedik road.—Beacon.—The black and red tower on Men   p. 53.
Groise rock has been rebuilt, and the summit is 13 feet above high
water.

PENERF ROAD.—Plateau de Piriac.—Beacon.—A   p. 54.
black tower has been built on Rothres rock, situated N.N.W. ¼ W., distant
about 8 cables from Piriac mill.*

Plateau des Mats.—Borenis rock.—The beacon on Borenis
rock has been washed away. A temporary buoy has been placed.

Halguen point.—Beacon.—A red stone tower 13 feet high   p. 58.
has been erected on the extremity of the rocks extending westward from
Halguen point, entrance to Vilaine river, with Penlan point bearing
N.N.E. ¼ E., distant 1½ miles.

CROISIC ROAD.—La Turbal.- Directions.—The two   p. 58.
lights exhibited at La Turbal, kept in line bearing E.N.E., will lead into
that harbour.*

Hergo Shoal.—Beacon.—A red stone tower has been erected on   p. 59.
Hergo shoal, entrance to Croisic, and the red buoy has been removed.

CHENAL DU NORD.—Le Pouliguen.—A beacon 20 feet   p. 59.
high, and surmounted by a vane, has been erected on La Vielle rock,
entrance to Le Pouliguen.*

The beacon is painted red on the south-west side, and black on the
north-east side.

BOURGNEUF BAY.- Shoals.—A rock with a depth of   p. 65.
4 feet at low water has been found lying N. by E. ¼ E. distant 1 1/10 miles
from Martroger beacon, south side of Bourgneuf bay. Also a bank of
2¼ fathoms, situated S.E. ¼ S. distant 2¼ miles from Pierre Moine
beacon.*

ILE D'YEU.—Corbeau rock.—Beacon.†—A tower 13 feet
high, painted black, and surmounted by a spherical vane with reflector,
has been built on Corbeau rock, distant about 1½ cables eastward of
Corbeau point, the eastern point of Ile d'Yeu.

· **PALLICE HARBOUR.**—Works are in course of construction   p. 75.
for the formation of a new harbour, at about one mile north-westward of
Pointe de Chef de Baie, entrance to La Rochelle. Vessels are forbidden

---

* *See* Admiralty chart :—Bourgneuf to I. de Groix, No. 2,646.

† *See* Admiralty charts :—Les Sables D'Olonne to Bourgneuf, No. 2,547 ; France,
west coast, Sheet II., No. 2,664.

to anchor or navigate within the limits marked out, viz., on the north by a line joining Saint-Marc beacon and a black buoy to the westward, marked Pallice No. 1; on the west by a line parallel to the coast, joining buoy No. 1 and two black buoys marked Nos. 2 and 3; and on the south by a line joining buoy No. 3 and the south pier.   No. 2 is a bell buoy.

At night, a red light, visible one mile, is shown from the coffer dams; and in foggy weather whistles will be sounded at intervals not exceeding two minutes.*

p. 81.   **GIRONDE RIVER.—LIGHTS.**—Grand Banc light vessel has been shifted 2 cables S.E. by E. of its former position; and now lies N. by W. ¾ W. distant about 5$\frac{9}{10}$ miles from Cordouan lighthouse.

p. 84.   **Passe du Nord.—Coubre bank.**—The south-east buoy of Coubre bank is conical, black, with one white band.†

Mauvaise shoal.—From an examination of this shoal, it has been found to have extended to the north-eastward, with a patch of 3½ fathoms, in mid-channel, from which La Coubre lighthouse bears S.E. by E. ¼ E distant 2½ miles.   Depths of 26 to 28 feet will be found both north and south of this patch.

p. 86.   **Directions.—Leading mark.**—Cordouan lighthouse kept in line with Grand Banc light vessel (new position), leads eastward of Mauvaise shoal.

INFORMATION RELATING TO CHAPTER III.

Variation in 1885.

Port Santona   -   -   17° 45' *W.*

pp. 124–130.   **BILBAO BAY.**—A mole is in course of construction, extending from the end of the old south-west sea-wall towards the bar, the inner part is constructed of iron; the outer portion will be of stone, having a signal tower thereon.   A small green light marks the extremity of the mole.‡

---

* *See* Admiralty chart :—France west coast, Pertius d'Antioche, Rochelle, &c., No. 2,746.
† *See* Admiralty chart :—France west coast, No. 2,664, scale m = 0·5 of an inch.
‡ *See* Admiralty chart :—Portugalete and Bilboa, No. 74.

According to a survey made by the harbour authorities, 1885, there is a least depth of 13 feet at low water on the bar. Vessels of 21 feet draught can cross at high water, smooth sea.

Nervion river.—Buoys.—Forty iron buoys have been placed in Nervion river, and ten more are to be placed. Of these, fourteen are mooring buoys, with moorings for large steamers, and are painted red. Docks are in course of construction. The semaphore is connected with Bilbao by telegraph.

Entering the river.—On sighting the semaphore at Galea point, vessels must show their number, to which the semaphore will answer with the same number on the mast, and at the yard arm another flag, indicating the number in turn given to the vessel for crossing the bar, which latter number the vessel shall keep on the masthead, and take her corresponding place among others to enter the port. There shall always be at least one cable's length between a vessel and the one immediately preceding her.

Electric lights indicating channel. — Thirty-two brush system, electric lights are exhibited at relative distances on the left (or south-western) shore of Nervion river, within the space comprised between the bar at the entrance and the anchorage off Desierto—a distance of about 5,700 yards. The seaward light, also the light at the extremity of Benedicta mole, are of greater power than the others.

As vessels can enter or leave the port with night tides during fine weather, these lights are exhibited from two hours before high water to two hours after. The signals made by the chief pilot from the tower on the south-west sea wall are—a fixed *red* light to mark the position of the tower, and a fixed *white* light shown on one or other side of the red light, to indicate whether vessels should alter course to the north-east, or the south-west side of the channel.

PORT SANTOÑA.—Wreck.—The steam-vessel *Provenzal* lies p. 139. sunk outside the entrance to port Santoña, in 8¾ fathoms at low water, with Fraile point bearing N.W. ¾ W., distant 7 miles, and is thus in a position dangerous to navigation.*

SAN MARTIN DE LA ARENA (SUANCES).—A buoy p. 150. marks the extremity of a breakwater in progress, extending from Marsan point, the inner east point of entrance to Suances.†

GIJON BAY.—Buoys.—Two iron mooring buoys painted white, p. 170. have been laid down in Gijon bay, from which the northern extremity of cape Torrens bears respectively N. 50° W., distant 4½ cables and N. 22° W.

* *See* Admiralty plan :—Port Santoña, No. 75.
† *See* plan on Admiralty chart:—Bayonne to Oporto, No. 2,728.

A A 2

distant 6 cables. A mooring buoy lies half a cable westward of the entrance to the port.

The red buoys have been removed.*

172.   **Bar.—Bad weather.—Signals.**—In bad weather, the following signals are used to direct vessels wishing to enter the harbour, and are shown from a mast on the top of the look-out of Santa Catalina. *See* remarks on Bar at p. 172.

1. A square flag - - -	Bad weather expected; vessels in the outer harbour should return to the basin.
2. A black ball - - -	The bar is dangerous. (Vessels entering the harbour when this signal is up will find the pilot inside the bar.)
3. Two square flags - - -	Impossible to cross the bar.
4. Two black balls -	Impossible to moor in the harbour.
5. A flag over a ball - - -	Vessels of light draught can enter. .
6. A flag under a ball -	Heavy vessels can enter. *See* note below.
7. A ball between two flags -	Send a boat to Musel bay, to endeavour to embark a pilot.
8. A flag between two balls -	Communicate the signals to the vessel which does not understand them.
9. A flag over two black balls -	Wait for the tide before entering the harbour. (If this signal is repeated it means wait until to-morrow.)
10. A flag under two black balls -	Signal the draught of the vessel, by hoisting the national flag as many times as the draught of the vessel, in feet; by the steam whistle; or by the International Code.
11. Two flags over a ball -	The outermost vessel is badly moored, and should come farther in.
12. Two flags under a ball -	The innermost vessel should get farther seaward.

---

* *See* Admiralty chart :—Gijon bay, No. 77.

The national flag at the foremast denotes that the signal is understood.

The code flag at the mainmast denotes that the signal is not understood.

Vessels with one mast hoist the national flag if the signal is understood, and both flags if not understood.

Note.—When the sea is very heavy, so that vessels entering the harbour cannot see the signals made from the pilot boat inside the bar, vessels are guided in the direction of the channel by means of a flagstaff furnished with an arm, placed on the pier of the new wet dock, named Fomento de Gijon. A black board or a blue flag attached to the arm, if shown westward of the flagstaff, denotes that the vessel is to steer more to the westward ; if shown eastward of the flagstaff, to steer more to the eastward ; and when the board or flag is moved in line with the flagstaff, it denotes that the vessel is in the channel, and that the flagstaff should be steered for. The bar should be crossed as quickly as possible.

Harbour.—The entrance to Gijon harbour, between Santa Catalina mole and the new mole to the southward is about 109 yards. A *fixed* white light is exhibited from the extremity of the new mole.   p. 174.

INFORMATION RELATING TO CHAPTER IV.

Variation in 1885.

Vigo bay   -   - 19° 45′ W.

CAPE FINISTERRE. — Semaphore. — The semaphore p. 222, 232. station established on cape Finisterre, painted white, and elevated 395 feet above the sea, is 44 yards northward of the lighthouse. Vessels should communicate by the International Code of Signals.*

Coruña and Corcubion are in telegraphic communication with each other; in connexion with the semaphore station at Finisterre.

Corcubion bay will accommodate six heavy ironclads lying in from   p. 234. 13 to 7½ fathoms water, at single anchor, with from 6 to 7 shackles of cable out.

PONTEVEDRA BAY.—The Spanish Government has given   p. 244. notice of the existence of a sunken rock, lying 8 cables westward of the south extreme of Onza island, at the entrance to Pontevedra bay.

This danger (*Pan de Centeno*) on which the steam vessel *Vizcaya* grounded, is a small black rock having a depth of 2½ fathoms, with from 6½ to 7 fathoms water close round it, increasing gradually to 13 fathoms.

---

* *See* Admiralty charts :—Bayonne to Oporto, No. 2,728 ; and cape Finisterre to cape St. Vincent, No. 87.

From the rock, the lighthouse on Salvora island bears N. 2° W.; cape Udra S. 67° E.; and the lighthouse on Faro island, Cies islands, S. 8° W.

p. 250.   **VIGO BAY.**— Telegraph Cable.— Information has been received from Captain Rawson, H.M.S. *Minotaur*, that a third telegraph cable is laid between Vigo and Camiñha (Camiña).*

At Vigo, the terminus of this cable is the same as that of the other cables, at point de la Lage; thence it is laid at about the distance of from 2 to 4 cables south-eastward of those cables, as far as the South channel entrance; from this position it takes a S.S.W. direction and passes cape Silleiro at the distance of about one mile.

Mariners are cautioned not to anchor in the vicinity.

Also, that two buoys, between which the telegraph cables are laid, have been placed off the town of Vigo.

The outer buoy, red with staff and ball, is moored in 11 fathoms water with point del Castro bearing S.E. by E. ½ E., distant 4 cables.

The inner buoy, red with staff and ball, is moored in 10 fathoms water, with point de la Lage (Vigo point) bearing South, distant 2 cables.

p. 251.   **Buoys.**—The following information has been received from the Spanish Government, 1884, relative to the buoyage of Vigo bay :—

North Shore.—Punta Subrido buoy is a cask buoy (provisional), painted black. Castros da Barra buoy is a conical buoy, painted black, and surmounted by a black and white globe. Bajo Borneira is marked by a bell buoy, painted black and red, with white globe. Bajo Zalgueiron is marked by a can buoy, painted black, with white globe. Punta Rodeira buoy is a can buoy, painted black and white in horizontal stripes, with white globe. Piedra de Pego is marked by a red triangular frame beacon, surmounted by a black and white cross.

South Shore.—Rondana shoal is marked by a conical buoy with globe, painted red. Cabo de Mar buoy is a conical buoy, painted red and white in vertical stripes, with white globe. Bouzas (El Cabezon) buoy is an inverted conical buoy, painted red.

Puerto de Bayona.—Monteferro buoy is a cask buoy painted red, moored in 8 fathoms, about three-quarters of a cable northward of Monteferro shoal (a 2¼ fathom patch between Estela de Tierre and Monteferro peninsula). Puerto Real buoy is an inverted conical buoy, painted red. Piedra Baiña (Sta. Marta) is marked by a red triangular frame beacon with white cross.

---

* *See* Admiralty charts:—Cape Finisterre to cape St. Vincent, No. 87; Bayonne to Oporto, No. 2,728; cape Finisterre to Vigo bay, No. 1,756; Vigo bay, No. 2,548.

The buoy, formerly marking Los Castros de Agoeiro, at the southern entrance of Vigo bay; also that marking Lobeira rock, in San Simon bay, have been removed.

Note.—These buoys are often damaged in bad weather, and are then temporarily replaced by others.

VIGO.—Landing.—There are two landing-places at Vigo, one at the north-west part of the town; the other at the north-east.

Weather Signals are made by means of cones and cylinders, shown from staffs on the roof of a house to the eastward of the cathedral.

INFORMATION RELATING TO CHAPTER V.

Variation in 1885.

Cape Roca   -   - 19° 0′ W.

BANK.—A bank, upon which a sounding of 28 fathoms was obtained from H.M.S. *Agincourt*, lies with cape Roca bearing S.E. by E. ¼ E. distant 12 miles.*   p. 274.

LISBON.—Time Signal.—The Portuguese Government has given notice that on the 15th August 1885, a new time signal will be established at the south-east angle of the Naval School, near the Marine observatory. The signal is a black ball 3¼ feet in diameter, which is hoisted half-mast as preparatory 5 minutes before signal, close up at 3 minutes before, and dropped at 1h. 0m. 0s. p.m. mean time at the Royal Astronomical observatory of Lisbon—equivalent to 1h. 36m. 44·7s. Greenwich mean time.†   p. 276.

The fall of the ball is effected automatically from the Royal Astronomical observatory of Lisbon, by means of electricity. The instant at which the said fall takes place will be registered chronographically, in order that the correction to be applied each day may be accurately known. These corrections will be published by the observatory in the *Folha Official* with the least possible delay.

Should the signal fail in accuracy, the fact will be indicated by the ball rising very slowly half-mast high, remaining in that position until 1h. 7m., when it will be hoisted close up a second time, and dropped at 1h. 10m. 0s.

---

* *See* Admiralty charts :—British islands to the Mediterranean sea, No. 1; Cape Finisterre to cape St. Vincent, No. 87.

† *See* Admiralty chart :—Entrance of the river Tagus, No. 89. Also, List of Time Signals, published by the Admiralty, 1880, pages 26, 27.

INFORMATION RELATING TO CHAPTER VI.

Variation in 1885.

Cadiz -   - 16° 0′ W.

p. 303.   **CADIZ BAY.—Telegraph Cable.**—The Canary island Telegraphic Company has laid the first section of a cable, commencing from the creek between Bermeja point and Cañuelo del Puerto, on the northern side of Cadiz bay, to a buoy moored with San Sebastian lighthouse bearing S. 40° E., distant 5¼ miles.

p. 304.   **Cadiz Harbour Entrance.—Los Cochinos Rocks.— Beacon.**—The Spanish Government has given notice that the bell buoy which previously marked the north-west edge of Los Cochinos shoal, south side of the main channel to Cadiz harbour, has been withdrawn; and that a beacon has been erected on that shoal, north-eastward of the rocks that uncover at low water.*

The beacon consists of an iron tube, 2½ feet in diameter and 19½ feet high, painted black and surmounted by a bright ball.†

Vessels entering Cadiz harbour by the main channel, should leave Los Cochinos and Las Puercas beacons, also El Fraile buoy, on the starboard hand.

p. 305.   **Buoys.**—El Fraile buoy, conical, with globe and base coloured black, lies in 4 fathoms water, with Las Puercas beacon bearing W. by N. ¼ N., distant 6¼ cables; and the extremity of San Felipe pier (extended about 1¼ cables) S. ¼ W., distant 6¼ cables.

El Diamante shoal is marked on its western edge by a boat buoy coloured red, lying in 5 fathoms water, with La Galera buoy, black, N.E., distant 8 cables; and La Puercas beacon, S.S.W. ¼ W., distant 9 cables.

The conical red buoy marking Cabezo de los Asnos, lies with Rota pier head N.E. ¼ E., and Las Puercas beacon S.S.E. ¼ E.

Cabezuela shoal buoy, red, lies in 3½ fathoms water, with Puntales castle S.S.W., distant 1 1/10 miles, and the extremity of San Felipe pier N.W. ¼ W.

p. 306.   Palma shoal buoy, black, lies in 4¾ fathoms water, with Puntales castle S. by W., distant 8 cables; and the extremity of San Felipe pier N.W. by N.

---

* *See* Admiralty charts:—Cape St. Vincent to Gibraltar strait, No. 92; Cadiz harbour with plan of the entrance, No. 86.

† This beacon has since been washed away, and had not been replaced in July 1882.

A LIST

OF

ADDITIONS AND ALTERATIONS TO LIGHTS

(*Corrected to May* 1885)

EMBRACED BY THE

SAILING DIRECTIONS

FOR THE

WEST COASTS OF FRANCE, SPAIN, AND PORTUGAL,

1881.

Page of Sailing Directions	No.	Name of Light.	Place.	Latitude. N.	Longitude. W.	Number and Colour of Lights.	Character of Light.	Interval of Revolution or Flash.	Miles seen in clear Weather.
26	161	BREST.	End of spit W. side Cameret bay.	48 17	4 55	1	Green.	F.	- -	4
31	161a	DOUARNENES BAY.	Point Millier.	48 6	4 38	1	White and red. *See Remarks.*	F.	- -	White 13 Red 9
24, 31	162b	AR-MEN ROCK (SAINTS).	On rock.	48 3	5 00	1	White.	F.	- -	20
37	173	PENFRET ISLAND	North point.	47 43	3 57	1	White with flash.	F. & Fl.	Four minutes {	Fl. 21 } F. 17 }
58	192a	LA TURBAL (TURBALLE).	Close to life-boat refuge house.	47 21	2 31	2	White. 40 yards apart.	F.	- -	7
58	193	PENLAN.	On the point.	47 31	2 30	1	White and red.	F.	- -	{ 13 9 }
58	193a	LA VILAINE RIVER.	Near Trehiguier and on Seal point.	47 30	2 27	2	Outer, white, inner, red.	F.	- -	9
61	196a	PORT POULIGUEN	Extremity of jetty.	47 16	2 26	1	Red.	F.	- -	5
66	206a	GOULET DE FROMANTINE {	100 yards S. of barricade of piles.	46 53	2 9	1	White.	F.	- -	5
			Back to back with la Croix beacon.	-	-	1	White.	F.	- -	10
68	211	ILE D'YEU. BRETON PORT.	Head of harbour.	-	-	1	White.	F.	- -	9
70	—	LES SABLES D'OLONNE.	-	-	-	—	-	-	-	-
72	221	ILE DE RE. BALEINES.	N.W. point.	46 15	1 34	1	White.	Fl	*See Remarks.*	24
72	222	ST. MARTIN PORT.	End of mole.	-	-	1	Green.	F.	- -	2
81	233	PALMYRE.	On the downs of the point.	45 41	1 9	1	Red and green alternately.	Alt.	Twenty seconds.	19
82	237	DE GRAVE.	South point of entrance.	45 34	1 4	1	White.	Fl.	Five seconds.	15
82	237a	ST. NICOLAS.	On the downs W. ¾ S. from Pointe de Grave lighthouse.	45 34	1 5	1	Green.	F.	- -	12
82	245	GART.	-	45 12	0 45	1	White and red. *See Remarks.*	F.	- -	6
82	246	PATIRAS ILE.	North point.	45 12	0 43	1	White.	Fl.	Four seconds.	18

No.	Colour, or any Peculiarity of Light-house.	Height in feet of centre of Lantern above High Water.	Height in feet of Building from Base to Vane.	Year lighted.	Character and Order of Illuminating Apparatus.	REMARKS.
161	Masonry.	35	29	1883	- - -	Shows the anchorage from S. 20° E. to N. 7° W.
161a	On keeper's house.	112	20	1881	- - -	Visible between S. 73° 45′ E. and N. 86° 45′ W. A sector of *white* light of 20½°, between Jaune and Vieille shoals. A sector of *red* light of 6° over Vieille shoal. A second sector of *white* light of 15° between Vieille shoal and Le Bouc rock. The light will be obscured through a sector of 16½° over Le Bouc rock and cape de la Chèvre. A third sector of *white* light of 105° over the bay of Douarnenez as far as the rocks of point Jument.
162b	- - -	94	110	1881	1st Ord.	Steam fog trumpet gives a blast of five seconds' duration every minute.
172	Square tower.	118	72	1836	D. 3d Ord.	In ordinary weather the short eclipses do not appear total within 6 miles.
192a	Iron supports.	33 / 24	20 / 22	{1882 / 1884}	- - -	Leading lights into harbour E.N.E.
193	Square tower.	66	-	{1844 / 1882}	- - -	*Red* from N. 19° E. to N. 71° E. ; *white* from N. 71° E. to S. 71° E.
193a	Square towers.	{ 25 / 68 }	-	1882	C.	Leading lights 480 yards apart; in line S. 49° E. The inner light is only visible over 28 degrees.
196a	Lamp-post.	23	18	-	D. - -	Visible between the bearings of North and N.W.
206a {	Black standard.	18	15	1881	D. - -	To proceed up the channel. Illuminates five-eighths of the horizon.
	Black shed.	39	20	1881	C. - -	To proceed down the channel. Illuminates about 80°.
211	Square tower.	66	39	- -	D. 4th Ord.	
—	- - -	-	-	- -	- - -	There are also two *red* lights near La Chaume. It is proposed to exhibit a light on St. Nicholas mole head to indicate depth over lock sill.
221	Octagonal tower.	166	154	1882	D. 1st Ord.	Shows a succession of groups of four flashes, the interval between two consecutive groups being three times as long as that between the flashes of one group.
222	- - -	25	21	1884	—	
233	On three pillars; the upper part black, the lower part and pillars white.	167	98	- -	Electric.	
237	Square.	85	82	- -	D. 3d Ord.	
237a	Square. Black.	71	—	—	—	
245	Iron beacon, white.	20	20	- -	D. 4th Ord.	*Red* in the direction of Mousset light.
246	Square tower.	72	59	- -	C. 4th Ord.	

WEST COASTS OF FRANCE, SPAIN, &c.

No.	Name of Light.	Place.	Latitude. N.	Longitude. W.	Number and Colour of Lights.		Character of Light.	Interval of Revolution or Flash.	Miles seen in clear Weather
260	CAPE HIGUERA.	On the cape.	43 24	1 46	1	Red.	*See* Remarks.		20
261	PORT PASAGES.	San Sebastian (San Pedro) tower on W. side.	. .	. .	1	Red.	F.	. .	6
		N. point of Bonanza mole, on E. side.	. .	. .	1	Green.	F.	. .	6
262	SAN SEBASTIAN.	Mount Igueldo.	43 20	2 0	1	Red.	Fl.	Two minutes.	15
265	SUMAYA.	Mount Atalaya.	43 19	2 15	1	White and green.	F.	. .	10
266	LEQUEITIO.	Santa Catalina de Lequeitio point.	43 23	2 32	1	Red.	F.	. .	10
269	BILBAO.	Signal tower on S.W. sea-wall.	. .	. .	1	Red.	F.	. .	. .
281	LLANES.	San Antonio south point.	43 27	4 46	1	Green.	F.	. .	9
—	GIJON.	End of new mole.	. .	. .	1	White.	F.	. .	. .
286	PENAS.	On the cape.	43 41	5 50	1	White and red alternately.	Rev.	Half minute.	21
287	AVILES.	Castillo point, north side of entrance.	43 38	5 56	1	Red.	F.	. .	10
292	PANCHA. NEAR RIVADEO PORT.	On island.	43 34	7 4	1	Red.	F.	. .	9
294	BARQUERO HARBOUR.	Conejera island.	43 46	7 39	1	Green.	F.	. .	9
331	ESPICHEL.	On the cape.	38 25	9 13	1	White.	F.	. .	18
336	CARTAYA BAR.	734 yards eastward of Rompido light.	. .	. .	2	White.	F.	. .	4
345	CADIZ.	On Las Puercas shoal.	. .	. .	1	White.	Occ.	*See* Remarks.	4
351	GIBRALTAR.	Near extremity of New mole.	36 7	5 21	1	Red with white sector.	F.	. .	8
367a	TANGIER.	On battery at S.E. corner of sea wall.	35 47	5 48	1	Red and white.	F.	. .	8
		Landing stage.	. .	. .	1	Green.	F.	. .	3

Nº	Colour, or any Peculiarity of Light-house.	Height in feet in centre of Lantern above high Water.	Height in feet of Building from Base to Vane.	Year lighted.	Character and Order of Illuminating Apparatus.	REMARKS.
29	Bluish-gray, white lantern.	190	69	1881	- - -	The light is eclipsed at alternate intervals of 10 and 50 seconds. Visible between S. 84° E. and N. 10° E.
31	Iron support.	15	- -	1884	—	
	Ditto.	15	- -	1884	- -	N. by E. ¼ E. 180 yards from southern light.
32	Tower white.	426	46	- -	D. 3d Ord.	
33	Gray. Octagonal.	139	39	1882	D. 5th Ord.	The light shows *green* towards the land between N.W. ¼ W. and E. ¼ N., and *white* in other directions. The white light is of less power than is usual with lights of the fifth order, as the greater part of it is concentrated to illuminate the bar beacon. A reflected light is shown from a beacon, in the form of a truncated cone, and buff coloured, surmounted by a globe (23 feet above high water) and cylinder painted white; it is situated 180 yards E. ¼ N. from Sumaya light-house, and the channel over Urola river bar is 87 yards eastward of the beacon.
28	Conical. Light colour. Lantern green.	148	43	- -	D. 5th Ord.	
29	Circular. White.	-	-	-	1883	- - -	Between the bar and Desierto anchorage 38 electric lights are also shown on the S.W. shore of the river, exhibited from 2 hours before to 2 hours after high water. Directing signals are made from the mole tower by a *white* light shown on one side or the other of the *red* light.
31	Octagonal. White.	64	26	- -	D. 6th Ord.	
—	- - -			1883	- - -	*Provisional light.* There is also a fixed red light at the end of dock, not perceptible until within the bar.
26	Circular.	340	33	- -	D. 1st Ord.	
27	Octagonal. Light yellow. Lantern green.	116	49	- -	D. 6th Ord.	
28	White.	79	29	- -	D. 5th Ord.	Eight feet above keeper's dwelling.
294	Gray. Lantern white. Conical.	273	24	- -	D. 6th Ord.	
331	Hexagonal.	625	100	- -	D. 1st Ord.	
336	On white perches.	{ 66, 56 }	{ 30, 23 }	- -	- - -	Leading lights over bar N. ½ W. The lights, which are frequently shifted, are 120 yards from the shore and 457 yards from the bar.
44	Black beacon.	16	- -	1881	- - -	Visible ten seconds, eclipsed twenty seconds.
51	Stone column.	28	32	- -	D. 4th Ord.	White sector, visible inshore between S.W. and N.W.
167a	Circular, white.	58	- -	1883	O.D. 5th Ord.	*Red* from S. 17° W. to S. 72° W. *White* from S. 72° W. over Tangier road.
	- - -	20	- -	1883		

INDEX.

Lightning Source UK Ltd.
Milton Keynes UK
UKHW020400180620
365183UK00012B/486